GREENBERG'S

GUIDE TO

LIONEL® TRAINS

1945 - 1969

Volume I:
Motive Power and Rolling Stock
Ninth Edition

PAUL V. AMBROSE

Based on Prior Editions by Bruce C. Greenberg

GREENBERG BOOKS
A Division of Kalmbach Publishing Co.

Ninth edition. First printing 1996

Printed in Hong Kong

Publisher's Cataloging in Publication
Prepared by Quality Books Inc.

Ambrose, Paul V.
    [Guide to Lionel Trains, 1945–1969]
    Greenberg's guide to Lionel trains, 1945–1969. Volume I, Motive power and
      rolling stock / Paul V. Ambrose. — 9th ed.
    p. cm.
    Includes index.
    ISBN 0-89778-503-7
    1. Railroads—Models. 2. Lionel Corporation. I. Greenberg, Bruce C. II. Title. III.
      Title: Guide to Lionel trains, 1945–1969. Iv. Title: Lionel trains, 1945–1969. V.
      Title: Motive power and rolling stock.
    TF197.G741996   625.1'9
                 QBI96-40007

CONTENTS

SPECIAL FEATURES OF THIS REVISED EDITION

A NEW LOOK AT POSTWAR LIONEL

This, the ninth edition of *Greenberg's Guide to Lionel Trains, 1945–1969, Volume I,* has been thoroughly revised. The last edition represented a streamlined approach to the vast array of Lionel postwar motive power, rolling stock, and accessories. This new edition further refines that approach. Every chapter and every entry has been rewritten. Alan Stewart rewrote Chapter 7 on flatcars, while Paul V. Ambrose, with the help of Harold J. Lovelock, was responsible for all the other chapters. Also, since the publication of the previous edition, new volumes in the postwar series have been published; their coverage has affected the information provided in the book you have in your hands.

COVERAGE OF POSTWAR LIONEL TRAINS IN GREENBERG GUIDES

Clearly, the arrival of the long-awaited *Volume VI: Accessories*, by Alan Stewart, makes the earlier edition of Volume I's chapter on accessories unnecessary. Also, after more than a decade of intensive and extensive research, *Volume VII: Selected Variations,* by Paul V. Ambrose and Harold J. Lovelock, offers detailed descriptions and photographs of every recognized variation of those categories of postwar Lionel production that needed the greatest clarification (coverage of the remaining categories is in preparation). It includes citation of part numbers and original boxes and packaging that would have properly accompanied a specific item; having these details often assures the validity of a model. This new Volume I

benefits from that research, though it does not include the same level of detail.

Another book that appeared since Volume I was last revised, *Volume V: Rare and Unusual*, by Paul V. Ambrose and Harold J. Lovelock, lives up to its title and offers pictures and commentary on unique items and even includes a chapter on fraudulent models. Such pieces are not included in Volume I, which continues to serve collectors as a streamlined reference to regular-production motive power and rolling stock.

The other volumes in this postwar series include *Volume II: Behind the Scenes*, which provides in-depth essays relating to postwar production, and *Volume III: Sets*, which gives a complete listing of all cataloged sets. *Volume IV: Uncataloged Sets,* the only reference book of its kind, addresses a most fascinating area of Lionel production and marketing strategy. Lionel's HO scale trains are covered in two Greenberg Guides by George Horan.

HOW THIS BOOK IS ORGANIZED

Every effort has been made to make this volume not only a more accurate presentation of Lionel postwar trains than ever before but also to offer this information in the most reader-friendly way. The listings have been written in a consistent manner, which we believe makes them much more informative and definitely much easier to follow.

Each chapter opens with an introduction that surveys all types of locomotives or cars within the category covered by that chapter. Detailed listings follow, and they are organized in one numerical sequence. As a consequence, collectors will more readily be able to locate a specific item.

The first chapter provides an overview of trucks, couplers, and other production details typical of Lionel's postwar era. It explains the descriptions of locomotive or car features that appear in the listings in the subsequent chapters. A Glossary of all special terms used in discussion of Lionel postwar models appears at the back of this volume. An Index of catalog numbers and numbers appearing on the actual cars follows, and it should help you locate a specific item. It also indicates where to find a photograph of that item.

Many new color and black-and-white photographs have been added in this edition to illustrate the development of Lionel production more accurately and clearly. There are new charts and sidebars to tell the often complicated stories behind particular lines.

DETERMINING VALUES

The purpose of this book is to provide comprehensive listings with current prices for Lionel motive power, rolling stock, and accessories in O and O27 gauges, cataloged between 1945 and 1969. We include those variations that have been authenticated. Values are reported for each item where there have been reported sales. The toy train values determined in this book should be taken as a guide to the marketplace. While they can be applied in general, collectors may find specific instances of wide variances.

Toy train values vary for a number of reasons. First, consider the *relative knowledge* of the buyer and seller. A seller, unaware that he has a rare variation, may sell it for the price of a common piece. Another source of price variation is *short-term fluctuation*, which depends on what is being offered at a given train meet on a given day. If four 773s are for sale at a small meet, we would expect that supply would outpace demand and lead to a reduction in price. A related source of variation is the *season* of the year. The train market is slower in the summer, and sellers may at this time be more inclined to reduce prices if they really want to move an item. Another important source of price variation is the relative strength of the seller's *desire to sell* and the buyer's *eagerness to buy*. Clearly a seller in economic distress will be more eager to strike a bargain. A final source of variation is the *personalities* of the seller and buyer. Some sellers like to quickly turn over items and therefore price their items to move; others seek a higher price and will bring an item to meet after meet until they find a willing buyer.

Train values in this book are based on reports of *obtained* prices, rather than asking prices. Generally, the prices reported here represent a "ready sale," or a price perceived as a good value by the buyer. They may sometimes appear lower than those seen on trains at meets for two reasons. First, items that sell often do so in the first hour of a train meet and therefore are no longer visible. (We have observed that much of the action at most meets occurs in the first hour.) The items that do not sell in the first hour have a higher price tag, and this price, although it may not represent the actual sale price, is the price observed. A related source of discrepancy is the willingness of some sellers to bargain over price.

Prices reported for scarce items and for desirable items in Like New condition reflect transactions between knowledgeable buyers and sellers, since these items infrequently are sold at train meets or shows.

Another factor that may affect prices is reconditioning done by the dealer. Some dealers take great pains to clean and service their pieces so that they look their best and operate properly. Others sell the items just as they have received them, dust and all. Naturally, the more effort the dealer expends in preparing his pieces for sale, the more he can expect to charge for them. This factor may account for significant price differences among dealers selling the same equipment.

From our studies of train prices, it appears that mail-order prices for used trains are generally higher than those obtained at train meets. This is appropriate considering the costs and efforts of producing a price list and packaging and shipping items. Mail-order items may sell at prices above those listed in this book. A final source of difference between observed prices and reported prices is region. Prices are currently lower in the Midwest.

We receive many inquiries as to whether or not a particular piece is a "good value." This book will help answer that question; but there is no substitute for experience in the marketplace. *We strongly recommend that novices do not make major purchases without the assistance of friends who have experience in buying and selling trains.* If you are buying a train and do not know whom to ask about its value, look for the people running the meet or show and discuss with them your need for assistance. Usually they can refer you to an experienced collector who will be willing to examine the piece and offer his opinion.

In the case where there is insufficient data upon which to establish a value, we indicate No Reported Sales (NRS) in the value column. Although some items may be rare or otherwise valuable, NRS alone does not indicate that a piece is a high-value item. In some cases, a new variation might be listed as NRS, simply because the item's scarcity could not be determined immediately.

CONDITION

For each item, we provide four price categories: **Good**, **Very Good**, **Excellent**, and **Like New**. These designations are part of a range defined by the Train Collectors Association as follows:

• **FAIR:** Well-scratched, chipped, dented, rusted, or warped.

• **GOOD:** Scratches, small dents, dirty.

• **VERY GOOD:** Few scratches, exceptionally clean, no dents or rust.

• **EXCELLENT:** Minute scratches or nicks, no dents or rust, all original with less than average wear.

• **LIKE NEW:** Only the faintest signs of handling and wheel wear with crisp, vibrant colors that show no evidence of polishing. Full information on outer and inner boxes for items appears in Volume VII, and a chart and illustration of all box types appears in Chapter 1 of this book.

• **MINT:** Brand new, absolutely unmarred, never run, all original and unused, in original box with any additional items that came with it, such as instruction sheets and factory inspection slip. An item may have been removed from the box and replaced in it, but it should show no evidence of handling. A Mint piece shows no fingerprints or evidence of discoloration.

We have included Like New in this edition because of the important trade in postwar items in this grade. We do not include Mint prices since too few of these pieces are offered to evaluate their worth; items that are truly Mint will bring an additional premium above the prices shown for Like New. See the cautions under "Buying and Selling Trains."

We do not show values for items in Fair or Restored condition. Fair items would be valued substantially below Good. We have not included Restored as a suggested value because such items are not a significant portion of the market for postwar trains. As a rough guide, however, we expect that Restored items will bring prices equivalent to Good or possibly Very Good. The term "professional restoration" refers to highly proficient technical work. There is disagreement among restorers as to what constitutes appropriate technique and finished product. There are substantial differences in the price that consumers are willing to pay for restored items.

It is a simple fact that there are more trains than boxes in the marketplace. Because most items surface at train meets without boxes, our listings are priced *without* boxes. A survey of postwar boxes and a discussion of the premiums they add to suggested values appear in Chapter 1.

BUYING AND SELLING TRAINS

It is the nature of a market for a seller to see his or her item in a very positive light; for example, it is common for a seller to seek a Like New price for a piece that is actually in Excellent condition. By contrast, a buyer will see the same item in a less favorable, more critical light. We strongly recommend that novices exercise extreme caution in any transaction, and that all collectors note the various cautions we include in this book and especially in Volumes V and VII regarding parts that are easily changed.

If you have trains to sell and sell them to a person planning to resell them, you cannot expect to achieve the prices reported in this book. Rather, you should expect to achieve about 50 percent of these prices for ordinary items in Good to Very Good condition (for highly desirable items in Excellent or better condition, a seller often receives a higher percentage of the prices suggested). It stands to reason that for your items to be of interest to a dealer, he or she must purchase them for considerably less than the prices listed here.

The danger posed by fakes and frauds is, unfortunately, a fact of collecting. Unethical people have chemically altered common pieces to change their colors and then offered them as rare variations. We urge readers to exercise extreme caution and consult an expert in purchasing Lionel equipment claimed to be a "factory error" or rare variation because of a difference in color. Volume V addresses this problem and presents information on genuinely rare variations.

Remember, the range of four values indicated in this volume are suggestions determined by the best information we have received from various sources at the time this book went to press.

In addition to noting the cautions offered here, enthusiasts interested in operating trains may have other purchasing requirements. Generally in the toy train field there is a lot of concern with exterior appearance and less concern with operation. If operation is important to you, ask the seller if the train runs satisfactorily. If the seller indicates any doubt about this, you should test it. Most train meets have test tracks provided for that purpose.

ACKNOWLEDGMENTS

The author appreciates the assistance his good friend, Harry Lovelock, provided when updating this volume. In addition, Alan Stewart applied his vast knowledge of postwar flatcars to revising Chapter 7. Joe Algozzini also shared his expertise on all aspects of postwar production and lent rolling stock that was photographed by Darla Evans for Chapter 4. Various suggestions and insights were shared by a number of knowledgeable collectors, including Ernie Chornyei, John Christopher, Phil Lonergan, Bob Morgan, Randy Okun, Steve Patterson, Bill Pike, and Ed Prendeville. Finally, the author is grateful for the information provided by collectors for all previous editions of this reference work.

Two other people deserve special thanks for the amount of work they contributed to this volume. First, Elsa van Bergen did her usual superb job of editing the manuscript and suggesting illustrative material. Roger Carp provided thoughtful overviews of prewar and postwar production for all but one of the chapters. These will help newcomers as well as longtime Lionel collectors better understand how the postwar product line was developed and marketed.

At Kalmbach Publishing Co., Mary Algozin copyedited and proofread the entire manuscript; Kristi Ludwig designed the cover; Sabine Beaupré designed the layout for the book; Sybil Sosin coordinated the editing, design, and printing; and Bob Thorson managed the final production of the book.

1

LIONEL POSTWAR PRODUCTION

Introduction by Roger Carp

Most of us who will read and use this guide once were youngsters who played with and cherished Lionel O gauge trains. We spent hours creating a world of our own in which freight cars transported all sorts of imaginary products and passenger cars carried people to destinations around the country. Our electric trains were treasured because they were more than mere toys. They were our key to the world around us.

Then we grew up. Along the way, most of us cast aside our trains. Often we gave them to a younger sibling or friend; sometimes we just forgot about them and learned later that our parents had donated them to charity or peddled them at a rummage sale. Losing these precious possessions didn't bother us too much. We had better things to do with our time: join athletic teams, finish homework, learn to drive, and discover the mysteries of the opposite sex.

Then we grew up some more. Jobs, military service, college, marriage, and children consumed our time and energy. But one day something hit us; we felt a longing to regain part of our childhood. That emotion led us back to Lionel trains. Perhaps we found our old trains still packed away in a closet or attic. More likely, they were gone, and we started acquiring the locomotives, rolling stock, and accessories that we had owned or dreamed of owning.

What's different, however, is that we can appreciate our trains more fully now than when we were kids. In our youth, we let them crash and threw away their boxes. We scarcely cared where they came from or who made them or why models changed over time. All that mattered was that our Lionel trains entertained us and ran reliably whenever we plugged in the transformer.

As we returned to collecting and operating vintage trains and accessories, we began asking questions about them. We wondered when our favorite models were manufactured and wanted to know how Lionel developed so complete a line of products in the postwar period. We compared models from the 1940s with those made in the following two decades to understand how production changed. We paid attention to the methods by which trains were decorated, the details that were added to or deleted from them, and the ways they were packaged.

In other words, we studied our postwar O and O27 gauge trains and discussed them with other collectors. As we did so, we learned about the company that had developed, manufactured, and marketed them. The more we learned, the more we appreciated Lionel's toy trains. As we never had as kids, we recognized how innovative the engineering staff at Lionel was in designing miniature versions of locomotives and rolling stock. We marveled at how electricity was used to power trains, fill and unload accessories, and generate the sounds of horns and whistles. "Those engineers must have been geniuses!" we exclaimed. And in many respects they were.

Brilliant in different ways were the executives who determined the extent and character of Lionel's product line each year. Beginning with a single outfit for the holiday season of 1945, they put together superb lines of O and O27 gauge trains that quickly became the most desirable toys a boy could receive. The range of models available was nothing short of extraordinary. Lionel offered steam, diesel, and electric locomotives representative of the biggest and most up-to-date motive power to be found on the principal railroads of America. Colorful, detailed, and realistic models of contemporary freight cars and passenger cars delighted children. Lionel might not always be the first with a particular piece, but generally it surpassed whatever competitors offered to maintain supremacy in the market.

The ten chapters that follow are intended to supplement the knowledge collectors and operators have acquired regarding the trains Lionel cataloged between 1945 and 1969. Each opens with an introduction designed to shed light on the kinds of models Lionel developed and how they changed. Detailed descriptions of each cataloged model as well as recognized variations follow, along with the latest and most comprehensive price information.

Some general trends should become apparent from reading these introductory overviews. First, Lionel's engineers used models from the late prewar period as the foundation of the line that was cataloged immediately after the war. A few of the stamped sheet-metal pieces in the earlier O27 line were modified with new trucks and couplers. More often, designers looked for inspiration to a series of near-scale die-cast freight cars when deciding what to revive in the late 1940s. Not everything they considered made it to mass-production, and we can only wish that Lionel had gone ahead with plans for another Hudson steam locomotive and a die-cast hopper.

Investigating the items that were cataloged in the late 1940s and early 1950s reveals a second trend. Advances in the injection-molding of thermoplastics significantly affected toy train design and production. Those improvements, along with advances in metal die-casting, electronics, powdered metallurgy, and paint masking and spraying, enabled Lionel to manufacture models that looked more realistic and operated in more sophisticated ways than ever before. Think of the company's magnificent F3s and Train Masters, 6464-series boxcars, and Bucyrus Erie cranes, among others: all exemplified the high degree of detail that injection-molding made possible. Other technological innovations enabled Lionel to offer steam locomotives that smoked and tenders that whistled, rolling stock with all sorts of animated features, and die-cast engines that pulled more cars.

New machinery and manufacturing techniques made it possible for Lionel to produce more realistic models of contemporary railroad equipment. An emphasis on realism, carried forward from the end of the prewar period, influenced the company's product line well into the 1950s. As a result, classic models of the Pennsylvania Railroad's GG1 electric and the New York Central's 4-6-4 Hudson joined the line. Then, answering challenges laid down by rivals, Lionel released detailed models of extruded aluminum streamlined passenger cars and modern boxcars. These long, beautiful models set standards that virtually no other manufacturer of toy trains approached at the time.

Sometime in the mid-1950s, however, a third trend emerged, due in large part to a significant shift in Lionel's marketing approach. Offering authentic yet often drab replicas became less important than bringing out colorful, entertaining toys. Sales personnel saw that children were changing, and they struggled to keep up with new demands. Thus in the 1940s, Lionel had emphasized the realism of its remote-control whistle and uncoupler. No outfit had received more publicity than the sophisticated Electronic Control Set, which used radio frequency waves to control how a train was directed, loaded, and coupled. But 10 years later, long after Lionel had quit trying to market the expensive Electronic Set, it boasted of the vibrant colors of its diesels and modern rolling stock. Improved painting techniques were responsible for

the gorgeous engines it cataloged. The company's wish to broaden the appeal of its electric trains culminated in the Lady Lionel, a set painted in pastel hues. Looking nothing like reality, it was supposed to appeal to little girls.

To say that Lionel abandoned its longtime commitment to authenticity wouldn't be fair. The multiple-color schemes used on its diesels and near-scale rolling stock certainly reflected an ongoing interest in realism; so too did Lionel's introduction of Super O gauge track in 1957. But when realism had to be compromised to satisfy the market, executives rarely hesitated. How else can we explain such whimsical pieces as a boxcar with swimming fish and an operating gondola featuring a police officer chasing a tramp? Cute they definitely were, but neither had much basis in reality.

Another method of satisfying children and maintaining a market for electric trains in the late 1950s and early 1960s was to link the toys to current events. One example was a set featuring a locomotive and some rolling stock decorated for the Alaska Railroad; cataloged in 1959, outfit 1611 was intended to capitalize on the excitement surrounding the admission of Alaska into the Union. Similarly, the popularity of westerns on television and widespread interest in the centennial of the Civil War spurred Lionel to develop models of a wood-burning locomotive and passenger cars from the late 19th century.

But this fourth trend of linking toy trains to social and cultural currents was best demonstrated by Lionel's introduction of trains with military or aeronautical elements. Sensing that Americans were enthralled by the space race, the company put out trains that reflected the national mood. Soon navy blue and olive drab became favorite colors for locomotives. Flatcars shipped military vehicles and sent satellites into orbit. Boxcars launched missiles, and cabooses carried medical personnel. Before long, it seemed, animation and action characterized virtually every piece included in the Super O outfits at the top of the line. The panoply of self-propelled motorized units that often had only a tangential basis in reality showed this trend at its extreme.

Unfortunately for Lionel, circumstances were changing faster than it was. The market for electric trains was declining, and nothing Lionel and its rivals did in the 1960s could alter this change. And so the final years of the postwar era witnessed a fifth trend. Lionel did its best to maintain production by cutting costs and reducing the size of its line. Details were eliminated, graphics removed, and parts cheapened on locomotives and rolling stock. To reach customers, Lionel tried just about anything, including the creation of many promotional sets available from leading merchandisers only. Mail-order firms and chain stores wanted unique items, and that led to an increase in the number of uncataloged pieces. Many of these locomotives and cars, although lacking the details found on earlier premium pieces, have taken on great interest for collectors.

Enthusiasts study these trends and search for the locomotives and rolling stock that reflect what fascinates them. The variety of pieces mass-produced by Lionel is astounding, and the number of variations can be mind-boggling. All of this is good news for collectors of postwar trains because it gives them more than enough to obtain, investigate, and analyze. This hobby can indeed become a lifetime pursuit, as the electric trains that we played with as youngsters consume our passions and challenge us to learn more about them.

POSTWAR TRUCKS AND COUPLERS

by Paul V. Ambrose

TYPE I: Staple-end (metal) trucks — **1945–51**
- Early coil couplers — 1945–mid 46
- Late coil couplers — mid 1946–48
- Magnetic couplers — 1948–51

TYPE II: Scout (combination) trucks — **1948–53**
- Scout couplers — 1948–51
- Magnetic couplers — 1950–53

TYPE III: Bar-end (metal) trucks — **late 1951–61, 1969**
- Early version with pivot stud — late 1951–61
- Late version attached with truck-mounting clip — 1955–58, 1969

Note: *All* bar-end trucks came with a magnetic coupler and a metal knuckle that was released by an armature flap; an extended tab was added to the flap in 1955 to facilitate hand-opening of the coupler. By 1958 bar-end trucks were virtually gone from the product line. However, because of the delay in the development of their AAR truck replacement, early versions with a ground washer at the pivot stud were used until 1961 on most operating and lighted cars that required either a sliding shoe or contact roller assembly.

TYPE IV: AAR (plastic) trucks — **1957–69**
- Early version with closed journal boxes — 1957–63
- Late version with open journal boxes — late 1963–69

Note: Operating couplers with AAR trucks also function on a magnetic principle. Instead of being released by an armature flap, the knuckle opens when a disk is drawn downward. Hence the sometimes-used term "disk-operating coupler."
    There are three distinctly different knuckles:

Metal knuckle attached with a silver pin	1957–62
Deldrin knuckle attached with a silver pin	late 1961–62
Deldrin knuckle with integral pivot points that eliminated the need for a knuckle pin	1962–69

Both early and late versions appear with a fixed coupler.

TYPE V: Arch-bar (plastic) trucks — **1959–69**

Note: These trucks were modeled from examples of the Civil War period; they *usually* appear with a fixed coupler. Some examples with operating couplers are passenger cars 1875, 1875W, and 1876.

TYPE VI: Six-wheel (combination) trucks — **1946–51**

Note: These trucks always came with coil couplers and appear exclusively with Madison passenger cars, the 2460 crane, and a few tenders, such as 2671W.

TYPE VII: 2400-series (O27 gauge and metal) passenger trucks — **1948–66**
- Early version with coil couplers — 1948–53
- Late version with magnetic couplers — 1954–66

TYPE VIII: 2500-series (O gauge and metal) passenger trucks — **1952–66**

TRUCKS AND COUPLERS
by Paul V. Ambrose

When collectors investigate Lionel production and seek to ascertain the number and types of variations that exist of particular cataloged pieces, they often look at trucks and couplers. The research and close examination of postwar trucks and couplers that went into preparing the revision of this volume—and publication of Volume VII, a more complete study of selected variations—reveal that there are eight types of trucks as well as numerous coupler modifications. The accompanying chart summarizes the eight basic types of trucks and the couplers used with them. As you see from this chart, trucks and couplers varied from all-metal to all-plastic to combinations of the two. The story of the evolution of postwar trucks is told in the accompanying series of photographs and captions. **Note:** Although the assignment of type numbers facilitates understanding of the development of trucks across the years, the detailed listings in the following chapters cite the type of truck by name for the convenience of the reader.

Body molds and heat-stamping don't lie—unless they are forgeries, of course—but trucks can. In examining a Lionel item for possible purchase, collectors must recognize that the trucks and couplers on a model may have been changed since it left the factory. Even trucks that were riveted to a plastic body mold or a metal frame can be changed and still look original if someone has the proper tools. Hobbyists frequently make repairs and change frames from one car to a similar one; when the frame is changed, the trucks and couplers often change as well.

Furthermore, Lionel habitually used leftover inventory until it was depleted, and so some models did leave the factory with parts that were not typical of the production of a certain time frame. Suggested values offered in this book do not depend on the type of truck or coupler present. Nevertheless, knowledge of the truck and coupler appropriate to that model can be used to help date the item or verify its authenticity.

The general trend of postwar technology reflects Lionel's tendency to cut costs wherever possible. Less-expensive fixed coupler trucks therefore replaced those with operating couplers whenever possible, and arch-bar trucks were a penny or so cheaper than AAR (Association of American Railroads) or Timken trucks (the name Timken is embossed on the side frames of AAR trucks). By 1958, bar-end trucks were becoming ancient history. After 1962 production, O27 gauge items came with only one operating coupler, and low-end production typically came with two fixed couplers.

All pre-1955 trucks came with a black knuckle pin; silver pins appeared in late 1955, and black pins continued to surface in 1956 as inventory was depleted. Truck Types IV, V, and a modified late version of VII used a snap-in roller carriage for the illumination of certain cars or when center-rail power was needed for a whistle tender.

Side view of Type I staple-end truck. This example has a coil coupler and the usual pivot stud.

Bottom view of Type I staple-end trucks. Left: The early coil coupler with thick axles. Right: Another example with early coil coupler but with typical axles.

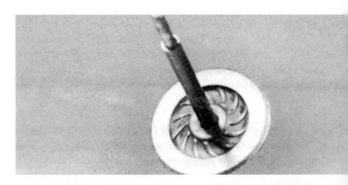

The earliest 1945 Type I trucks came with whirly wheels. Note that the axle end has been turned down, creating a collar to control wheel gauging.

Side view of other Type I staple-end trucks. Left: An example with
late coil coupler. Right: A version with magnetic coupler. Note
that both trucks have the typical pivot stud.

*Side view of a Type III bar-end truck. The example shown is a 1955
version that eliminated the pivot stud. This style of truck was fastened to the car with a truck-mounting clip.*

Bottom view of Type I staple-end trucks. Left: 1946–47 era, with
late coil coupler activated through a sliding shoe by a 1019 or an
RCS. Right: The last version of the staple-end truck with a magnetic coupler. (Note the hole in the activator flap and the rivet
with the flared end down.)

*Bottom view of Type III bar-end trucks. Left: Pre-1955 version with-
out the extended tab on the armature flap. The example shown
was attached by means of a pivot stud, and included a metal plate
that was necessary to attach the truck assembly to certain cars,
such as the 6511 pipe car. Right: The 1955 version with an extended
tab to facilitate uncoupling. Note that both trucks have the rivet
that attaches the armature flap with the round head down.*

The Type II Scout truck consisted of a stamped-metal frame into
which plastic side frames were pressed.

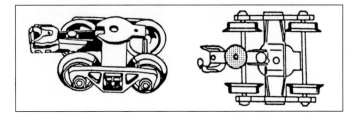

Side and bottom views of Type IV early AAR trucks.

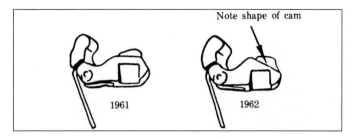

Bottom view of the two Delrin knuckles used with Type IV trucks. Pre-1962 production used a metal knuckle.

Side and bottom views of the Type V arch-bar trucks with disk-operating coupler.

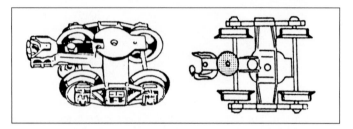

Side view of the Type VII truck.

Underside of Type VII O27 gauge passenger truck (left) and O gauge passenger truck (right).

Side view of the Type VIII truck.

STAMPING
by Alan Stewart

Heat-stamping uses a reel of colored tape moved via a film "carrier"; the item to be stamped is held in position with a tool just below the tape. The heated die (with whatever shape or lettering is to be printed) is pressed against the back of the tape, forcing the colored side onto the part to be decorated. The heat melts the color onto the part and usually causes indentations in the paint and the plastic. Metal parts, like the cab numbers of many die-cast steam locomotives, also can be heat-stamped.

There are several variables in the heat-stamping process, only one of which is the heat. A critical part of the setup is adjusting the die closure to just "kiss" the surface of the part. Too light and you get only partial color transfer; too heavy and the centers of the letters "O" and "A" fill in. The lettering can be burned in so deep as to make it look like a branded cow! The procedures and tooling required by this process are the reasons heat-stamped fakes are not usually found. Be aware, however, that the color of original heat-stamping can be chemically changed. Some unscrupulous persons do this with acids and dyes and try to pass them off as rare variations! Usually, however, it is easier to change the color of a painted car and leave the heat-stamped lettering, which is much more difficult to affect. But the important feature, aside from the "cratering" around the edges of a heat-stamped decoration, is that the decoration has a smooth, uniform appearance. Paint from the tape is actually transferred to the part.

Rubber-stamping, on the other hand, transfers ink applied to the stamp from a pad or roller, to the part. This leaves a "grainy" appearance to the decoration.

Heat-stamped decoration is much more durable than the rubber-stamped kind. It is also more attractive. Lionel went to the trouble and expense of using it extensively. The 6356 New York Central stock car and 6464-125 New York Central boxcar are two examples of rolling stock that was decorated with both techniques, and they are common enough for most collectors to have an example of each.

NEW DATES AND BUILT DATES
by Paul V. Ambrose

Although Lionel's offerings included imaginary road names, such as Lionel Lines tenders and Bronx Zoo box cars, among others, many models were based on railroad prototypes. In reproducing these real cars, Lionel used

Examples of the many styles of cardstock boxes used during the postwar period. Top to bottom, left to right: (1) side view, Art Deco; (2) side view, Early Classic; (3) side view, Middle Classic; (4) top view, OPS Classic; (5) side view, Late Classic with the stock number deleted from the sides; (6) end view, Bold Classic; (7) end view, Late Classic; (8) top view, Perforated Picture; (9) bottom view, same for both Orange Perforated and Orange Picture; (10) top view, Orange Perforated; (11) top view, Orange Picture; (12) bottom view, Cellophane-front; (13) top view, Cellophane-front; (14) side view, early version of Hillside Orange Picture that showed only the new corporate name "The Lionel Toy Corporation"; (15) side view, typical version of Hillside Orange Picture; (16) top and bottom views, same for both Hagerstown and Hillside checkerboard; (17) end view, Hagerstown Checkerboard; (18) end view, Hillside Checkerboard. B. Myles Collection.

authentic heralds and dimensional data, including "CAPY", "LD LMT", and other markings. It also included "BUILT" dates and "NEW" dates on many models. Our listings of variations cite this feature.

On actual rolling stock, the built date refers to the original construction of a car and the new date indicates when it was rebuilt or refurbished. So when these dates appear on a Lionel model, they add realism. Be aware, however, that they do *not* necessarily indicate Lionel's production dates.

Two examples may be helpful. The X2458 Pennsylvania boxcar is marked "NEW 3-41", although Lionel offered it from 1946 through 1948. It is possible that the real Pennsylvania Railroad boxcar replicated by Lionel had been rebuilt in March 1941, and this information was reproduced on the model. The 6014 Frisco boxcar is marked "BLT. 7-57", but Lionel made it from 1957 to 1969. In addition, Lionel stamped its 3361 log dump car and 6362 rail truck car "336155" and "636255", respectively, throughout the life span of the cars. However, the "55" had nothing to do with the catalog or stock number; it was the year (1955) that Lionel released these cars.

ORIGINAL BOXES
by Paul V. Ambrose

Any collectible item is considered complete only when it is in the box or packaging it came in (assuming it was

originally packaged in some manner). A rare edition of a book is more valuable with its original jacket and binding, and the same is true of model trains. Unfortunately, this fact was not always appreciated; not too long ago, collectors considered outfit and inner component boxes expendable and often threw them out. Many collectors shunned boxes because of storage problems or because dampness and age had taken their toll.

When reviewing the range of suggested values provided by the staff of Kalmbach Publishing Co., remember that, generally speaking, an individual component box adds 10 to 15 percent to the value of an item, and a master carton (the outer box) is valued at 10 to 15 percent of the worth of the appropriate contents of motive power. Of course the condition of the box should be at least equal to that of the item(s) it contains. Some boxes are so scarce that they are more valuable than their common contents.

The accompanying chart lists all the boxes that properly came with postwar Lionel—the terms used are those widely known to collectors; they are shown in the photograph. Remember that many low-priced and promotional items came unboxed as outfit components and there are items for which a component box does not exist.

POSTWAR PAPER-TYPE (CARDSTOCK) BOXES

by Paul V. Ambrose

ART DECO: The original postwar component box with bold blue lettering that touched the tops and bottoms of the blue frames and outlines.

EARLY CLASSIC: The most notable box of the postwar era, introduced in 1948 for the O27 line with smaller lettering; the city names "NEW YORK", "CHICAGO", and "SAN FRANCISCO"; has the stock number printed on all four sides.

MIDDLE CLASSIC: Same as Early Classic, except the city name "SAN FRANCISCO" was eliminated. It was used from mid-1949 through 1955.

OPS CLASSIC: Same as Middle Classic, but with the inclusion of a preprinted OPS (Office of Price Stabilization) stamp. It was used in 1952.

LATE CLASSIC: Same as Middle Classic, except that the stock number was eliminated from the four sides. It was used from 1956 through 1958.

BOLD CLASSIC: Same as Late Classic, but with a much bolder-faced print on the end flaps. It was used for part of the 1958 product line.

GLOSSY CLASSIC: A scarce box that surfaced in 1958. It was made in the Classic design, but it was printed on coated stock similar to what was introduced in 1959. The 3424 Wabash brakeman, for example, occasionally came in this type of box, as did a 260 bumper and the 3366-100 white horses.

ORANGE PERFORATED: A dramatic change in graphics that was a total departure from the Classic design. The box was orange coated stock that had a tear-out perforated front panel. It was used in 1959 and 1960.

PERFORATED PICTURE This box occasionally surfaced in 1961 and 1962. It was not routinely used but was simply a means by which to deplete unfinished, perforated-front "raw" stock. It sometimes appears with a rolling stock item, but its use was most prevalent for early-issue Presidential passenger cars.

ORANGE PICTURE: A variation of the Orange Perforated without perforations and with a picture of a steam and F3 locomotive on the front, and the city names "NEW YORK" and "CHICAGO". It was used from 1961 and 1964 and included the phrase "THE LIONEL CORPORATION".

HILLSIDE ORANGE PICTURE: Similar to Orange Picture, but "HILLSIDE, N.J." (the location of the Lionel plant) replaced "NEW YORK" and "CHICAGO". It was used for part of the 1965 product line and included the new (in 1964) corporate name "THE LIONEL TOY CORPORATION".

CELLOPHANE-FRONT: This was Lionel's first attempt to make package contents visible by adding a cellophane window to the front of the box. The window was used in 1966, and the stock number was no longer printed on the end flaps as part of the manufacturing process; it was now rubber-stamped.

HAGERSTOWN CHECKERBOARD: Another dramatic change in graphics. This 1968 component box had a Lionel checkerboard pattern with "HAGERSTOWN, MARYLAND" printed at the bottom of the end flaps. Lionel moved their operations to Hagerstown for the years 1967 and 1968. The 6014-series boxcars, the SP-type cabooses, and the 6464-series boxcars all utilized the same size box, and the stock numbers were applied with a rubber stamp. Exceptions to box size were made for the large 6560 crane and the small 260 bumper; Hagerstown Checkerboard graphics were used on boxes sized appropriately for these items, and the stock numbers were type-stamped rather than rubber-stamped.

HILLSIDE CHECKERBOARD: Same as Hagerstown Checkerboard, except that "HILLSIDE, NEW JERSEY" replaced "HAGERSTOWN, MARYLAND" in 1969.

LAST RESORT: When everything else was depleted, Lionel sometimes reverted to using a plain generic white or "last resort" box during the late 1960s. Most were rubber-stamped, but an occasional type-stamped example does surface.

2

STEAM LOCOMOTIVES

Introduction by Roger Carp

At the dawn of the post–World War II era, the steam locomotive ruled the Lionel line, just as it did nearly all the railroads in the United States. To be honest, it was even more entrenched at Lionel in 1945. Prototype railroads were adding diesel-powered locomotives to their rosters, and some made extensive use of electric units. But the largest manufacturer of toy trains took a different approach and committed its resources to steamers. During the final years of the prewar period, Lionel actually dropped O and O27 gauge models of electrics and assembled an all-steam roster.

The company's infatuation with steam locomotives had several sources. First and foremost, Joshua Lionel Cowen, its founder and president, loved these engines. He thought they were beautiful and powerful, and firmly believed that every boy in America shared his sentiments. And on this point he was surely correct. In the early 1940s and again following the war, youngsters clamoring for Lionel trains couldn't take their eyes off its array of large and small steam locomotives. They loved the intricate detail, the operating lights and whistle, and the moving parts that characterized Lionel's offerings. So a second element in the firm's commitment to steam was that in bringing out improved models it was meeting the market's demands.

Two other factors explained Lionel's emphasis on steam. Diesel and electric locomotives might be making inroads on rail lines across America, but steam still prevailed right before and after the war. If anything, the 1930s and 1940s represented a landmark era for steam, with enormous, awe-inspiring locomotives being built, including some unforgettable streamlined ones. Kids glimpsed steam engines every day, and they dreamed of having miniature versions on their tabletop layouts or their bedroom floors. Fortunately for Lionel, advances in technology enabled it to turn youngsters' dreams into reality. Until the early 1930s, engineers had no alternative to stamping and blanking sheet metal in order to mass-produce Standard and O gauge locomotives. The engines Lionel designed were not, therefore, authentic scale models. The advent of metal die-casting technology changed this situation and made it possible to create rugged models with more detail than previously imagined. Another breakthrough, the invention of a reliable, realistic whistle, only bolstered the appeal of Lionel's steamers.

Lionel had capitalized on its superior die-casting techniques and innovative use of electrical features to introduce some classic O gauge models of contemporary steam locomotives in the late 1930s. Having a cadre of dedicated draftsmen and model makers working under the direction of chief engineer Joseph Bonanno didn't hurt either, especially when they had at their fingertips blueprints lent by railroads. From the drawing boards of this brilliant staff came models of a streamlined Pennsylvania Railroad Torpedo and an impressive 2-6-2 at the lower end of the fleet and a scale New York Central Hudson and Pennsy switcher at the top. "No compromises necessary!" declared a prewar catalog. "Lionel locomotives look right and *are* right. They're scale models in appearance as well as in performance." The conclusion was plain: If the engines pulling the train were accurate and dependable, so must everything else Lionel offered.

The same philosophy held sway when the war ended. With only months to prepare an outfit for merchants heading into the holiday season, Lionel needed a good-looking, reliable prewar locomotive to update with its new staple-end trucks equipped with coil couplers. Executives settled on the 224, a zinc-alloy die-cast model with a 2-6-2 wheel arrangement, cataloged as part of the O gauge line between 1938 and 1941. They paired the engine with the 2466 tender, also a slightly modified carryover. A noteworthy piece in its own right, the 2466 attested to the strides Lionel had made in compression-molding phenolic plastics prior to the war.

From all accounts, the revised 224 served its purpose, but Lionel promised much more for 1946. If the one locomotive available in 1945 reflected what the company felt compelled to do to revive interest in its trains, the models advertised in the consumer catalog a year later showed what it really wanted to accomplish now that peace had returned. More specifically, Lionel's goals were threefold in 1946: perfect new features that would set its locomotives apart from competitors', install those features on brand-new and established models, and offer distinctive engines for both the O and O27 gauge lines. By and large, the company met all three goals.

The innovation that drew the most comment from consumers and within the trade was a smoking mechanism. It relied on a special bulb installed in top-of-the-line locomotives; smoke pellets were dropped onto the bulb, where they were heated until they dissolved. The effect was somewhat disappointing, because the amount of smoke wasn't great. Still, as had been true with a remote-control whistle in the late 1930s, Lionel was the pioneer. Engineers also kept improving the design and operation of its remote-control knuckle coupler. A third step forward was the introduction of an elaborate control, directional, and uncoupling system utilizing radio frequency waves. This system, developed by Joseph Bonanno, came installed in a four-car freight outfit known as the 4109WS Electronic Control Set. All components were equipped with receivers to respond to an operator's commands.

While some members of the engineering department busied themselves with the smoking mechanism or the Electronic Set, others worked feverishly to bring out the new models demanded by sales executives. Typically, designers studied prewar offerings to see what could be modified for the product line without looking antiquated. They concentrated on an 0-4-0 switcher (the 1662 updated as the 1665) and an O27 gauge 2-4-2 (the 204 updated as the 1654). In addition, they studied what was getting attention on the major railroads in the Northeast, where Lionel's market was strongest. A trio of magnificent new O gauge steam locomotives resulted from the engineers' efforts, along with two incredible might-have-beens.

Because its headquarters were located in New York City, Lionel had for decades been keenly aware of what engines and passenger trains ran on the Pennsylvania Railroad and the New York Central. This trend influenced two of the new locomotives for 1946. Just two years earlier, the Pennsy had ordered a huge turbine-driven 6-8-6 engine from Baldwin Locomotive Works. This beast, the sole member of the S2 class, never amounted to much—it pulled only scattered passenger trains prior to being retired in 1952. But all the publicity given the Turbine intrigued Lionel, and its designers announced O and O27 gauge versions (the 671 and 2020, respectively). This giant, boasting a whistle, smoke unit, and double worm-drive Atomic Motor, dominated the year's line. Lionel even adapted this model to provide motive power for the Electronic Set (the 671R).

Also new for the O27 line exclusively was a sleek and shiny model of the New York Central's streamlined class J-3a Hudson. The 221 featured a die-cast boiler painted gray and rubber-stamped silver, along with a 221T or 221W sheet-metal tender with striking decaled lettering and striping. Modeled after the engines that pulled the *Empire State Express*, the 221 brought back memories of

the O gauge pressed-steel and enameled Commodore Vanderbilt streamlined Hudson that was cataloged from 193? through 1939.

The Turbine, advertised as the top-of-the-line O2? locomotive, fell to midrange among O gauge motive power. That's because Lionel had so much more to offer. Engineers set their sights on updating the stately 226, a die-cast 2-6-4 painted black and cataloged between 1938 and 1941. They adapted its boiler, installed an extra set of driving wheels (to make it a 2-8-4), fitted it with the latest trucks and couplers, and put in an Atomic Motor and smoking mechanism. The engine, numbered 726, was teamed with the scale-proportioned 2426W tender. With its separate steps and handrail, die-cast whistle box, and six-wheel trucks, this tender stood out as the finest of its time. Lionel christened this locomotive the Berkshire after a prototype on the Boston & Albany, a subsidiary of the New York Central, and designated it as the motive power for three outstanding outfits.

But Lionel had still bigger plans for 1946. The consumer catalog depicted modified versions of two notable prewar steamers, the 203 Pennsylvania Railroad class B6 0-6-0 switcher and 763 New York Central class J-1 4-6-4 Hudson. To be sure, neither had been the premium version of those respective models, but both would have been excellent additions to the postwar O gauge roster. Sadly for Lionel enthusiasts, the updated items (the 40? and 703, respectively) weren't mass-produced. Mystery surrounded the decision not to manufacture them. Perhaps orders from distributors and dealers failed to meet expectations. Or high-level executives might have worried that offering additional motive power would only hurt sales of the new Turbine and Berkshire. Whatever the reason, Lionel simply reported that updated versions of its scale-detailed locomotives, like those of the prewar die-cast hopper and caboose also shown in the 1946 catalog, were not going to be made.

Difficult as it might be to believe, 1946 was the watershed year for Lionel's postwar steam locomotives. Never again would it bring out three new models in a single year, certainly not ones collectors salute as classics. Although the company produced other desirable engines, Lionel, like prototype railroads, kept diverting more of its resources to diesels. Naturally, the shift wasn't abrupt. For example, 1947 saw some noteworthy developments, as engineers ironed out problems with the Berkshire and Turbine and heralded an improved smoke unit. They also modified the 225 steamer, a 2-6-2 cataloged from 1938 through 1942. The new engine, assigned the numbers 67? in O gauge and 2025 in O27, was promoted as a replica of the Pennsy's class K4 Pacific. Youngsters probably didn't care that the actual locomotive had a 4-6-2 wheel arrangement, but this error suggested that realism was becoming less of a priority for Lionel.

The growing emphasis on marketing toys that families could afford no matter what their budget had a major impact on the steam engine and tender introduced in 1948. Ignoring the O gauge roster, engineers gratified the wish of sales personnel for an inexpensive train to counter the inroads being made by Louis Marx and Company. They devised the 1001 Scout locomotive, a 2-4-2 with Lionel's first injection-molded plastic boiler. A year later, perhaps because executives felt uncomfortable relying so heavily on plastic, they substituted a die-cast boiler and renumbered this stripped-down model as the 1110. As kids learned, however, the Scout's real problems were mechanical, not aesthetic. Its plastic-case motor and unreliable reversing unit inundated Lionel's service stations with repairs and tarnished the reputation of its engineering department.

As though to make amends for the Scout, a group of engineers conducted experiments involving magnetism and powdered metallurgy. Their labors culminated in the development of what Lionel called Magnetraction, a process that increased a locomotive's pulling power and enabled it to stay on track better. Sintered-iron wheels were the key to enhanced performance, and by 1950 many steamers had received these improved parts. Lionel renumbered engines to reflect this change, with the Turbine becoming the 681 and the Berkshire becoming the 736, for example. From this time on, Magnetraction became standard on most Lionel locomotives. An exception was 1952, when shortages of Alnico magnetic material caused by the Korean War forced Lionel to release versions of the Turbine and the Berkshire (the 671RR and 726RR, respectively) as well as a reissued 675 and 2025 that lacked Magnetraction.

Happy as Lionel's engineering staff and sales force were about Magnetraction, they could have guessed it would be overshadowed by the return of a near-scale model of the New York Central's 4-6-4 Hudson. Lionel flirted with this in 1946, but abandoned its plans. Four years later, however, to mark the firm's golden anniversary, it brought back a version of what many observers claimed was its finest O gauge steam engine. The 773 boasted the latest features, particularly Magnetraction and a smoking mechanism. True, it wasn't entirely to scale and didn't even have all the details of the 763. Nonetheless, enthusiasts lauded the 773 and its 2426W tender as a classic and have prized it ever since.

Sad to say, Lionel removed this masterpiece after only a year. Yet the executives who put together the product line wanted to do more with the 4-6-4 wheel arrangement. Consequently, in 1950 they instructed engineers to design a modified Hudson for the O27 line. The new model, numbered 2046, shared a New York Central heritage with its O gauge counterpart. Its boiler casting derived from one developed for the 726. The 2046, which came with a 2046W Lionel Lines tender, ran through 1951, was replaced in 1952 by a twin lacking Magnetraction (the 2056), and returned to the line for 1953.

Hudsons definitely stayed on the minds of engineering and sales personnel for the next few years. They began in 1953 by cataloging another type of Hudson with the 2046. Whereas the latter used a casting based on a New York Central boiler, the new 685 and its O27 partner (the 2055) had one that captured the look of an Atchison, Topeka & Santa Fe Railway prototype. These steam engines came with the usual smoke, whistle, and headlight, along with a 6026W Lionel Lines tender. Then in 1954 Lionel replaced the 685 in the O gauge line by the all-but-identical 665. That Santa Fe-type 4-6-4, cataloged through 1959, differed from its predecessor in having a feedwater heater in front and later being teamed with a 2046W tender. An O27 version, the 2065, was available from 1954 through 1956. As if matters weren't confusing enough, Lionel also introduced an O gauge version of the 2046. The 646, which ran through 1958, also came with a 2046W tender.

After 1955, the last year Lionel offered the 682 deluxe Turbine, it de-emphasized the role of steam locomotives in its O gauge line. Diesels predominated as motive power for the biggest, most expensive outfits. Having a Berkshire, a Hudson or two, and occasionally something else seemed enough. The situation was different in O27. Lionel maintained an extensive line that included 2-6-4s with and without smoke and Magnetraction (the 2037 and 2016, respectively) and two Hudsons. Designers supplemented it in 1955 with a reissued 0-4-0 switcher (the 1615) and in 1957 with a 2-4-2 decorated for the Pennsylvania Railroad (the 250). They also rolled out a 2037 with a 1130T tender, both painted pink and lettered blue, to pull the pastel Girls' Set in 1957 and 1958.

But the biggest story of the late 1950s for Lionel's steam enthusiasts broke in 1957, when the 746 was introduced. Amid the diesels and electrics in the brand-new Super O line, Lionel brought out a stunning replica of the Norfolk and Western Railway's class J 4-8-4 Northern. Loaded with such features as illuminated marker lights and a liquid smoke generator, the streamlined 746 proved that, as the consumer catalog insisted, "steam locos can be right up to the minute in power and design."

Language like this suggested that Lionel had initiated and solidly backed the development of what many collectors consider its most desirable postwar steam locomotive. The truth was somewhat different, as no evidence has surfaced that the company planned another highly detailed and expensive steamer. But in 1956, John Van Dyck, an O gauge modeler living in Virginia, contacted Lionel regarding one of his locomotives. He had converted a 726 Berkshire into a replica of the streamlined Norfolk and Western J that he often glimpsed near his home. Van Dyck sent his modified engine and tender to Lionel, and its engineering staff took over and finished the 746.

Through 1959, the J, with its brilliant red striping and yellow lettering, pulled top-of-the-line freight sets. Strangely, these Super O outfits usually included space and military rolling stock that hinted at a future world in which steam locomotives had no place. The same uneasy juxtaposition of yesterday and tomorrow appeared in 1959 when, in the midst of proclaiming itself to be the toy maker of the space age, Lionel issued its first model of a 19th-century locomotive and tender. Two models of a 4-4-0 General were cataloged through 1962: the Super O gauge 1872 had a smoking mechanism and Magnetraction, the O27 1862 did not.

The motivation for offering an antique train most likely stemmed from a wish to capitalize on the nation's fascination with the Wild West and the upcoming centennial of the Civil War. Lionel knew that Thomas Industries, a small firm established in New Jersey, had made O gauge models of 19th-century locomotives in the late 1940s and 1950s, but never considered it much of a threat. Of more concern might have been news that two rivals, The A. C. Gilbert Company and Louis Marx and Company, planned to introduce old-time train sets in 1959. Lionel had no choice but to respond in hopes of preventing the S gauge American Flyer Frontiersman or the O27 Wm. Crooks set from stealing customers.

After the J and the General, the 1960s were anticlimactic for Lionel's steam roster. That's appropriate, remembering that nearly all the real steam engines still around were being sent to scrap yards or museums. The high point for Lionel came in 1964, when it brought back the 773 Hudson for a final two-year run, this time with the 773W tender. Otherwise, the 1960s deserved attention only because of the assortment of O27 gauge 2-4-2s available. These plastic models, descendants of the Scout locomotives, appeared with a range of numbers, coupled to different tenders, in cataloged and uncataloged sets. Nearly all the engines had a light, some came with a smoking mechanism, and a fair number were equipped with Magnetraction. Painted stripes embellished a few of them, as did tenders lettered for the Baltimore and Ohio, Pennsy, or the Southern Pacific.

200-SERIES SCOUT ENGINE BODY TYPES, METAL-CASE MOTORS

Chart by Paul V. Ambrose, H. Lovelock, and A. Stewart

Type	No.	Year Issued	Distinguishing Characteristics
I	1130	1953	Small generator detail at top rear of boiler No E-unit slot Small smokestack Thin running board with plugged hole Plain boiler front Solid cowcatcher
II	250	1957	Same as Type I, except thick running board
III	248 249	1958	Same as Type I, except thick running board Curved E-unit slot added to top of boiler
IV	247	1959	Small generator detail at top rear of boiler Curved E-unit slot Large smokestack Thick running board with plugged hole Condenser detail added below headlight Solid cowcatcher
V	247	1959	Similar to Type IV, except thick running board with open hole and see-through generator
VI	243 244	1960	Small generator detail removed Curved E-unit slot Large smokestack Thick running board with plugged hole Condenser detail below headlight Solid cowcatcher restored

Note: Metal-case motors were secured through the top of the boiler with a 6/32 by 6/17 motor-mounting screw, and had a conventional E-unit with a metal reversing lever.

From *Greenberg's Guide to Lionel Trains 1945–1969, Vol. VII*

200-SERIES SCOUT ENGINE BODY TYPES, PLASTIC-CASE MOTORS

Chart by Paul V. Ambrose, H. Lovelock, and A. Stewart

Type	No.	Year Issued	Distinguishing Characteristics
VII	245 246	1959	Small generator detail at top rear of boiler Reverse lever slot at center line of boiler Large smokestack Thick running board Condenser detail below headlight See-through cowcatcher Threaded motor-mounting pin
VIII	233 235 236 237 238 242 246	1969	Similar to Type VII, except small generator detail removed, solid cowcatcher restored, knurled motor-mounting pin
IX	239 241 251	1965	Incorporated the changes made to Type VIII, except with die-cast boiler. Last production use of "old" tooling that began with 1654 in 1946.
X	237 238 240 242	1964	A completely new tool designed for plastic rather than die-casting. Similar to previous types with finer detailing. The most noticeable characteristics are thin running board and absence of the bell platform.

Note: All plastic-case motors were secured with a motor-mounting pin that went crosswise through the body at running-board height.

From *Greenberg's Guide to Lionel Trains 1945–1969, Vol. VII*

Lionel's move from steam motive power for its O gauge line paralleled the abandonment of steam on prototype railroads. But collectors appreciate the superb models Lionel did develop and pay increasing attention to the diverse locomotives produced for the O27 gauge line at the end of the postwar era. Like all of Lionel's steamers, they keep alive memories of the time when steam was sovereign.

TENDERS

Collectors often overlook the tenders that belong with steam locomotives. This is unfortunate because the values cited in the listings that follow require a locomotive to have its correct tender. We must, therefore, be familiar with the eight types of tenders marketed during the postwar period. All eight are described in detail, with their variations shown in photographs, in *Greenberg's Guide to Lionel Trains, 1945–1969, Volume VII: Selected Variations.*

Semiscale Tenders

The semiscale die-cast tender was a carryover design from the prewar period; all postwar models were designated 2426W. The detail and ornamentation included with the tender were exceptional; the deck handrail was attached with stanchions and nuts, and separate screw-fastened steps appeared at each of the four corners. The 1946–1947 version utilized a metal-body whistle, while 1948–1950 production came with a plastic-body whistle. Being the top-of-the-line tender, 2426W was paired exclusively with the top-of-the-line engines, which were the 726 Berkshire (1946–1949) and the 773 Hudson (1950).

Early Coal Tenders

The design for the early coal tenders with plastic bodies originated in the prewar period; all examples are identified with mold number 1666T-4. As a group, these tenders are difficult to analyze and chronicle, and Lionel's policy of numbering the underframes, usually by rubber-stamping them in silver, was inconsistent.

The railing detail on 2466 and 6466 tenders was designated by a suffix: "T" or "W" models generally came without a railing, and "WX" examples came with deck railing only. Premium tenders 671W, 2020W, and 6020W came with railing on the deck and at the four corners. Hobbyists and dealers make body and frame changes regularly and often erroneously assemble tenders. The color of lettering underwent several changes. Early postwar production came with white heat-stamped lettering (the same as prewar), which was soon changed to silver. About 1949, however, the lettering reverted to white.

Truck and coupler information followed the norm. However, some 6000-series tenders from 1948, such as 6020W and 6466W, still came with coil couplers as Lionel depleted inventory.

Sheet-metal Tenders

Originally developed for low-cost sets in the early 1940s, the sheet-metal body style was carried forward to the postwar period to serve the same purpose. The body and frame are joined by a series of slots and flexible tabs. It is difficult to disjoin and reassemble a sheet-metal tender—the tabs are apt to break.

Slope-back Tenders

There are two distinctly different versions of slope-back tenders. The early models, 2403B and 6403B, used a prewar design and featured die-cast bodies, ringing bells, and exceptional detailing. They are identified by die number 2203T-4 on the inside of the body. Unfortunately, the die-cast version was discontinued after the 1949 product year; in 1955 the style was resurrected as the vastly inferior plastic-body 1615T.

The plastic body, embossed with mold number 1615-52, was cataloged in various forms for the remainder of the postwar period. The slope-back tender was further cheapened in 1963 with the introduction of the tab frame that eliminated the rear step and the need for a screw to attach the body to the chassis. Comparing a 2403B with a 1061T, a stranger to the hobby would have difficulty believing they were made by the same company.

Streamlined Tenders

The Lionel version of the streamlined tender was introduced in 1948; by and large, the style was copied generally from the model used by the Pennsylvania Railroad with its twenty-wheel steam turbine locomotive. All regular-production items were "W" or whistle tenders.

As opposed to some Lionel tenders, the original tooling used for this one did *not* include a body mold number.

Late 1940s and early 1950s production utilized many different underlying colors of plastic for the body mold, while subsequent production used mainly black; a notable exception is the 746W Norfolk and Western, which regularly came in dark red, mottled plastic. The body underwent subtle changes over time.

Small Streamlined Tenders

The small streamlined tender was introduced in 1954 as the 1130T to replace the 6066T as a low-end set component. The stock number designation resulted from the original pairing of the tender with the 1130 engine. Because of their specific purpose, none ever came with a whistle; all versions were strictly nonwhistle "T" tenders.

All bodies from the series were molded from black plastic and identified on the inside with mold number 1130-27. The pink 1130T-500 tender from the Girls' Set is the most valued item in the series. Another interesting piece is an uncataloged example from the mid-1960s with Southern Pacific lettering.

Square Tenders

The 6026 or square-body style was introduced in 1953 and touted as a freight tender. The body was not copied from a prototype but incorporated the designs of several tenders used on real railroads. The basic tender body does not have a body mold number. Examples with "6026W" heat-stamped on the sides began to appear around 1957. All square tenders came with chemically blackened frames and followed the normal progression of box, truck, and coupler modifications.

The General Tenders

The General tenders made their debut in 1959 with the 1862 and 1872 wood-burning locomotives. Lionel engineers took a step into the past and copied a Civil War design. All tenders were named for the Western & Atlantic Railroad and shared the same unique galvanized tab frame and rubberized wood pile.

LISTINGS OF STEAM LOCOMOTIVES

221: 1946–47. 2-6-4; painted die-cast body with silver rubber-stamped cab number; ornamental sand dome and safety valve; wire handrails; full complement of driving hardware; sheet-metal pilot and trailing trucks; sliding shoe pickup; three-position E-unit; lighted with oversized headlight lens. 221T or 221W sheet-metal tender with unique New York Central decaled lettering. Values assume whistle tender.

Note: The 221, with its distinctive Henry Dreyfuss-

221 (A) with 221T tender with typical New York Central decaled lettering.

Three different versions of the 224 locomotive. Top: The prewar version with a long drawbar and prewar tender. Observe the prewar trucks on the tender. Middle: 224 (A) with 2466W Lionel Lines tender. Notice how the items are coupled; the locomotive drawbar fits into

a slot in the tender floor. Bottom: 224 (B) with 2466WX Lionel Lines tender. Observe the rounded cab floor that projects beyond the cab (compare with example on the middle shelf). R. Swanson Collection.

	Gd	VG	Ex	LN

designed gladiator-style shroud, is patterned after the famous streamlined Hudson-type engine used by the New York Central for its *20th Century Limited* runs. This locomotive was intended for use on O27 gauge track only. If operated on O gauge layouts, it tends to lose contact with the power rail while going over switches and crossings. This can cause the E-unit to trip, stopping the train. Be aware that 1946 production has a thinner pilot than 1947 models do.

(A) 1946; gray body and cast-aluminum drivers.

	Gd	VG	Ex	LN
	60	100	125	180

(B) Same as (A) except with typical black drivers.

	Gd	VG	Ex	LN
	60	75	100	150

(C) 1947; black body and nickel-rimmed black drivers.

	Gd	VG	Ex	LN
	50	65	90	130

224: 1945–46. 2-6-2; black-painted die-cast body with metal number plate on cab; ornamental movable bell and ornamental whistle; wire handrails; nickel-rimmed Baldwin disk drivers with full complement of driving hardware; die-cast pilot and trailing trucks; three-position E-unit; lighted

These locomotives are shown with proper component boxes and appropriate master cartons. To most collectors these very scarce boxes are worth far more than the accompanying engine and tender. Top: 236 with 1130T Lionel Lines tender. Middle: 243 with 243W Lionel Lines tender. Bottom: 244 with 244T Lionel Lines tender. F. Davis Collection.

	Gd	VG	Ex	LN

with headlight lens; 2466W or 2466WX early coal tender.

Note: The postwar 224 and 1666 share the same boiler casting.

(A) 1945; blackened handrails and squared cab floor (the same as prewar) with long drawbar. The unique 1945 model 2466W tender came with blackened deck railing and did *not* include a drawbar; the engine drawbar fit into an oval hole stamped into the tender frame.

	80	95	110	175

(B) 1946; silver handrails and typical rounded cab floor with shorter drawbar that coupled to the tender in the usual manner.

	80	90	110	150

233: 1961–62. 2-4-2 Scout engine; Type VIII black-painted plastic body (see chart of Scout types at beginning of this chapter) with white heat-stamped cab number; liquid smoke unit; Magnetraction; plastic motor with two high-power magnets; two-position reverse; lighted with headlight lens; 233W square whistle tender.

	50	85	105	175

235: Uncataloged, 1961. 2-4-2 Scout engine; Type VIII black-painted plastic body with white heat-stamped cab number; liquid smoke unit; Magnetraction; plastic motor with one high-power magnet; two-position reverse; lighted with headlight lens; 1050T slope-back or 1130T streamlined tender. Extremely scarce.

	80	125	160	250

236: 1961–62. 2-4-2 Scout engine. Type VIII black-painted plastic body with white heat-stamped cab number; liquid smoke unit; Magnetraction; plastic motor with one

high-power magnet; two-position reverse; lighted with headlight lens; 1050T slope-back or 1130T streamlined tender.

	18	30	45	60

237: 1963–66. 2-4-2 Scout engine; Type VIII or X black-painted plastic body with white heat-stamped cab number; marker jewels; liquid smoke unit; plastic motor with traction tire; two-position reverse; lighted with headlight lens; 1061T or 1062T slope-back, 242T or 1060T streamlined, or 234W square whistle tender.

Note: Except for their numbers, 237 and 238 are identical. The engines were numbered differently because 238 (cataloged 1963–64) always came with a whistle tender, while 237 during the same two years regularly came with a nonwhistle tender. A whistle tender adds $25, $40, $60, and $100 to the respective prices.

	Gd	VG	Ex	LN
(A) Type VIII body.	25	35	60	70
(B) Type X body.	25	35	60	70

238: 1963–64. 2-4-2 Scout engine; same as 237, but came only with 234W square whistle tender.

Note: An example of 238 is far more difficult to obtain than 237. We have also verified an unpainted 238, but are not able to determine if the variation was planned or simply a factory error.

	Gd	VG	Ex	LN
(A) Type VIII body.	75	125	150	250
(B) Type X body.	75	125	150	250

239: 1965–66. 2-4-2 Scout engine; Type IX black-painted die-cast body with cab numbers as described below;

Top: 233 with 233W Lionel Lines tender. Middle: 235 with 1130T Lionel Lines tender. Bottom: 236 with 1130T Lionel Lines tender. T. Randazzo Collection.

	Gd	VG	Ex	LN

marker jewels; liquid smoke unit; plastic motor with traction tire; two-position reverse; lighted with headlight lens; 234W square whistle or 242T streamlined tender. Values assume whistle tender.

(A) White heat-stamped cab number.

| | 65 | 90 | 140 | 190 |

(B) Large white rubber-stamped cab number.

| | 100 | 125 | 175 | 225 |

(C) Small white rubber-stamped cab number.

| | 60 | 85 | 130 | 175 |

240: Uncataloged, 1964. 2-4-2 Scout engine; Type X black-painted plastic body with white heat-stamped cab number; marker jewels; liquid smoke unit; plastic motor with traction tire; two-position reverse; lighted with headlight lens; 242T streamlined tender. Originally issued with Sears military set 9820. **130 175 260 350**

241: Uncataloged, 1965–66. 2-4-2 Scout engine; Type IX black-painted die-cast body with white rubber-stamped cab number; marker jewels; liquid smoke unit; plastic motor with traction tire; two-position reverse; lighted with headlight lens; 234W square whistle tender.

(A) White-painted full-width running board stripe.

| | 75 | 125 | 165 | 250 |

(B) White rubber-stamped narrow running board stripe. **75 125 165 250**

242: 1962–66. 2-4-2 Scout engine; Type VIII or X black-painted plastic body with white heat-stamped cab number; plastic motor with traction tire; two-position reverse; lighted with headlight lens; 242T or 1060T streamlined tender, or 1061T or 1062T slope-back tender. Exclusively a low-end cataloged and uncataloged set component; never offered for separate sale.

| (A) Type VIII body. | 20 | 40 | 60 | 80 |
| (B) Type X body. | 20 | 40 | 60 | 80 |

243: 1960. 2-4-2 Scout engine; Type VI black-painted plastic body with white heat-stamped cab number; liquid smoke unit; metal motor; two-position E-unit; lighted with headlight lens; ballast weights front and rear; 243W square whistle tender.

Note: The 243 engine is identical to 244, except for the number; the items were numbered differently because 243 always came with a whistle tender, while 244 was paired with a nonwhistle tender. **70 100 150 200**

244: 1960–61. 2-4-2 Scout engine; same as 243, except it came with 244T slope-back or 1130T streamlined tender.

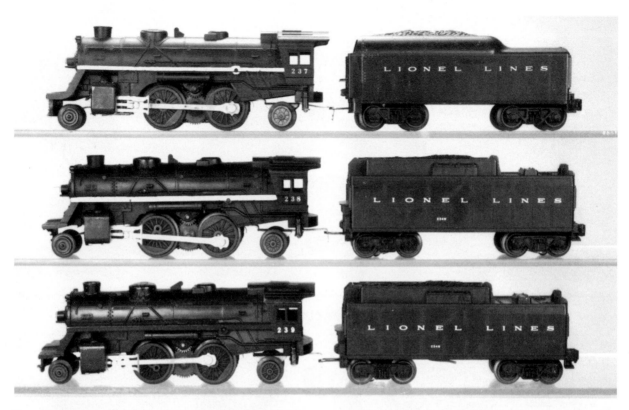

Top: 237 (B) with 1130T Lionel Lines tender. Middle: 238 (A) with 234W Lionel Lines tender. Bottom: 239 (A) with 234W Lionel Lines tender. P. Lonergan Collection.

Top: 240 with 242T Lionel Lines tender. Middle: 241 (B) with 1062T Lionel Lines tender. Bottom: 242 (B) with 242T Lionel Lines tender. M. Yeaton Collection.

Top: 243 with 243W Lionel Lines tender. Middle: 244 with 244T Lionel Lines tender. Bottom: 245 with 1130T Lionel Lines tender. K. Rubright Collection.

	Gd	VG	Ex	LN

Note: Except for the number, the 244 and 243 engines are identical; the items were numbered differently because 243 was matched with a whistle tender, while 244 came with a nonwhistle tender.

	25	30	40	50

245: Uncataloged, 1959. 2-4-2 Scout engine; Type VII black-painted plastic body with white heat-stamped cab number; Magnetraction; plastic motor with two low-power magnets; threaded motor-mounting pin; two-position reverse; lighted with headlight lens; ballast weights front and rear; 1130T streamlined tender.

Note: 245 was the only Scout engine that came with *both* Magnetraction and ballast weights.

	35	50	70	100

246: 1959–61. 2-4-2 Scout engine; Type VII or VIII commonly black-painted plastic body with white heat-stamped cab number; Magnetraction; plastic motor with one low-power magnet; two-position reverse; lighted with headlight lens; 244T slope-back or 1130T streamlined tender.

(A) 1959: Type VII body; motor with smooth bottom; threaded motor-mounting pin similar to older Scout motor.

	25	35	45	55

(B) 1960; Type VIII; usually with redesigned motor with serrated bottom; knurled motor-mounting pin.

	25	35	45	55

247: 1959. 2-4-2 Scout engine; Type IV or V black-painted plastic body with blue-painted running-board stripe and white heat-stamped cab number; liquid smoke unit; metal motor; two-position E-unit; lighted with headlight lens; ballast weights front and rear; 247T streamlined tender lettered "BALTIMORE AND OHIO".

	Gd	VG	Ex	LN
(A) Type IV body.	30	50	65	100
(B) Type V body.	30	50	65	100

248: Uncataloged, 1958. 2-4-2 Scout engine; Type III black-painted plastic body with white heat-stamped cab number; metal motor; two-position E-unit; not lighted but with headlight lens; ballast weights front and rear; 1130T streamlined tender.

Note: Except for the number and absence of running-board stripe, 248 is identical to 249.

	30	50	65	100

249: 1958. 2-4-2 Scout engine; same as 248, except for number and red-painted running-board stripe; came with 250T streamlined tender lettered "PENNSYLVANIA".

	20	30	50	60

250: 1957. 2-4-2 Scout engine; Type II unpainted black plastic body with red-painted running-board stripe and white heat-stamped cab number; metal motor; three-position E-unit with lever pointing down; lighted

Top: 246 (B) with 1130T Lionel Lines tender. Middle: 247 (B) with 247T Baltimore and Ohio tender. Bottom: 248 with 1130T Lionel Lines tender. J. Amanda Collection.

Top: 249 with 250T Pennsylvania tender. Middle: 250 with 250T Pennsylvania tender. Bottom: 251 with 1062T Lionel Lines tender. M. Bryan Collection.

	Gd	**VG**	**Ex**	**LN**

with headlight lens; ballast weights front and rear; 250T streamlined tender lettered "PENNSYLVANIA".

	20	**25**	**40**	**50**

251: Uncataloged, 1966. 2-4-2 Scout engine; Type IX black-painted die-cast body with white rubber-stamped cab number; marker jewels; plastic motor with traction tire; two-position reverse; lighted with headlight lens; 1062T slope-back tender. Extremely scarce.

	140	**225**	**280**	**450**

637: 1959–63. 2-6-4; black-painted die-cast body with white rubber-stamped cab number; ornamental bell; spoked drivers with drive rods and side rods only; sheet-metal trailing truck; Magnetraction; three-position E-unit; lighted with headlight lens; smoke. 2046W or 736W streamlined tender.

Note: Amazingly, Lionel touted this item as a Super O

engine when it shares the same boiler casting with 2036, 2026 (1951 model), 2037, 2016, 2018, 2037-500, and 2029.

	60	**90**	**160**	**225**

646: 1954–58. 4-6-4; black-painted die-cast body; most often with four-window cab; hinged boiler front with reinforcing wedges; ornamental bell; wire handrails; spoked drivers with full complement of driving hardware; earliest production with die-cast trailing truck that was replaced with sheet-metal trailing truck with plastic side frames; Magnetraction; three-position E-unit; lighted with headlight lens; smoke. 2046W streamlined tender.

Note: The 646 is a hybrid engine; it utilized the same boiler casting as the 736 Berkshire but was fitted with a 4-6-4 Hudson wheel arrangement. The boiler casting and wheel arrangement were shared with 2046 and 2056.

637 with 2046W Lionel Lines tender. Note the raised number board and heat-stamped "2046W" on tender side, indicative of late 1950s production.

Top: 646 (B) with 2046W Lionel Lines tender. This early example of the tender does not have a raised number board on the side. The chassis has been switched on this tender; the early 2046W came only with metal trucks. This example has AAR trucks. Bottom: 665 (B) with 6026W Lionel Lines tender.*

SUMMARY OF STEAM TURBINES

1946	2020 / 2020W 671 / 671W 671R / 4671W	All tenders are short 2466-type. No tender numbers. No E-unit lever. Receptacles for E-unit wire on motor brushplate. Smoke bulb. Thick nickel rims on all drivers. Extruded wheel weights. Horizontal motor, no Magnetraction. 671R has black Electronic decal on round turbine housing.
1947	2020 / 2020W 671 / 671W 671R / 4671W	Tenders have numbers on underside. E-unit lever in cab. No receptacles for E-unit wire on motor brushplate (except 671R). Smoke heater unit. Slanted motor. Thick nickel rims on all drivers. No Magnetraction. 671R has black Electronic decal moved to location under, and forward from, engineer's window.
1948	2020 / 6020W 671 / 2671W 671R / 4671W	6020W tender is same as 2020W. Thin blackened rims on front and rear drivers. No rims on center drivers. Tender 2671W is long, low, streamlined water scoop type. It has long (6") "PENNSYLVANIA" lettering, open light ports in back, and twelve wheels. 671R Electronic decal same as 1947.
1949	2020 / 6020W 671 / 2671 W 671 R / 4671W	No rims on any of the drivers.
1950	681 / 2671W	Has Magnetraction and inset wheel weights.
1951	681 / 2671W	Same as 1950.
1952	681 / 2671W	Same as 1952.
	671 / 2046W-50	No Magnetraction. No magnet in frame. Inset wheel weights. The 2046-50 has eight wheels; otherwise very similar to 2671W.
	671RR / 10467W-50 (two variations)	Numberboard re-printed with "RR" under "671"; otherwise same as 671 above. Most 671RRs do not have Magnetraction; a few of them do.
1953	681 / 2046W-50	Same as 1950, except with 2046W-50 eight-wheel tender.
1954	682 / 2046W-50	Extra valve gear linkage. White stripe down side of engine. 2046W-50 tender has short (5⅝") "PENNSYLVANIA" lettering and filled-in light ports in back.
1955	682 / 2046W-50	Same as 1954.

From Greenberg's Guide to Lionel Trains, 1945–1969, Volume II

(A) Large silver rubber-stamped cab number.

| | 125 | 175 | 250 | 350 |

(B) Small white rubber-stamped cab number.

| | 125 | 175 | 250 | 350 |

(C) Small white heat-stamped cab number.

| | 125 | 175 | 250 | 350 |

665: 1954–56, 1966. 4-6-4 Santa Fe–type Hudson; black-painted die-cast body with external feedwater heater tank on boiler front; ornamental bell and ornamental whistle; wire handrails; full complement of driving hardware; trailing truck with plastic side frames; Magnetraction; three-position E-unit; lighted with headlight lens; smoke. 6026W square tender, or 2046W or 736W streamlined tender.

Note: This engine is identical with 2065 and has the same boiler casting as 685 and 2055.

(A) White rubber-stamped cab number.

| | 100 | 175 | 245 | 320 |

(B) White heat-stamped cab number.

| | 100 | 160 | 230 | 300 |

671: 1946 (1947–49 model described in next entry). 6-8-6 model of Pennsylvania Railroad S2 steam turbine (see chart); black-painted die-cast body without E-unit slot,

	Gd	VG	Ex	LN

and flat outer surface on turbine housing; silver rubber-stamped cab number; wire handrails; thick nickel rims on *all* drivers with side rod only; horizontally mounted motor with brushplate marked "LIONEL ATOMIC / PRECISION MOTOR" with two female receptacles for E-unit jack; three-position E-unit with jack that plugs into brushplate (one receptacle on brushplate locks the E-unit in forward, neutral, or reverse, while the other jack activates the unit for sequential, transformer-controlled forward-neutral-reverse); lighted with prism lens; smoke with early smoke bulb unit. 671W early coal tender.

Note: Lionel offered 671S conversion kit to update 1946 models with heater-type smoke units. Engines that retain the original smoke bulb arrangement are considerably scarcer than converted models. Except for the number, this engine is identical with the 1946 model of 2020 that was cataloged for the O27 gauge line.

(A) "6200" rubber-stamped on boiler front keystone.
| | 120 | 175 | 250 | 350 |

(B) "6200" heat-stamped on boiler front keystone.
| | 120 | 175 | 250 | 350 |

(C) "6200" decal on boiler front keystone.
| | 80 | 125 | 200 | 300 |

671: 1947–49 (1946 model described above). 6-8-6 model of Pennsylvania Railroad S2 steam turbine; black-painted die-cast body featuring revised boiler casting with E-unit slot, rounded outer surface on turbine housing, and additional piping detail; silver rubber-stamped cab number; wire handrails; "6200" decal on boiler front keystone; side rod only; slant-mounted motor; typical three-position E-unit; lighted with usual headlight lens; smoke with usual resistance coil unit. 671W early coal tender or 2671W streamlined tender.

Note: Except for the number, this engine is identical with the 1947–49 model of 2020 that was cataloged for the O27 gauge line. See also 681.

(A) 1947; "LIONEL / PRECISION MOTOR" with tubular brushplates; thick nickel rims on *all* drivers.
| | 120 | 175 | 250 | 350 |

(B) 1948; same motor as (A), but thin blackened rims on first and fourth drivers only.
| | 200 | 275 | 375 | 500 |

(C) 1949; new slant-mounted motor, whereby the brushes were now integrated with the back plate; no rims on any drivers. | | 115 | 150 | 225 | 300 |

671R: 1946–49. 6-8-6 model of Pennsylvania Railroad S2 steam turbine; unique engine included with Electronic Control sets; silver rubber-stamped cab number appearing *only* as "671"; the 671R incorporated the other yearly changes made to turbines (see 671 entries above). Unique 4424W (stock number used in 1946) or 4671W early coal tender; light gray Electronic Control decal; frame with two Electronic Control receivers—one for whistle operation and other for control of locomotive E-unit.

Note: The following information is taken from the Lionel Service Manual. 671R is a standard 671 adapted

to electronic control by a special brushplate equipped with two jacks and a plug. A number of 671Rs made in 1946 are not equipped with a E-unit lever; on these locomotives the E-unit coil is grounded permanently and can be disconnected only at the "high" side by removing the plug from jack no. 1.

For conventional nonelectronic operation, the plug from the motor brushplate is inserted into jack no. 1, thus connecting the E-unit coil to the contact rollers of the locomotive. The E-unit indexes whenever current in the track is momentarily interrupted, whether by accident or operation of the direction control.

For electronic operation, the E-unit coil is disconnected from the locomotive contact rollers by removing the motor plug from jack no. 1 (the motor plug is then usually inserted in jack no. 2 to keep it out of the way). Instead, the E-unit coil is connected to the electronic receiver in the tender by inserting the plug from the tender in jack no. 1. Since the relay contained in the electronic receiver is normally open, the E-unit is not energized and the E-unit indexes only when the proper button on the electronic transmitter is pressed and released.

(A) Same as 1946 model of 671 (above); black Electronic Control decal on flat outer surface of turbine housing. | 130 | 220 | 315 | 450 |

(B) Transition piece without E-unit slot combining 1946 and 1947 features; usually with "671" heat-stamped on boiler front keystone. | 130 | 220 | 315 | 450 |

(C) Same as 1947–49 model of 671, but with unique brushplate (part no. 671RM-5) needed to receive the jack connection from tender; black Electronic Control decal moved to flat surface above first wheel of trailing truck.
| | 130 | 220 | 315 | 450 |

671RR: 1952. 6-8-6 model of Pennsylvania Railroad S2 steam turbine; black-painted die-cast body; silver rubber-stamped cab number; wire handrails; "6200" decal on boiler front keystone; one-piece sintered iron drivers with inset wheel weights; side rod only; *no* Magnetraction (visible hole through frame between first and second drivers); three-position E-unit; lighted with headlight lens; smoke. 2046WX (2046W-50) streamlined tender.

Note: The 671RR was the Korean War issue of the 681 *without* Magnetraction (described later). Because of inventory on hand, some 1952 examples reached the marketplace with Magnetraction.

(A) Cab numbered only "671".
| | 130 | 200 | 260 | 330 |

(B) Cab numbered "671 / RR".
| | 150 | 225 | 300 | 400 |

675: 1947–49 (1952 model described below). 2-6-2; black-painted die-cast body with silver rubber-stamped cab number; ornamental bell; wire handrails; smokestack is separate piece; nickel-rimmed Baldwin disk drivers with full complement of driving hardware; die-cast trailing truck; three-position E-unit; lighted with headlight lens; smoke. 2466WX or 6466WX early coal tender.

671R (A) with 4671W Lionel Lines tender. The example pictured is the 1946 model of the steam turbine that was included with the Electronic Control Set. Notice that the Electronic Control decal was placed on the flat outer surface of the turbine housing. H. Holden Collection.

All 671R Electronic Control Turbines were numbered "671" beneath the window and had distinctive decals on both the locomotive and tender. Note the radio receiver under the tender and the placement of the Electronic Control decal above the first wheel of the trailing truck on the locomotive. The example shown above appears as 671R (C) in our listings. H. Holden Collection.

	Gd	VG	Ex	LN

Note: This engine has the same boiler casting as 2025 and 2035. Except for the three-digit O gauge designation, it is identical with the 1947–49 model 2025. Many of the variations pertain to the decoration on the keystone that was cast into the boiler front, which is readily interchangeable.

(A) 1947; large unpainted aluminum smokestack, plain pilot, "675" rubber-stamped on boiler front keystone.
80   125   180   240

(B) Same as (A), except "675" heat-stamped on boiler front keystone. **80   120   165   220**

(C) Same as (A), except "675" decal on boiler front keystone. **80   120   165   220**

(D) Same as (A), except "5690" decal on boiler front keystone. **80   120   165   220**

(E) 1948–49; black-painted smokestack, pilot with simulated knuckle; "5690" decal on keystone.
80   120   165   220

675: 1952 (1947–49 model described above). 2-6-4; black-painted die-cast body with silver rubber-stamped cab number; "5690" decal on boiler front; black-painted smokestack, which is a separate piece; ornamental bell; wire handrails; spoked drivers with full complement of driving hardware; pilot with simulated knuckle; sheet-metal trailing truck; three-position E-unit; lighted with headlight lens; smoke. 2046W streamlined tender.
Note: Has same boiler casting as 2025 and 2035. Internally, the engine is comparable to 2035, not the 1947–49 model of 675. **80   125   200   260**

	Gd	VG	Ex	LN

681: 1950–51, 1953. 6-8-6 model of Pennsylvania Railroad S2 steam turbine; black-painted die-cast body; wire handrails; "6200" decal on boiler front keystone; one-piece sintered-iron drivers with inset wheel weights; side rod only; Magnetraction; three-position E-unit; lighted with headlight lens; smoke. 2671W or 2046WX (2046W-50) streamlined tender. See also 671RR.
Note: The number on the turbine was changed from 671 to 681 in 1950 with the introduction of Magnetraction.

(A) Silver rubber-stamped cab number.
120   200   260   375

(B) White heat-stamped cab number.
120   200   260   375

682: 1954–55. 6-8-6 model of Pennsylvania Railroad S2 steam turbine; black-painted die-cast body with white-painted running board stripe; white heat-stamped cab number; wire handrails; "6200" decal on boiler front keystone; one-piece sintered-iron drivers with inset wheel weights; side rod only with valve gear linkage attached to first driver; Magnetraction; three-position E-unit; lighted with headlight lens; smoke; 2046 WX (2046W-50) streamlined tender. **210   300   415   600**

685: 1953. 4-6-4 Santa Fe–type Hudson; black-painted die-cast body with plain boiler front; ornamental bell and ornamental whistle; wire handrails; full complement of driving hardware; trailing truck with plastic sideframes; Magnetraction; three-position E-unit;

675 (E) (1947–49 model) with 6466WX Lionel Lines tender.

Magnetraction was a feature included with the 681 and 682 models of the Turbine. Top: 681 (A) with 2671W Pennsylvania tender. Bottom: 682 with 2046-50W Penn- *sylvania tender. Observe the valve gear linkage attached to the first driver.*

Top: 685 (A) with 6026W Lionel Lines tender. Bottom: 726 (B) (1947–49 model) with 2426W Lionel Lines tender.

	Gd	VG	Ex	LN

lighted with headlight lens; smoke. 6026W square tender.

Note: Identical with 2055 and has same boiler casting as 665 and 2065.

(A) White rubber-stamped cab number.

	125	225	300	525

(B) White heat-stamped cab number.

	115	200	265	450

726: 1946 (1947–49 model described below). 2-8-4 Berkshire; black-painted die-cast body without E-unit slot; small sand dome; silver rubber-stamped cab number; hinged boiler front; ornamental movable bell and ornamental whistle; wire handrails with turned stanchions; plain pilot with hexagonal flagstaffs on pilot beam; nickel-rimmed Baldwin disk drivers with full complement of driving hardware; die-cast pilot and trailing trucks; horizontally mounted motor with brushplate marked "LIONEL ATOMIC / PRECISION MOTOR" with two female receptacles for E-unit jack; three-position E-unit with jack that plugs into brushplate (one receptacle on brushplate locks the E-unit in forward, neutral, or reverse, while the other jack activates the unit for sequential, transformer-controlled forward-neutral-reverse); lighted with headlight lens; smoke with early smoke bulb unit. 2426W semiscale tender.

Note: Lionel offered 726S conversion kit to update 1946 models with heater-type smoke units. Engines that retain the original smoke bulb arrangement are considerably scarcer than converted models.

	275	350	450	600

726: 1947–49 (1946 model described above). 2-8-4 Berkshire; black-painted die-cast body featuring revised boiler casting with E-unit slot; large sand dome; silver rubber-stamped cab number; hinged boiler front; ornamental movable bell and ornamental whistle; wire handrails; hexagonal flagstaffs on pilot beam; nickel-rimmed Baldwin disk drivers with full complement of driving hardware; die-cast pilot and trailing trucks; slant-mounted motor; typical three-position E-unit; lighted with head-

light lens; smoke with usual resistance coil unit. 2426W semiscale tender.

(A) 1947; "LIONEL / PRECISION MOTOR" with tubular brush holders; plain pilot.

	270	340	430	52?

(B) 1948; same as (A), except pilot with simulated knuckle.

	265	325	424	50?

(C) 1949; new slant-mounted motor whereby the brushes were now integrated with the back plate; pilot with simulated knuckle.

	265	325	425	50?

726RR: 1952. 2-8-4 Berkshire; black-painted die-cast body with either three-window or four-window cab; silver rubber-stamped cab number; hinged boiler front typically with reinforcing wedges; ornamental movable bell and ornamental whistle; wire handrails; spoked drivers with full complement of driving hardware; die-cast pilot and trailing trucks; *without* Magnetraction; three-position E-unit; lighted with headlight lens; smoke. 2046W streamlined tender.

Note: The 726RR was the Korean War issue of the 1950–51 model of 736 (described below).

(A) Cab numbered only "726" in larger print.

	210	330	385	52?

(B) Cab numbered "726 / RR" in smaller print.

	210	330	385	52?

736: 1950–51, 1953–68. 2-8-4 Berkshire; black-painted die-cast body; hinged boiler front; ornamental movable bell and ornamental whistle; wire handrails; spoked drivers with full complement of driving hardware; die-cast pilot truck; Magnetraction; three-position E-unit; lighted with headlight lens; smoke. 2671WX, 2046W, or 736W streamlined tender.

Note: The Berkshire underwent a number change in 1950 as Magnetraction was introduced. The 736 served as the backbone of Lionel steam power through 1966 and was cataloged as a separate-sale item in 1968. Because of the length of time it was manufactured, the 736 was constantly evolving. Some of the pertinent variables follow.

Cab window: 1950–51 (and 726RR in 1952) typically three-window style with rear horizontal frame omitted. Because of the Berkshire number change in 1950, we assume Lionel wanted to make the model appear "different" from previous issues. Most later production reverted to the typical four-window frame.

Cab number: 1950–51 production had large and fancy "736" rubber-stamped in silver. From 1953 through the remainder of production, the "736" was smaller and typically heat-stamped in white. However, some late 1960 production was rubber-stamped in white in the same size as the heat stamp.

Boiler front: In 1952 two reinforcing wedges were cast onto the plate below the headlight to prevent breakage. The wedged boiler front would remain for the balance of postwar production.

Trailing truck: Through 1954 all examples were die-cast. 1955 and later models came as the sheet-metal version with plastic side frames.

All 726 Berkshire production (left) featured a silver rubber-stamped cab number. 1950–1951 production of the 736 (right) also used a rubber-stamped cab number in the same style as the 726. Note the three-window cab arrangement on the model at right.

LIONEL 726–736 SERIES STEAM LOCOMOTIVES
2-8-4 Berkshire Type (226 Boiler Derivative)—Variations Chronology, 1946–1966

Model year		1946	1947	1948	1949	1950–1951	1952	1953–1954	1955–1956	1957–1960	1961–1966[1]
Cab number		"726" rubber-stamped—silver				"736" RS —silver	"726" or "726RR" RS— silver	"736" heat-stamped—white, thinner typeface			
Electrical	Motor	726M-1 "Atomic"	671M-1		681-000						
	Drive	Horizontal, dual worm	30° slant, single worm								
	Brushes	Tubular receptacles			Receptacles integrated with motor back plate						
	E-unit	Horizontal, spring ret., jack plug	Vertical, gravity return, lever through top of boiler								
	Collector assembly	4-screw cast mount	2-screw, stamped mount							1-screw, smaller stamped mount	
	Smoke unit	Lamp type, 18V	Resistance wire-heating element								
Wheels	Drivers	Zinc, lettered "Baldwin Disc", steel tires				Sintered iron, 1-piece, spoked					
	Axles	Bottom drop-out	Through-frame								
	Traction aid	None	Ballast weight			Magnetized drivers	None	Magnetized drivers			
	F and R trucks	Cast-metal frames—front and rear						Rear—new-style stamped frame, plastic side frames			
	Pilot plate	2-screw mounted	Staked to pilot/steam chest casting, access hole for screw								
Castings	Boiler	Short dome, open detail	Long sand dome, filled valve gear hanger detail, cast stanchion posts								
	Cab windows[2]	3- and 4-window		4-window			3- and 4-window	3-window	3- and 4-window		
	Frame	Open bottom	Closed bottom, simulated lower, boiler and suspension added			Magnet cavity, iron side plates	Cavity, no side plates	Magnet cavity, iron side plates			
	Pilot	No simulated coupler	Cast, simulated coupler and lift-pin assembly								
	Boiler front	2 small mounting lugs—top and bottom, 2 notches horizontally opposite				1 large mounting lug—top only, 1 notch at locking snap					
	Smokebox door	No headlamp brace, hole in headlamp base plate						Cast headlamp brace, baseplate hole deleted			
Hardware	Side rods	Notch in eccentric crank, coupling flat (nickel-plated in early years; cadmium-plated ca. 1953-on)									
	Handrails	Turned stanchions with nuts	Cotter pin attachment								
	Flagstaffs	Hexagon base (transition date unclear)							Round base		
	Headlamp lens	Flat plastic disk					Solid Lucite				
	Draft gear	Engine and tender close coupled				Lengthened ¼"					
Tender	Frame number	2426W					2671WX	2046W			736W
	Body style	Large die-cast derivation of prewar 2226W				1-piece plastic streamlined Pennsylvania type with water scoop					
	Misc. details	Plastic coal pipe, turned stanchions, wire handrails					3 backup lamp holes	Backup lamp holes filled; numberboards added to sides			
	Lettering	RS "LIONEL LINES," silver or white in 1946, silver only 1947–49					"LIONEL LINES" small type	"LIONEL LINES"—new typeface, larger			"PENNSYLVANIA"
	Trucks	6-wheel, plastic side frames						4-wheel, cast-metal side frames			4-wheel, all plastic
	Coupler	Electromagnetic					Spring-loaded plate (manual tab added in 1955)				Plastic, metal disk, no tab
	Whistle	Cast-metal housing horizontal motor shaft		Plastic housing, vertical motor shaft								
Misc.	Major variants	1946	1947	1948–49		1950-51	1952 (2 varieties)	1953–54	1955–56		
	Catalog price	N/A	$37.50		$42.50		$43.50 ($45.00 in 1956)			$47/$49	$50/$60

[1]Not manufactured after 1966, sold until 1968
[2]3- and 4-window variations are known to exist in many (possibly all) 226 derived boiler-cab castings (i.e., 646, 276, 736, 2046, 2056).
From *Greenberg's Guide to Lionel Trains, 1945–1969, Volume II*

New 1952 production of the Berkshire (left) was numbered "726 / RR"; the example on the right is typical for all production 1953–1966. Note the three-window cab arrangement on the 726RR.

Reinforcing wedges were added to the 736 boiler front for all new 1952 and later Berkshire production.

The pilot on 1946–1947 production of the Berkshire is shown at left. Beginning in 1948 a simulated knuckle was added to the 726 and would remain for the entire postwar production of the 736.

Flagstaffs appear on most Berkshire production through 1956. Early hexagonal-based version is at left, while late round-based version is at right.

Shown above are the three motors used to power the Berkshire. Top: 1946 "Lionel Atomic / Precision Motor" with tubular brush holders. Middle: 1947–1948 slant-mounted "Lionel / Precision Motor" with tubular brush holders. Right: 1949–1966 new slant-mounted motor that integrated the brushes into the back plate assembly.

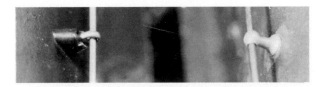

The 1946 model of the 726 (right) featured turned handrail stanchions. Beginning in 1947 (left) all Berkshire handrails were attached with cotter pins.

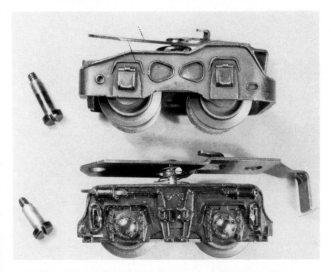

A die-cast trailing truck (top) appeared with all Berkshire models through 1954. Beginning in 1955 the plastic side frame version (bottom) became the norm.

Gd VG Ex LN

Flagstaffs: These accent pieces appear on the pilot bar of most production through 1956; however, some engines from this period surface with no evidence of ever having flagstaffs attached. Flagstaffs came in two styles—hexagonal-based (early) and round-based (late)—and some were randomly painted black.

Collector assembly: Through 1956 the collector assembly utilized wide arms and rollers and was attached by two screws. A new assembly appeared in 1957; it came with narrow arms and rollers and was attached by one screw.

(A) 1950–51; silver rubber-stamped cab number; three-window cab; plain boiler front; flagstaffs; die-cast trailing truck. **250 325 450 625**

Gd VG Ex LN

(B) 1953–54; white heat-stamped cab number; four-window cab; reinforced boiler front; flagstaffs; die-cast trailing truck. **250 300 400 525**

(C) 1955–56; same as (B), except sheet-metal trailing truck with plastic side frames. **250 300 400 525**

(D) 1957–68; white heat-stamped cab number; reinforced boiler front; flagstaffs discontinued; sheet-metal trailing truck with plastic side frames; revised collector assembly with narrow rollers and attached by one screw. **250 300 400 525**

(E) Same as (D), except white rubber-stamped cab number. **250 300 400 525**

746: 1957–60; 4-8-4 model of Norfolk and Western Railway class J Northern; black-painted die-cast body with wide red-painted running board stripe outlined in yellow; yellow rubber-stamped number on running board stripe; ornamental bell and ornamental whistle; wire handrails; unique main rod and eccentric rod assemblies; Magnetraction; three-position E-unit; lighted with headlight lens; liquid smoke unit. 746W streamlined tender.

(A) Tender with short stripe. **500 850 1195 1750**

(B) Tender with long stripe. **580 900 1275 2000**

773: 1950, 1964–66. 4-6-4 New York Central–type Hudson in 1:48 scale; black-painted die-cast body with white rubber-stamped cab number; hinged boiler front; ornamental movable bell, ornamental whistle, ornamental turbo generator, and hexagonal flagstaffs on pilot beam; wire handrails; unique spoked drivers with full complement of driving hardware; die-cast pilot and trailing trucks; three-position E-unit engaged or disengaged from brushplate assembly; lighted with headlight lens; smoke.

Note: The 773 was the grandchild of the more detailed prewar 700E and 763 and was designed to run on O gauge track. Also note that the rubber-stamped cab number is typically larger on the 1964 model.

(A) 1950; valve guide on steam chest; 2426W semi-scale tender. **700 950 1400 1800**

(B) 1964; no valve guide on steam chest; 736W streamlined tender. **455 650 900 1200**

726RR (B) with 2046W Lionel Lines tender. This model was the Korean War issue of the Berkshire without Magnetraction. F. Davis Collection.

Top: 736 (A) with 2671WX Lionel Lines tender. The diminutive letters on the tender are indicative of the

1950–1951 production. Bottom: 746 (B) with 746W Norfolk and Western long-stripe tender.

	Gd	VG	Ex	LN

(C) Same as (B), except with 773W streamlined tender. **500 750 1100 1400**

1001: 1948. 2-4-2 Scout engine. The highly detailed 1001 was the first plastic steam engine body ever used by Lionel. Unpainted black plastic body commonly with white heat-stamped cab number; side rods and crossheads; plastic motor with Baldwin disk drive wheels and tubular brass contact rollers; two-position reverse with aluminum lever; lighted but without headlight lens; threaded motor-mounting pin; 1001T sheet-metal tender lettered "LIONEL SCOUT".

Note: There also exists an extremely scarce die-cast engine numbered "1001", but it is *not* a 1001 body style. The engine alluded to is a 1101 body that was erroneously marked "1001". See 1101.

(A) Silver rubber-stamped cab number; very scarce and assumed to be the earliest production. **50 75 110 150**

(B) White heat-stamped cab number. **22 30 40 65**

1050: Uncataloged, 1959. 1001-type 0-4-0 Scout engine; unpainted black plastic body with white heat-stamped cab number; side rods and crossheads; plastic motor; forward only; lighted with headlight lens; threaded motor-mounting pin; 1050T slope-back tender. Surprisingly, although the 1050 is a very scarce engine, it has been virtually neglected by collectors for many years. **50 75 125 150**

1060: Advance catalog, 1960–62. 1001-type 2-4-2 Scout engine; unpainted black plastic body with white heat-

stamped cab number; side rods and crossheads; improved plastic motor; forward only; lighted with headlight lens; knurled motor-mounting pin; 1050T slope-back or 1060T streamlined tender.

Note: A modification was made to the boiler front around 1961. Because of the likelihood of breaking, the elongated rainshield over the headlight that was part of the original 1948 design was shortened. The shorter version would be the norm for the future 1060, 1061, and 1062 production. A 1050T tender, because of frame and truck configurations, adds $3, $5, $7, and $10, respectively, to the values listed here.

(A) Long rainshield over headlight. **12 20 30 40**

(B) Short rainshield over headlight. **12 20 30 40**

1061: Advance catalog, 1963; consumer catalog 1964, 1969. 0-4-0 or 2-4-2 1001-type Scout engine; unpainted black plastic body typically with white heat-stamped cab number; side rods only; plastic motor with or without traction tire; forward only; not lighted and without headlight lens; knurled motor-mounting pin; 1061T or 1062T slope-back tender, or 1060T or 242T streamlined tender.

Note: Slope-back tenders were either lettered "LIONEL LINES" or unlettered and are valued equally. The values provided below assume *any* of the above-mentioned tenders.

(A) Most common version, as described above. **12 20 30 40**

(B) Scarce variation without number; an occasional uncataloged set component. **40 75 110 150**

The 1:48 scale 773 was the grandchild of the more detailed prewar 700E and 763. The original Lionel design was based on a model operated by the New York Central Railroad, hence the often-used term New York Central–type

Hudson. Top: 773 (A) with 2426W Lionel Lines tender. Bottom: 773 (C) with 773W New York Central tender. Note that the water scoop on most 773W tenders is reversed—no doubt an assembly error at the factory.

	Gd	VG	Ex	LN

(C) 1969; instead of being heat-stamped, the 1061 number was printed in white on a piece of black paper and glued to the cab sides. Very scarce.

	75	125	190	250

1062: 1963–64. 0-4-0 or 2-4-2 1001-type Scout engine; unpainted black plastic body with white heat-stamped cab number; side rods only; plastic motor with or without traction tire; two-position reverse with fiber lever; lighted with headlight lens; knurled motor-mounting pin; 1061T or 1062T slope-back tender, or 1060T or 242T streamlined tender, or moderately scarce streamlined tender lettered "SOUTHERN PACIFIC".

Note: All tenders, except an example with Southern Pacific lettering (which adds a premium), are valued equally.

	12	18	30	40

1101: Uncataloged, 1948. 2-4-2 Scout engine; black-painted die-cast body with silver rubber-stamped cab number; ornamental nickel bell and whistle; metal motor with drive rods and solid crossheads; sliding contact assembly; three-position E-unit with lever projecting through top of boiler near cab; lighted but without headlight lens; motor secured crosswise with threaded mounting screw; 1001T sheet-metal tender lettered "LIONEL SCOUT".

(A) Cab erroneously rubber-stamped in silver with "1001"; very scarce.

	160	225	340	450

(B) Cab properly numbered "1101"; this engine is a common variation.

	20	28	42	60

1110: 1949, 1951–52. Modified 2-4-2 Scout engine; black-

773 (1950 version) steam cylinder with slide valve guide.

773 (1964 version) steam cylinder without slide valve.

	Gd	VG	Ex	LN

painted die-cast body with silver rubber-stamped cab number; no ornamental trim; plastic motor; two-position reverse with fiber lever projecting through top of boiler along center line between the sand and steam domes; lighted but without headlight lens; motor secured crosswise with threaded mounting pin; sheet-metal tender lettered "LIONEL SCOUT".

Note: The body casting for 1110 is similar to 1654 and 1655 but *not* interchangeable; the more noticeable modifications made to the 1654 die were plugging the ornamental bell and whistle slots, and repositioning the reverse lever slot and motor-mounting screw hole.

(A) Early 1949 production; Baldwin disk drive wheels and aluminum reverse lever.

	20	30	48	60

(B) Later 1949 production; spoked drive wheels.

	10	15	32	40

(C) Early 1951 production assembled with leftover 6110 body castings that are easily identified by a circular hole in the boiler front above the headlight.

	12	20	38	45

	Gd	VG	Ex	LN		Gd	VG	Ex	LN

(D) Later 1951–52 production, with usual body that shows faint outline above the headlight where the air-draft hole added for 6110 was plugged.

	Gd	VG	Ex	LN
	12	**20**	**38**	**45**

(E) Examples sometimes appear with metal motor adapted to fit the body. Some metal motors may have even been installed at the factory, but most were Lionel Service Station replacements.

	Gd	VG	Ex	LN
	10	**15**	**32**	**40**

Top: 1001 (B) with 1001T Lionel Scout tender. Bottom: 1050 with 1050T Lionel Lines tender. M. Sokol Collection.

Top: 1060 (A) with 1060T Lionel Lines tender. Middle: 1061 (A) with 1061T unmarked tender. Bottom: 1062 with 1062T Lionel Lines tender. M. Yeaton Collection.

	Gd	VG	Ex	LN

1120: 1950. Modified 2-4-2 Scout engine; black-painted die-cast body with silver rubber-stamped cab number; no ornamental trim; plastic motor; Magnetraction; two-position reverse with fiber lever projecting through top of boiler along center line between the sand and steam domes; not lighted and without headlight lens; motor secured crosswise with threaded mounting pin; 1001T sheet-metal tender lettered "LIONEL SCOUT".

Note: The body for 1120 is identical to the 1949 body of 1110; the number was changed because of the addition of Magnetraction.

	Gd	VG	Ex	LN
	15	20	30	45

1130: 1953–54. The predecessor to the 200-series 2-4-2 Scout engines; usually Type I black-painted plastic body with cab numbers as described below; metal motor; three-position E-unit with lever pointing down; lighted with headlight lens; ballast weights front and rear; motor secured through top of boiler near cab with 6/32" by 7/16" motor-mounting screw; 6066T early coal, or 1130T streamlined tender.

Note: The old tooling that originated with 1654 and was last used for die-casting as 2034 was extensively reworked to add detail for use with plastic.

(A) Extremely scarce variation assembled from unused 2034 die-cast bodies; silver rubber-stamped cab number.

	Gd	VG	Ex	LN
	75	125	210	250

(B) Plastic body with silver rubber-stamped cab number.

	Gd	VG	Ex	LN
	16	20	35	45

(C) Plastic body with white heat-stamped cab number.

	Gd	VG	Ex	LN
	35	50	75	100

1615: 1955–57. 0-4-0 switcher; black-painted die-cast body; raised "B6" on one side of boiler casting; wire handrails; front step; full complement of driving hardware; three-position E-unit; lighted with headlight lens; magnetic coupler on front; drawbar with grounding spring. 1615T slope-back tender.

Note: This engine is a reissue of 1656, which was last cataloged in 1948–49; the boiler casting is the same, except 1615 now came with a different motor and was paired with a plastic-body tender. See entries for 1665, 1656, and 1625.

(A) White rubber-stamped cab number.

	Gd	VG	Ex	LN
	85	145	200	300

(B) White heat-stamped cab number.

	Gd	VG	Ex	LN
	85	145	200	300

1625: 1958. 0-4-0 switcher; black-painted die-cast body; raised "B6" on one side of boiler casting; wire handrails; front step; full complement of driving hardware; three-position E-unit; lighted with headlight lens; fixed plastic coupler on front; drawbar with grounding spring. 1625T slope-back tender.

Note: Except for the fixed-plastic coupler, this engine is identical with 1615. See entries for 1665, 1656, and 1615.

(A) White rubber-stamped cab number.

	Gd	VG	Ex	LN
	90	150	225	325

	Gd	VG	Ex	LN

(B) White heat-stamped cab number.

	Gd	VG	Ex	LN
	90	150	225	325

1654: 1946–47. The original 2-4-2 Scout-type engine; black-painted die-cast body with silver rubber-stamped cab number; ornamental nickel bell and whistle; wire handrails; metal motor with drive rods and solid cross heads, and side rods; sliding contact assembly; three-position E-unit with lever projecting through top of boiler near cab; lighted with headlight lens; motor secured crosswise with threaded mounting screw; 1654T or 1654W sheet-metal tender lettered "LIONEL LINES".

(A) With 1654T nonwhistle tender.

	Gd	VG	Ex	LN
	30	40	60	75

(B) With 1654W whistle tender.

	Gd	VG	Ex	LN
	35	50	80	100

1655: 1948–49. 2-4-2 Scout engine; black-painted die-cast body with silver rubber-stamped cab number; ornamental nickel bell and whistle; wire handrails; improved metal motor with drive rods and solid crossheads, and side rods; sliding contact assembly; three-position E-unit with lever projecting through top of boiler near cab; lighted with headlight lens; motor secured crosswise with threaded mounting screw; 6654W sheet-metal tender lettered "LIONEL LINES".

	Gd	VG	Ex	LN
	35	50	70	100

1656: 1948–49. 0-4-0 switcher; black-painted die-cast body with silver rubber-stamped cab number; raised "B6" on one side of boiler casting; ornamental bell; wire handrails; front step; full complement of driving hardware; three-position E-unit; lighted with headlight lens; coil coupler on front. 2403B or 6403B slope-back tender.

Note: This engine is identical with 1665 except for the motor.

	Gd	VG	Ex	LN
	130	210	295	400

1665: 1946. 0-4-0 switcher; black-painted die-cast body with silver rubber-stamped cab number; raised "B6" on one side of boiler casting; ornamental bell; wire handrails; front step; full complement of driving hardware; three-position E-unit; lighted with headlight lens; coil coupler on front. 2403B slope-back tender.

Note: A female jack assembly was positioned inside the cab to receive two connecting wires from the tender; the left-hand jack connects the front coil coupler of the engine to the pickup shoe on the tender, while the other wire provides an electrical ground connection, which is necessary because the engine does not have a front pilot truck. See entries for 1656, 1615, and 1625.

	Gd	VG	Ex	LN
	150	250	350	500

1666: 1946. 2-6-2; black-painted die-cast body; ornamental bell and ornamental whistle; wire handrails; nickel-rimmed spoked drivers with full complement of driving hardware; die-cast trailing truck; three-position E-unit; lighted with headlight lens. 2466W early coal tender.

Note: The postwar 1666 and 224 have the same boiler casting. The 1666 was not cataloged in 1947, but entries

Top: 1101 (B) with 1001T Lionel Scout tender. Second: 1110 (B) with 1001T Lionel Scout tender. Third: 1120 with 1001T Lionel Scout tender. Bottom: 1130 (B) with 1130T Lionel Lines tender with Scout trucks. K. Rubright Collection.

	Gd	VG	Ex	LN

in the Lionel Service Manual indicate there was 1947 production. Furthermore, the engine was included in a special spring 1947 promotional set, 3105W, shown on page 3 of the 1947 advance catalog.

(A) 1946; metal number plate on cab; hatches on sand dome; blackened handrails; movable bell; die-cast pilot truck; screw-mounted pilot and steam chest.

	50	85	135	180

(B) Same as (A), except silver handrails.

	50	85	135	180

(C) 1947; silver rubber-stamped cab number; smooth sand dome; silver handrails; solid bell; sheet-metal pilot truck; pilot and steam chest affixed to posts in boiler casting.

	50	85	135	180

(D) Same as (C), but with an "X" about ⅜" high stamped on the left firebox door inside the cab.

	50	85	135	180

1862: 1959–62. 4-4-0 model of Civil War General; gray-painted plastic boiler with tile red–painted cab and cowcatcher; gold heat-stamped lettering; sand dome, steam dome, gold ornamental bell, and extremely fragile black ornamental whistle; without boiler banding and piping detail; wire handrails; ballast weight but no Magnetraction; two-position E-unit; lantern with light. 1862T General tender.

Note: This model was the less expensive O27 gauge counterpart to the premium 1872. See 1872 and 1882.

	100	160	225	300

	Gd	VG	Ex	LN

1872: 1959–62. 4-4-0 model of Civil War General; gray-painted plastic boiler with tile red–painted cab and cowcatcher; gold heat-stamped lettering; sand dome, steam dome, gold ornamental bell and extremely fragile black ornamental whistle; boiler banding and piping detail; wire handrails; Magnetraction and ballast weight; three-position E-unit; lantern with light; liquid smoke unit. 1872T General tender.

Note: The handrail along the body of all General engines forms part of the circuit carrying electric current to the headlight. The front lantern is easily changed; however, early production came with a tile red lantern while later production was black. The 1872 was a premium model and cataloged as a Super O item.

(A) Gray smokestack.	100	200	300	410
(B) Black smokestack.	100	200	300	410

1882: Uncataloged, 1960. 4-4-0 model of Civil War General; black-painted plastic boiler with orange-painted cab and cowcatcher; gold heat-stamped lettering; sand dome, steam dome, gold ornamental bell and extremely fragile black ornamental whistle; without boiler banding and piping detail; wire handrails; ballast weight but no Magnetraction; two-position E-unit; black lantern with light. 1882T General tender.

Note: Except for color, this engine is identical with 1862. See also 1872.

The unique 1882, 1882T, 1887, and 1885, along with

Top: 1615 (B) with 1615T Lionel Lines tender. Bottom: 1625 (B) with 1625T Lionel Lines tender. K. Rubright Collection.

Top: 1655 with 6654W Lionel Lines tender. Middle: 1666 (B) with 2466W Lionel Lines tender. Bottom: 1666 (C) with 2466W Lionel Lines tender. D. Gould Collection.

1656 with 2403B Lionel Lines tender.

	Gd	VG	Ex	LN

the common 1866, were part of the highly collectible uncataloged Halloween General outfit. (See *Greenberg's Guide to Lionel Trains 1945–1969, Volume IV: Uncatalogued Sets.*)

	200	300	420	625

2016: 1955–56. 2-6-4; black-painted die-cast body; ornamental bell; spoked drivers with drive rods and side rods only; sheet-metal trailing truck; no Magnetraction; three-position E-unit; lighted with headlight lens; *without* smoke. 6026W square tender.

Note: Has the same boiler casting as 2036, 2026 (1951 model), 2037, 2018, 2037-500, 637, and 2029.

(A) White rubber-stamped cab number.

	50	90	125	180

(B) White heat-stamped cab number.

	50	90	125	180

2018: 1956–59. 2-6-4; black-painted die-cast body; ornamental bell; spoked drivers with drive rods and side rods only; sheet-metal trailing truck; no Magnetraction; three-position E-unit; lighted with headlight lens; smoke. 6026T square tender, 1130T small streamlined tender,

A comparison of two postwar 1666 locomotives. Note the bell and hanger on the 1666 (B) at left and the single-piece bell on the 1666 (C) at right. Also note the hatches on the top of the forward dome of the left locomotive. T. Riley Collection.

or 6026W square tender. Values assume whistle tender.

Note: This engine has the same boiler casting as 2036, 2026 (1951 model), 2037, 2016, 2037-500, 637, and 2029.

(A) White rubber-stamped cab number.

	60	85	120	175

(B) White heat-stamped cab number.

	60	85	120	175

2020: 1946 (1947–49 model described below). 6-8-6 model of Pennsylvania Railroad S2 steam turbine; black-painted die-cast body without E-unit slot, and flat outer surface on turbine housing; silver rubber-stamped cab number; wire handrails; thick nickel rims on *all* drivers with side rod only; horizontally mounted motor with brushplate marked "LIONEL ATOMIC / PRECISION MOTOR" with two female receptacles for E-unit jack; three-position E-unit with jack that plugs into brushplate (one receptacle on brushplate locks the E-unit in forward, neutral, or reverse, while the other jack activates the unit for sequential, transformer-controlled forward-neutral-reverse); lighted with prism lens; smoke with early smoke bulb unit. 2020W early coal tender.

Note: Lionel offered 671S conversion kit to update 1946 models with heater-type smoke units. Engines that retain the original smoke bulb arrangement are considerably scarcer than converted models. Except for the number, this engine is identical to the 1946 version of 671 cataloged as O gauge.

(A) "6200" rubber-stamped on boiler front keystone.

	100	140	200	290

(B) "6200" heat-stamped on boiler front keystone.

	100	140	200	290

(C) "6200" decal on boiler front keystone.

	100	140	200	290

2020: 1947–49 (1946 model above). 6-8-6 model of Pennsylvania Railroad S2 steam turbine; black-painted die-cast body featuring revised boiler casting with E-unit slot, rounded outer surface on turbine housing, and additional piping detail; silver rubber-stamped cab number; wire handrails; "6200" decal on boiler front keystone; side rod

1862 General with 1862T W & A.R.R. tender. B. Myles Collection.

1872 General with 1872T W & A.R.R. tender. F. S. Davis Collection.

1882 General with 1882T W & A.R.R. tender.

	Gd	VG	Ex	LN

only; slant-mounted motor; typical three-position E-unit; lighted with usual headlight lens; smoke with usual resistance coil unit. 2020W or 6020W early coal tender.

Note: Except for the number, this engine is identical with the 1947–49 model 671 cataloged for the O gauge line.

(A) 1947; "LIONEL / PRECISION MOTOR" with tubular brushplates; thick nickel rims on *all* drivers.

	100	140	200	290

(B) 1948; same motor as (A), but thin blackened rims on first and fourth drivers only.

	100	140	200	290

(C) 1949; new slant-mounted motor, whereby the

	Gd	VG	Ex	LN

brushes were integrated with the back plate; no rims on any drivers.

	100	140	200	290

2025: 1947–49 (1952 model described below). 2-6-2; black-painted die-cast body with silver rubber-stamped cab number; smokestack is separate piece; ornamental bell; wire handrails; nickel-rimmed Baldwin disk drivers with full complement of driving hardware; die-cast trailing truck; three-position E-unit; lighted with headlight lens; smoke. 2466WX or 6466WX early coal tender.

Note: This engine has the same boiler casting as 675 and 2035. Except for the four-digit O27 gauge designation, it is identical with the 1947–49 model 675. Many of

1666 (B) has the typical postwar rounded cab floor and a metal number plate.

The very last postwar 1666 production featured a rubber-stamped cab number. See 1666 (C) in the listings.

	Gd	VG	Ex	LN

the variations pertain to the decoration on the keystone that was cast into the boiler front, which by design is readily interchangeable.

(A) 1947; large unpainted aluminum smokestack, plain pilot; "2025" rubber-stamped on boiler front keystone.

| | 70 | 100 | 140 | 200 |

(B) Same as (A), except "2025" heat-stamped on boiler front keystone.

| | 70 | 100 | 140 | 200 |

(C) Same as (A), except "2025" decal on boiler front keystone.

| | 70 | 100 | 140 | 200 |

(D) Same as (A), except "5690" decal on boiler front keystone.

| | 70 | 100 | 130 | 180 |

(E) 1948–49; black-painted smokestack, pilot with simulated knuckle; "5690" decal on boiler front keystone.

| | 70 | 100 | 130 | 180 |

2025: 1952 (1947–49 model described above). 2-6-4; black-painted die-cast body with silver rubber-stamped cab number; "5690" decal on boiler front keystone; black-painted smokestack, which is a separate piece; ornamental bell; wire handrails; spoked drivers with full complement of driving hardware; pilot with simulated knuckle; sheet-metal trailing truck; three-position E-unit; lighted with headlight lens; smoke. 6466W early coal tender.

Note: This engine has same boiler casting as 675 and 2035. Internally, the engine is comparable to 2035, not the 1947–49 model of 2025.

| | 70 | 100 | 130 | 180 |

2026: 1948–49 (1951–53 model described below). 2-6-2; black-painted die-cast body with silver rubber-stamped cab number; ornamental bell and ornamental whistle; wire handrails; steel-rimmed spoked drivers with full complement of driving hardware; die-cast trailing truck; sliding shoe pickup; three-position E-unit; lighted with headlight lens; smoke. 6466WX early coal tender.

Note: This engine is very different from the 1951–53

model. This example of 2026 resulted from the relatively minor updating of the 1666 die.

| | 60 | 80 | 115 | 140 |

2026: 1951–53 (1948–49 model described above). 2-6-4; black-painted die-cast body; ornamental bell; spoked drivers with drive rods and side rods only; sheet-metal trailing truck; contact roller pickup; three-position E-unit; lighted with headlight lens; smoke. 6066T, 6466T, or 6466W early coal tender. Values assume whistle tender.

Note: This engine is different from the 1948–49 model and uses the boiler developed for 2036 in 1950. Also has the same boiler casting as 2037, 2016, 2018, 2037-500, 637, and 2029. See 2036 entry for more details.

(A) 1951–52; silver rubber-stamped cab number.

| | 60 | 80 | 115 | 140 |

(B) 1953; white heat-stamped cab number.

| | 60 | 80 | 115 | 140 |

2029: 1964–69. 2-6-4; black-painted die-cast body with white heat-stamped cab number; ornamental bell; spoked drivers with drive rods and side rods only; sheet-metal trailing truck; tire traction; two-position E-unit; lighted with headlight lens; smoke. 1060T small streamlined tender, 234T, typical 234W, or scarce 234W square tender lettered "PENNSYLVANIA". The 234W Pennsylvania tender alone is valued $300 in Like New condition. Values assume common whistle tender.

Note: This engine has the same boiler casting as 2036, 2026 (1951 model), 2037, 2016, 2018, 2037-500, and 637.

(A) As described above.

| | 70 | 90 | 125 | 160 |

(B) 1968; bottom plate reading "THE LIONEL TOY CORPORATION, HAGERSTOWN, MARYLAND 21740", with "JAPAN" embossed on the trailing truck.

| | 100 | 120 | 145 | 180 |

Top: 2016 (B) with 6026W Lionel Lines tender. Middle: 2018 (B) with 6026W Lionel Lines tender. Bottom: 2020 (C) (1947–49 model) with 6020W Lionel Lines tender.

	Gd	VG	Ex	LN

2034: 1952. Modified 2-4-2 Scout engine with additional modifications from last use as the 1951–52 version of 1110; black-painted die-cast body with silver rubber-stamped cab number; metal motor; three-position E-unit with lever pointing down; lighted with headlight lens; motor secured through top of boiler near cab with ⁶⁄₃₂" by ⁷⁄₁₆" motor-mounting screw; 6066T early coal tender.

Note: The modifications made to the tooling for the 2034 body included plugging the reverse-lever slot, the railing holes along the boiler, the circular hole in the boiler front, and the motor-mounting pin holes along the running board. Also, a motor-mounting screw hole was added to the top of the boiler.

(A) Early production; open motor-mounting pin holes.

	25	30	50	70

(B) As described in main entry.

	20	25	45	60

2035: 1950–51. 2-6-4; black-painted die-cast body with white heat-stamped cab number; "5690" decal on boiler

1946 model of 2020 steam turbine with 2020W Lionel Lines tender. Observe that the engine does not have an E-unit lever projecting through the boiler top. See listing for further information. H. Holden Collection.

Top: 2025 (A) (1947–1949 model) with 2466WX Lionel Lines tender. Middle: 2026 (1948–1949 model) with 2466WX Lionel Lines tender. Bottom: 2029 (A) with 234W Lionel Lines tender. P. West Collection.

	Gd	VG	Ex	LN

front keystone; black-painted smokestack, which is a separate piece; ornamental bell; wire handrails; sintered-iron spoked drivers with full complement of driving hardware; pilot with simulated knuckle; sheet-metal trailing truck; Magnetraction; three-position E-unit; lighted with headlight lens; smoke. 6466W early coal tender.

Note: This engine has the same boiler casting as 675 and 2025; it was given a new number in 1950 with the introduction of Magnetraction. The Lionel Service Manual states there are major internal differences between the 1950 and 1951 versions in the motors and smoke units.

(A) 1950; has "half-moon" eccentric crank.

	65	**95**	**175**	**225**

(B) 1951; has "two-pin" eccentric crank.

	65	**95**	**175**	**225**

2036: 1950. 2-6-4; black-painted die-cast body with silver rubber-stamped cab number; ornamental bell; spoked drivers with drive rods and side rods only; sheet-metal trailing truck; Magnetraction; three-position E-unit; lighted with headlight lens; *without* smoke. 6466W early coal tender.

Note: A new boiler debuted with this engine, and it would stay in the product line for the remainder of postwar production. Instead of being a new tool, casting most likely resulted from a reworking of the 2026 die, which was descended from the 1666 tooling. The 2036 boiler was used for the 2026 (1951 model), 2037, 2016, 2018, 2037-500,

637, and 2029. However, beginning with production of 2037 in 1953, a whistle was added to the top left side of the tooling above the third driver.

	65	**90**	**150**	**200**

2037: 1953–55, 1957–63. 2-6-4; black-painted die-cast body; ornamental bell; spoked drivers with drive rods and side rods only; sheet-metal trailing truck; Magnetraction; three-position E-unit; lighted with headlight lens; smoke. 6066T, 6026T, or 1130T nonwhistle tender, or 6026W, 233W, or 234W square whistle tender. Values assume whistle tender.

Note: This engine has the same boiler casting as 2036, 2026 (1951 model), 2016, 2018, 2037-500, 637, and 2029. Beginning in 1953, a whistle was added to the top left side of the tooling above the third divider; it would remain for the balance of postwar production.

(A) White rubber-stamped cab number.

	80	**110**	**150**	**200**

(B) White heat-stamped cab number.

	60	**90**	**125**	**170**

2037-500: 1957–58. 2-6-4; pink-painted die-cast body from the 1587S Lady Lionel (better known as the Girls' Set); ornamental bell; spoked drivers with drive rods and side rods only; sheet-metal trailing truck; Magnetraction; three-position E-unit; lighted with headlight lens; smoke. 1130T-500 small streamlined tender.

Note: This engine has the same boiler casting as

2037 (B) with 6026W Lionel Lines tender.

2037-500 (B) with 1130T-500 Lionel Lines tender. Exclusive component of the Girls' Set. L. Nuzzaci Collection.

Top: 2046 (B) with 2046W Lionel Lines tender. Middle: 2055 (B) with 6026W Lionel Lines tender. Bottom: 2056 with 2046W Lionel Lines tender. M. Yeaton Collection.

Top: 2034 (A) with 6066T Lionel Lines tender. Middle: 2035 (B) with 6466W Lionel Lines tender. Bottom: 2036 with 6466W Lionel Lines tender. A. Bartus Collection.

	Gd	VG	Ex	LN

2036, 2026 (1951 model), 2016, 2018, 2037, 637, and 2029.

(A) Blue rubber-stamped cab number.

	360	600	800	1100

(B) Blue heat-stamped cab number.

	360	600	800	1100

2046: 1950–51, 1953. 4-6-4; black-painted die-cast body; hinged boiler front; ornamental bell; wire handrails; spoked drivers with full complement of driving hardware; Magnetraction; three-position E-unit; lighted with headlight lens; smoke. 2046W streamlined tender.

Note: The 2046 is a hybrid engine; it utilized the same boiler casting as the 736 Berkshire but was fitted with a 4-6-4 Hudson wheel arrangement. The same boiler casting and wheel arrangement appear with the 2056 and 646.

(A) 1950–51; silver rubber-stamped cab number; typically has three-window cab; die-cast trailing truck.

	135	185	235	300

(B) 1953; white heat-stamped cab number; usually with four-window cab; usually with reinforced boiler front (see 736 entry above); trailing truck die-cast or sheet-metal with plastic side frames.

	135	185	235	300

2055: 1953–55; 4-6-4 Santa Fe–type Hudson; black-painted die-cast body with plain boiler front; ornamental bell and ornamental whistle; wire handrails; full complement of driving hardware; trailing truck with plastic side frames; Magnetraction; three-position E-unit; lighted with headlight lens; smoke. 6026W square tender or 2046W streamlined tender.

Note: This engine is identical with 685 and has the same boiler casting as 665 and 2065.

(A) White rubber-stamped cab number.

	75	130	195	280

(B) White heat-stamped cab number.

	75	130	195	280

2056: 1952. 4-6-4; black-painted die-cast body with silver rubber-stamped cab number; usually with four-window cab; hinged boiler front; ornamental bell; wire handrails; spoked drivers with full complement of driving hardware; *without* Magnetraction; three-position E-unit; lighted with headlight lens; smoke. 2046W streamlined tender.

Note: The 2056 was the Korean War issue of the 2046 (described above). The model is a hybrid; it utilized the same boiler casting as the 736 Berkshire but was fitted with a 4-6-4 Hudson wheel arrangement. See 646 and 2046 entries.

	105	175	250	350

2065: 1954–56. 4-6-4 Santa Fe–type Hudson; black-painted die-cast body with external feedwater heater tank on boiler front; ornamental bell and ornamental whistle; wire handrails; full complement of driving hardware; trailing truck with plastic side frames; Magnetraction; three-position E-unit; lighted with headlight lens; smoke

2065 (B) with 2046W Lionel Lines tender.

6110 with 6001T Lionel Lines tender.

	Gd	VG	Ex	LN

6026W square tender or 2046W streamlined tender.

Note: This engine is identical with 665 and has the same boiler casting as 685 and 2055.

(A) White rubber-stamped cab number.

	100	150	225	300

(B) White heat-stamped cab number.

	100	150	225	300

6110: 1950. Modified 2-4-2 Scout engine; black-painted die-cast body with silver rubber-stamped cab number; no ornamental trim; plastic motor with Magnetraction; two-position reverse with fiber lever projecting through top of boiler along center line between the sand and steam domes; not lighted and without headlight lens; unique smoke assembly from which smoke is driven out of the stack by air forced through a circular hole in the boiler front above the headlight because of the forward motion of the engine; motor secured crosswise with threaded mounting pin; 6001T early coal tender.

Note: Except for the hole in the boiler front, the 6110 body is identical to 1110 and 1120.

	15	20	35	50

3

DIESEL LOCOMOTIVES, ELECTRIC LOCOMOTIVES, AND MOTORIZED UNITS

Introduction by Roger Carp

In beauty and authenticity, the models of diesel and electric locomotives Lionel marketed during the postwar era were in a class of their own. These O and O27 gauge pieces captured the color and detail of all sorts of prototype engines manufactured by virtually ever major builder of the time. As never before, Lionel depended on dazzling the children and their families who bought train sets. That is, reliable performance was only part of what the company promised with its diesel and electric locomotives. More to the point, these models offered style and elegance. Their multiple-color paint schemes and flashy graphics represented something novel and modern for Lionel. It's little wonder that kids pleaded for these models and collectors prize them so highly today.

Diesel and electric locomotives also reflected a more aggressive marketing approach on the part of Lionel. Sales executives saw in these models opportunities to reach more consumers than ever. They weren't content to market one or two kinds of prototypes or offer limited, even generic decoration. Instead, Lionel invested in tooling and painting equipment that enabled it to catalog several different types of diesels and electrics in an enormous variety of road names and paint schemes. It sought to represent the latest locomotives used on railroads in every part of the United States, including both large and small systems. Furthermore, the firm brought out models that were aimed at every price level. Diesels and electrics showed how forward-thinking both Lionel's engineering staff and its sales force could be.

The same ingenuity was equally if not more evident in the array of motorized units that Lionel developed. Whereas most diesels and electrics showed how expertly the company could blend realism with imagination, its small auxiliary models attested to the skill with which its designers could create self-propelled toys. For above all else, the motorized units were delightful, whimsical toys, sure to bring a smile to any child or adult. Their charm survived long after Lionel quit making them, and they also are in great demand today.

Of course, when World War II ended, Lionel wasn't looking so far into the future. Executives wanted to satisfy merchandisers by having a basic outfit and a few accessories for the holiday season of 1945. Even before they accomplished this feat they were gazing ahead to the next year as a time when Lionel could expand its product line in every sense. As far as locomotives were concerned, the company's plan was to emphasize steam, just as it had at the close of the prewar period. The biggest, newest steam engines would highlight the 1946 catalog and engineers put in long hours to finish O and O27 gauge models of the Pennsylvania Railroad's spectacular 6-8-6 Turbine and a 2-8-4 Berkshire. They also talked of modifying versions of the scale-proportioned Pennsy 0-6-0 switch engine and New York Central 4-6-4 Hudson that had glorified the prewar line.

But an all-steam roster caused problems, no matter how much the company's founder, Joshua Lionel Cowen, might have approved. Simply put, times were changing on railroads around the United States and Lionel would have to change, too, if it wanted to dominate the toy train market. Progress on most prototype railroads meant purchasing diesel-powered engines and relying less on steam. On selected lines electric locomotives gained in importance. Children watched the latest motive power on their favorite railroads and expected toy manufacturers to provide detailed, dependable models of what they saw. Should Lionel hesitate, other firms, particularly The A. C. Gilbert Company, definitely would intervene to conquer the market.

Thus in 1947 Lionel picked up where it had left off about 20 years before. It cataloged a handsome model of a highly publicized workhorse of an electric locomotive. Before the Great Depression, that had meant offering Standard and O gauge replicas of the bipolar electric used by the Chicago, Milwaukee, St. Paul & Pacific Railroad. After World War II, Lionel stayed in the forefront of the hobby by mass-producing a legendary O gauge model of a legendary electric, the Pennsylvania Railroad's class GG1. True, the GG1 had been around for more than a decade by this time. Yet it still looked contemporary, thanks to the sleek, elongated curves of its design, executed by the famous industrial designer Raymond Loewy. Lionel couldn't have made a better choice for an electric to reproduce in miniature.

The 2332 GG1 represented a fascinating blend of tradition and change at Lionel. It could be perceived as the descendant of the New York Central boxcab and Milwaukee Road bipolar, the electrics that dominated the line throughout the second and third decades of the century. As they most likely had with those different models, Lionel's designers worked from blueprints provided by the owner to bring out a shortened yet striking model of a celebrated electric associated with only a single railroad. Of course, technological advances enabled the firm to market a more realistic engine in the 1940s than it had previously. Earlier models had consisted primarily of straight lines and square shapes, the best that could be produced by stamping sheet metal; the 2332 had the flowing lines and an elongated body that were possible because it was die-cast. Improved decoration also distinguished the GG1. After a brief, initial trial with black, Lionel painted the body Brunswick green and affixed rubber-stamped gold striping and lettering as well as a decaled Pennsy keystone herald.

To understand how the GG1 upheld tradition at Lionel, it should be compared less with older electrics and more with the big steamers cataloged right up to its release. Like the 700E New York Central or even the 671 Turbine, the GG1 was a dark, almost black engine associated with a prominent railroad based in the Northeast. Since it belonged to only that road, there was no purpose in decorating a model for Lionel Lines. So Lionel proceeded to letter the 2332 for its owner. However, as was true with various steam locomotives, this O gauge piece featured only spartan decoration. Even if left unchanged, Lionel's GG1 might have continued to attract buyers for several years, but it had a key drawback that sales personnel couldn't ignore. There wasn't much reason for a kid living in the Midwest or on the West Coast to be terribly excited about a model of a locomotive he wasn't ever going to see in his neighborhood.

The real break with the past occurred in 1948, when Lionel released the first of its popular models of the F3 diesel manufactured by the Electro-Motive Division of General Motors. Difficult as it might be to understand now, the F3 represented a gamble on Lionel's part, one that the company might not have taken had support not come from outside the firm. J. L. Cowen didn't care for diesels and might have been reluctant to bless the decision of his son, Lawrence, newly installed as president of the firm, to add an O gauge replica of one to the line. They had no idea how kids and their families would react to a model of so newfangled a locomotive, one missing the action and drama of a steamer.

Several lucky breaks encouraged Lionel to proceed. General Motors agreed to underwrite a portion of the tooling costs in exchange for seeing its emblem on the model. The New York Central was willing to meet the same conditions, as long as the new 2333 featured its name. This arrangement satisfied Lionel, and an F3 painted in the Central's two-tone gray lightning-bolt scheme with rubber-stamped white stripes made its debut in 1948. But it looked, well, drab: just one more dark locomotive for the O gauge market.

What transformed the 2333 from an ugly duckling into a lovely swan was the decision of the Atchison, Topeka & Santa Fe Railway to contribute to its development. In return for that assistance, representatives requested that Lionel catalog a version with its road name and herald. Nothing could have benefited Lionel more. At the time, the Santa Fe's silver, red, and yellow warbonnet paint scheme was unsurpassed in majesty. The public associated it with the glimmering streamlined trains that symbolized the thrills of living in the West, crossing midwestern prairies and southwestern towns until they reached the ultimate destination of southern California. The sophistication of movie stars intermingled with the timeless beauty of native American crafts. Such were the images conjured up by the Santa Fe and its crack passenger trains pulled by warbonnet F units.

Children across the country, even in the Midwest and Northeast where the New York Central reigned supreme, clamored for the Santa Fe F3s. Lionel must have been taken aback by the success of its new model, the first O gauge locomotive with an injection-molded body. With production supervisors and assembly workers struggling to make enough F3s to meet the demand, everyone at Lionel knew they had something that would long win praise. Over the next 18 years, even though the company underwent significant changes and experimented with its product line, it didn't dare remove the Santa Fe F3 from its catalog. Details might be eliminated and decoration simplified, but this champion survived.

Once the Cowens had climbed aboard the diesel bandwagon, they had no wish to jump off. In 1949 Lionel released O and O27 gauge versions of another Electro-Motive Division diesel, this time an NW2 switch engine (the 622 and 6220, respectively). The choice was curious. Perhaps General Motors had inserted stipulations in its agreement with Lionel that compelled the latter to roster a second EMD prototype. At least as important was the action of a competitor. General Models Corporation, based in Chicago, brought out an O gauge model of the NW2 in the summer of 1948. Worried about losing sales to this newcomer, Lionel sent examples of the GMC switcher to its factory in northern New Jersey for engineers to dis-assemble and study. Then they pushed ahead with a model of their own.

The end product was a rugged, detailed replica painted black and heat-stamped white. Though the 1949 catalog showed it lettered for Lionel Lines and the 1950 catalog depicted a New York Central version, the only models mass-produced were decorated for the Santa Fe. Both the O and O27 switchers were available with a bell that rang. This feature, which captivated children and annoyed adults, had been around since the late prewar era, but no previous postwar engine had been equipped with it. The GG1 and F3 came with horns, and most steamers boasted a remote-control whistle.

More than its chiming bell, what set the 622 apart from its peers (including the 6220) was a brand-new feature that Lionel called Magnetraction. Engineers had been conducting experiments involving powdered metal in hopes of reconstructing the wheels and axles used on locomotives. They wanted to bolster the magnetism of those parts and thereby endow miniature engines with greater pulling power. Of the locomotives cataloged in 1949, only the 622 had Magnetraction. Success inspired Lionel to add this feature to more engines in 1950 and still more in 1951 until virtually every O and O27 model (except those at the bottom of the line) came with it.

Besides Magnetraction, Lionel's golden anniversary year of 1950 heralded the introduction of a new diesel. This time designers concentrated on broadening the O27 line with a replica of the FA type manufactured by the American Locomotive Company (Alco). As was true of Lionel's F3s, the 2023 came in an AA combination that consisted of identical powered and dummy units. Decorated for the Union Pacific, their injection-molded plastic bodies were painted a vivid shade of yellow (the roof was gray) and heat-stamped red. Lionel equipped these desirable diesels with Magnetraction as well as operating lights and a horn and sold them either separately or as set components. They looked best with the three matching passenger cars included in the highly prized 1464W Anniversary Set.

After bringing out new diesels for three consecutive years, Lionel rested from its labors in 1951. Perhaps sales executives doubted the wisdom of expanding the roster, or restrictions caused by the Korean War might have limited their options. Whatever the reason, the only new product the company could offer in 1951 was a modified 2023, now painted silver and heat-stamped black.

Such minimal activity contrasted with the accomplishments of Lionel's rivals. In 1950 Louis Marx and Company had capitalized on the popularity of the Santa Fe's warbonnet scheme and used it for lithographing a tin O27 model of a different Electro-Motive diesel, the FT. Marx also offered its own F3, decorated in a Southern Pacific scheme. The A. C. Gilbert Company also trusted that the warbonnet sold diesels. Starting in 1950, it cataloged S gauge models of Alco's sleek PA and PB that were painted and lettered for the Santa Fe. (Lionel

also introduced a B unit for its diesel in 1950.) Meanwhile, Gilbert's American Flyer line forged ahead of Lionel with the first toy version of a diesel road switcher, Electro-Motive's GP7.

Lionel answered these challenges only indirectly in 1952 and 1953. Instead of bringing out brand-new models, it expanded its roster by decorating diesels for more railroads. For example, the 2031 Rock Island and 2032 Erie Railroad AA units joined the Union Pacific engines (renumbered as 2033) in the FA stable. All three were cataloged from 1952 through 1954, as were a pair of NW2 switchers. This model, dropped from the line in 1951, was reinstated the next year with a Santa Fe model (renumbered as 623) and its Chesapeake and Ohio companion (the 624). Nice as they were, these pieces couldn't help being overshadowed by another F3. Arriving in 1952 was the 2345, a lovely AA combination painted silver and orange and heat-stamped black for the Western Pacific. Available as a separate-sale item only, it's one of the most desirable F3s.

Just when kids thought Lionel had regained momentum, they discovered nothing new in the consumer catalog for 1953. Instead, it described only the same Alcos and diesel switchers and showed the Santa Fe, New York Central, and Western Pacific F3s with fewer details and new numbers (2353, 2354, and 2355, respectively).

Disappointed consumers looked elsewhere and found Lionel's competitors busy. Marx announced an O27 gauge model of Electro-Motive's popular E7 and added a Baltimore and Ohio unit to its list of F3s. Gilbert offered new versions of its S gauge PA, this time painted and lettered for fictional yet exciting trains, such as the *Silver Streak*, the *Rocket*, the *Silver Flash*, and the *Comet*. Assuredly the most significant of Lionel's rivals in 1953 was American Model Toys, a firm in Indiana that brought out its own O gauge diesel, a model of an Electro-Motive Division F7. This handsome piece came decorated for several railroads, including the Chicago and North Western, New York Central, Pennsylvania, Santa Fe, and the Southern Railway. The most attractive AMT diesel might have been the one painted and lettered for a specific train, the *Texas Special*, which ran between St. Louis and San Antonio over the Missouri-Kansas-Texas Railroad and the St. Louis-San Francisco Railway.

As though curious to see what others might devise, Lionel watched and waited through 1953. Then it responded with a line that some observers praise as its finest of the postwar era. The outstanding new locomotive for 1954 was the 2321 Fairbanks-Morse Train Master. This enormous model, painted gray and maroon and rubber-stamped yellow and maroon, captured in O gauge the heft and detail of one of the largest and most powerful diesel locomotives then being built. The dual-motored 2321 came decorated for the Delaware, Lackawanna & Western and featured operating lights and couplers, a horn, and Magnetraction. Lionel pictured this giant on the cover of its catalog to show how important it was.

Also making their debut in 1954 were a couple of F3s

whose decoration indicated just how seriously Lionel took AMT. First there was the 2245, a single-motored model (cataloged as O27) painted and lettered for the *Texas Special*. The fact that Lionel went to the trouble to decorate an AB combination for a specific passenger train left no doubt it wanted to engage American Model Toys in head-to-head competition. Next came the 2356, which consisted of an AA combination painted green and gray and rubber-stamped yellow with a Southern Railway decal. Cataloging these F3s, along with its New York Central and Santa Fe models, meant that Lionel's big diesels represented almost every region of the country. More important, they overshadowed the product lines of every rival.

All but buried at the back of the 1954 catalog was another newcomer to the line, one that would revolutionize it over the next decade. There, Lionel introduced the 50 section gang car. This small, self-propelled auxiliary unit sped around the track until one of its bumpers struck an object. Then the vehicle reversed direction, and the figures perched on it changed position. The concept of such an independent unit was brilliant, as it created a whole new type of product for Lionel to develop and market. Kids loved the gang car and its many successors, and collectors pursued them avidly. Further, the gang car reflected Lionel's willingness to compromise standards and make items that were imaginative toys rather than realistic models. Viewed as a whole, the 1954 line proved that Lionel could pursue the twin goals of designing toys and building near-scale models.

How skillfully Lionel could accomplish these aims was shown again and again over the next three years. In 1955, its engineers unveiled a road switcher to challenge the American Flyer locomotive. Like Gilbert's model, the 2028 was designated a GP7. It boasted an unpainted Tuscan red body with rubber-stamped Pennsylvania Railroad graphics. Along with this O27 gauge model, Lionel released two other road switchers: the 2328, decorated for the Chicago, Burlington & Quincy; and 2338, which represented the Milwaukee Road. These two units were equipped with Magnetraction, operating couplers and lights, and a working horn; the 2028 had only a single light and lacked the horn. The most desirable of these GP7s was a variation of the 2338 with a solid orange band around its cab.

For Lionel, 1955 stood out in other ways. More F3s and NW2s were available, as was a stunning version of the Train Master decorated for the Virginian Railway. Moreover, following an absence of four years, a GG1 was cataloged. The 2340 came in Brunswick green or Tuscan red; either way, it was a gorgeous addition to the line, especially when pulling the streamlined cars packed with the 2254W *Congressional* outfit. Also in 1955, Lionel offered its first trolley in almost half a century. Other manufacturers, in particular Minitoys, had made O gauge trolleys after World War II. With the 60, Lionel sought to control that part of the toy train market. This yellow and red model of a Birney trolley used the frame of a gang car, so that it worked in the same manner as a motorized unit.

A year later, Lionel still directed its attention to small niches in the market. It sought to fill them with models of specialized General Electric locomotives; this fact suggested that Lionel had negotiated some kind of licensing agreement with GE. To start, there was the 520 80-ton electric, whose appearance hearkened back to the box-cabs Lionel had manufactured in the second and third decades of the century. Another electric, the 2350 New Haven EP-5, broadened the O gauge line with the elegance of its black, orange, and white scheme. The third GE prototype was a 44-ton diesel that pulled freight or passenger cars. Three versions were offered in 1956, including the 628 Northern Pacific and 629 Burlington, both of which came equipped with working headlights.

With these General Electric locomotives, Lionel reached the peak of its diesel production. By 1956 it was cataloging models of virtually every major type of modern locomotive. Indeed, its depth became even greater when the 41 United States Army gas turbine switch engine and the 51 New York Navy Yard Vulcan switcher were cataloged. Lionel didn't offer a model of a Baldwin prototype as Gilbert did or an Alco switcher as Marx did. All the same, it probably couldn't have expanded its product line without hurting its own sales.

Consequently, beginning in 1956 and continuing through the next few years, Lionel concentrated on developing more motorized units and increasing the paint schemes available on its best-selling F3 and NW2 diesels. The variety of self-propelled pieces is nothing short of phenomenal. First came the 3360 operating burro crane and 3927 track cleaning car in 1956. They were followed by the 42 Picatinny Arsenal switcher, 53 Denver and Rio Grande Western snowplow, and 55 Tie-Jector in 1957; and the 52 fire car, 54 ballast tamper, 56 Minneapolis and St. Louis mine transport, and 68 executive inspection car in 1958. Also back in 1956, Lionel brought out the 400 Budd Rail Diesel Car, a self-propelled passenger car similar to the models developed by American Model Toys and Marx.

During the last years of the 1950s, Lionel held the line on new diesel development while cutting corners on the models already in the line. New road names were available for the O and O27 gauge F3s, for example, including the highly collectible 2373 Canadian Pacific in 1957 and the 2379 Denver & Rio Grande Western in 1957 and 1958. Then Lionel dropped these beauties and kept only the 2242 New Haven and 2383 Santa Fe, both introduced in 1958 with many details missing. Details also were removed from the NW2 switchers beginning in 1955, although the number of road names cataloged increased significantly over the next six years.

Nowhere was the procedure of eliminating details, simplifying decoration, and adding road names more evident than with the Alco FA. Lionel had discontinued this fine O27 diesel after 1954, only to reissue it in a less elaborate form three years later. Engines produced from 1957 through 1969 had thinner, less durable bodies than their predecessors. Engineers plugged the locomotive's portholes

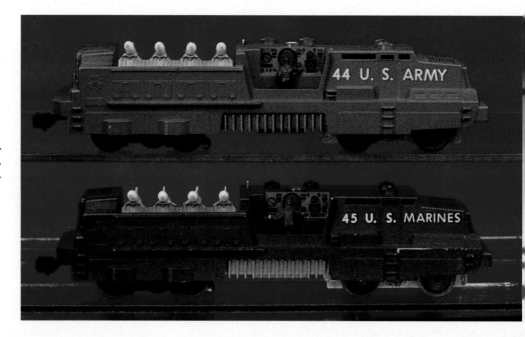

Top: 44 (A) U.S. Army mobile missile launcher. Bottom: 45 U.S. Marines mobile missile launcher. E. Dougherty Collection.

	Gd	VG	Ex	LN

and marker light slots and removed the headlight lens. Not surprisingly, the FAs cataloged during the 1960s looked cheap and performed poorly, suggesting that quality had slipped in importance at Lionel. Most still were equipped with Magnetraction, but often only via one axle. Fewer had an operating horn or a light in both AA units.

Even though inexpensive FAs came to dominate the Lionel product line during the 1960s, a handful of premium diesels and electrics remained in the catalog. An F3 and a Train Master were available, as were the desirable GG1 and EP-5 electrics. A mix of collectible and common GP7 and virtually identical GP9 models also appeared. For that reason, collectors shouldn't ignore this last part of the postwar era. Still, when compared with the finest years of diesel and electric locomotive development at Lionel, the 1960s lose most of their luster. The ingenuity and expertise demonstrated by the engineers who designed the earlier locomotives and motorized units were great. No finer testaments to their work survived than the F3s, Train Masters, and GG1s made by Lionel.

41 UNITED STATES ARMY (Motorized Unit): 1955–57. 2-4-2 gas turbine switcher; unpainted black body with white heat-stamped lettering and stylized Transportation Corps logo on cab; ornamental horn; headlight lens each end; chemically blackened side rails; chemically blackened high end rails; three-position E-unit; no light; operating couplers; window struts often broken or repaired. **100 130 150 200**

42 PICATINNY / ARSENAL (Motorized Unit): 1957. 2-4-2 gas turbine switcher; unpainted olive body with white heat-stamped lettering; ornamental horn; headlight lens each end; white-painted side rails; chemically blackened

high end rails; three-position E-unit; no light; operating couplers; window struts often broken or repaired.
150 225 300 400

44 U.S. ARMY (Motorized Unit): 1959–62. Mobile missile launcher; blue-painted body with white heat-stamped lettering; gray missile launcher with four missiles; rubberized blue man at control panel; Magnetraction; three-position E-unit; red light on roof; fixed die-cast coupler at one end only.

Note: Lionel apparently erred on this model: the molded plastic bottom interfered with the pawl on the E-unit. To remedy this problem, a small rectangular hole was cut in the bottom just below the E-unit. Early units do not have this cutout (A. Stewart comment).

(A) Light gray missile launcher.
110 150 205 290
(B) Dark gray missile launcher.
110 150 205 290

45 U.S. MARINES (Motorized Unit): 1960–62. Mobile missile launcher; olive-painted body with white heat-stamped lettering; gray missile launcher with four missiles; rubberized blue man at control panel; Magnetraction; three-position E-unit; red light on roof; fixed die-cast coupler at one end only. **125 190 225 340**

50 LIONEL (Motorized Unit): 1954–64. Self-powered section gang car; unpainted orange body and brushplate cover lettering; most typically with very dark blue heat-stamped ornamental horn; three rubberized crewmen (figure closest to end rotates with directional change); most commonly with U-shaped bumper brackets with blue rubberized bumpers; direction controlled by bumper-operated slide.

A group of motorized units. Top: 41 United States Army, 42 Picatinny Arsenal, and 51 Navy Yard. Middle: Scarce 53 (B) Rio Grande, most common 53 (A) with the letter "a" reversed, and 56 M St L mine transport. Bottom: 57 A E C, 58 Great Northern, and 59 U.S. Air Force Minuteman. The window struts on these pieces are easily broken; consequently, the engines must be handled with great care. Broken or repaired struts substantially lessen values. L. Nuzzaci Collection.

Gd   VG   Ex   LN

Note: Because of a long production life, variations are common. Some of the variables follow.

Bodies: On most 1954 production, the brushplate cover matched the body; however, on post-1954 models it usually was a shade darker than the body.

Ornamental Horn: 1954 production had a two-piece horn centered on the brushplate cover. Beginning in 1955 the horn was moved to the right, and new production began using a less expensive one-piece horn.

Bumpers: The very earliest production came with gray bumpers that were soon replaced by the common blue variety. Some blue bumpers from the very last runs were slightly larger than previous examples.

Bumper brackets: The original bumper bracket was U-shaped. Sometime in the early 1960s the shape was changed to an inverted L.

Crewmen: On the common variety the two fixed crewmen were blue and the rotating man olive. The scarce variation has the colors reversed, with the fixed crewmen olive and the rotating man blue.

Lettering: Most production came with very dark blue lettering that in some instances appeared as black. How-

ever, some 1954 production was heat-stamped with medium blue lettering.

The most accepted collectible variations are as follows:

(A) Earliest production with center horn, gray bumpers, olive fixed crewmen and blue rotating man.

| | 350 | 400 | 450 | 500 |

(B) Same as (A), except with common blue bumpers.

| | 30 | 60 | 90 | 120 |

(C) Center horn, blue bumpers, blue fixed crewmen and olive rotating man. **30   50   75   100**

(D) Most common version with off-center one-piece horn, blue bumpers, blue fixed crewmen and olive rotating man. **30   45   55   70**

(E) Same as (D), except with inverted L-shaped bumper bracket. **30   45   60   80**

51 NAVY YARD/NEW YORK (Motorized Unit): 1956–57. 2-4-2 Vulcan switcher; unpainted blue body with white heat-stamped lettering; ornamental bell; headlight lens each end; chemically blackened side rails; chemically blackened low end rails; three-position E-unit; no

Two versions of the 55 Tie-Jector. The left example does not have the slot behind the door, while the right one does. The slot provided ventilation for the motor. Early Tie-Jectors without the slot often show evidence of bin melting. L. Nuzzaci and R. Lord Collections.

	Gd	VG	Ex	LN

light; operating couplers; window struts often broken or repaired. **100 150 190 250**

52 FIRE CAR (Motorized Unit): 1958–61. Unpainted red body with white heat-stamped lettering; ornamental bell; rubberized fireman figure on white seat with "deluge nozzle" (seat swivels with directional change); gray compressor and hose assembly with retractable hose; retractable white outriggers; red warning light; rubberized bumpers; direction controlled by bumper-operated slide.

Note: When found today, the foam lamp pad usually has deteriorated beyond repair, causing the light bulb to shift, which melts the plastic body.

105 165 225 300

53 RIO GRANDE (Motorized Unit): 1957–60. 2-4-2 Vulcan switcher with snow plow; unpainted black body with yellow-painted cab sides and black heat-stamped lettering; most typically unpainted yellow snow plow; ornamental bell; headlight lens each end; yellow-painted side rails; chemically blackened low end rails; three-position E-unit; no light; operating coupler rear end; window struts often broken or repaired.

(A) Backwards "a" in Rio Grande; most common production. **180 250 330 450**
(B) Correct "a" in Rio Grande; scarce.
370 520 680 900

54 BALLAST TAMPER (Motorized Unit): 1958–61, 1966–69. Unpainted yellow body with black heat-stamped lettering; ornamental horn; flexible antenna on rear; gray housing with red tampers; rubberized blue man in cab; forward only; no light; fixed plastic coupler.

Note: Two activator track clips were included with the item to trip the on-off lever. When in the tamping mode, the unit is geared to operate at half speed.

100 160 225 300

55 TIE-JECTOR (Motorized Unit): 1957–61. Unpainted red body with white heat-stamped lettering; "PRR" keystone logo; item actually numbered "5511";

ornamental horn; rubberized blue man in cab; forward only; no light; fixed plastic coupler.

Note: Along with twenty-four wood ties, two activator track clips were included with the item to trip the on-off lever. Pulling more than a single car could cause the motor to overheat.

(A) As described above. **120 170 235 290**
(B) Same as (A), but orange tint to body.
150 225 290 400
(C) Same as (A), but horizontal slot in wall behind the motorman; the slot provided ventilation for the motor
120 170 235 290

56 M St L / MINE TRANSPORT (Motorized Unit): 1958. 2-4-2 Vulcan switcher; red-painted body with white-painted cab sides and red heat-stamped lettering; ornamental bell; headlight lens each end; white-painted side rails; chemically blackened low end rails; three-position E-unit; no light; operating couplers, window struts often broken or repaired. **250 400 560 725**

57 AEC (Motorized Unit): 1959–60. 2-4-2 Vulcan switcher; unpainted white body with red-painted cab sides and white heat-stamped lettering; stylized Atomic Energy Commission logo on cab; ornamental bell; headlight lens each end; chemically blackened side rails; chemically blackened low end rails; three-position E-unit; no light; operating couplers; window struts often broken or repaired. **325 500 750 1000**

58 GREAT NORTHERN (Motorized Unit): 1959–61. 2-4-2 Vulcan switcher with snow blower; unpainted green body with white-painted cab sides and green heat-stamped lettering; Great Northern logo on cab; unpainted green snow blower rotates when switcher is in motion; ornamental bell; headlight lens each end; white-painted side rails; chemically blackened low end rails; three-position E-unit; no light; operating coupler at rear end; window struts often broken or repaired. **325 450 650 800**

59 U.S. AIR FORCE/MINUTEMAN (Motorized Unit): 1962–63. 2-4-2 gas turbine switcher; unpainted white

Top: 52 fire car, 54 ballast tamper, and 3360 burro crane. Bottom: 55 Tie-Jector, 69 maintenance car, and 68 executive inspection car. L. Nuzzaci and R. Lord Collections.

	Gd	VG	Ex	LN

ody with blue heat-stamped lettering; red heat-stamped "59"; blue and red heat-stamped star and stripe logo on cab; ornamental horn; headlight lens each end; chemically blackened side rails; chemically blackened high end rails; three-position E-unit; no light; operating couplers; window struts often broken or repaired.

	300	425	600	750

60 LIONELVILLE RAPID TRANSIT (Motorized Unit): 1955–58. Four-wheel Birney-style trolley; unpainted yellow body with heat-stamped lettering; unpainted red roof; trolley pole (pole rotates with directional change); silhouetted window inserts; lighted; direction controlled by bumper-operated slide.

Note: Though cataloged through 1958, production was probably complete by late 1956. Be aware that trolley bodies, roofs, poles, and even the stamped-steel motorman silhouettes are completely interchangeable. This no doubt accounts for the numerous variations reported. Below are some of the variables.

Bodies: Heat-stamped black (earliest) or blue lettering.

Roofs: Early production with roof slots at each end. Later models had four additional vents along the edges of the clerestory. The Lionel Service Manual, on a page dated 11-55, stated, "For 1956 production the No. 60 Trolley was redesigned to provide cooling vents in the roof. . . ." In addition, an aluminized paper reflector was added to the underside of the roof to prevent roof damage due to the combination of bulb and motor heat (J. Algozzini comment).

Light: Trolley illuminated by shock-mounted lamp. Early production with partially painted silver lamp, to prevent excessive glare through the roof. Later production used an unpainted lamp when the underside of roof was fitted with an aluminized paper reflector.

Bumpers: Early production with two-part spring bumper; later production with solid one-piece bumper.

Trolley pole holders: Early production with square top; later production with splines (grooves relating to grooves on a shaft).

Motorman silhouettes: In early production metal silhouettes of a motorman were attached to the ends of the bumper slide to simulate changing of the motorman's position with each change of direction.

Original boxes: Boxes are either from 1955 and 1956 (Classic design) or 1956 (corrugated). Instruction sheets dated 8-55 or 2-56.

The most accepted collectible variations are as follows:

(A) Earliest production with black lettering; metal motorman silhouettes; no clerestory vents; two-part spring bumpers.

	150	220	300	460

(B) Same as (A), without motorman silhouettes.

	150	220	300	460

(C) Most common version with blue lettering; no clerestory vents; two-part spring bumpers.

	100	150	195	240

(D) Same as (C), but with solid one-piece bumper.

	125	175	220	275

(E) Blue lettering; with clerestory vents; solid one-piece bumper.

	125	175	220	275

65 HANDCAR (Motorized Unit): 1962–66. Unpainted yellow body with raised yellow lettering integral to body

Top: Three different versions of the 50 section gang car. Left to right, 50 (C), 50 (D), and 50 (E). The item on the right has inverted L-shaped bumper brackets; note that the heat-stamped decoration is missing from the side shown.
Bottom: Three versions of the 60 Birney-style trolley. Left to right, 60 (D), 60 (B), and 60 (E). Observe the black lettering on the center example and the one-piece bumper and clerestory vents on the model to the right. L. Nuzzaci Collection.

This is the two-piece spring bumper used on the earlier production of the 60 trolley. The final production of the trolley had a one-piece bumper. R. Bartelt photograph.

	Gd	VG	Ex	LN

mold (one side marked "THE LIONEL CORPORATION / NEW YORK NEW YORK" and other side marked "HANDCAR No 65"); red pump handle; two vinyl motormen; one direction only.

Note: As the unit moves along the track, the motormen raise and lower their arms in a pumping manner. Be aware that the vinyl material used for the figures has often caused a destructive chemical reaction with the car body that causes the area where they stand to appear to "melt" away.

	Gd	VG	Ex	LN
(A) Dark yellow body.	150	275	400	525
(B) Light yellow body.	170	325	450	600

68 EXECUTIVE INSPECTION CAR (Motorized Unit): 1958–61. Facsimile of 1958 DeSoto station wagon; red-painted body (gray body mold) with cream-painted side panel and roof (plastic bumpers front and rear); no decoration on body; two-position E-unit controlled by switch knob on roof; lighted front and rear (two lamp sockets). **200 250 350 450**

69 MAINTENANCE CAR (Motorized Unit): 1960–62. Self-powered signal service car; unpainted black body cover with white heat-stamped lettering (maintenance car does *not* appear on body); dark gray brushplate cover; light gray platform assembly with rubberized man and red sign marked "DANGER" and "SAFETY FIRST" in white lettering (sign rotates with directional change); inverted L-shaped bumper brackets with blue rubberized bumpers; direction controlled by bumper-operated slide. **175 240 310 450**

202 UNION PACIFIC (Diesel): 1957. Alco A unit; orange-painted body with black heat-stamped lettering; closed pilot; one-axle Magnetraction; two-position E-unit; light. **60 80 100 125**

204 SANTA FE (Diesel): 1957. Alco AA units; dark blue-painted body with wide yellow-painted upper stripe and cab roof and yellow heat-stamped lettering; red roofline stripe and additional red stripe below wide yellow upper

	Gd	VG	Ex	LN

tripe, and narrow red and yellow stripes on lower body; arge wraparound nose decal; open pilot with small ledge; wo-axle Magnetraction; three-position E-unit; light in *both* units. **75 100 150 225**

205 MISSOURI PACIFIC (Diesel): 1957–58. Alco AA units; blue-painted body with white heat-stamped lettering; open pilot with small ledge; two-axle Magnetraction; three-position E-unit; light.

(A) Pilots with factory-installed painted nose supports. **90 125 180 250**

(B) Common production without nose supports. **75 100 160 225**

208 SANTA FE (Diesel): 1958–59. Alco AA units; dark blue-painted body with wide yellow-painted upper stripe and cab roof and yellow heat-stamped lettering; red roofline stripe and additional red stripe below wide yellow upper stripe, and narrow red and yellow stripes on lower body; large wraparound nose decal; open pilot with small ledge; two-axle Magnetraction; three-position E-unit; light; horn. **78 100 165 225**

209 NEW HAVEN (Diesel): 1958. Alco AA units; black-painted body with wide orange-painted upper stripe and

wide white-painted lower stripe; white and orange heat-stamped lettering and large wraparound white and orange nose emblem; open pilot with small ledge; two-axle Magnetraction; three-position E-unit; light; horn. **350 425 775 900**

210 TEXAS SPECIAL (Diesel): 1958. Alco AA units; red-painted body with white-painted lower stripe; red heat-stamped lettering and white heat-stamped star on nose; open pilot with small ledge; two-axle Magnetraction; three-position E-unit; light. **110 160 210 260**

211 TEXAS SPECIAL (Diesel): 1962–63, 1965–66. Alco AA units; red-painted body with white-painted lower stripe; red heat-stamped lettering and white heat-stamped star on nose; open pilot with large ledge; powered unit usually with weight; traction tires; two-position E-unit; light

(A) 1962; one-axle Magnetraction and powered unit without weight. **80 130 180 230**

(B) All other production as described above. **80 130 180 230**

212 SANTA FE (Diesel): 1964–66. Alco AA units; silver- and red-painted body in warbonnet scheme with black heat-stamped lettering; nose decal; open pilot with large

Top: 202 Union Pacific and 212 (A) United States Marine Corps. Middle: 209 New Haven AA units. Bottom: 212 (B) United States Marine Corps and rare matching 212T dummy unit with open pilot. E. Dougherty Collection.

Top: 205 (B) Missouri Pacific AA units. Bottom: 204 Santa Fe AA units.

The Evolution of Lionel Alcos
by Paul V. Ambrose

The first Alco—the Lionel diesel locomotive modeled on the 1500-horsepower FA units built by the American Locomotive Company for the Union Pacific Railroad—appeared in 1950 to mark Lionel's 50th anniversary. Over the years two distinctly different styles of Alcos evolved. The early models, the epitome of design and engineering excellence, were offered through 1954. (See listing 2023 and subsequent ones.) In 1957 the 200-series Alcos appeared, becoming more and more inferior to the original units.

All early Alcos came in an AA combination; the powered and nonpowered bodies were identical. The powered unit contains a single motor; Lionel exerted special effort to enable them to negotiate tightly curved O27 gauge track and switches. Also included in the powered unit were an E-unit and operating horn. Both units were equipped with electromagnetic operating couplers at the pilot ends and nonoperating couplers at the back ends.

Alco frames were die-cast and had rear steps staked to the underside. All trucks included separately attached die-cast side frames. The 1950–1951 production of 2023 models also included a metal step attached to pilot side frames on both units. This realistic detail was discontinued with 1952 production. In 1953 Lionel added a raised, dime-sized detail to the roof above the motor to reinforce the roof and prevent warping that might occur during the cooling process after the body was ejected from the mold.

Individual boxes do not exist for early Alcos. Instead, the master carton included a large folded insert that separated the units and fillers to protect couplers. These master cartons are datable by graphics and/or a year date.

In operation and quality of construction, the 200-series introduced in 1957 was a far cry from the earlier models; by 1959 the Alco clearly was a poor cousin to its predecessors. Although the 200-series body mold was basically the same as that used for early Alcos, there were some noticeable cost-saving changes. Not only was the body molding thinner, but Lionel designers plugged the marker lens slots and three open portholes along the sides, eliminated the headlight lens, and added an integral pilot to the lower portion of the nose area. All 200-series Alco couplers were fixed and die-cast. The frames were stamped steel, and most were chemically blackened.

All models equipped with an opening for a front coupler had a coupler bar or strut, and this was very fragile. Aware of the problem, Lionel produced a nose support, a metal front piece to be used for service repair of broken coupler bars. In 1960 the coupler bar was reinforced with a larger molded ledge.

For more information on Alcos, including descriptions and illustrations of all variations and explanation of the motors used, see *Greenberg's Guide to Lionel Trains 1945–1969, Volume VII.*

Top: 208 Santa Fe AA units. Middle: 210 Texas Special AA units. Bottom: 211 Texas Special AA units.

	Gd	VG	Ex	LN

edge; powered unit usually with weight; traction tires; two-position E-unit; horn.

Note: It is common to find a mixed combination of one of each of the two variations described below.

(A) Bodies with built date appearing as "BLT 8-57 / BY LIONEL".

	78	100	150	225

(B) Bodies with "BLT / BY LIONEL".

	78	100	150	225

212 UNITED STATES MARINE CORPS (Diesel): 1958–59. Alco A unit; painted body with two narrow white side-detailing stripes and white heat-stamped lettering; closed pilot; one-axle Magnetraction; two-position E-unit; light.

(A) Dark blue-painted body.

	75	100	150	225

(B) Medium blue-painted body. This variation is distinctly lighter than (A) and was usually the powered unit paired with the extremely scarce 212T. See next listing.

	100	150	225	280

212(T) UNITED STATES MARINE CORPS (Diesel): Uncataloged, 1958. Alco dummy A unit; dark blue-painted body with two narrow white side-detailing stripes and white heat-stamped lettering; *open* pilot with small ledge.

Note: This is an extremely valuable and scarce item.

On a page dated 12-58 the Lionel Service Manual states, "a limited number of A(T) units were made for a special outfit."

	285	350	575	700

213 MINNEAPOLIS & ST. LOUIS (Diesel): 1964. Alco AA units; red-painted body with medium-width white stripe centered on side; white heat-stamped lettering that includes "The Peoria Gateway" in a circle. Open pilot with large ledge; powered unit most often with weight; traction tires; two-position E-unit; light.

	75	125	175	300

215 SANTA FE (Diesel): Uncataloged, 1965–66. Also A unit; silver- and red-painted body in warbonnet scheme with black heat-stamped lettering; nose decal; open pilot with large ledge; weight; traction tires; two-position E-unit; light.

Note: Verified examples of an AA combination from uncataloged sets *always* came with a nonweighted 212T dummy A unit. An AB combination utilizing a 218C Santa Fe B unit has also been confirmed.

(A) AA combination with 212T; built date on 215 body appearing as "BLT 8-57 / BY LIONEL".

	75	100	165	200

(B) AA combination with 212T; built date on 215 body appearing as "BLT / BY LIONEL".

	75	100	165	200

Top: 213 M & St L AA units. Middle: 216 Burlington. Bottom: Uncataloged 216 M & St L properly paired with 213T M & St L dummy A unit. K. Rubright Collection.

	Gd	VG	Ex	LN

(C) AB combination with 218C; either style of built date. **80 110 180 225**

216 BURLINGTON (Diesel): 1958. Alco A unit; silver-painted body with two narrow red side-detailing stripes and red heat-stamped lettering; open pilot with small ledge; two-axle Magnetraction; three-position E-unit; light. **100 150 310 400**

216 MINNEAPOLIS & ST. LOUIS (Diesel): Uncataloged, 1965. Alco A unit; red-painted body with medium-width white stripe centered on side; white heat-stamped lettering that includes "The Peoria Gateway" in a circle; open pilot with large ledge; weight; traction tires; two-position E-unit; light.

Note: Verified examples of an AA combination from uncataloged sets *always* came with a nonweighted 213T dummy A unit. However, a 216 *may* also have come as a single A unit in another uncataloged set.

(A) Single A unit. **75 100 140 175**
(B) AA combination with 213T. **90 125 200 275**

217 B and M (Boston and Maine) (Diesel): 1959. Alco AB units; black-painted and typically unpainted blue body with white roofline stripe and predominantly white heat-

stamped lettering with "M" accented in black; stylized B and M logo on side (full road name *not* spelled out); open pilot with small ledge; two-axle Magnetraction; three-position E-unit; light.

Note: The 217C was the first issue of an Alco B unit. Blue is the most common color for body molds. However blue is susceptible to fading, and some items may even turn to a shade of teal. But distinctly different teal examples also exist that do *not* appear to be time-faded. Some AB units do not match as a result of this variation, but they are legitimate pairs. Mixed combinations with one blue body mold and one teal are also found.

(A) Paired blue bodies. **75 100 185 225**
(B) Paired teal bodies. **75 100 185 225**

218 SANTA FE (Diesel): 1959–63. Alco AA units; silver- and red-painted body in warbonnet scheme with black heat-stamped lettering; all built dates appearing as "BLT 8-57 / BY LIONEL"; nose decal; open pilot; two-axle Magnetraction; three-position E-unit; light; horn.

Note: The 218 usually came as an AA pair; however, with outfit 1649, cataloged in 1961, the pairing was an AB combination. The Santa Fe nose decal comes in two variations: common is yellow with red accents at the four corners, on the scarce decal the background is solid yellow.

217 Boston and Maine AB units.

Top: 212 (A) Santa Fe AA units. Second: Uncataloged 215 (B) Santa Fe properly paired with 212T Santa Fe dummy A unit. Third: 218 (A) Santa Fe AA units. Fourth: Uncataloged 220 (A)

Santa Fe AA units. Bottom: 223 and 218C Santa Fe AB units. This pairing occurred in outfit 11385, cataloged in 1963. M. Yeaton Collection.

Top: 219 Missouri Pacific AA units. Middle: 221 Rio Grande and 221 United States Marine Corps. Bottom: 221 Santa Fe and 232 New Haven. E. Dougherty Collection.

	Gd	VG	Ex	LN

(A) AA units; pilots with small edge; yellow and red nose decals. — 70 100 170 200

(B) AA units; pilots with large ledge; yellow and red nose decals. — 70 100 170 200

(C) AA units; solid yellow nose decals; the collectibility of this variation is due to the solid yellow decals (pilot information is inconsequential). — 100 125 200 250

(D) AB units; because this pairing occurred in 1961, the pilot of the A unit came with a large ledge. — 70 100 170 200

(218C) SANTA FE (Diesel): 1961–63. Alco B unit; silver-painted body with narrow yellow and red stripes on lower body and black heat-stamped lettering; built date appearing as "BLT BY / LIONEL"; matches any Santa Fe Alco A unit with warbonnet scheme.

Note: The 218C was the only B unit from the Alco series that did *not* include a number on the body. — 40 50 80 100

219 MISSOURI PACIFIC (Diesel): Uncataloged, 1959. Alco AA units; unpainted blue body with white heat-stamped lettering; open pilot with small ledge; two-axle Magnetraction; two-position E-unit; light. — 68 100 150 225

	Gd	VG	Ex	LN

220 SANTA FE (Diesel): Uncataloged, 1960; consumer catalog 1961. Alco AA units or A unit; silver- and red-painted body in warbonnet scheme with black heat-stamped lettering; all built dates appearing as "BLT 8-57 / BY LIONEL"; nose decal; open pilot; two-axle Magnetraction; three-position E-unit; light.

Note: A 220 A unit was paired with a 218C Santa Fe B unit on page 48 of the 1961 consumer catalog, but we have never verified this AB pairing in an outfit. However, we do have verification of the AA combination, and a 220 A unit has been reported with an uncataloged set. It is possible to find a mixed combination of one each of the two pilot variations described below.

(A) AA combination; pilots with small ledge. — 100 150 225 275

(B) AA combination; pilots with large ledge. — 100 150 225 275

(C) Single A unit; either pilot variation applicable. — 75 100 135 175

221 RIO GRANDE (Diesel): 1963–64. Alco A unit; unpainted yellow body with black roofline stripe and three narrow black stripes on lower body; black heat-stamped lettering; closed pilot with ledge; no ornamental horn; traction tire; two-position E-unit; no light; usually without frame box.

Top: 222 Rio Grande and 2024 Chesapeake and Ohio. Bottom: 224 United States Navy AB units. L. Nuzzaci Collection.

	Gd	VG	Ex	LN

Note: In the dismal 1960s, cost reduction was the order of the day. All Alcos manufactured prior to 1963, even those without Magnetraction, included two geared axles. But new 1963 low-end models included only one geared axle. 35 45 75 100

221 SANTA FE (Diesel): Uncataloged, 1964. Alco A unit; unpainted olive body with white heat-stamped lettering; closed pilot with ledge; no ornamental horn; typically forward only; no light; usually without frame box.

Note: This is an extremely scarce engine. The 221 Santa Fe headed at least one uncataloged set and possibly more. 175 250 420 550

221 UNITED STATES MARINE CORPS (Diesel): Uncataloged, 1964. Alco A unit; unpainted olive body with two narrow white side-detailing stripes and white heat-stamped lettering; closed pilot with ledge; no ornamental horn; traction tire; two-position E-unit; no light; usually without frame box. 100 150 255 325

222 RIO GRANDE (Diesel): Advance catalog 1962. Alco A unit; yellow-painted body with black roofline stripe and three narrow black stripes on lower body; black heat-stamped lettering; closed pilot with ledge; no ornamental horn; traction tire; forward only; light; no frame box. 35 45 75 100

223 SANTA FE (Diesel): 1963. Alco AB units; silver- and red-painted body in warbonnet scheme with black heat-stamped lettering; "BLT 8-57 / BY LIONEL"; nose decal; open pilot with large ledge; one-axle Magnetraction; two-position E-unit; light; horn.

Note: The Santa Fe B unit did *not* include a number. See 218C. 85 125 185 275

224 UNITED STATES NAVY (Diesel): 1960. Alco AB units; blue-painted body with white heat-stamped lettering; open pilot with large ledge; two-axle Magnetraction; three-position E-unit; light. 100 150 200 250

225 CHESAPEAKE & OHIO (Diesel): 1960. Alco A unit; dark blue-painted body with yellow heat-stamped lettering and yellow heat-stamped "C and O" herald on nose; open pilot with large ledge; two-axle Magnetraction; two-position E-unit; light.

Note: The 225 does *not* come with the yellow roofline stripe that is present on C & O models 230 and 2024. 65 100 120 150

226 B and M (Boston and Maine) (Diesel): Uncataloged, 1960. Alco AB units; black-painted and most often unpainted blue body with white roofline stripe and predominantly white heat-stamped lettering with "M" accented in black; stylized B and M logo; open pilot; two-axle Magnetraction; three-position E-unit; light; horn.

(A) Pilot with small ledge; unpainted blue area on body of both units. 85 100 190 225

(B) Pilot with large ledge; unpainted blue area on body of both units. 85 100 190 225

(C) Pilot with large ledge; A unit with gray body mold that is *painted* both black and blue; unpainted blue area on body of B unit. 100 150 225 300

227 CANADIAN NATIONAL (Diesel): Uncataloged, 1960. Alco A unit; green-painted body with two narrow yellow side-detailing stripes and yellow heat-stamped lettering; closed pilot with ledge; weight; forward only; light.

Note: Aside from the ballast weight riveted to the rear of the body, this engine has no traction aid. 78 100 160 200

Top: 225 Chesapeake & Ohio. Middle: 226 Boston and Maine AB units. Bottom: 227 Canadian National and 228 Canadian National.

	Gd	VG	Ex	LN

228 CANADIAN NATIONAL (Diesel): Uncataloged, 1960. Alco A unit; green-painted body with two narrow yellow side-detailing stripes and yellow heat-stamped lettering; open pilot; two-axle Magnetraction; two-position E-unit; light.

	Gd	VG	Ex	LN
(A) Pilot with small ledge.	70	100	140	180
(B) Pilot with large ledge.	70	100	140	180

229 MINNEAPOLIS & ST. LOUIS (Diesel): 1961–62. Alco A unit in 1961 and Alco AB units in 1962; red-painted body with medium-width white stripe centered on side; white heat-stamped lettering that includes "The Peoria Gateway" in circle; open pilot with large ledge; one-axle Magnetraction; two-position E-unit; light; horn.

	Gd	VG	Ex	LN
(A) Single A unit.	60	90	120	150
(B) AB units.	95	160	225	300

230 CHESAPEAKE & OHIO (Diesel): 1961. Alco A unit; dark blue-painted body with yellow roofline stripe and yellow heat-stamped lettering; closed pilot with ledge; two-axle Magnetraction; two-position E-unit; light.

Note: The 230 does *not* have the C and O nose herald that is present on the 225 model.

	Gd	VG	Ex	LN
	55	80	105	135

231 ROCK ISLAND (Diesel): 1961–63. Alco A unit; black-painted body with white roofline stripe and white heat-stamped lettering with white heat-stamped Rock Island herald on nose; open pilot with large ledge; two-axle Magnetraction; two-position E-unit; light.

	Gd	VG	Ex	LN
(A) Body without red-painted middle stripe.				
	125	175	250	350
(B) Body with red-painted middle stripe.				
	50	75	100	125

232 NEW HAVEN (Diesel): 1962. Alco A unit; orange-painted body with two narrow black side-detailing stripes; white and black heat-stamped lettering; closed pilot with ledge; two-axle Magnetraction; two-position E-unit; light.

	Gd	VG	Ex	LN
	65	100	130	160

520 LIONEL LINES (Electric): 1956–57. GE 80-ton boxcab electric; unpainted red body with white heat-stamped lettering; single plastic pantograph; chemically treated sheet-metal frame; three-position E-unit; no light; operating coupler at one end and fixed die-cast coupler at other end.

Note: The pantograph is the key part to this locomotive. Its fragile molded plastic was easily damaged. The pantograph was also easy to remove, and thus easy to lose (A. Stewart comment). This locomotive is a close model of a boxcab electric sold by GE to the Chile Exploration Company for use in its copper mines. The Lionel model is surprisingly accurate, right down to the air tanks

Top: 229 M & St L AB units. Bottom: 230 Chesapeake & Ohio and 231 (A) Rock Island.

	Gd	VG	Ex	LN

atop the cab and the portholes. Its number was exactly the same as the 520 shown on the prototype.

(A) Black pantograph. **70 105 140 157**
(B) Copper-colored pantograph.
80 115 150 200

600 M K T (Missouri-Kansas-Texas) (Diesel): 1955. EMD NW2 switcher; unpainted red body with white heat-stamped number and medallion; gold ornamental bell and silver ornamental horn; early sheet-metal frame without skirt; not lighted; operating couplers; one- or two-axle Magnetraction; three-position E-unit with lever pointing down. The Lionel Service Manual stated that only a few thousand units were produced with two-axle Magnetraction; the great majority came with one-axle Magnetraction.

(A) Gray-painted frame with yellow-painted platform railings and chemically blackened steps.
240 350 450 600

520 (B) Lionel Lines boxcab electric. Notice the copper-colored pantograph.

(B) Gray-painted frame with chemically blackened platform railings and steps.
200 300 400 500
(C) Black-painted frame with chemically blackened platform railings and steps. **90 130 170 225**
(D) Chemically blackened frame, platform, railings, and steps; most common version.
90 130 170 225

601 SEABOARD (Diesel): 1956. EMD NW2 switcher with operating horn; black- and red-painted body with three stripes and white heat-stamped lettering; Seaboard medallion decal; gold ornamental bell and silver ornamental horn; early sheet-metal frame with skirt; not lighted; operating couplers; two-axle Magnetraction; three-position E-unit with lever pointing down. Cataloged as O gauge.

(A) Red stripes on body with square ends.
80 125 170 225
(B) Red stripes on body with rounded ends.
80 125 170 225

602 SEABOARD (Diesel): 1957–58. EMD NW2 switcher with operating horn; black- and red-painted body with three red stripes with rounded ends and white heat-stamped lettering; Seaboard medallion decal; gold ornamental bell and silver ornamental horn; early sheet-metal frame with skirt; lighted; fixed plastic couplers; two-axle Magnetraction; three-position E-unit with lever pointing down.

Note: The presence of a light meant that this diesel required a new front platform, modified to include a lamp socket. Cataloged as O27 gauge.
85 140 195 250

610 ERIE (Diesel): 1955. EMD NW2 switcher; black-painted body with yellow heat-stamped number and Erie

Top: 600 (D) M K T and 601 (B) Seaboard. Middle: 602 Seaboard and 610 (C) Erie. Bottom: 611 (B) Jersey Central and 613 Union Pacific L. Nuzzaci Collection.

	Gd	VG	Ex	LN

medallion; gold ornamental bell and silver ornamental horn; early sheet-metal frame without skirt; not lighted; operating couplers; one- or two-axle Magnetraction; three-position E-unit with lever pointing down. The Lionel Service Manual stated that only a few thousand units were produced with two-axle Magnetraction; the great majority came with one-axle Magnetraction.

(A) Yellow-painted frame with yellow-painted platform railings and chemically blackened steps.

	280	430	590	900

(B) Black-painted frame with chemically blackened platform railings and steps.

	85	120	160	220

(C) Chemically blackened frame, platform railings, and steps; most common version.

	85	120	160	220

(D) Very scarce body variation (frame inconsequential) with nameplate on each side. A mold modification was made in 1956 to include nameplates on all future production; this shell was a Lionel Service Department replacement body.

	150	200	275	350

611 JERSEY CENTRAL (Diesel): 1957–58. EMD NW2 switcher; unpainted blue body with orange-painted detail; white heat-stamped lettering on nameplates and blue heat-stamped number and Jersey Central medallion on cab. This is the only NW2 with two primary colors of lettering; gold ornamental bell and silver ornamental horn; early sheet-metal frame with skirt; lighted; fixed plastic couplers; one-axle Magnetraction; three-position E-unit with lever pointing down.

Note: The presence of a light meant that this diesel required a new front platform, modified to include a lamp socket.

(A) Royal blue body with dark blue lettering.

	120	150	205	325

(B) Medium blue body with dark blue lettering.

	120	150	205	325

(C) Medium blue body with medium blue lettering.

	120	150	205	325

613 UNION PACIFIC (Diesel): 1958. EMD NW2 switcher; yellow- and gray-painted body with red heat-stamped lettering (cab lettering different on each side); "NEW 7-58" on sides near nose; "U.P." and "613" on front of nose; gold ornamental bell and silver ornamental horn; early sheet-metal frame with skirt; lighted; fixed plastic couplers; two-axle Magnetraction; three-position E-unit with lever pointing down.

	125	200	415	500

614 ALASKA RAILROAD (Diesel): 1959–60. EMD

	Gd	VG	Ex	LN

NW2 switcher; blue-painted body with yellow heat-stamped lettering and Eskimo figure; yellow brake superstructure; early sheet-metal frame with skirt; lighted; fixed plastic couplers but only cab end self-centering; one-axle Magnetraction; two-position E-unit with lever pointing up.

Note: The brake superstructure is secured by two molded tabs; one goes into the front center window of the cab, the other fits into the slot normally used for the ornamental bell. A mold modification was made on the top of the body to include an E-unit slot; even if plugged, this slot is discernible on all later-production NW2 switchers.

(A) "BUILT BY / LIONEL" outlined in yellow on lower sides of body near nose; very scarce.

	250	350	450	600

(B) Body without yellow outline.

	120	160	200	250

616 SANTA FE (Diesel): 1961–62. EMD NW2 switcher with operating horn; black-painted body with white-painted safety stripes and white heat-stamped lettering and Santa Fe medallion; no ornamental trim according to the Lionel Service Manual, although some examples have been observed with a gold ornamental bell; open ornamental horn slot; early sheet-metal frame with skirt; lighted with headlight lens; fixed plastic couplers; two-axle Magnetraction; three-position E-unit with lever pointing down.

(A) Body with open E-unit and bell slots.

	85	125	175	250

(B) Body with open bell slot and plugged E-unit slot.

	200	300	380	500

(C) Body with plugged E-unit and bell slots.

	200	300	380	500

617 SANTA FE (Diesel): 1963. EMD NW2 switcher with operating horn; black-painted body with white-painted safety stripes and white heat-stamped lettering and Santa Fe medallion; plugged E-unit slot; black ornamental bell and silver ornamental horn; radio wheel; marker lens; lighted with headlight lens; fixed plastic couplers; two-axle Magnetraction; three-position E-unit with lever pointing down.

Note: This model was trimmed with details that had last been used on 6250 in 1955. The 617 was a transition piece; it was the only diesel switcher that came with two distinctly different frames.

(A) Early sheet-metal frame with skirt; die-cast side frames.

	120	150	250	325

(B) Late sheet-metal frame; die-cast side frames.

	120	150	250	325

621 JERSEY CENTRAL (Diesel): 1956–57. EMD NW2 switcher with operating horn; unpainted blue body with orange heat-stamped number and blank nameplates; orange Jersey Central medallion decal; gold ornamental bell and silver ornamental horn; early sheet-metal frame with skirt; not lighted; operating couplers; one-axle Magnetraction; three-position E-unit with lever pointing down.

	Gd	VG	Ex	LN
(A) Royal blue body.	60	75	145	200
(B) Dark navy blue body.	85	100	190	250

622 A.T. & S.F. (Santa Fe) (Diesel): 1949–50. EMD NW2 switcher with ringing bell; black-painted body with white heat-stamped lettering; GM and Santa Fe medallion decals; black ornamental bell and silver ornamental horn; radio wheel; marker lens; wire handrail along hood; black-painted die-cast frame with wire handrail detail; lighted with headlight lens, front and rear; coil couplers; two-axle Magnetraction (1949 models with magnetized axles and 1950 production with magnets cemented to truck frame); three-position E-unit.

Note: There are two sizes of GM decals and two distinctly different colors of Santa Fe medallion decals. Many variations are possible because of variations in decals, the possibility of two different frames, and the "622" heat-stamped on the lower front of some bodies. The 622 was never featured in the consumer catalog as Santa Fe, but as "LIONEL" in 1949 and "NEW YORK CENTRAL" in 1950. Identical to 6220 except for number.

(A) Large GM decal on cab below number; "622" on body front.

	170	200	350	450

(B) Large GM decal on cab below number; without "622" on body front.

	170	200	350	450

(C) Small GM decal on lower sides near nose; without "622" on body front.

	150	175	325	400

623 A.T. & S.F. (Diesel): 1952–54. EMD NW2 switcher; black-painted body with white heat-stamped lettering; small GM and Santa Fe medallion decals; black ornamental bell and silver ornamental horn; radio wheel; marker lens; wire handrail along hood; black-painted die-cast frame with wire handrail detail; lighted with headlight lens, front and rear; coil couplers; two-axle Magnetraction; three-position E-unit.

(A) Ten stanchions attach wire handrail to body.

	95	120	200	250

(B) Three stanchions attach wire handrail to body.

	95	120	200	250

624 CHESAPEAKE & OHIO (Diesel): 1952–54. EMD NW2 switcher; blue-painted body with unpainted yellow smokestacks and yellow heat-stamped cab number; "CHESAPEAKE & OHIO" and C and O medallion decals; black ornamental bell and silver ornamental horn; radio wheel; marker lens; wire handrail along hood; blue-painted die-cast frame with yellow-painted stripe and wire handrail detail; lighted with headlight lens, front and rear; coil couplers; two-axle Magnetraction; three-position E-unit. The large Chesapeake & Ohio decal is prone to flaking; Like New must have decals intact.

(A) Ten stanchions attach wire handrail to body; small GM decal on lower sides near nose.

	110	150	270	325

(B) Three stanchions attach wire handrail to body; usually without small GM decal.

	110	150	270	325

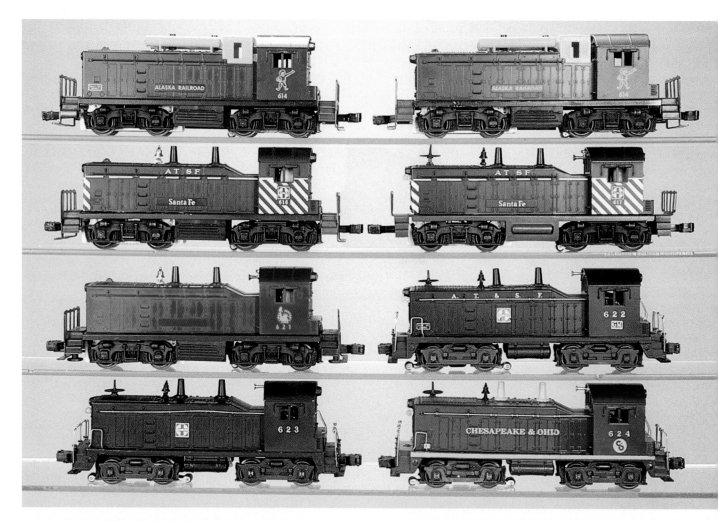

Top: 614 (A) and (B) Alaska Railroad. Second: 616 (A) Santa Fe and 617 (B) Santa Fe. Third: 621 A) Jersey Central and 622 (B) Santa Fe. Bottom: 623 (B) Santa Fe and 624 (A) Chesapeake & Ohio.

This photo shows the transition from the early sheet-metal frame and die-cast side frames for diesel switcher trucks to the late sheet-metal frame and plastic side frames. Top: 616 (A) Santa Fe with the early frame and die-cast side frames. Middle: 617 (B) Santa Fe with the late frame and die-cast side frames. Bottom: 634 (A) Santa Fe with the late frame and plastic side frames.

	Gd	VG	Ex	LN

(C) Distinctly different lighter blue–painted body with three stanchions; Lionel Service Department replacement cab. **200 300 450 550**

625 LEHIGH VALLEY (Diesel): 1957–58. GE 44-ton switcher; unpainted red body and black-painted details with white heat-stamped lettering and white lower stripe; LV diamond herald (road name not spelled out); ornamental horn and ornamental bell; headlight lens both ends; black-painted frame; one-axle Magnetraction; three-position E-unit; light at one end; fixed plastic couplers. **75 120 150 190**

626 BALTIMORE AND OHIO (Diesel): 1957. GE 44-ton switcher; unpainted blue body with yellow heat-stamped lettering and yellow lower stripe; ornamental horn and ornamental bell; headlight lens both ends; yellow-painted frame; one-axle Magnetraction; three-position E-unit; light at one end; operating couplers. **120 225 375 600**

627 LEHIGH VALLEY (Diesel): 1956–57. GE 44-ton switcher; unpainted red body with white heat-stamped lettering and white lower stripe; LV diamond herald (road name not spelled out); ornamental horn and ornamental bell; headlight lens both ends; black-painted frame; typically one-axle Magnetraction; three-position E-unit; no light; operating couplers. **80 110 145 200**

628 NORTHERN PACIFIC (Diesel): 1956–57. GE 44-ton switcher; unpainted black body with yellow heat-stamped lettering and yellow lower stripe; Northern Pacific herald; ornamental horn and ornamental bell; headlight lens both ends; yellow-painted frame; one-axle Magnetraction; three-position E-unit; light at one end; operating couplers.
(A) True black body. **80 110 145 200**
(B) Blue-black body. **80 110 145 200**

629 BURLINGTON (Diesel): 1956. GE 44-ton switcher; silver-painted body with red heat-stamped lettering and red lower stripe; Burlington Route herald; ornamental horn and ornamental bell; headlight lens both ends; red-painted frame; one-axle Magnetraction; three-position E-unit; light at one end; operating couplers.
Note: Substantial premium for fresh-looking silver paint. **110 200 350 650**

633 SANTA FE (Diesel): 1962. EMD NW2 switcher; blue-painted body with yellow-painted safety stripes and yellow heat-stamped lettering and Santa Fe medallion; no ornamental trim; plugged ornamental bell and horn slots; late sheet-metal frame with plastic side frame trucks; lighted; unique motor truck with traction tire, but no front coupler; rear collector truck with fixed die-cast coupler; two-position E-unit with lever pointing up. **100 150 215 325**

634 SANTA FE (Diesel): 1963, 1965–66. EMD NW2 switcher; blue-painted body with yellow heat-stamped lettering and Santa Fe medallion; yellow-painted safety stripes on 1963 models (stripes eliminated from 1965–66 production); no ornamental trim; plugged ornamental bell and horn slots; typically open marker lens holes; late sheet-metal frame with plastic side frame trucks; lighted; motor truck with traction tire and fixed plastic coupler; rear collector truck with fixed die-cast coupler; two-position E-unit with lever pointing up.
Note: Apparently Lionel was experiencing traction problems on models without Magnetraction and developed a ballast weight that attached to the underside of the hood; the use of the weight required a body mold modification to accept two screws that secured the weight. This modification did *not* appear on the 1963 model but was present on 1965 and later production.
(A) Body with safety stripes; without marker lens holes. **80 125 185 275**
(B) Body with safety stripes; with marker lens holes. **80 125 185 275**
(C) Body without safety stripes; with marker lens holes; most common version. **55 75 120 200**

635 UNION PACIFIC (Diesel): Uncataloged, 1965. EMD NW2 switcher; yellow-painted body with predominantly red heat-stamped lettering (cab lettering different on each side); "NEW 7-58" on sides near nose; white heat-stamped "U.P." and "635" on front of nose; no ornamental trim; plugged ornamental bell and horn slots; open marker lens holes; body with weight; late sheet-metal frame with plastic side frame trucks; motor truck with traction tire and fixed plastic coupler; rear collector truck with fixed die-cast coupler; two-position E-unit with lever pointing up. **60 100 160 200**

(645) UNION PACIFIC (Diesel): 1969. EMD NW2 switcher; unpainted yellow body with red heat-stamped lettering (cab lettering different on each side); no ornamental trim; plugged ornamental bell and horn slots; open marker lens holes; body with weight; late sheet-metal frame with plastic side frame trucks; motor truck with traction tire and fixed plastic coupler; rear collector truck with fixed die-cast coupler; two-position E-unit with lever pointing up.
Note: Most interestingly, the 645 is *not* numbered; it is similar to 635, except for being unpainted and not having "NEW 7-58," "U.P.," or a number on the front. **60 90 130 200**

1055 TEXAS SPECIAL (Diesel): Advance catalog, 1959–60. Alco A unit; red-painted body with white heat-stamped lettering; closed pilot; ornamental horn; weight; forward only; light; frame box.
Note: Aside from the ballast weight riveted to the rear of the body, this engine has no traction aid.
(A) Smooth pilot. **30 45 60 100**
(B) Pilot with ledge. **30 45 60 100**

Stanchions attached the decorative wire handrail along the upper body of early NW2 switchers. The change from ten stanchions to three occurred in 1953. Top: 624 (A) Chesapeake & Ohio with ten stanchions. Bottom: 624 (B) Chesapeake & Ohio with three stanchions.

	Gd	VG	Ex	LN

1065 UNION PACIFIC (Diesel): Advance catalog, 1961. Alco A unit; yellow-painted body with red roofline stripe and red heat-stamped lettering; closed pilot with ledge; usually without ornamental horn; weight; forward only; light; usually without frame box.

Note: Aside from the ballast weight riveted to the rear of the body, this engine has no traction aid.

	35	55	90	120

1066 UNION PACIFIC (Diesel): Uncataloged, 1964. Alco A unit; unpainted yellow body with red roofline stripe and red heat-stamped lettering; closed pilot with ledge; no ornamental horn; traction tire; forward only; no light according to the Lionel Service Manual, but examples with the correct motor truck have been observed with a light assembly; no frame box.

Note: The 1066 was the cheapest Alco unit that Lionel could produce.

	50	75	105	125

2023 UNION PACIFIC (Diesel): 1950. Alco AA units; yellow-painted body and gray-painted roof with red heat-stamped lettering; narrow red roofline stripe; window shell; headlight lens; ornamental horn; marker lenses numbered "2023"; nose decal; gray-painted die-cast frame with narrow red stripe; pilot truck side frames with step; Magnetraction; horn; three-position E-unit; light in both units; always packaged in master carton. Collectors frequently refer to this pair as the "Anniversary Alcos."

Note: As with any new item, Lionel experimented with decorating schemes, especially with the yellow and gray 2023. Decorating particulars are discussed with each variation.

(A) Earliest production; gray nose and gray-painted

side frames for the trucks. These units are a true postwar rarity: There are many more fraudulent examples in the marketplace than there are legitimate pairs. Black body mold with the roof and nose areas masked to retain the gray base coat while the rest of the shell was painted yellow.

	1600	2000	2800	3500

(B) Black body mold with only the roof area masked to retain the gray base coat; gray-painted side frames for the trucks.

	200	275	400	550

(C) Same as (B), except for common black-oxidized side frames for the trucks.

	150	200	330	450

(D) Most common version with yellow body mold and black-oxidized side frames for the trucks. The body and nose areas were masked to retain the yellow base coat before the roof was painted gray.

Note: Yellow paint applied to yellow body molds did not age well; even Mint examples often appear "milky" and blotched.

	150	175	295	425

2023 UNION PACIFIC (Diesel): 1951. Alco AA units; silver-painted body and gray-painted roof with black heat-stamped lettering; narrow black roofline stripe; window shell; headlight lens; ornamental horn; marker lenses numbered "2023"; nose decal; silver-painted die-cast frame with narrow black stripe; pilot truck side frames with step; Magnetraction; horn; three-position E-unit; light in both units; always packaged in master carton.

	150	175	295	425

2024 CHESAPEAKE & OHIO (Diesel): 1969. Alco A unit; unpainted dark blue body with yellow roofline stripe and yellow heat-stamped lettering; open pilot with large ledge; traction tire; two-position E-unit; light.

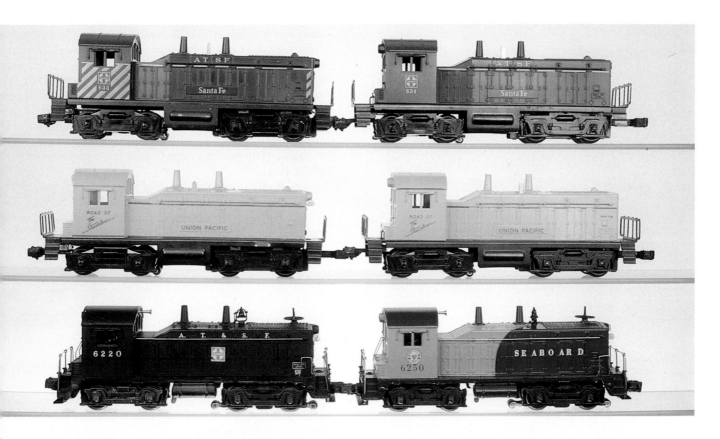

Top: 633 Santa Fe and 634 (C) Santa Fe. Middle: 645 Union Pacific and 635 Union Pacific. Bottom: 6220 (B) Santa Fe and 6250 (C) Seaboard. L. Nuzzaci Collection.

All five center-cab diesels. Top: Red and black 625 Lehigh Valley and 626 Baltimore and Ohio. Middle: All-red 627 Lehigh Valley and 628 Northern Pacific. Bottom: 629 Burlington. L. Nuzzaci Collection.

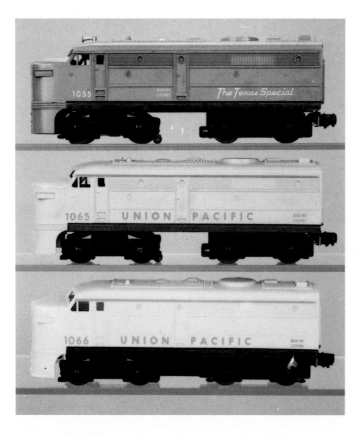

Top: 1055 (A) Texas Special. Middle: 1065 Union Pacific. Bottom: 1066 Union Pacific.

	Gd	VG	Ex	LN

Note: The 2024 bodies often appear with a headlight lens.

	30	45	80	100

2028 PENNSYLVANIA (Diesel): 1955. EMD GP7 road switcher; unpainted Tuscan red body with rubber-stamped lettering; rubber-stamped "PRR" herald on cab; typically gold-painted frame; Magnetraction; three-position E-unit; light in cab end only; operating couplers; no other premium features.

The 2028 was the first issue in the series; it came with three frame variations:

(1) Three rivets on each side to attach railing.
(2) Welded handrails with three-rivet holes on each side.
(3) Welded handrails with no rivet holes.
See comments by Alan Stewart, page 77.

Note: Many bodies have been relettered; original rubber-stamped lettering did not wear well.

(A) Gold lettering on body.

165	300	410	600

(B) Yellow lettering on body.

140	250	375	500

(C) White lettering on body.

140	250	375	500

(D) Scarce example with tan-painted frame; typically with welded handrails with three rivet holes; body data inconsequential.

250	400	565	800

(2031) ROCK ISLAND (Diesel): 1952–54. Alco AA units; black-painted body with wide red-painted middle stripe and white heat-stamped lettering; window shell; headlight lens; ornamental horn; marker lenses numbered "2031"; small nose decal; black-painted die-cast frame with narrow white stripe; Magnetraction; horn; three-position E-unit; light in both units; always packaged in master carton.

Note: The number "2031" does *not* appear anywhere on the body.

(A) Bodies with smooth roof over motor area.

150	275	380	450

(B) Bodies with raised, dime-sized detail over motor area.

150	275	380	450

(C) Same as (B), but minor variation on the nose whereby the front-facing portions of the marker lens slots that contain the running lights are *not* painted red.

150	275	380	450

(2032) ERIE (Diesel): 1952–54. Alco AA units; black-painted body with narrow yellow stripe; window shell; headlight lens; ornamental horn; marker lenses numbered "2032"; nose decal and Erie medallion and "BUILT BY / LIONEL" decals on sides; black-painted die-cast frame with narrow yellow stripe; Magnetraction; horn; three-position E-unit; light in both units; always packaged in master carton.

Note: The 2032 does *not* include any heat-stamped lettering, and the number "2032" does *not* appear anywhere on the body. Typical placement of side decals are Erie medallion decal centered midway between the cab door and side door; built decal positioned on lower side about 2" from rear of body.

(A) Bodies with smooth roof over motor area.

125	150	250	325

(B) Bodies with raised, dime-sized detail over motor area.

125	150	250	325

2033 UNION PACIFIC (Diesel): 1952–54. Alco AA units; silver-painted body with black heat-stamped lettering; window shell; headlight lens; ornamental horn; marker lenses numbered "2033"; nose decal; silver-painted die-cast frame; Magnetraction; horn; three-position E-unit; light in both units; always packaged in master carton.

Note: The 2033 did *not* include a pinstripe along either the roofline or the frame that was present on the 2023 model.

(A) Bodies with smooth roof over motor area.

155	200	350	450

(B) Bodies with raised, dime-sized detail over motor area.

155	200	350	450

2041 ROCK ISLAND (Diesel): 1969. Alco AA units; unpainted black body with wide red-painted middle stripe and white roofline stripe; white heat-stamped lettering; open pilot with large ledge; traction tire; two-position E-unit; light.

All early-production Alcos (those made between 1950 and 1954) came in an AA combination. Top: 2023 Union Pacific in silver. Second: Yellow and gray 2023 (D) with yellow nose. Third: Very rare yellow and gray 2023 (A) with gray nose. Bottom: 2033 (A) Union Pacific. L. Nuzzaci and R. Lord Collections.

	Gd	VG	Ex	LN

Note: The catalog illustration featured a Rock Island nose herald with the 2041, but the herald was eliminated from regular production. Be aware that an abundance of partially decorated 2041 bodies are available in the marketplace. Furthermore, 2041 bodies often appear with a headlight lens. **60   85   120   175**

2240 WABASH (Diesel): 1956. EMD F3 AB units; blue-painted body with gray-painted roof and upper quarter and white silk-screened lower quarter and thin, interrupted center-side stripe; louvered roof and closed portholes; yellow heat-stamped lettering; Wabash decal on nose; one-piece ornamental horns, molded cab door ladder, window shell, number boards, and headlight lens; blue chassis with blue-painted pilot and chemically blackened side frames; single vertical motor; Magnetraction; three-position E-unit; lighted; horn; operating coupler on pilot and die-cast fixed couplers at all other ends.

Note: Aside from being totally painted, the 2240 B unit has a less-than-full-length center-side stripe. Compare the photographs of the 2240 B unit and the 2367

model. Because it had a single motor, the 2240 was designated as O27 gauge in the consumer catalog.
400   600   800   1100

2242 NEW HAVEN (Diesel): 1958–59. EMD F3 AB units; distinctive silver, white, orange, and black checkerboard paint scheme; louvered roof and closed portholes; orange heat-stamped lettering; white heat-stamped "N / H" on nose; one-piece ornamental horns, molded cab door ladder, window shell, number boards, and headlight lens; silver chassis with black-painted pilot and chemically blackened side frames; single vertical motor; Magnetraction; three-position E-unit; lighted; horn; operating coupler on pilot and die-cast fixed couplers at all other ends.

Note: Even though the 2242 had a single motor, it was cataloged as a Super O item.
500   800   1200   1500

2243 SANTA FE (Diesel): 1955–57. EMD F3 AB units; silver and red warbonnet paint scheme with red, yellow, and black rubber-stamped detailing stripes; louvered roof

Observations on the 2028
by Alan Stewart

The 1955 advance and consumer catalogs both show the 2028 with no side handrails; the Rowland pulp paper catalogs for dealers showed correct Pennsylvania Railroad markings but no side rails. The riveted handrail version was manufactured first, followed by the welded version with holes still present, and finally the welded version with no holes. The riveted handrails were a rework, the result of feedback from dealers and a last-minute decision to put handrails on the economy model. (The 1529 set locomotive has welded handrails with rivet holes. The 2328 and 2338 locomotives, also introduced in 1955, most likely did not come with anything but welded handrails.)

The 1955 consumer catalog mentions that the 2028 is painted in the correct Pennsylvania maroon and gold colors. This and set 1529 indicate that gold lettering came first. This collector has a tan frame variation of the 2028 that has welded rails with rivet holes, which he believes is the result of a single painting error rather than an attempt to improve appearance or cut costs. Its scarcity and handrails indicate that this locomotive came in midrun, which points to a quickly caught error in the paint department.

The 2028 cab came with white or silver lettering as well, but the lettering appeared to be white when viewed under a magnifying glass. Also observed are yellow-lettered examples with rivets, with holes, and plain welded. The white and yellow letters apparently were later attempts by Lionel to find a way out of the problem of fading gold letters. At any rate, the tan frame and white-lettered versions most likely have frames with holes. The white-lettered version probably preceded the yellow-lettered and represents only part of an attempt to create more durable lettering.

Note: A photograph of the 2028 Pennsylvania appears with the 2327 and 2328.

2031 (B) Rock Island. K. Rubright Collection.

Top: 2032 (B) Erie. Middle: 2041 Rock Island. Look closely and observe the differences between the fine-quality Erie model (early 1950s production) on the top shelf and an example of 1969 production such as the 2041. Bottom: Uncompleted 2041 Rock Island bodies. These bodies may have been released through a Lionel Service Station and mounted on frames, or they may be factory errors. E. Dougherty Collection.

In 1953, a dime-sized detail (bottom) was added to the Alco tooling to reinforce the roof and prevent warping. P. Lonergan Collection.

	Gd	VG	Ex	LN

and closed portholes; black heat-stamped lettering and small heat-stamped "GM" on door panel; wraparound Santa Fe decal on nose; one-piece ornamental horns, molded cab door ladder, window shell, number boards, and headlight lens; silver chassis with silver-painted pilot and chemically blackened side frames; single vertical motor; Magnetraction; three-position E-unit; lighted; horn; operating coupler on pilot and die-cast fixed couplers at all other ends.

Note: The 2243 was cataloged as O27 gauge in 1955–56 but given O gauge designation in 1957.

(A) Early 1955 production with raised molded cab door ladder; usually with a gray body mold.

	375	500	610	770

(B) Typical molded cab door ladder.

	300	400	495	650

(C) Late 1957 market distribution of inventory; orange body mold that is easily distinguished because of the raised molded cab door ladder.

	300	400	495	650

(2243C) (SANTA FE) (Diesel): 1955–57. EMD F3 B unit; silver-painted body with red, yellow, and black rubber-stamped detailing stripes on lower side; rubber-stamped Indian head logo, but Santa Fe name does *not* appear on body; louvered roof and closed portholes; silver chassis and chemically blackened side frames; die-cast fixed couplers; sometimes identified with "2243C" rubber-stamped on underside of chassis.

Note: This B unit was the mate to the 2243 powered unit, but it was not cataloged for separate sale. Also matches 2383 AA units for which no B unit was made.

	100	160	220	300

2245 THE TEXAS SPECIAL (Diesel): 1954–55. EMD F3 AB units; glossy red-painted body with white silk-screened lower quarter; louvered roof and typically with open portholes with snap-in lenses; unpainted red lettering shows through white and white-painted lettering on red achieved with the use of unique reverse-out silk-screen mask and white-painted star on nose; combination MKT and Frisco decal; two-piece ornamental horns, cab door ladder, window shell, number boards, and headlight lens; silver chassis; single motor; Magnetraction; three-position E-unit; lighted; horn; operating coupler on pilot and die-cast fixed couplers at all other ends.

Note: The 2245 was the first F3 unit to be offered with a single motor; cataloged as O27 gauge.

(A) 1954; horizontally mounted motor; chassis with red-painted pilot and silver-painted side frames with steps.

	300	400	550	825

(B) 1955 production with 1954 bodies but revised chassis with vertically mounted motor; silver-painted pilot and chemically blackened side frames.

	300	400	550	825

(C) Later 1955; the same as (B), except B unit with closed portholes. *Caution: Be extremely dubious of any A unit with closed portholes.*

	430	610	835	1250

2321 LACKAWANNA (Diesel): 1954–56. F-M Train Master; gray-painted body with maroon-painted lower-side stripe and two yellow rubber-stamped stripes; maroon rubber-stamped lettering; F-M logo decal each side; nose decal each end; ornamental horn each side; lens piece each end; applied wire handrails; twin motors; Magnetraction; three-position E-unit; light both ends; horn; operating couplers.

Note: The usual first step in the decorating process was to paint the entire body maroon and then repaint the gray areas. It might have been too difficult to properly mask the maroon roof, leading the production department to repaint the roof while the other gray areas of the body were being painted. Furthermore, most 1954 and some 1955 production came with light brackets shaped like an inverted L. Earliest production came with an engraved battery plate cover while subsequent examples included a blank plate with an instruction sticker. *Caution:* Beware of screw-hole cracks.

(A) Earliest production; maroon roof.

	400	600	800	1100

(B) Most common production; gray roof.

	300	390	500	725

2322 VIRGINIAN (Diesel): 1965–66. F-M Train Master; typically unpainted blue body with wide yellow-painted upper and lower stripes, crisscross-painted ends; yellow rubber-stamped lettering; F-M logo decal each side; nose decal each end; ornamental horn each side; lens piece each end; applied wire handrails; twin motors; Magnetraction; three-position E-unit; light both ends; horn; operating couplers.

Note: This reissue is very similar to 2331; the most noticeable difference is the use of green wire for the armature windings. *Caution:* Beware of screw-hole cracks.

(A) Typical blue body painted *both* yellow and blue. Scarce.

	400	600	825	1050

(B) Most common production; described above.

	300	495	625	900

2328 BURLINGTON (Diesel): 1955–56. EMD GP7 road switcher; silver-painted body with black rubber-stamped lettering; rubber-stamped Burlington Route herald on cab; ornamental horn each side; headlight lens and number boards each end; red-painted frame; Magnetraction; three-position E-unit; light both ends; horn; operating couplers.

Note: Substantial premium for fresh-looking silver paint.

	200	300	425	675

2329 VIRGINIAN (Electric): 1958–59. GE E-33 or EL-C rectifier; blue-painted body with yellow-painted upper stripe; yellow heat-stamped lettering; ornamental horn; headlight lens and number boards each end; nose decal at cab end; single pantograph; yellow-painted frame; single motor; Magnetraction; three-position

Continued on page 86

Observations on F3 A and B Units
by Richard Lord, with information from Raymond Sorensen and Joseph Algozzini

The F3s evolved over the years and changed greatly since their introduction in 1948. Some of the changes improved the product, while others tended to mute the bold design statement of the first F3s. The mechanical and technological alterations are generally considered to be advances. The later F3s ran more quietly and functioned better than the early ones.

Lionel issued the first 2333 New York Central and Santa Fe models with rubber-stamped Santa Fe or New York Central lettering, which did not hold up well. It replaced them with heat-stamped versions sometime during the 1949 production year. The early celluloid porthole windows used on the 2333 Santa Fe and New York Central models were apt to fall out of the window openings; as a result, the company replaced them around 1952 by plastic snap-in porthole inserts. (The New York Central model also carried a 2333 number, but in the Lionel Service Manual its parts carry a 2334 prefix.) The styrene plastic used as of 1951 improved the paint adherence of the cabs.

Lionel made other changes for the sake of economy and ease of production, and these are seen as "cheapening" the product. These include the elimination of cab detail or reduction in its authenticity. The fine paint schemes of the later F3s compensated for these simplified cabs.

The F3s are among the most expensive Lionel postwar trains to collect. To complicate matters, the F3 market is rife with reproduction parts and cabs.

This explanation of mechanical features will assist the F3 collector in determining whether or not a particular piece is original. For additional information on these models, see *Lionel's Postwar F3's.*

MOTORS: Lionel used two types of motors on the F3s—horizontal and vertical. The horizontal motor had the power shaft running sideways, which powered gears downward to the wheels. The horizontal motor had two types of brushplates—an early 1948-type, with a fiberboard plate and protruding brush holders containing coiled brush springs, and a later plastic molded brushplate in which the brushes were integrated into the brushplate and did not extend outward from it (V-shaped brush springs were used instead of the earlier coiled variety). Vertical motors had an armature shaft that ran down and turned a worm gear on the drive wheel axle.

HORN LOCATION: Lionel's designers first placed the operating horn of the F3 in the powered unit. In the earliest (1948) 2333 models, a Z-shaped bracket fastened this horn to the rear of the frame. The bracket held a rubber washer at the top where the horn sat. By 1950 a heat-stamped bracket with "feet" on each end had replaced this arrangement; it was mounted across the rear motor from one side of the frame to the other. However, because of motor vibrations the horn did not operate as well as it might. As a result, Lionel moved the horn to the non-powered A unit in the 1953 and 1954 productions. With the

invention of the vertical motor in 1955, it placed the horn back in the powered unit. The horn in the single-motored F3s was always in the powered unit.

LAMP: The operating nose lamp of the F3 was first a clip-on type fastened to the frame by two tabs. In 1953 and after, the lamp housing was cast into the frame.

FRAMES: Prior to 1955, the frames on the A units were cast metal with the number 2333-20 and the wording "MADE IN U.S. OF AMERICA THE LIONEL CORPORATION NEW YORK". In 1955 the number changed to 2243-38. The B-unit frames were molded plastic with "GENERAL MOTORS TYPE F-# DIESEL ELECTRIC UNIT MADE IN U.S. OF AMERICAN THE LIONEL CORPORATION NEW YORK". The early B units also had rubber-stamped numbers on the frame; later B units did not.

Before 1955, the battery plate was stamped in black lettering: "TO OPERATE HORN INSERT A SIZE 'D' FLASHLIGHT CELL HERE" and in bolder print "CAUTION REMOVE CELL WHEN LOCOMOTIVE IS NOT IN USE." Beginning in 1955, a black rectangular sticker with white lettering was applied to the battery cover; it read "TO OPERATE HORN INSERT A SIZE 'D' CELL HERE. REMOVE CELL BEFORE STORING LOCOMOTIVE." The screw on the battery plate prior to 1955 was a flathead type with ridged edges (for gripping); it changed to a slotted roundhead type without grip ridges.

PILOT: The pilot was comprised of several parts screwed together. In 1955 and after Lionel eliminated the screws and "staked" the pilot assembly together. The pilot had a notch in the bar that ran underneath the coupler. The notch was the result of two lips that extended down from the pilot bar. In 1954 Lionel eliminated the lips and notch because the lips tended to catch on switches in turns. This interference with switch boxes was a recurring problem, especially on O27 track.

TRUCKS: Before 1955, the F3 trucks were painted and screwed together; their footsteps were fastened by screws. They also had a coil coupler with sliding shoe, and a dual pickup roller fastened to one of them. In 1955 and after, Lionel blackened the trucks by means of an oxidation process, staked them together, and eliminated the footsteps. The coil coupler gave way to a magnetic coupler with no sliding shoe, and each truck had its own pickup roller.

Also before 1955, the A-unit pilot truck carried an identification plate that read "LIONEL" accompanied by the Lionel "L" logo. The rear truck was molded with the wording "MADE IN U.S. OF AMERICA THE LIONEL CORPORATION NEW YORK". The B unit used the dummy A-unit rear truck. The truck construction beginning in 1955 was vastly different and had no lettering.

GENERAL MOTORS LOGO: From 1948 through 1952, a General Motors logo was decaled to the Santa Fe,

New York Central, and Western Pacific F3s. In 1953 and after, it was heat-stamped. Curiously, the Lionel Service Manual lists three separate GM decals for the 1948–52 F3s. The 2333 and 2343 Santa Fe units used part 2333-104; the 2334 and 2344 New York Central units used parts 2333-104 and 2334-23; and the 2345 Western Pacific used part 622-126—the same decal first used on the 622 switcher. Color and size account for the differences, but reports have surfaced of F3s with the "wrong" decals. This occurred when Lionel ran out of a specific decal for one model and substituted a decal from another until the correct one was available. Therefore, the type of decal should not affect the value of the pieces very much.

ROOF VENTS: Prior to 1953, the diesel roof vents were a realistic wire mesh–screen type that was attached to the cab by an unusual double speed nut from within the cab. From 1953 on, Lionel eliminated the mesh screen and molded the vents into the plastic cab, beginning with the 2353/54/55 models.

PORTHOLES WITH LENSES: From 1948 through 1954, the F3s had open portholes with plastic lenses. (**Note:** Lionel's official name for the lenses was "side window.") From 1948 to 1951, the lens was a celluloid contact lens–type cap that was easily lost. These lenses tend to yellow with exposure to light and air, a point to consider when determining authenticity.

From 1951 through 1954, Lionel changed the lens to a plastic snap-in type. (This type of lens was used with the first 1955 production of the 2245 Texas Special as well.) There was a slight change in the shape of the plastic lens in 1953 for ease of assembly. In 1955, designers eliminated the portholes with lenses; thereafter the portholes were molded into the cab.

The 2356 Southern Railway carried over certain features not found on other F3s for a particular catalog year. For example, during 1955 the portholes with lenses were eliminated, but the Southern still had them. It even had portholes with lenses in 1956, while all other F3s did not. Could Lionel have used up old stock on the Southern and continued cataloging that model until it sold what had already been produced? The answer is yes. During the same years, the green GG1 was not made, but it was available to dealers because Lionel had a plentiful back stock.

Also, collectors have noted different versions of the Texas Special. The first was a 1954 version with portholes, silver frame and trucks, and red pilot. Some 1955 production had filled-in portholes on the B unit, silver frame and pilot on the A unit, and black trucks on both units. The latter version is consistent with the F3 changes that occurred in 1955. This is the only time Lionel substantially changed and continued an F3 road name without also changing its catalog number.

NOSE GRAB IRONS: Lionel placed nose grab irons on all F3s from 1948 through 1952; thereafter, it eliminated them and the holes in the body.

SIDE LADDERS: The F3s from 1948 through 1954 had a snap-on simulated black plastic ladder. Lionel eliminated it in 1955, afterwards molding a side ladder into the plastic cab. The earliest version was distinctly larger than later models.

ORNAMENTAL HORNS: Prior to 1955, the ornamental horn was a two-piece assembly locked into place underneath the cab. The die-cast horn piece was attached to a black sheet-metal bracket with tabs folded over from the inside of the cab. Beginning in 1955, the horn was a one-piece die-cast snap-in type. (The first horn had no die-casting, but had a stamped base and machined horn. A. Stewart comment.)

CAB-FASTENING TECHNIQUES: From 1948 through 1952, three screws fastened the cab to the frame. Beginning in 1953, a smaller screw fastened the cab nose to the chassis, and the rear of the cab had a clip with two prongs that gripped the end of the frame to fasten the rear of the cab. This change was the result of the problem that Lionel had with stripped screw holes in the F3 cab rears. However, the company had only substituted one problem for another. If the rear brackets, which were riveted to the plastic cab, were bent up too sharply because they gripped the frame end too tightly, the cab shell could crack when the cab was removed from the frame for servicing. Many cabs produced from 1953 onward show signs of such cracking—some beyond repair.

STAMPING: The principal means of lettering and numbering F3 cabs was heat-stamping. This process left a depression in the cabs as the heat melted the plastic. Another method was rubber-stamping, which left no such depression under normal conditions. In addition, some F3s had a combination of heat- and rubber-stamping. For example, the 2368 Baltimore & Ohio had heat-stamped lettering and numbers, but the lines were rubber-stamped.

A caution regarding heat-stamping: On some F3s like the 2368, the stamping process appears to have been rubber-stamped although actually the lettering and numbers were heat-stamped. Heat-stamping cannot always be determined by feel. One way to detect it is to hold the cab sideways to see the surface of the cab in natural light. If you use a magnifying glass, you will see depressions, especially at the corners and edges of letters. It takes a keen and trained eye to tell heat-stamping from rubber-stamping when the touch of the heat-stamping tool is lighter than normal.

The evolution of F3s included still other change. Lionel experimented with materials and part types, and some of them appeared on F3s. For example, it tried to reduce the vibrations in F3 motor gears. In 1954 and 1955 the company tried a nylon idler gear, which was still too noisy. The vibration problem was later solved by means of the vertical motor. This and other hard-to-detect changes in F3s should be of little or no concern in an examination, as most of the changes occurred at times when major alterations were made—chiefly in 1953 and 1955. (As usual, there is an exception—as noted in the differences in the 1948 and 1949 production runs of the 2333 Santa Fe and New York Central models.)

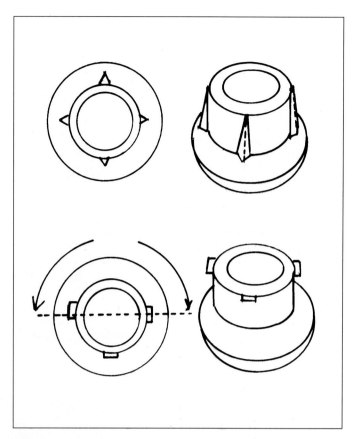

Two versions of the General Motors decal—large on top, small on bottom. G. Stern photograph.

2343-133 has four "crushable" wedges placed 90 degrees apart. 2353-11 has three catches molded in. Opposing ones are about 170 degrees apart.

The 2363 Illinois Central (left) from 1955 features a raised ladder; the 2379 Denver and Rio Grande Western (right) from 1957 features the flush ladder. From Lionel's Postwar F3's.

From left: Western Pacific 2355 (1953) with no roof dimple, 2245 Texas Special (1954) with dimple behind grilles (interestingly, painted over a Santa Fe war-bonnet), and 2373 Canadian Pacific (1957) with dimple and grille starting to fill in. From Lionel's Postwar F3's.

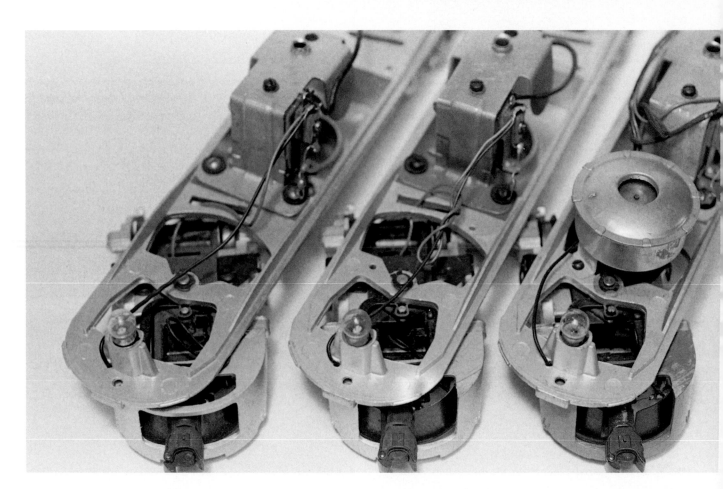

The power units shown here are from 1953 and 1954. The pilots illustrate the production history. From left: 1953, bar over coupler, notched pilot bottom, and no holes for horn bracket; 1954, no bar, still notched, and holes for horn bracket (left front and right rear of second opening over truck); and 1954, bar gone, notch removed, and horn installed. From Lionel's Postwar F3's.

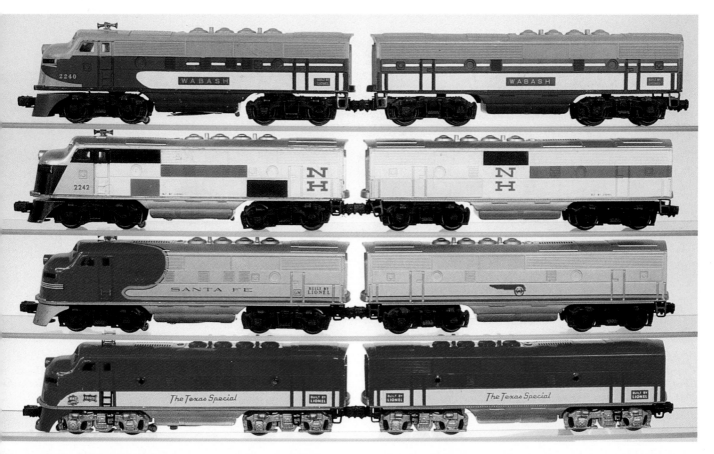

The F3 AB combinations shown here were usually cataloged as O27 units and have only a single motor in the A unit. Top: 2240 Wabash AB units. Second: 2242 New Haven AB units. Third: 2243 Santa Fe AB units. Bottom: 2245 (A) Texas Special AB units. The 2242 was cataloged only as a Super O locomotive (1958–1959), while the 2243 was cataloged as O27 (1955–1956) and O (1957). L. Nuzzaci Collection.

The F3 series started in 1948 with the 2333 (C) Santa Fe AA units shown on the top shelf and the 2333 (C) New York Central AA units on the middle shelf. Note the differences between the "BUILT BY / LIONEL" and General Motors decals on the top with those same features on the 2343 (A) Santa Fe AA units on the bottom shelf. L. Nuzzaci Collection.

Top: 2344 (A) New York Central AA units. Middle: 2345 Western Pacific AA units. Bottom: 2353 (A) Santa Fe AA units from 1953–1955. Note the fine details on the F3 models, such as two-part ornamental horns, open portholes, grab irons on the nose (except on the Santa Fe), and ornamental ladders on both the body and the trucks. L. Nuzzaci Collection.

Top: 2354 (A) New York Central AA units. Middle: 2355 Western Pacific AA units. Bottom: 2356 (B) Southern AA units. Note that the grab irons found on the front of the earlier F3s were deleted from these models. L. Nuzzaci Collection.

Top: 2363 (A) Illinois Central AB units. Middle: 2367 (A) Wabash AB units. Bottom: 2368 (A) Baltimore and Ohio AB units Note the missing details on these post-1954 F3 models. One-piece ornamental horns, filled portholes, and molded cab door ladders had became the norm. L. Nuzzaci Collection.

Top: 2373 (A) Canadian Pacific AA units. Middle: 2378 (A) Milwaukee Road AB units. Bottom: 2379 (A) Rio Grande AB units. A matching F3 B unit was never made for the Canadian Pacific. L. Nuzzaci Collection.

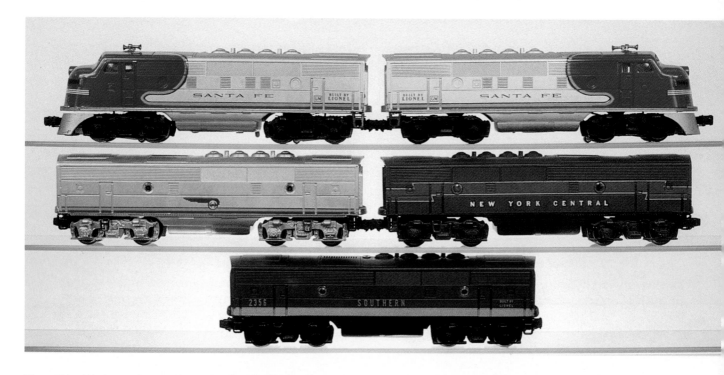

Top: 2383 (A) Santa Fe AA units. Middle: 2343C (B) Santa Fe and 2344C (B) New York Central B units. Bottom: 2356C Southern B unit. The three F3 B units shown were sometimes included in sets to make an ABA combination, and each was available for separate sale. L. Nuzzaci Collection.

	Gd	VG	Ex	LN

E-unit; light both ends; horn; operating couplers.

	Gd	VG	Ex	LN
	315	540	750	1000

2330 PENNSYLVANIA (Electric): 1950. GG1; green-painted die-cast body with five rubber-stamped gold stripes; gold heat-stamped lettering; small PRR keystone decal centered at upper quarter of sides; small keystone nose decal numbered "2330" at each end; headlight lens, running lights, and ornamental horn each end; two pantographs; twin motors; Magnetraction; three-position E-unit; light both ends; horn; operating coil couplers.

	625	900	1550	2400

2331 VIRGINIAN (Diesel): 1955–58. F-M Train Master; bodies and lettering described below; crisscross-painted ends; F-M logo decal each side; nose decal each end; ornamental horn each side; lens piece each end; applied wire handrails; twin motors, Magnetraction; three-position E-unit; light both ends; horn; operating couplers.

Note: Some early 1955 production came with light brackets shaped like an inverted L and an engraved battery plate cover. *Caution:* Beware of screw-hole cracks.

(A) Gray body painted *both* yellow and black; gold rubber-stamped lettering. Scarce.

	720	1150	1400	1750

(B) Gray body painted *both* yellow and blue; yellow rubber-stamped lettering. Very scarce.

	600	900	1200	1600

(C) Unpainted blue body with wide yellow-painted

upper and lower stripes; yellow rubber-stamped lettering.

	400	600	900	1200

2332 PENNSYLVANIA (Electric): 1947–49. GG1; painted die-cast body with five rubber-stamped stripes; gold rubber-stamped lettering; small PRR keystone marking centered at upper quarter of sides; small keystone nose decal numbered "2332" at each end; headlight lens, running lights, and ornamental horn each end; two pantographs; single angle-mounted motor; no Magnetraction; three-position E-unit; light both ends; harsh-sounding AC vibrator box horn: operating coil couplers.

(A) Black body; rubber-stamped keystone; gold stripes.

	900	1400	2000	3000

(B) Black body; rubber-stamped keystone; "silver" stripes.

	900	1400	2000	3000

(C) Black body; keystone decal; gold stripes.

	900	1400	2000	3000

(D) Brunswick green body; rubber-stamped keystone; gold stripes.

	320	475	800	1000

(E) Brunswick green body; rubber-stamped keystone; "silver" stripes.

	320	475	800	1100

(F) Brunswick green body; keystone decal; gold stripes. Most common version.

	320	450	750	1000

2333 NEW YORK CENTRAL (Diesel): 1948–49. EMD F3 AA units; black body mold with dark gray and light gray lightning-bolt paint scheme with white rubber

Top: 2321 (A) Lackawanna F-M Train Master with maroon roof. Bottom: 2321 (B) Lackawanna with gray roof.

Top: 2322 (B) Virginian Train Master. Middle: 2341 (A) Jersey Central in high-gloss orange. Bottom: 2341 (B) Jersey Central in flat orange. E. Dougherty Collection.

Top: 2331 (A) Virginian Train Master with yellow-painted body and black-painted stripe and roof. Middle: 2331 (C) with unpainted blue stripe and roof and yellow-painted bands. Bottom: 2331 (B) dull blue-painted stripe and roof and yellow-painted bands on a gray body mold. The color of the body is readily determined when the model is held upside-down. E. Dougherty Collection.

	Gd	VG	Ex	LN

stamped detailing stripes; wire-cloth ventilator on roof and open portholes with lenses; white lettering; New York Central decal on nose and black-and-white GM decal; two-piece ornamental horns, cab door ladder, window shell, number boards, headlight lens, and grab irons on nose; gray chassis with gray-painted pilot and side frames with steps; twin horizontal motors; *no* Magnetraction; three-position E-unit; lighted both units; horn in powered unit; operating coupler on pilots and die-cast fixed couplers at other ends.

Note: The same 2333 number was assigned to the Santa Fe (see next listing). Also, the placement of the GM decal was not consistent. Earliest production (according to the illustration in the Lionel Service Manual) had the decal placed above "BUILT BY / LIONEL"; subsequent production placed the decal on the door in front of "BUILT BY / LIONEL". Furthermore, factory errors and out-of-stock situations were inevitable; examples exist with improper red-and-white GM decals that "should" have been exclusive to the Santa Fe model. Portholes for the 2333 were oversized and conical and had to be forced into place with a special punch and die. Finally, a compatible F3 B unit did not appear until 1950 (see 2344C).

(A) Earliest production with large rubber-stamped lettering; GM decal above "BUILT BY / LIONEL".

	425	**750**	**1000**	**1500**

(B) Large rubber-stamped lettering; GM decal on door panel in front of "BUILT BY / LIONEL".

	425	**750**	**1000**	**1500**

(C) Heat-stamped lettering in the usual size; typical placement of GM decal on door panel in front of "BUILT BY / LIONEL".

	295	**450**	**700**	**1000**

2333 SANTA FE (Diesel): 1948–49. EMD F3 AA units; black body mold with silver and red warbonnet paint scheme with red, yellow, and black rubber-stamped detailing stripes; wire-cloth ventilator on roof and open portholes with lenses; black lettering; wraparound Santa Fe decal on nose and red-and-white GM decal; two-piece ornamental horns, cab door ladder, window shell, number boards, headlight lens, and grab irons on nose; silver chassis with silver-painted pilot and silver-painted side frames with steps; twin horizontal motors; *no* Magnetraction; three-position E-unit; lighted both units; horn in powered unit; operating coupler on pilots and die-cast fixed couplers at other ends.

Note: The same 2333 number was assigned to the New York Central (see previous listing). Also, the placement of the GM decal was not consistent. Earliest production (according to the illustration in the Lionel Service

Continued on page 91

Top: 2028 (A) Pennsylvania GP7 road switcher with post-factory horn and wire railings. Middle: 2328 Burlington. Bottom: 2337 Wabash. Note that the example pictured has an erroneous operating coupler at the cab end. L. Nuzzaci Collection.

Top: 2338 (D) common Milwaukee Road GP7 with intermittent orange stripe and dark rubber-stamped logo. Middle: 2338 (A) rare Milwaukee Road with unpainted orange stripe across cab and red rubber-stamped logo. Notice that the number "2338" is black, as opposed to white on the common version. Bottom: 2339 Wabash. L. Nuzzaci Collection.

Top: 2346 Boston and Maine GP9. Middle: Rare 2347 Chesapeake & Ohio GP7 made exclusively for Sears. Bottom: 2348 M & St L GP9. L. Nuzzaci and R. Lord Collections.

Top: 2349 Northern Pacific GP9. Middle: 2359 Boston and Maine GP9. Bottom: 2365 Chesapeake & Ohio GP7. L. Nuzzaci Collection.

2329 Virginian rectifier electric. L. Nuzzaci Collection.

	Gd	VG	Ex	LN

Manual) had the decal placed *above* "BUILT BY / LIONEL"; subsequent production placed the decal on the door panel in front of "BUILT BY / LIONEL". Portholes for the 2333 were oversized and conical and had to be forced into place with a special punch and die. Finally, a compatible F3 B unit did not appear until 1950 (see 2343C).

(A) Earliest production with rubber-stamped lettering; GM decal above "BUILT BY / LIONEL"; nickel-plated rear step assembly (same as pilot coupler shield).

	275	400	625	1000

(B) Rubber-stamped lettering; GM decal above "BUILT BY / LIONEL"; typical chemically blackened rear step assembly.

	275	400	625	1000

(C) Rubber-stamped lettering; GM decal on door panel in front of "BUILT BY / LIONEL".

	275	400	625	1000

(D) Heat-stamped lettering; typical placement of GM decal on door panel in front of "BUILT BY / LIONEL".

	375	600	1000	1300

(E) Preproduction display model with unpainted, clear plastic body; intact examples have red, yellow, and black rubber-stamped detailing stripes and were fully trimmed (including appropriate decals).

	1500	2200	3500	—

2337 WABASH (Diesel): 1958. EMD GP7 road switcher; unpainted blue body with gray-painted upper quarter and roof and white-painted lower quarter and front stripe; white heat-stamped lettering; Wabash decal on cab; ornamental horn each side; headlight lens and number boards each end; black-painted frame; Magnetraction; three-position E-unit; light both ends; horn; fixed plastic couplers. Cataloged as O27 gauge. See also 2339.

	110	200	315	450

2338 THE MILWAUKEE ROAD (Diesel): 1955–56. EMD GP7 road switcher; unpainted orange body with black-painted upper half, roof, and cab; heat-stamped lettering, most typically with white "2338" and black "BUILT BY / LIONEL"; rubber-stamped Milwaukee Road herald on cab; ornamental horn each side; headlight lens and number boards each end; black-painted frame; Magnetraction; three-position E-unit; light both ends; horn; operating couplers.

(A) Earliest production; orange translucent body with orange band bisecting the cab; red rubber-stamped herald; black heat-stamped "2338." **Note:** The rubber-stamped herald did not adhere well to the shiny, unpainted orange surface.

	800	1300	1800	2100

(B) Orange translucent body with black-painted cab; dark brown or dark cherry rubber-stamped herald.

	150	200	250	400

(C) Same as (B), except inside of body painted black. Because the early-production bodies were translucent, interior illumination showed through. Lionel, to temporarily solve the problem, began to paint interiors black until the translucent bodies were depleted.

	150	200	250	400

(D) Opaque orange body; dark brown or dark cherry rubber-stamped herald. Most common production.

	150	200	250	400

(E) Same as (D), except distinctly different glossy black paint.

	180	225	350	475

2339 WABASH (Diesel): 1957. EMD GP7 road switcher. Same as 2337, except operating couplers. Cataloged as O gauge.

(A) Royal blue body mold.

	165	210	325	500

(B) Navy body mold.

	165	210	325	500

2340 PENNSYLVANIA (Electric): 1955. GG1; painted die-cast body with five rubber-stamped gold stripes; gold heat-stamped lettering; small PRR keystone decal centered at upper quarter of sides; small keystone nose decal numbered "2340" at each end; headlight lens, running lights, and ornamental horn each end; two pantographs; twin motors; Magnetraction; three-position E-unit; light both ends; horn; operating coil couplers.

(A) Tuscan red body. Headed the *Congressional* passenger set; cataloged as 2340-1.

	700	1000	1800	2600

(B) Brunswick green body. Cataloged as 2340-25.

	650	950	1700	2400

2341 JERSEY CENTRAL (Diesel): 1956. F-M Train Master; unpainted blue body with wide orange-painted upper and lower stripes; white heat-stamped lettering;

	Gd	**VG**	**Ex**	**LN**

F-M logo decal each side; nose decal each end; ornamental horn each side; lens piece each end; applied wire handrails; twin motors; Magnetraction; three-position E-unit; light both ends; horn; operating couplers.

Note: Beware of fraudulent examples; *extreme caution advised*. Most bogus pieces have been silk-screened, but fraudulent heat-stamped items have also been observed. Also, beware of screw-hole cracks.

(A) High-gloss orange. Scarce. Be aware that it is possible to "gloss" a dull version with paste wax or furniture spray.

	Gd	**VG**	**Ex**	**LN**
(A) High-gloss orange	1100	1500	2300	3500
(B) Dull orange.	950	1300	2000	2750

2343 SANTA FE (Diesel): 1950–52. EMD F3 AA units; silver and red warbonnet paint scheme with red, yellow, and black rubber-stamped detailing stripes; wire-cloth ventilator on roof and open portholes with lenses; black heat-stamped lettering; wraparound Santa Fe decal on nose and red-and-white GM decal; two-piece ornamental horns, cab door ladder, window shell, number boards, headlight lens, and grab irons on nose; silver chassis with silver-painted pilot and silver-painted side frames with steps; twin horizontal motors; Magnetraction; three-position E-unit; lighted both units; horn in powered unit; operating coupler on pilots and die-cast fixed couplers at other ends.

Note: A matching 2343 B unit (see 2343C) was introduced in 1950. Further note that for 1950–51 production, bodies were molded in black plastic (common) or yellow (scarce), while most 1952 production came with a gray body mold.

(A) 1950–51 production with large GM decal and open portholes with glued lenses.

	Gd	**VG**	**Ex**	**LN**
(A)	250	400	675	1300

(B) 1952 production typically with small GM decal and open portholes with snap-in lenses.

	Gd	**VG**	**Ex**	**LN**
(B)	250	400	675	1300

(2343C) (SANTA FE) (Diesel): 1950–55. EMD F3 B unit; silver-painted body with red, yellow, and black rubber-stamped detailing stripes on lower side; rubber-stamped Indian head logo, but Santa Fe name does *not* appear on body; open portholes with lenses; silver chassis and silver-painted side frames with steps; die-cast fixed couplers; usually identified with "2343C" rubber-stamped on underside of chassis.

(A) 1950–51 model with wire-cloth ventilator on roof and open portholes with glued lenses; matches 2333 and 2343.

	Gd	**VG**	**Ex**	**LN**
(A)	100	200	250	400

(B) 1952 model with wire-cloth ventilator on roof and open portholes with snap-in lenses; matches 2343.

	Gd	**VG**	**Ex**	**LN**
(B)	100	200	250	400

(C) 1953–55 model with louvered roof and open portholes with snap-in lenses; matches 2353.

	Gd	**VG**	**Ex**	**LN**
(C)	90	175	215	325

2344 NEW YORK CENTRAL (Diesel): 1950–52. EMD F3 AA units; Dark gray and light gray lightning-bolt paint scheme with white rubber-stamped detailing stripes; wire-cloth ventilator on roof and open portholes with lenses; white heat-stamped lettering; New York Central decal on nose and black-and-white GM decal; two-piece ornamental horns, cab door ladder, window shell, number boards, headlight lens, and grab irons on nose; gray chassis with gray-painted pilot and gray-painted side frames with steps; twin horizontal motors; Magnetraction; three-position E-unit; lighted both units; horn in powered unit; operating coupler on pilots and die-cast fixed couplers at other ends.

Note: A matching 2344 B unit (see 2344C) was introduced in 1950. Further note that for 1950–51 production bodies were molded in either black plastic (common) or yellow (scarce), while most 1952 production came with a gray body mold.

(A) 1950–51; large GM decal and open portholes with glued lenses.

	Gd	**VG**	**Ex**	**LN**
(A)	290	400	600	900

(B) 1952; typically with small GM decal and open portholes with snap-in lenses.

	Gd	**VG**	**Ex**	**LN**
(B)	290	400	600	900

(2344C) NEW YORK CENTRAL (Diesel): 1950–55. EMD F3 B unit; Dark gray and light gray lightning-bolt paint scheme with white rubber-stamped detailing stripes; white heat-stamped lettering; open portholes with lenses; gray chassis and gray-painted side frames with steps; die-cast fixed couplers; usually identified with "2344C" rubber-stamped on underside of chassis.

(A) 1950–51; wire-cloth ventilator on roof and open portholes with glued lenses; matches 2333 and 2344.

	Gd	**VG**	**Ex**	**LN**
(A)	120	225	300	475

(B) 1952; wire-cloth ventilator on roof and open portholes with snap-in lenses; matches 2344.

	Gd	**VG**	**Ex**	**LN**
(B)	120	225	300	475

(C) 1953–55; louvered roof and open portholes with snap-in lenses; matches 2354.

	Gd	**VG**	**Ex**	**LN**
(C)	110	200	250	350

2345 WESTERN PACIFIC (Diesel): 1952. EMD F3 AA units; silver-painted body with orange-painted nose and middle side stripe; wire-cloth ventilator on roof and open portholes with snap-in lenses; black heat-stamped lettering; Western Pacific decal on nose and small black-and-white GM decal; two-piece ornamental horns, cab door ladder, window shell, number boards, headlight lens, and grab irons on nose; silver chassis with silver-painted pilot and silver-painted side frames with steps; twin horizontal motors; Magnetraction; three-position E-unit; lighted both units; horn in powered unit; operating coupler on pilots and die-cast fixed couplers at other ends.

Note: The 2345 pair does *not* have a matching B unit.

	Gd	**VG**	**Ex**	**LN**
	1100	1400	2075	3000

2346 BOSTON AND MAINE (Diesel): 1965–66. EMD GP9 road switcher; blue-painted body with black-painted cab and ends; white heat-stamped lettering; black and

Continued on page 100

One Legend Begets Another: A Close Look at the GG1
by Richard Shanfeld and Joseph Sadorf,
with contributions from Jerome Butler, Raymond Dennis, and James Pauley

Lionel had always made good models of electrics in the prewar era: New York Central center-cab electrics and the magnificent models of Milwaukee Road bipolar electrics so well exemplified by the Standard gauge 381 and 402 models. The Milwaukee Road prototypes were so strong that they could outpull any steam engine, even the most powerful compounds. Lionel's problem was that these models could not be updated into the postwar era because the stamped sheet-metal technology that produced them was rapidly being abandoned for die-casting techniques. Even with a tradition of electric engines, what electric locomotive could lend itself to die-casting and still tap a large potential market?

It was great good fortune for both Lionel and train collectors everywhere that there was such a prototype for Lionel to model. This was the Pennsylvania Railroad's sleek, streamlined GG1 electric, which had established itself as a legendary performer since it first began running under the Pennsylvania's catenary in 1934. This massive locomotive had twelve drive wheels, which supplied awesome tractive effort for the heaviest freight trains. In addition, it could take long strings of passenger cars and maintain high-speed express service better than any steam engine. These engines ran on 11,000-volt, 25-cycle AC; they were so reliable that it seemed all they needed was an occasional trip to the wash racks.

Besides, with their sleek Raymond Loewy design, the GG1s were a great expression of confidence in the future. (Loewy designed the Pennsy's streamlined K4 steam engine as well, also modeled by Lionel, and such diverse symbols of corporate America as the Exxon logo, the Oreo cookie, the Coca-Cola soda fountain, the Studebaker Starlight coupe, and the Avanti.) They sang under their catenary for nearly 50 years before they were retired, and quite a number have been preserved for posterity.

The first Lionel model of the GG1, the 2332, made its debut in 1947. It immediately became a favorite with toy train enthusiasts. It had a die-cast body shell finished in a rich Brunswick green with gold striping and lettering, just like its prototype. Except for its lack of scale length—a compromise necessary because the engine had to negotiate the 30-inch diameter of O gauge track—Lionel's GG1 was an accurate model. The 2332 had a rugged single motor mounted at an angle; even today it is noted as a smooth runner by collectors. It could not, however, pull the heavy trains so easily handled by the twin-engine versions with Magnetraction; in fact, the 2332 had trouble pulling its cataloged consist of three Madison cars. It had lights at both ends and two pantographs, which were insulated from the body shell by a fiber washer on a center mounting stud. (The white rubber insulators were decorative.) The operator could even reroute the wiring so the motor got its power from overhead catenary! So intent was Lionel on presenting a realistic model that it even tried to duplicate the sound of the GG1's harsh air horn by mounting a vibrator box inside the chassis. If the harsh buzz of the 2332's horn sounded like a stick rattling inside a plastic box, that was no accident. That was exactly the sound Lionel wanted to create!

In many ways, the 2332 was a kind of test run for the models that were to follow in 1950 and afterwards. There are two persistent controversies concerning the early production of these engines. First, a small number of these locomotives were made in flat black instead of dark Brunswick green. These black locomotives had rubber-stamped keystones instead of the later water-soluble decals, but the striping and keystones were not well applied. The "silver" keystones on the sides (and their red rubber-stamped counterparts) are usually badly blurred. To add to the confusion, some early Brunswick green GG1s came with these rubber-stamped keystones.

The second controversy revolves around the apparent silver color of the striping and lettering. It may well be that all the 2332s were originally stamped in gold. According to one plausible scenario, the ink used in the rubber-stamped striping and lettering had an unfortunate tendency to oxidize over the years into what, at first glance, looks like silver paint. The silver stamping and lettering was probably the result of a chemical reaction. Lionel used a paint shade known as Illinois bronze and mixed it with real silver to form the ink used on the GG1. The bronze flake, made from copper and brass, gave the gold appearance; the silver added brightness.

Unfortunately for Lionel, contaminants in the vehicle varnish led to oxidation that caused the bronze mix to turn black—leaving the silver, which was unaffected by the chemical reaction. The same reaction occurred on prewar pieces, which did not have the added silver. For example, the original gold stamping on the 309 and 310 passenger cars turned black. Examination in natural light of a 2332 stored in its box since it was new showed striping and lettering in a color resembling that of pale dry ginger ale. A few

2332 locomotives with this paint formulation have turned up in their original boxes in Like New or Mint condition. These examples clearly show the original color to be a pale gold, not silver. Even when new, many examples of the 2332—whatever the variety—show faded central striping.

There are many construction differences between the single-motored 2332 and the double-motored 2330, 2340, and 2360 models that followed in 1950 and afterwards. The front trucks of the 2332 differed from all the double-motored GG1s in that the area around the mounting screw hole was stamped in a triangular shape. Unlike later GG1s, the 2332 had nickel rims on its center truck wheels. The end trucks of the 2332 used electrical coil uncouplers, as did all the later GG1s (except the Fundimensions revivals, which used magnetic mechanical uncouplers). The pickup shoes for the uncouplers on the end trucks were close to the coupler ends of the trucks, until a transition was made in 1961 with the 2360 Tuscan red model, when the pickup shoes were placed closer to the mounting screw away from the coupler itself. The reasons for the change probably related to production costs, since the 3662-1 automatic refrigerated milk car used the same pickup shoe found on the 2360 models produced in 1961 and afterwards.

A few of the earliest 2332 locomotives have turned up with motor brushplates made of red thermoset compound rather than the usual black. Other such brushplates were used on late 1946 and early 1947 examples of the 671/2020 Turbines and the 726 Berkshire. There has been much speculation about whether these were special models (both were part 671M-5). There is further speculation on the reason for the difference in color. Most likely the Atomic Motor theme inspired the red color, but it looked unattractive on a black locomotive. Lionel simply used leftover red brushplates on 2332s where they were not visible (A. Stewart comment).

The harsh vibrator box horn of the 2332 gave way to a 1.5-volt battery-operated horn in all the double-motored GG1s. The battery horn, which used a D-size dry cell, was activated by a relay that used the whistle control DC voltage (about 5 volts) to close the circuit. Since the battery was comparatively hard to replace (the operator had to disassemble the front truck), many later GG1s were stored with the battery inside the locomotive. When the battery leaked, severe corrosion of the body shell and frame resulted. (None of the Fundimensions GG1s were equipped with a horn.)

For collectors, there is a special caution about battery leakage in the GG1. When examining a 2330, 2340, or 2360 for battery damage, be sure to check the window area at the top of the cab in addition to the bottom frame and body cavity. If a model was stored wheels-up in its box with the battery still installed—an easy thing to do—any leakage from the battery would drain towards one of the window areas, where the metal casting is very thin. Unfortunately, such acid leakage has actually eaten away the entire window area of some examples.

The single-motored 2332 had its motor mounted at an angle driving a single axle, and it did not have Magnetraction. All later GG1 models had Magnetraction and two vertically mounted motors, one for each six-wheel power truck, driving the wheels through spur gears. The 2332 had an E-unit slot on top cut into a half-circle; all other GG1s had a straight E-unit slot. In addition, a large flathead screw secured the 2332's single motor at the top of the body shell; all later models lacked this method of mounting. In the early production of the 2332 shells, the cab was shimmed by a brass washer $1/16$ inch thick where the motor was mounted to the inside of the cab. This was necessary to correct the mounting post for the motor truck, which had been cast too short in early runs.

The 2330 GG1, made only in 1950, represented a radical departure from its predecessor. Lionel added not only a better-sounding horn, but a second motor and Magnetraction. As with the NW2 switchers introduced that year, Lionel used separately mounted magnets on the power trucks instead of the later magnetic drive axles. Occasionally, one of these magnets would rub against the power truck frame and rob the locomotive of some of its performance. On the switchers, the only way to correct this was to file the magnet down carefully, since the magnets were applied with a special baked cement at the factory and could not be moved. The correction was much easier to make on the GG1, by prying the magnet out and carefully regluing it to the frame. However, removing and replacing the magnet destroyed some of the magnetic flux, since the magnets were originally magnetized at the factory only after they had been installed. Binding could also occur when one of the bushings on a power truck wheel was pressed too far into the frame. The Lionel Service Manual recommended spacer washers to solve that problem. The mechanical elements of the 2330 ran unchanged through all the later models of the GG1; the differences were only in the body shells from then on.

The frame of the new Magnetraction GG1 was made in two pieces, as opposed to the four-piece construction of the 2332. The 2332 used a separate plate for each pilot truck; the motor and nonpowered trucks were also separate pieces. The 2330 used a one-piece metal stamping to mount both of its power trucks, one of the pilot trucks, the horn with its relay, and the E-unit. The second part was a small plate that covered the battery and acted as a battery contact. This plate, which also held the other pilot truck, was stamped from steel.

There were some cosmetic differences between the 2330 and the 2332. The five stripes running across the side of the body were slightly lower on most 2330s and

were interrupted by the two ladders vertically mounted on the body shell. Although the striping continued to be rubber-stamped, the lettering and numbering were now heat-stamped. Experience has shown that the rubber-stamped lettering and numbering on the 2332 wore off as the model was handled. That is why many 2332s have had their stripes and numbers restored, most often by silk-screening, which Lionel seldom used in its production. The heat-stamped lettering and numbering were much more durable. Collectors should always handle a GG1 by its trucks, not its lettering or striping. In addition, avoid using newspaper or other printed paper for storage because the inks will react with the bright coloring, be absorbed into the stripes and lettering, and dull them. Florist's paper or Teflon-coated plastic bags are better for storage, especially when a small pouch of moisture absorbent silica is added to the box. (These pouches are used in photography and electronics.)

The graduated-height air vents of the 2332 and the marker lights shaped like squares retreating to rectangles were retained on the 2330. The triangular mounting screw hole on the end of pilot trucks of the 2332 gave way to a rounded semicircular plate around the mounting hole of the 2330 and its later models.

The GG1 was not produced between 1951 and 1954—a curious turn of events, since Lionel enjoyed its greatest sales successes in those years. However, the locomotive returned in 1955 with the 2340, which had the same mechanical features as the 2330. This time, the Brunswick green GG1 had a new Tuscan red partner to match the new 2254W *Congressional* passenger outfit offered that year. The aluminum passenger cars that came with the Tuscan GG1 had flat channels instead of fluted channels immediately above the windows; maroon striping was mounted in the channels. The *Congressional* set represented Lionel at its best; the sight of these cars pulled by the Tuscan 2340 would impress anyone.

There were no other cosmetic changes between the 2330 and the 2340; the Lionel Service Manual listed the body part numbers as 2340-30 for the Tuscan version and 2340-31 for the Brunswick green version. The suffix numbers Lionel used for marketing purposes were 2340-1 for the Tuscan version and 2340-25 for the green; the original box part numbers were 2340-10 for the Tuscan version and 2340-27 for the green. These numerical differences help collectors identify the correct boxes and parts for their particular 2340s, not to mention the later 2360s, which had their own parts nomenclatures.

The last number for the GG1, the 2360, appeared in 1956 and subsequently developed several interesting variations. In 1956 the 2360 was cataloged as a five-stripe locomotive in either Tuscan red or Brunswick green, just like the 2340. However, Lionel made several small yet significant changes over time to the body shell casting.

In previous models the air vents at the front sides were graduated in height in four distinct steps. Beginning with the 1961 version of the 2360, these vents became even in height all the way across the body. Incredibly, this body change followed the practice of the Pennsylvania Railroad, which made the same change to the real locomotives in the late 1950s! The company made other changes to the casting in 1961. On earlier GG1s, the marker lights had been placed in a square housing that came back into two rectangular boxes. With the 2360 from 1961, these marker lights were teardrop-shaped, as on the prototype. Also, the posts into which the pantograph insulators fit were strengthened by being made broader than their predecessors.

These changes did not, however, occur right away or all at once; so it is possible to date the differing models of the 2360 with some precision. The green 2360 did not show any of the cosmetic changes, though it was cataloged from 1956 to 1958. (The Lionel Service Manual

Two versions of the 2360. The upper locomotive (C) has side ventilator screens that differ in height, while on the lower locomotive (D), the ventilator screens are approximately the same height. R. Shanfeld Collection.

lists the body shell numbers as 2360-7 for the Tuscan version and 2360-26 for the green. Significantly, a parts sheet dated 11/59 lists the 2360-26 body shell as "obsolete.") Perhaps only one run of the Brunswick green 2360 was made or leftover 2340 green-painted body shells were numbered as 2360 models, even though it continued to be available through 1958. The green 2360 never used the body shell that went through cosmetic changes and differing paint styles.

The Tuscan 2360, however, shows many changes, beginning in 1957 when the GG1 was offered in Tuscan in only one set; after that year, Lionel merely cataloged the GG1 to help dealers dispose of existing stock. The earliest Tuscan 2360 models used the older-style body shell, five stripes, and heat-stamped lettering and numbering. Then new lettering and striping appeared on the older-style cab: One large single rubber-stamped gold stripe replaced the five narrow stripes, and the lettering in "PENNSYLVANIA" was made much larger, as was the locomotive number. The Pennsylvania Railroad had introduced this single-striped and large keystone scheme on the prototypes in 1955.

On the first version of this new decorating scheme, all striping was rubber-stamped. The numbers and lettering were large and heat-stamped. However, in 1961 a second version emerged; the only difference was that the lettering and numbering were heat-stamped, while the single stripe was painted. Usually, Lionel designated a new number for any locomotive that underwent changes such as these. In this case, the firm probably had a large number of leftover body castings after 1955. Therefore, the new number 2360 was put into effect anyway and Lionel painted the leftover castings into green or Tuscan versions as the market demanded. The company did not need the new body die until later, when it had exhausted the supply of older shells. That did not occur until the next model of the GG1 came out.

Although the original box is marked "2360-10", the 1957 consumer catalog identified the Tuscan single-striped GG1 as 2360-1. This locomotive was part of set 2293W, a Super O freight set. The green GG1 was still available; it was listed in the 1957 catalog as 2360-25. Most likely, these were 1956 green locomotives being depleted. The 1958 catalog listed both GG1s for sale again; this time it illustrated the green 2360-25 locomotive at the top of pages 28 and 29, but showed the incorrect 2360-1 above the front pantograph. This was corrected in the separate-sale entry at the bottom of page 28 of that catalog (J. Algozzini comment). In this case, both versions were probably leftover production. Apparently Lionel made no GG1s in 1958, although the GG1 appeared in the catalog to help dealers deplete their stocks. (Remember, 1958 was a severe recession year, and Lionel was cutting back its operations considerably.)

As usual, the catalog illustrations were models of inaccuracy. The 1957 catalog illustration clearly used the older body style for the drawing. However, the green GG1 illustrated in the 1958 catalog was a curious blend of the old and the new body styles. The marker lights appeared to be those of the older body shell, but the air vents looked as though they were all in the same height, as on the newer body shell. The 1961 catalog illustrations were poorly rendered drawings based on the older body shell; the vents were clearly graduated in height, but the marker lights looked like the newer, teardrop-shaped ones.

After a two-year absence, the 2360 returned in 1961, this time only in the Tuscan single-striped version. Finally, Lionel introduced the new body shell features with these production runs. The lettering and numbering were heat-stamped, as before, and the single stripe was painted onto the body shell. Sometime in 1962 and 1963, the last years for production of the GG1, the company made one further change. The lettering and numbering were no longer heat-stamped; instead, water-transfer decals were used. These examples represented the last stage of production for the postwar GG1.

Alan Stewart believes that none of the stripes on GG1s were rubber-stamped but were actually painted on using a mask. This would explain how Lionel managed to get the stripe to curve around and down at the ends and to penetrate details such as the air vents. One can see how the mask had cutouts for the ladders that did not closely match the actual body detail—the stripes stop short. Original striping is continuous with no seams or breaks. This is one telltale sign of most restriping jobs.

Few Lionel locomotives have found more favor—or more controversy—than the GG1s. All kinds of variations, some suspect and others genuine, have turned up in collector circles. Some single-striped versions have small keystones on the sides; some five-striped versions have large keystones. Many repainted and restriped locomotives exist, owing to both wear of the original decor and the popularity of the locomotive. At least three separate manufacturers or restorers have made repaints of the GG1 body shells; these usually can be detected by the silk-screened stripes, letters, and numbers. Lionel never used silk-screening as a decorative technique in the postwar era. Quite a number of paint color variations have turned up, even in the later models. "Odd" versions of the GG1 should be approached with care, and expert advice is a must before purchase.

GG1 Major Variations

Engine Number	Color	Year(s) Mfg.	Numbering and Lettering	Stripes	Side Keystone	End Keystone	Side Ventilation
2332	black	1947	Rubber-stamped: gold or silver	Five rubber-stamped: gold or silver	Rubber-stamped or gold and red decal	Rubber-stamped or gold and red decal with engine number in keystone	Graduated
2332	green	1947–49					
2330	green	1950	Heat-stamped: gold	Five rubber-stamped: gold	Red and gold keystone	Red and gold decal with engine number in keystone	
2340 (A)	Tuscan	1955					
2340 (B)	green	1955					
2360 (A)	Tuscan	1956					
2360 (B)	green	1956					
2360 (C)	Tuscan	1957–58	Heat-stamped: numbers and letters	One rubber-stamped: large gold	Large red and white decal	Red and white decal with engine number in keystone	Same height
2360 (D)	Tuscan	1961					
2360 (E)	Tuscan	1961–62					
2360 (F)	Tuscan	1962–63	Decaled large numbers and letters in three sections	Painted stripe, much brighter			

Top: Black 2332 (A) Pennsylvania GG1 with gold stripes and rubber-stamped keystone. Middle: Dark green 2332 (E) Pennsylvania GG1. Bottom: Dark green 2332 (F) Pennsylvania GG1 with keystone decal. R. Shanfeld Collection.

Top: 2332 (F) Pennsylvania GG1 with keystone decal. This example is a distinctly glossier green than the norm. Bottom: 2330 Pennsylvania GG1 R. Shanfeld Collection.

Top: Tuscan red 2340 (A) GG1. Middle: Green 2340 (B) GG1 (cataloged as 2340-25). Introduced in 1955, the 2340 mechanically is quite similar to the 2330 with dual motors, Magnetraction, and a battery-powered horn. Bottom: Tuscan 2360 (A). The 2360 was introduced in 1956 and initially retained the mechanical features and decorating scheme of the 2340. R. Shanfeld Collection.

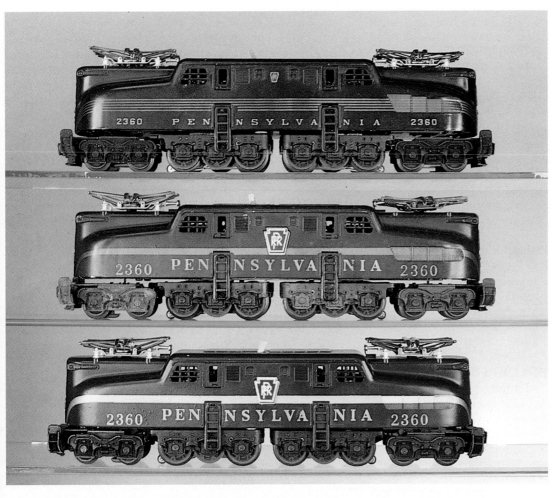

Introduced in 1956, the 2360 initially was made with five stripes in both Tuscan red and Brunswick green. The green version (B) is shown on the top shelf. Then Lionel replaced the five stripes on the Tuscan model with a single stripe, retaining the uneven height air vents. In 1961, Lionel changed the air vents and marker light detail. On the middle shelf is 2360 (C), and on the bottom is 2360 (D). R. Shanfeld Collection.

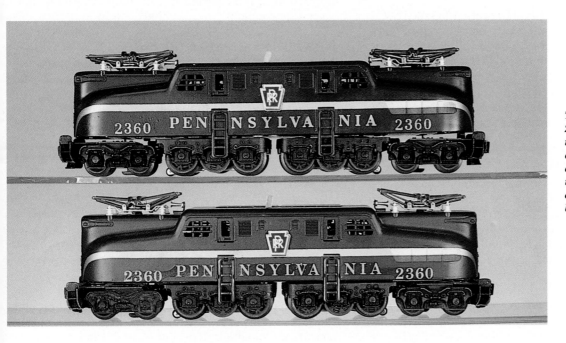

The last two versions of the 2360. The 1962 model (E) on top has a single gold stripe and heat-stamped lettering and numbers. The lower unit (F) from 1962–63 has decaled lettering and numbers. R. Shanfeld Collection.

	Gd	VG	Ex	LN

white heat-stamped BM logo; ornamental horn each side; headlight lens and number boards each end; white-painted frame; Magnetraction; three-position E-unit; light both ends; horn; operating couplers. **145 225 290 450**

2347 CHESAPEAKE & OHIO (Diesel): Uncataloged; 1965. EMD GP7 road switcher; blue-painted body with yellow heat-stamped lettering; heat-stamped C and O herald on cab; ornamental horn each side; headlight lens and number boards each end; yellow-painted frame; Magnetraction; three-position E-unit; light both ends; horn; operating couplers. Made exclusively for Sears.

Note: Even in mint condition, the handrails look as if they have been "touched up" (A. Stewart comment). *Caution:* Because of the exceedingly high price this item commands, forgeries are quite common. Most forgeries are made from rubber-stamped bodies, such as the 2028 and 2328, because there is no evidence of heat-stamping, which could present a problem. Look for loose-fitting ornamental horns, silk-screened lettering, and a repainted frame. Ask the seller to remove the cab from the frame so both parts can be examined individually. **1400 2200 2900 4000**

2348 MINNEAPOLIS & ST LOUIS (Diesel): 1958–59. EMD GP9 road switcher; red-painted body with white-painted middle side stripe and blue-painted cab roof; heat-stamped lettering (red on white and white on red); heat-stamped Peoria Gateway herald on cab; ornamental horn each side; headlight lens and number boards each end; black-painted frame; Magnetraction; three-position E-unit; light both ends; horn; operating couplers.

175 275 425 500

2349 NORTHERN PACIFIC (Diesel): 1959–60. EMD GP9 road switcher; predominantly black-painted body with unique gold-painted crescent and ends separated by red-painted stripe; gold heat-stamped lettering; red heat-stamped "RADIO / EQUIPPED" behind cab; ornamental horn each side; headlight lens and number boards each end; gold-painted frame; Magnetraction; three-position E-unit; light both ends; horn; operating couplers.

200 295 415 550

2350 NEW HAVEN (Electric): 1956–58. GE EP-5 rectifier; most typically black-painted body (black body mold) with orange-painted upper stripe and white-painted lower stripe; heat-stamped lettering and nose decoration described below; ornamental horn, headlight lens, number boards, and windshields each end; two pantographs; single motor; Magnetraction; three-position E-unit; light both ends; horn; operating couplers.

Note: It was evidently difficult to maintain consistent quality on the painted nose versions, so Lionel introduced a decal to solve this problem. It was an adhesive-backed decal—most unusual for Lionel—rather than a water-based one. Unfortunately, the adhesive-backed decals are more easily faked, but they were more durable than the nose decals used on the 2358, 2345, and 2378

(A. Stewart comment). Cracks in the noses of the EP-5s are growing more prevalent with time. The body mounting brackets were riveted to the plastic shell at each end, and the headlight lenses were pressed in just above them. This stress, transmitted to the shell through the mounting bracket during handling, along with the aging of the plastic, conspires to cause increasingly common vertical cracks from the bottom up to the headlight lens. Versions with decaled fronts tend to mask this problem.

(A) Orange "N", black "H", orange "NEW HAVEN", painted nose trim. Very scarce.
900 1300 1600 2000
(B) Same as (A), except adhesive-backed nose trim decal. Scarce. **600 900 1200 1500**
(C) White "N", orange "H", white "NEW HAVEN", painted nose trim. **390 600 800 1100**
(D) Same as (C), except adhesive-backed nose trim decal. Most common version. **220 370 500 600**
(E) Similar to (D), except the upper orange and lower white stripes go *completely* through the doorjambs. Probable 1958-production replacement body. See this item on the third shelf of the photograph of 2350s.
500 800 1100 1400
(F) Same as (D), with typical decorating scheme, but yellow body mold. **500 800 1100 1400**

2351 THE MILWAUKEE ROAD (Electric): 1957–58. GE EP-5 rectifier; unpainted yellow body with black-painted upper quarter and roof and wide dark red–painted middle side stripe; yellow heat-stamped lettering; ornamental horn, headlight lens, number boards, and windshields each end; two pantographs; single motor; Magnetraction; three-position E-unit; light both ends; horn; operating couplers. **200 350 575 700**

2352 PENNSYLVANIA (Electric): 1957–58. GE EP-5 rectifier; painted body with gold rubber-stamped stripe and gold-painted heat dissipater on roof (body mold either yellow or Tuscan red); gold heat-stamped lettering; large PRR keystone decal on middle of side; ornamental horn, headlight lens, number boards, and windshields each end; two pantographs; single motor; Magnetraction; three-position E-unit; light both ends; horn; operating couplers.
(A) Tuscan red body. **225 375 550 750**
(B) Chocolate brown body.
230 400 575 800

2353 SANTA FE (Diesel): 1953–55. EMD F3 AA units; silver and red warbonnet paint scheme with red, yellow, and black rubber-stamped detailing stripes; louvered roof and open portholes with snap-in lenses; black heat-stamped lettering and small heat-stamped "GM" on door panel; wraparound Santa Fe decal on nose; two-piece ornamental horns, cab door ladder, window shell, number boards, and headlight lens, but *no* grab irons on nose; silver chassis with silver-painted pilot and silver-painted side frames with steps; twin horizontal motors; Magnetraction; three-position E-unit; lighted both units; horn

	Gd	VG	Ex	LN

in nonpowered (trailer) unit; operating coupler on pilots and die-cast couplers at other ends.

Note: For matching B unit see 2343C (C). In 1953, Lionel changed the method of attaching the body to the chassis; the end (opposite the nose) was attached by a two-prong bracket, which eliminated the need for the two interior mounting bosses. Furthermore, beginning with 1954 production, the notch at the bottom of the pilot was removed; the revised pilot had a smooth bottom. More interesting, however, was a minor exterior modification made to the F3 body mold in 1954. A round "dimple" was added to the roof directly behind the roof vents. It helped conceal the sink mark at the sprue location and was present on all future production of F3 bodies.

(A) Bodies without dimple behind roof vents.

	270	400	625	950

(B) Bodies with dimple behind roof vents.

	270	400	625	950

(2353C) (SANTA FE) (Diesel): Not made. Appropriately numbered B unit *not* designated; for B unit that matched 2353, see 2343C (C). Amazingly, Lionel did *not* renumber the Santa Fe B unit when it made the 1953 changes to the F3 AA units.

2354 NEW YORK CENTRAL (Diesel): 1953–55. EMD F3 AA units; dark gray and light gray lightning-bolt paint scheme with white rubber-stamped detailing stripes; louvered roof and open portholes with snap-in lenses; white heat-stamped lettering and small heat-stamped "GM" on door panel; New York Central decal on nose; two-piece ornamental horns, cab door ladder, window shell, number boards, and headlight lens, but *no* grab irons on nose; gray chassis with gray-painted pilot and gray-painted side frames with steps; twin horizontal motors; Magnetraction; three-position E-unit; lighted both units; horn in nonpowered (trailer) unit; operating coupler on pilots and die-cast fixed couplers at other ends.

Note: For matching B unit see 2344C (C). See the Note with 2353 for description of the changed method of attaching the body to the chassis and the addition of a dimple to the body mold.

(A) Bodies without dimple behind roof vents.

	270	425	650	1000

(B) Bodies with dimple behind roof vents.

	270	425	650	1000

(2354C) NEW YORK CENTRAL (Diesel): Not made. Appropriately numbered B unit *not* designated; for B unit that matched 2354, see 2344C (C). Amazingly, Lionel did *not* renumber the New York Central B unit when it made the 1953 changes to the F3 AA units.

2355 WESTERN PACIFIC (Diesel): 1953. EMD F3 AA units; silver-painted body with orange-painted nose and middle side stripe; louvered roof and open portholes with snap-in lenses; black heat-stamped lettering and small heat-stamped "GM" on door panel; Western Pacific decal on nose; two-piece ornamental horns, cab door ladder, window shell, number boards, and headlight lens, but *no* grab irons on nose; silver chassis with silver-painted pilot and silver-painted side frames with steps; twin horizontal motors; Magnetraction; three-position E-unit; lighted both units; horn in nonpowered (trailer) unit; operating coupler on pilots and die-cast fixed couplers at other ends.

Note: The 2355 pair does *not* have a matching B unit. In 1953, Lionel changed the method of attaching the body to the chassis; the end (opposite the nose) was attached by a two-prong bracket, which eliminated the need for the two interior mounting bosses.

	800	1300	1900	2800

2356 SOUTHERN (Diesel): 1954–56. EMD F3 AA units; green-painted body with gray-painted lower-side stripe and front with yellow rubber-stamped detailing stripe; louvered roof and open portholes with snap-in lenses; yellow rubber-stamped lettering; Southern decal on nose; two-piece ornamental horns, cab door ladder, window shell, number boards, and headlight lens, but *no* grab irons on nose; black chassis with black-painted pilot and black-painted side frames with steps; twin horizontal motors; Magnetraction; three-position E-unit; lighted both units; horn in nonpowered (trailer) unit; operating coupler on pilots and die-cast fixed couplers at other ends.

Note: For matching B unit see 2356C. See the Note with 2353 for description of the changed method of attaching the body to the chassis and the addition of a dimple to the body mold.

(A) Earliest production (or simply the depletion of existing inventory) without dimple behind roof vents.

	600	1200	1500	2000

(B) Most typical production with dimple behind roof vents.

	500	1100	1400	1800

2356C SOUTHERN (Diesel): 1954–56. EMD F3 B unit; green-painted body with gray-painted lower-side stripe and yellow rubber-stamped detailing stripe; louvered roof and open portholes with snap-in lenses; yellow rubber-stamped lettering; black chassis and black-painted side frames with steps; die-cast fixed couplers.

Note: The Southern was the only B unit from the entire F3 series to be numbered on the body; the number appears as "2356".

	160	250	350	525

2358 GREAT NORTHERN (Electric): 1959–60. GE EP-5 rectifier; orange- and green-painted body (gray body mold) with three narrow yellow stripes; orange-painted heat dissipater on roof; yellow heat-stamped "GREAT NORTHERN" and yellow "BLT BY / LIONEL" and "2358" that are part of nose decal; ornamental horn, headlight lens, number boards, and windshield each end; two pantographs; single motor; Magnetraction; three-position E-unit; light both ends; horn; operating couplers.

Note: Original water-transfer GN nose decals are almost always flaking. Be aware that many engines have

	Gd	VG	Ex	LN

been "redecaled" with adhesive-backed or water-transfer reproductions. Look for telltale gray spots around the edges of the nose decal. This indicates that the original decal has been removed, taking some of the paint with it (A. Stewart comment). A substantial premium can be obtained for examples with near top-condition decals, as the Like New price demonstrates.

	350	750	1100	1750

2359 BOSTON AND MAINE (Diesel): 1961–62. EMD GP9 road switcher; blue-painted body with black-painted cab and ends; white heat-stamped lettering; black-and-white heat-stamped BM logo; ornamental horn each side; headlight lens and number boards each end; white-painted frame; Magnetraction; three-position E-unit; light both ends; horn; operating couplers.

	185	200	300	400

2360 PENNSYLVANIA (Electric): 1956–58, 1961–63. GG1; painted die-cast body with stripe(s) described below; most typically gold heat-stamped lettering; PRR keystone decal centered at upper quarter of sides; small keystone nose decal numbered "2360" at each end; headlight lens, running lights, and ornamental horn each end; two pantographs; twin motors; Magnetraction; three-position E-unit; light both ends; horn; operating coil couplers.

Note: A die modification was made in 1961 that changed the side ventilators from a graduated style to one in which the ventilators were the same height.

(A) 1956; Tuscan red body with five rubber-stamped gold stripes. Headed the 1956 *Congressional* passenger set; cataloged as 2360-1.

	600	1050	1800	2700

(B) 1956–58; Brunswick green body with five rubber-stamped gold stripes. Cataloged as 2360-25.

	575	1000	1300	1900

(C) 1957–58; Tuscan red body with single large *rubber*-stamped gold stripe; most typically large keystone side decal; still retained the graduated side ventilators from the original design.

	500	900	1500	2100

(D) 1961; same as (C), but ventilators are same height.

	500	900	1500	2100

(E) 1961–62; Tuscan red body with single large gold-painted stripe; large keystone decal; ventilators are same height.

	500	900	1300	1750

(F) 1962–63; same as (E), but large decaled lettering and numbers.

	500	900	1300	1750

Top: 2352 (A) Pennsylvania EP-5. Bottom: 2358 Great Northern EP-5. L. Nuzzaci Collection.

Top: 2350 (C) New Haven with painted nose trim. Second: 2350 (D) New Haven with decaled nose trim. Third: 2350 (E) New Haven with orange and white stripes through door. Bottom: 2350 (A) New Haven with orange "N" and black "H". Note that the nose rivets are visible on examples with painted nose trim. E. Dougherty Collection.

Top: 2350 (B) New Haven EP-5 with large orange "N". Middle: 2350 (D) with large white "N". Bottom: 2351 Milwaukee Road. L. Nuzzaci and R. Lord Collections.

	Gd	VG	Ex	LN

2363 ILLINOIS CENTRAL (Diesel): 1955–56. EMD F3 AB units; brown-painted body with orange lower quarter and yellow rubber-stamped detailing stripes; louvered roof and closed portholes; rubber-stamped lettering; Illinois Central decal on nose; one-piece ornamental horns, raised molded cab door ladder, window shell, number boards, and headlight lens; black chassis with black-painted pilot and chemically blackened side frames; twin vertical motors; Magnetraction; three-position E-unit; lighted; horn; operating couplers on pilot and die-cast fixed couplers at all other ends.

Note: The Illinois Central A unit body was molded in gray plastic, while the B unit body was molded in orange plastic.

(A) Early (1955) production with unpainted orange area on B unit and most typically with brown rubber-stamped lettering. **Note:** Black often appears as brown on an unpainted surface or with an insufficient quantity of ink.

	500	1000	1500	2000

(B) Later production with orange-painted area on B unit and most typically with black rubber-stamped lettering.

	450	900	1350	1800

2365 CHESAPEAKE AND OHIO (Diesel): 1962–63. EMD GP7 road switcher; blue-painted body with yellow heat-stamped lettering; heat-stamped C and O herald on cab; ornamental horn each side; headlight lens and number boards each end; yellow-painted frame; Magnetraction; three-position E-unit; light both ends; no horn; fixed plastic couplers.

	135	250	400	500

2367 WABASH (Diesel): 1955. EMD F3 AB units; blue body (A unit blue-painted, B unit unpainted) with gray-painted roof and upper quarter and white silk-screened lower quarter and thin, interrupted center side stripe; louvered roof and closed portholes; most typically yellow heat-stamped lettering; Wabash decal on nose; one-piece ornamental horns, raised molded cab door ladder, window shell, number boards, and headlight lens; blue chassis with blue-painted pilot and chemically blackened side frames; twin vertical motors; Magnetraction; three-position E-unit; lighted; horn; operating coupler on pilot and die-cast fixed couplers at all other ends.

Note: Aside from having an unpainted blue body, the 2367 B unit has a full-length thin center-side stripe. Compare this item with 2240 B unit in the photograph.

(A) As described above.

	400	800	1200	1600

(B) Scarce variation of B unit, with yellow rubber-stamped lettering; "BUILT BY / LIONEL" on the *same* end of the body, unlike the heat-stamped models, which had "BUILT BY / LIONEL" on opposing ends.

	500	1000	2000	3000

	Gd	VG	Ex	LN

2368 BALTIMORE AND OHIO (Diesel): 1956. EMD F3 AB units; most typically unpainted blue body with gray-painted roof and white-painted nose and upper quarter and black-painted lower-side stripe accented with yellow heat-stamped lettering; *no* decal on nose, but nose rubber-stamped with blue and yellow stripes that join to the side stripes; one-piece ornamental horns, molded cab door ladder, window shell, number boards, and headlight lens; black chassis with black-painted pilot and chemically blackened side frames; twin vertical motors; Magnetraction; three-position E-unit; lighted; horn; operating coupler on pilot and die-cast fixed couplers at all other ends.

(A) As described above.

	800	1750	2500	3200

(B) Scarce variation with gray body mold (A unit only) that is blue-painted along with the other usual painted colors. Most likely a Lionel Service Station replacement body.

	1000	2000	3000	4000

2373 CANADIAN PACIFIC (Diesel): 1957. EMD F3 AA units; gray-painted body with dark brown–painted roof and lower quarter and thin yellow heat-stamped detailing stripes; louvered roof and closed portholes; yellow heat-stamped lettering; wraparound Canadian Pacific decal on nose; one-piece ornamental horns, molded cab door ladder, window shell, number boards, and headlight lens; black chassis with black-painted pilot and chemically blackened side frames; twin vertical motors; Magnetraction; three-position E-unit; lighted both units; horn in powered unit; operating coupler on pilots and die-cast fixed couplers at other ends.

Note: The 2373 pair does *not* have a matching B unit.

(A) As described above.

	950	1500	2100	3000

(B) Raised molded cab door ladder; usually with an orange body mold.

	950	1500	2100	3000

2378 THE MILWAUKEE ROAD (Diesel): 1956. EMD F3 AB units; unpainted gray body with red-painted stripe and yellow heat-stamped detailing stripes; louvered roof and closed portholes; yellow heat-stamped lettering; large wraparound Milwaukee Road decal on nose; one-piece ornamental horns, molded cab door ladder, window shell, number boards, and headlight lens; black chassis with black-painted pilot and chemically blackened side frames; twin vertical motors; Magnetraction; three-position E-unit; lighted; horn; operating coupler on pilot and die-cast fixed couplers at all other ends.

(A) AB units with yellow roofline stripe.

	1050	1800	2600	3200

(B) AB units without yellow roofline stripe.

	1000	1700	2400	3000

(C) Mixed AB units usually with yellow roofline stripe on B unit. It appears that more B units than A units were produced with the stripe.

	1000	1700	2400	3000

2379 RIO GRANDE (Diesel): 1957–58. EMD F3 AB units; yellow-painted body with green-painted nose and silver-painted roof and lower-side stripe; louvered roof and closed portholes; black heat-stamped lettering and detailing stripes; wraparound Rio Grande decal on nose; one-piece ornamental horns, molded cab door ladder, window shell, number boards, and headlight lens; black chassis with black-painted pilot and chemically blackened side frames; twin vertical motors; Magnetraction; three-position E-unit; lighted; horn; operating coupler on pilot and die-cast fixed couplers at all other ends.

(A) As described above.

	600	800	1100	1600

(B) Raised molded cab door ladder; usually with an orange body mold.

	600	800	1100	1600

2383 SANTA FE (Diesel): 1958–66. EMD F3 AA units; silver and red warbonnet paint scheme with red, yellow, and black rubber-stamped detailing stripes; louvered roof and closed portholes; black heat-stamped lettering and small heat-stamped "GM" on door panel; wraparound Santa Fe decal on nose; one-piece ornamental horns, molded cab door ladder, window shell, number boards, and headlight lens; silver chassis with silver-painted pilot and chemically blackened side frames; twin vertical motors; Magnetraction; three-position E-unit; lighted both units; horn in powered unit; operating coupler on pilots and die-cast fixed couplers at other ends.

Note: The 2383 pair was not offered with a B unit; however, the 2243 B unit is a near-perfect match.

(A) As described above.

	300	500	650	800

(B) Some mid-1960s production surfaced with red-orange bodies; all items that we have examined are time-faded, most probably due to inferior paint, and are *not* considered variations by most collectors. Listed here for reference.

	300	500	650	850

3360 BURRO (Motorized Unit): 1956–57. Self-propelled operating crane; most typically unpainted yellow body and boom with red heat-stamped lettering; fixed die-cast couplers.

Note: The 3360 is an interesting and complex unit. Besides being able to travel forward or backward or stand in a neutral position, its cab, through a unique slip-clutch mechanism, can mechanically rotate, and the block-and-hook assembly can be raised or lowered. Only one activator track-clip was included with it.

	150	265	340	400

3927 LIONEL LINES (Motorized Unit): 1956–60. Track-cleaning car; unpainted orange body with black heat-stamped lettering (lettering appears blue until placed under bright incandescent light); ornamental horn; on-off switch projects upward through body; movable black wiper carriage; motor-driven sponge and plate assembly on underframe; fixed die-cast coupler.

Note: The motor on 3927 does *not* power the wheels; the unit must be pulled by a separate engine. A complete

3927 Track-cleaning car.

	Gd	VG	Ex	LN

unit includes a set of cotton track-wiping cylinders and two rubberized bottles of cleaning fluid with removable caps. Bottles are rubber-stamped "LIONEL / TRACK / CLEANER".

	60	90	120	160

6220 A.T. & S.F. (Diesel): 1949–50. EMD NW2 switcher with ringing bell; identical to 622, except for number; designated as O27 gauge because of the four-digit number. See 622 for complete description. The 6220 was never illustrated correctly in the consumer catalog. It was shown with "LIONEL" in 1949; while the 1950 catalog listed 6220 as the proper engine for outfit 1457B, it showed 622 with "NEW YORK CENTRAL" markings in the artist's rendering of the set.

(A) Ten stanchions attach wire handrail to body; large

	Gd	VG	Ex	LN

GM decal on cab below number.

	170	200	350	450

(B) Ten stanchions attach wire handrail to body; small GM decal on lower sides near nose.

	150	175	325	400

(C) Three stanchions attach wire handrail to body; small GM decal on lower sides near nose; Lionel Service Department replacement cab dates about 1954.

	150	175	325	400

6250 SEABOARD (Diesel): 1954–55. EMD NW2 switcher; blue- and orange–painted body with unpainted blue smokestacks and blue heat-stamped cab number; Seaboard medallion decal and Seaboard lettering as described below; black ornamental bell and silver ornamental horn; radio wheel; marker lens; wire handrail along hood with three stanchions; blue-painted die-cast frame with wire handrail detail; lighted with headlight lens, front and rear; coil couplers; two-axle Magnetraction; three-position E-unit.

(A) "SEABOARD" decal (tends to flake, therefore Like New must have decals intact). Most common version.

	125	175	300	450

(B) Closely spaced rubber-stamped "SEABOARD"; very scarce variation. This was the first run of the rubber-stamped versions.

	350	500	650	800

(C) Widely spaced rubber-stamped "SEABOARD".

	125	175	300	400

4

BOXCARS, REFRIGERATOR CARS, AND STOCK CARS

Introduction by Roger Carp

No freight train, real or miniature, ever seemed complete without a boxcar or two as well as a refrigerator car or stock car. That's why, almost from the moment Lionel began marketing an O gauge line of electric trains in the second decade of this century, it offered replicas of these popular freight cars. Children liked them, especially if the cars had doors that opened so the models could be packed with small toys or figures. Then young engineers could imagine their train was carrying furniture, automobiles, cattle, or various other products to town.

A demand for boxcars and similar O and O27 gauge rolling stock had special influence during the postwar decades. No other toy seemed as important to youngsters during the late 1940s and 1950s as an electric train. Lionel's sales force worked diligently to keep up with the public's desire for trains. Doing so meant bringing out more than exciting locomotives and innovative accessories. It involved introducing and manufacturing extensive lines of rolling stock, particularly models of the freight cars children saw daily and wanted on their miniature railroads. And at the top of their list were boxcars.

The array of boxcars cataloged by Lionel was amazing. They came in different sizes with an enormous range of paint schemes and road names. Supplementing the list of boxcars were refrigerator and stock cars. There might be fewer of them than boxcars, but these models also featured attractive decoration and realistic details. Even better, a number of them could be operated, so that kids could pretend they were unloading milk cans or horses. Late in the 1950s, when interest in electric trains started to dwindle, Lionel devised some cars with spectacular animation. Rolling stock cataloged during the final decade of the postwar era claimed to be transporting fish, harboring gun-toting outlaws, and launching helicopters.

It's not difficult to understand, therefore, why so many of today's toy train collectors and operators focus on Lionel's boxcars, refrigerator cars, and stock cars. They appreciate their beauty and enjoy their special effects. Experienced hobbyists realize that the great assortment of models cataloged by Lionel does more than give them memorable pieces to run on layouts or display on shelves. It sheds light on shifts in marketing and manufacturing at Lionel so that a quarter-century after the postwar period, the ingenuity and foresight of engineers and sales executives can be applauded.

Of course, all of this praise rushes the story. When World War II ended in August 1945 and toy companies received permission to revive their product lines, Lionel wanted only to have a train set ready for the Christmas season. Key personnel admitted that any outfit had to have a boxcar, so they set about to complete one. Using something from the prewar line seemed obvious, and they had some superb models to choose from. During the 1930s, Lionel offered rosters of small and larger O gauge freight cars that included colorful boxcars, stock cars, and refrigerator cars made of stamped sheet metal and painted in bright enamel tones. From 1938 through 1942, it also cataloged versions of these models equipped with automatic magnetic couplers. One was an operating boxcar (the 3814) that appeared to unload boxes of merchandise.

To the discerning eyes of Lionel's sales and engineering staffs, none of these cars would do. Regardless of how visually appealing the 2655 Lionel Lines boxcar or the 2814R Lionel Lines refrigerator car might be, they and all their companions looked too much like old-fashioned toys to satisfy the public after the war. The company needed something bigger and more realistic to entice consumers. Executives responsible for assembling the postwar line must have breathed sighs of relief after remembering the spectacular O gauge boxcars Lionel had announced in 1940 and 1941.

Advances in the use of compression-molded phenolic plastics (typically referred to by a brand name, Bakelite) enabled designers to create a 10¾-inch–long scale-detailed model of a single-door boxcar decorated for the

Pennsylvania Railroad. New in 1940, the 714 featured a die-cast zinc-alloy frame and stamped-steel parts, including sprung Bettendorf trucks and highly detailed couplers. Its Bakelite body was painted Tuscan red and rubber-stamped white. Unfortunately, the car's scale couplers were not compatible with those used elsewhere in the product line. To overcome this problem, Lionel advertised the 2954, a version of the Pennsy boxcar equipped with tinplate trucks and automatic magnetic couplers.

Pleased by the favorable response the single-door boxcars received, Lionel asked its engineers to modify the body slightly to create something new for 1941. They answered with a 9-inch–long Pennsylvania Railroad boxcar with a sheet-metal body and die-cast ends. What truly set the 2758 apart from the cars released the previous year were its sets of sliding double doors. In fact, the consumer catalog explained, these features separated it from other boxcars because they identified it as one of the up-to-date cars designed to transport automobiles.

The notion that the double-door automobile car was something special still carried weight in 1945. Planners of the postwar line selected it as the sole boxcar cataloged for that year. They gave it newly designed trucks and couplers, not to mention a new number (the X2458). However, when the time came to fill orders, Lionel decided to use up its leftover inventory of prewar models. For that reason, the boxcars initially sold had bodies marked "X2758". Before long in 1946, items with the new number were ready; Lionel cataloged the X2458 Pennsy automobile boxcar through 1948.

Engineers followed the same procedure of returning a prewar item to the line when they brought out an operating boxcar in 1946. In reality, the 3854 automatic merchandise car was a new item based on an earlier model, the 714 and 2954 single-door Pennsylvania Railroad boxcars. It featured a solenoid-powered mechanism that was used in conjunction with a section of remote-control track to hurl plastic cubes from a door to simulate a boxcar having packing crates unloaded. This mechanism, which had been installed on the prewar 3814, was slightly revised after the war and added to both Lionel's scale-detailed boxcar and a brand-new smaller version (the O27 gauge 3454). Both sizes of the merchandise car were cataloged through 1947, although the value of the 3854 far exceeds that of its cousin. In fact, this superb freight car, the only one in the postwar line to be made of Bakelite, is among the most desirable of all the regular-production rolling stock manufactured by Lionel between 1945 and 1969.

Also in 1946, Lionel introduced a new line of single-door boxcars that became the backbone of the O27 line for the next several years. To produce these cars, designers relied on injection-molding thermoplastics, a process that enabled them to add details and produce large quantities of rolling stock at reasonable prices. First came versions of the X2454 that were painted orange and heat-stamped black with Pennsylvania Railroad graphics. Another model was painted silver and equipped to be an operating merchandise car.

The most common example of the X2454, which was cataloged into 1947, featured, in addition to its Pennsy decoration, advertising for Baby Ruth candy bars. This wasn't novel, since Lionel had been putting the Baby Ruth name on O27 boxcars since 1935. The move was a brilliant one, though no record exists of how Lionel and Curtiss, which produced Baby Ruth, hammered out their licensing agreement. The idea of having a toy advertise a brand of candy made good sense, however much dentists might have protested. Besides the common version of the postwar Baby Ruth, Lionel created a special model, the 4454, which came with a radio receiver so it could function as a component of the 4109WS Electronic Control Set.

The big news for 1947 wasn't a boxcar but a refrigerator car. By and large, a reefer shouldn't capture much interest, but Lionel's was far from ordinary. The 3462 automatic refrigerated milk car represented yet another breakthrough for Lionel ("one of the most remarkable cars ever manufactured," boasted the consumer catalog). Designed by an outside inventor, it used a solenoid to enable a figure to push tiny metal milk cans from the refrigerator car onto a metal platform. The animation was simple yet captivating. Lionel had a terrific addition to its O and O27 lines. So successful was the milk car that in various forms it stayed in the line for the next 13 years. Millions of these operating refrigerator cars reportedly were sold.

Somewhat surprisingly, Lionel seemed satisfied to continue to advertise the 2458 as its only exclusively O gauge boxcar in 1947 and 1948. No additional road names were mass-produced, even though the 1948 catalog depicted examples decorated for the Atchison, Topeka and Santa Fe and the Southern Pacific. Instead, the low end of the line was the focus of attention as the company introduced its inexpensive Scout freight sets to compete with the electric trains marketed by Louis Marx and Company. Among the rolling stock developed for the Scout line was a brand-new boxcar. It measured 8½ inches long and had an unpainted plastic body fastened to a metal frame. The X1004, decorated for the Pennsy with Baby Ruth graphics added, had double doors that didn't open.

Having all but ignored boxcars in 1948, Lionel's engineers made up for lost time the following year. To start, they took the New York Central and Santa Fe 9¼-inch boxcars brought out in 1948 (both numbered as X6454 to reflect their new magnetic couplers) and invested them with life. Capitalizing on the trusted solenoid mechanism, they used remote control to open one of the car's doors and push forward a figure mounted inside. The two versions of the X3464 dazzled children and adults alike. Meanwhile, the X6454 series gained three road names. Versions decorated for the Erie Railroad, Pennsylvania, and Southern Pacific joined the fleet.

Collectors haven't always paid these 9¼-inch boxcars the respect they deserve. After all, they do seem somewhat drab, especially when compared with later, multiple-colored models. With one exception, they came painted in solid shades of brown or orange and had rudimentary white, black, or brown lettering. In fairness, Lionel aimed to replicate what typically was found on railroads during the 1940s. And brown was the norm. So it makes better sense to recognize that the styling and realistic decoration of the X6454-series cars were state-of-the-art for the time. Acquiring examples of virtually all of these boxcars doesn't take much time or expense, though desirable variations exist. Among these are the orange X6454 Baby Ruth with brown-painted doors and the identical X6454 New York Central.

Another noteworthy development in 1949 was Lionel's first postwar stock car. And like the refrigerator car, it came as part of an enchanting operating accessory. Probably as soon as the company's sales staff realized how well the 3462 was selling, they began pleading with the engineering department to come up with something similar. At last in 1949, Frank Pettit, Lionel's industrious and imaginative development engineer, presented it with an operating stock car. Using a mechanism that vibrated a metal tray within the car, it moved miniature cattle out one of the doors, down a ramp, through a stockyard, and back inside the car. Though not as dependable as the milk car, the 3656 operating cattle car was a favorite from the start and remained in the catalog through 1955.

With a number of 9¼-inch boxcars in its line, along with the operating stock car and milk car, Lionel can't be blamed for channeling its energies elsewhere in the early 1950s. But inactivity and indifference are what competitors hope for, and before long Lionel found itself slipping behind a few newcomers. It wasn't simply that Athearn and Bob Peare Engineering brought out O scale boxcar kits. What mattered was that these two firms, among others, offered miniature replicas of the latest rolling stock that featured bright, multiple-color paint schemes and flashy heralds. More troublesome to Lionel was American Model Toys. This small firm in Indiana introduced ready-to-run, near-scale models of contemporary boxcars and stock cars that it directed at the youngsters who owned O gauge trains. By 1952, it was obvious that Lionel had allowed itself to fall behind and would have to hurry to regain momentum.

Whatever worries Lionel's executives might have felt as 1953 dawned were gone by the time the year ended. First, they enlivened the X6454 series with the 3474, a stunning operating replica of the Western Pacific's new boxcar painted silver with a large orange feather splashed across each of its sides. Ironically, this attractive car, such a departure from earlier entries in the series, marked its demise. Concerned that the X6454 cars looked short and dull next to the offerings of other firms, Lionel had instructed its engineers to design a near-scale model to challenge the boxcars from American Model Toys. They exceeded all expectations in bringing out four cars, each measuring 10⅝ inches from coupler to coupler. Although their decoration was somewhat sparse (solid colors with heralds and slogans in a second color), these four 6464 boxcars compared favorably to their predecessors and were immediate hits.

From such humble beginnings emerged a glorious legend. Rather than content itself with the four 6464 boxcars, Lionel more than doubled the number of cars in 1954. And the new 6464-125 New York Central Pacemaker and 6464-150 Missouri Pacific Eagle bested every rival in the line when it came to colorful graphics. This trend continued over the next few years, as Lionel was determined to retain the loyalty of boxcar lovers. Advances in injection-molding and paint-masking enabled it to mass-produce models of the latest and most eye-catching cars. Technology was keeping pace with marketing, as executives sought to make their trains appealing to children rather than adult hobbyists. Kids and their parents responded to the colors and play value of the 6464 boxcars; realism was of secondary importance. Even so, the cars brought out year after year in the middle and late 1950s reached a wide audience.

Today, the 6464 series is the most desirable of all the groups of postwar Lionel rolling stock to collect. It also has been studied extensively by people eager to learn how body shells, frames, and graphics changed and to surmise why. With all the attention given to the twenty-nine boxcars cataloged between 1953 and 1969, it's not surprising that their prices continue to rise. The most desirable models in the series are the 6464-510 New York Central and 6464-515 Missouri-Kansas-Texas (both sold only as parts of the pastel 1587S Lady Lionel, the so-called Girls' Set, cataloged in 1957 and 1958) and the 6464-325 Baltimore & Ohio/Sentinel car, available for just one year and only as a separate-sale item. Notable variations include the solid-shield 6464-300 Rutland and gray-body 6464-375 Central of Georgia as well as the 6464-1 Western Pacific with red lettering and the 6464-175 Rock Island with black lettering.

Once Lionel had designed a longer body shell for its boxcars, engineers felt free to experiment in an effort to broaden the product line. For example, by fitting sets of double doors to it they created an up-to-date version of the automobile boxcar. Cars decorated for the Baltimore and Ohio (the 6468) and the New Haven (the 6468-25) were cataloged between 1953 and 1958. The most desirable of these handsome cars was the 6468X, a Tuscan red version of the Baltimore and Ohio that was available in just the 1535W O27 freight outfit cataloged in 1955. Also in 1953, engineers revised the X3464 series of operating boxcars by adapting the mechanism to fit into the longer boxcars. Through 1958, Lionel offered versions of 6464 boxcars in which the familiar little blue man would stride forward whenever his remote-controlled mechanism was activated. All seven of the 3484 and 3494 cars looked good, with the last two models (the 3494-550 Monon and 3494-625 Soo Line) being especially desirable.

Engineers also set about modifying Lionel's refrigerator and stock cars. First came the striking 6356 New York Central two-level stock car and 6672 Santa Fe reefer in 1954. Offering these near-scale cars with prototype road names represented a simple yet notable improvement for Lionel. Then in 1955 there was the 3662, a larger version of the automatic milk car, and the 6352, a special model with a bin to hold and unload the plastic ice cubes used with the 352 ice depot accessory. And a year later, Lionel announced a new operating stock car (the 3356 Santa Fe Railway Express Agency). This time, it carried miniature horses and worked with an improved corral.

With so many near-scale boxcars and associated models in its line by 1956, there seemed nowhere for Lionel's designers to go. And who could have been disappointed if they had quit inventing at this point? But collectors know that some of the most charming and imaginative operating boxcars had yet to appear. Over the next 6 years, the firm would release exciting, entertaining pieces whose value keeps increasing.

Already in 1956, Lionel had introduced the 3530 Electro Mobile Power boxcar, which delivered electricity to a removable searchlight, along with the classic 3424, a Wabash boxcar with an animated figure on top. As the car was pulled under an overhead telltale pole placed in front of a tunnel or bridge, the little brakeman ducked to avoid striking his head. When the car had passed through and reached a second pole, he resumed standing. It was a delightful addition to the line, one providing action that was more realistic and amusing than anything cataloged by Lionel's main rival, the S gauge American Flyer line manufactured by The A. C. Gilbert Company. Not even the operating boxcar announced by Gilbert in 1956 compared with the 3424, though it was fascinating that both companies devised boxcars with animated figures on their roofs about the same time.

Later in the 1950s, Lionel released stock cars that transported chickens and featured a figure who appeared to be sweeping debris from the 3434 poultry dispatch. On another model, the 3428 United States Mail car, he delivered a sack of mail on command. Another special boxcar, the 3435 traveling aquarium, relied on incredible graphics to suggest a car filled with swimming fish on their way to an aquarium or a seafood market. These cars, as well as a version of the operating horse car designed to look as though it were carrying ponies for a circus act (the 3366), left no doubt that Lionel wanted to bring fun to families considering the purchase of an electric train.

The search for customers in a shrinking market led Lionel to try another approach in the late 1950s. It had never stopped offering an 8½-inch boxcar, although all references to its being a Scout car disappeared after 1952. Then the X6014 Pennsylvania Railroad/Baby Ruth model was packed with low-end O27 sets. Perhaps someone realized that the free advertising given by the X6014 might appeal to other enterprises and bring in needed revenue. These cars could be made without much expense because they had unpainted injection-molded plastic bodies with minimal heat-stamped decoration.

A rash of 6014 and similar 8½-inch boxcars appeared between 1957 and 1963. The cataloged 6024 advertising Nabisco Shredded Wheat entered the line with uncataloged versions of the 6014 decorated for Chun King Chinese foods and RCA Whirlpool washers and dryers. Over the next few years boxcars were introduced that advertised Bosco chocolate syrup, Wix automotive oil filters, Airex fishing tackle (made by a subsidiary of Lionel), Swift meats, Stokely-Van Camp's pork and beans, and Libby's tomato juice. A few of these cars had slots molded into their roof to encourage children to deposit coins in them. The concept of a piggy bank on railroad trucks was clever, but never quite caught on. As a result, prices for these cars, like those for just about all the 8½-inch boxcars, remain low.

As Lionel struggled to sell electric trains in the 1960s, it reissued a few of the 6464-series boxcars previously dropped from production and invented some operating boxcars with a military aspect. The 6470 explosives car arrived in 1959, ready to be assembled and then "blown up" when struck by a missile from an accessory. Joining it two years later was the similar 6448 target car. Not surprisingly, Lionel eventually cataloged a car to be used with the exploding boxcar. The roof of the 3665 Minuteman opened to reveal a missile poised to be shot at its unsuspecting companions.

During the same years that Lionel was developing the boxcars of the future, it offered stock cars that brought back memories of the Wild West. The 3370 featured a sheriff and outlaw shooting at each other, and the 6473 horse transport carried a load of horses whose heads bobbed as the car traveled around. These cars, like the 3376 Bronx Zoo with a giraffe sticking its head out of the roof, showed how creative Lionel's engineers could be when given the freedom to design what essentially were toys.

Some of these boxcars and stock cars surely can be derided as downright silly. A few observers may complain that the Bronx Zoo and the traveling aquarium were sad reminders of how far Lionel had slipped since introducing the realistic 6464 series. Seen from another perspective, though, the animated, toylike cars of the late 1950s and early 1960s reveal great inventiveness and carry on the tradition inaugurated by the 3462 automatic refrigerated milk car or even the 3814 automatic merchandise car from the prewar period. Indeed, Lionel's engineers probably showed more creativity than ever as the market for O gauge trains declined after 1958. If children did not appreciate the colorful and innovative stock cars and boxcars it cataloged in the 1960s, today's enthusiasts prize them.

9¼-INCH BOXCARS

Lionel introduced the 9¼-inch plastic-body boxcar in 1946, and the styling and decorating schemes were state-of-the-art for the time. The body style would be a basic part of the product line through 1952, at which time it was permanently retired in favor of the more-to-scale 6464 series.

The 9¼-inch boxcar entries are dispersed in this chapter's numerical sequence. They are: X2454, X3454, X3464, 3474, X4454, and X6454. Note that Lionel introduced a 9¼-inch stock car (operating model 3656) in 1949 and a nonoperating version (model 6656) in 1950. In later years the nonoperating version was sometimes modified to action cars such as the 3370 and 3376.

8½-INCH BOXCARS

The nonopening double-door 8½-inch boxcars, introduced as 1004 in 1948, came in many road names, colors, and body types. The bodies are attached to metal frames by a screw at one end and a single slot at the other end that fits over a square-tab projecting from the frame. The chart shown here is applicable to the following stock numbers: 638-2361, 1004, 3357, 6004, 6014 (all models), 6034, 6044, and 6050 (all models).

6464 BOXCARS

The 6464-series boxcars are the most collected of any postwar category. The listings have been revised to emphasize details and make the descriptions consistent regarding painted versus unpainted and heat-stamped versus rubber-stamped. Less emphasis is placed on trucks, couplers, and doors. These boxcars followed the same truck and coupler modifications as other items in the product line (see Chapter 1).

The 6464 body-type chart on the next page includes terms and details cited in the following listings. Remember, these cars are generally 10⅝ inches; this length has *not* been cited in the entries.

Since collectors can change doors easily and often, in most instances doors have no bearing on the value or collectibility of a 6464-series boxcar. The Lionel factory used or adapted inventory to specific needs, such as installing black doors on a 6464-900 New York Central when the supply of jade green–painted doors was temporarily depleted. Only four regular-production doors warrant any premium; of these, only the following three add modest value to the car: single-block yellow doors with gray-painted stripe for the 6464-150 Missouri Pacific; multi-block unpainted solid red doors for the 6464-275 State of Maine; and single-block silver- and aqua blue–painted doors for the 6464-325 Baltimore & Ohio / Sentinel. The only doors that add substantial value are the yellow and green "split-door" models for the 6464-300 Rutland.

638-2361 STOKELY-VAN CAMP'S: Uncataloged, 1962–64; 8½" nonopening double-door boxcar with coin slot; unpainted red body with white and yellow heat-stamped lettering; can on left, and "PORK AND BEANS" and number on right; usually with fixed coupler arch-bar trucks. First issued with set 19142, Stokely-Van Camp's promotional outfit from 1962. (See *Greenberg's Guide to Lionel Trains, 1945–1969, Volume IV: Uncatalogued Sets.*) This car was the first use of the Type IIa body (see box).

Note: The odd, seven-digit number of this boxcar long perplexed collectors until H. Carter and M. Goldey

NONOPENING DOUBLE-DOOR 8½-INCH BOXCARS

Revised by H. Lovelock

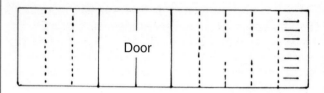

Type I

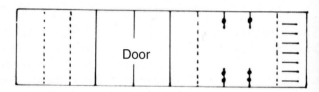

Type IIa.
Solid catwalk

Type IIb.
Two plug marks on catwalk
(plug holes open when used for 3357)

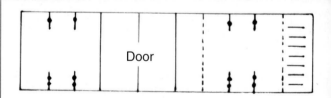

Type III.
All examples with two plug marks on catwalk
(plug holes open when used for 3357)

Note: *All* body types sometimes come with a coin slot in the catwalk. For appropriate information, see each entry.

OBSERVATIONS ON 6464 BOXCARS

by Dr. Charles Weber (revised by A. Stewart and P. Ambrose)
Illustrations by Bruce Kaiser

Body Types

To facilitate description of individual cars, each panel has been assigned a number and each row of rivets a letter. The chronology of the types is as follows:

Type I	1953–54
Type IIa	1954–55
Type IIb	1955–58
Type III	Late 1958–59
Type IV	1960–69.

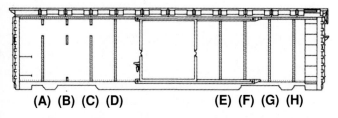

(A) (B) (C) (D)   (E) (F) (G) (H)

Type I. The car has three incomplete columns of rivets (A, B, and C). All three are broken near the top; column B is also broken near the bottom.

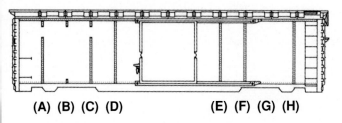

(A) (B) (C) (D)   (E) (F) (G) (H)

Type II. Introduced in 1954. Columns A, B, C, and G are incomplete. A, B, and C are broken near the top as in Type I. Column B has only three rivets at the top and two at the bottom. All the rivets in column G are deleted.

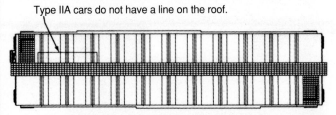

Type IIA cars do not have a line on the roof.

Two versions of Type II cars can be distinguished by the presence or absence of lines on the roof on the brake-wheel end, which corresponds to the area of the ice hatch on the 6352 operating ice car. Type IIa cars do not have lines on the roof, whereas a die modification was made in 1955 to accommodate the ice hatch on the 6352, hence the Type IIb mold with faint roof lines.

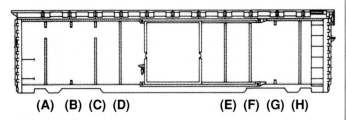

(A) (B) (C) (D)   (E) (F) (G) (H)

Type III. Introduced in the late 1958. Column A has a break near the top (four rivets down). B has only three rivets at top and two at the bottom. C has a break near the top. G has only two rivets at the top and two at the bottom. Type III has interior roof ribs.

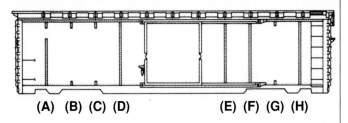

(A) (B) (C) (D)   (E) (F) (G) (H)

Type IV. Introduced in 1960. Same as Type III, but Column C has only three rivets at the top and two at the bottom. Type IV has roof ribs.

Changes in Doors

Pre-1955 production 6464 boxcars came with single-block (1953) doors. In 1955, a multiblock door was designed to accommodate the graphics on the new 6464-275 State of Maine boxcar. Lionel used these multiblock doors for the remainder of the series through 1969, but single-block doors surfaced as late as 1957 as the company continued to deplete existing inventory. Doors are easily and often changed; with few exceptions, no additional value should be placed on a door type.

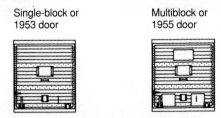

Single-block or 1953 door   Multiblock or 1955 door

Identification of doors helps in dating boxcars. For example, a 6464-25 Great Northern has only single-block doors and a 6464-825 Alaska has only multiblock doors. Items such as the 6464-300 Rutland from 1955–57 can surface with either type of door.

	Gd	**VG**	**Ex**	**LN**

discovered that 638-2361 was Stokely-Van Camp's corporate office telephone number (the exchange MElrose 8 translates numerically to 638).

	Gd	VG	Ex	LN
(A) Type IIa red body.	25	30	50	70
(B) Type IIb red body.	25	30	50	70
(C) Type III light red body.	25	35	50	70

X1004 BABY RUTH: 1948–52. 8½" nonopening double-door Type I boxcar; unpainted orange body with blue heat-stamped lettering; PRR logo and technical data on left; Scout trucks with Scout couplers.

	Gd	VG	Ex	LN
(A) Earlier production; "Baby Ruth" in outlined lettering.	5	8	12	16
(B) 1950–52; "Baby Ruth" in solid lettering.	5	8	12	16

X2454 BABY RUTH: 1946–47. 9¼" boxcar; light orange–painted body with black heat-stamped lettering; brown-painted metal doors; PRR logo and technical data on right; brake wheel; frame with steps at the four corners; staple-end trucks with coil couplers.

	Gd	VG	Ex	LN
	7	15	22	30

X2454 PENNSYLVANIA: 1946. 9¼" boxcar; light orange–painted body with black heat-stamped lettering car also numbered "65400"; PRR logo and technical data on right; brake wheel; frame with steps at the four corners; staple-end trucks with coil couplers.

	Gd	VG	Ex	LN
(A) Light orange–painted metal doors.	70	110	180	225
(B) Brown-painted metal doors.	60	100	160	200

X2458 PENNSYLVANIA: 1946–48. 9¼" double-door automobile car (prewar design); brown-painted stamped steel body with die-cast ends and white heat-stamped lettering; also numbered "61100"; PRR logo and most technical data on left; metal doors painted to match body; separate black metal ladder attached to each side; brake wheel; most typically on frame with steps at the four corners; bottom base assembly that included air reservoir, valves, and brake cylinder; staple-end trucks with coil couplers.

	Gd	VG	Ex	LN
(A) With rivet below "8" in "X2458".	15	25	50	75

(B) Without rivet below "8" in "X2458". Sometime around 1947 a single rivet was removed from the tooling because it interfered with the alignment of the heat-stamp plate for the number.

	Gd	VG	Ex	LN
	15	25	50	75

Top: 638-2361 (A) Stokely-Van Camp's. Middle: X1004 (A) Baby Ruth and X1004 (B) Baby Ruth. Bottom: 3357 (A) **hydraulic platform maintenance car and 3370 (A) Wells Fargo. J Algozzini Collection.**

A selection of 9¼-inch boxcars manufactured in 1946 and 1947. Top: X2454 (A) Pennsylvania (orange door) and X2454 (B) Pennsylvania (brown door). Middle: *X2454 Baby Ruth and X4454 Baby Ruth with Electronic Control decal. Bottom: 3454 (C) automatic merchandise car. R. Swanson Collection.*

X2458 (A) Pennsylvania and X2758 Pennsylvania. E. Dougherty Collection.

	Gd	VG	Ex	LN

X2758 PENNSYLVANIA: 1945–46. Same as X2458, except for number. Bodies most probably painted and assembled before the war but fitted with earliest version of postwar trucks and couplers; ultimately depleted as 1946 set components. **15 25 50 75**

3356 SANTA FE: 1956–60, 1964–66. Operating horse car from 3356 Operating Horse Car and Corral Set; unpainted green body and sliding doors each side with yellow heat-stamped lettering; car also lettered "RAILWAY EXPRESS / AGENCY INC"; operating doors at the far ends (one side only) lower or raise when electrical contact is made or broken; horses move back and forth from car to corral by vibrator action; brake wheel.

Note: A complete set includes the necessary operating hardware, a horse corral, and a set of nine black horses. The corral has two parts: unpainted white corral and unpainted brown and green-painted ramp assembly. Because of its fragility, the corral is valued approximately 50 percent more than the most common version of the car. Values are for car only.

(A) 1956–60. "BLT 5-56 / BY LIONEL" in lower right of side; brake wheel on right when viewed from operating door side; bar-end trucks. Most common version.

40 60 85 100

(B) Same as (A), except brake wheel on left when viewed from operating door side.

40 65 90 110

(C) 1964–66. Without any built date information; brake wheel on left when viewed from operating door side; AAR trucks with operating couplers.

40 65 90 110

Top: 3356 (A) Santa Fe operating horse car and 3366 operating circus car. Second: 6352 (A) Pacific Fruit Express and 6356 (C) N Y C stock car. Third: 6376 Lionel Lines circus car and 6434 poultry dispatch. Bottom: 6572 (B) Railway Express Agency refrigerator and 6556 Katy M-K-T stock car. L. Nuzzaci Collection.

	Gd	VG	Ex	LN

3357 HYDRAULIC PLATFORM MAINTENANCE CAR: 1962–64. 8½" nonopening double-door operating boxcar; unpainted blue body with white heat-stamped lettering; commonly referred to as "cop and hobo car"; AAR trucks; 1962 and mid-1963 production came with two operating couplers; later production typically had with one fixed and one operating coupler.

Note: A complete example requires original rubberized cop and hobo, gray superstructure for car, and separate bridge assembly. Most often the operating components were packaged in a separate box numbered "3357-23" or "3357-27". The manufacture of this car required a modification to the Scout boxcar tooling, hence the introduction of the Type IIb body.

	Gd	VG	Ex	LN
(A) Type IIb body.	20	40	65	90
(B) Type III body.	20	40	65	90

3366 CIRCUS CAR: 1959–61. Operating circus car from 3366 Operating Circus Car and Corral Set; unpainted white body and sliding doors each side with red-painted roof walk and red heat-stamped lettering; operating doors at the far ends (one side only) lower or raise when electrical contact is made or broken; horses move back and forth from car to corral by vibrator action; brake wheel on left when viewed from operating door side; bar-end trucks.

Note: Unpainted white plastic has a tendency to turn cream-colored; cars with white bodies and cream doors (or vice versa) are common. Substantial premium for pure white example. A complete set includes the necessary operating hardware, a horse corral, and a set of nine white horses. The corral (same design as 3356) has two parts: unpainted white corral and unpainted gray and red-painted ramp assembly.

	Gd	VG	Ex	LN
(A) Car and corral.	125	150	250	300
(B) Car only.	50	75	100	150

3370 WELLS FARGO: 1961–64. Modified 9¼" (short) stock car; unpainted green body with yellow heat-stamped lettering; also lettered Western & Atlantic; nonopening doors; sheriff and outlaw alternately bob up and down as car moves along track. The movement is caused by a unique assembly with a cam on one axle, an actuator lever and pawl, and a ratchet wheel.

(A) AAR trucks with operating couplers.

	Gd	VG	Ex	LN
	18	35	58	80

(B) Arch-bar trucks with operating couplers as a set component for General outfits.

	Gd	VG	Ex	LN
	18	35	58	80

	Gd	VG	Ex	LN

3376 BRONX ZOO: 1960–66, 1969. Modified 9¼" (short) stock car; unpainted body with heat-stamped lettering; nonopening doors; counterweighted yellow giraffe head protruding through roof bobs down as car approaches a "tell-tale signal" (as described in the Lionel Service Manual); typically AAR trucks with operating couplers into 1963, then usually one fixed and one operating coupler for the remainder of production.

Note: Giraffe produced with and without spots and is interchangeable with other giraffe cars. Price for car only; for cam and telltale pole, add $20 to $25 to values.

(A) Blue body with white lettering.

	20	30	55	70

(B) Green body with yellow lettering; designated "3376-160".

	35	75	110	135

(C) Scarce 1969 production of blue body with yellow lettering.

	110	210	310	475

3386 BRONX ZOO: Uncataloged, 1960; modified 9¼" (short) stock car; unpainted blue body with white heat-stamped lettering; same as 3376, except with fixed coupler arch-bar trucks.

	25	45	65	90

	Gd	VG	Ex	LN

3424 WABASH: 1956–58. Unique operating 6464 Type IIb brakeman car; unpainted blue body with unpainted white multiblock doors; white heat-stamped lettering; Wabash flag logo on right; bracket assembly that secures rubberized brakeman projects through roof; brake wheel; bar-end trucks.

Note: A complete car comes with two pole-support assemblies with track clips and two telltale poles. Generally, a car with a white brakeman has a white pickup shoe, and a car with a blue brakeman has a blue shoe.

(A) Dark blue body (usually with white brakeman).

	30	50	80	110

(B) Medium blue body.

	30	50	80	110

3428 UNITED STATES MAIL: 1959–60. 6464-type operating boxcar; red- (including roof and ends), white- and blue-painted body with black heat-stamped lettering on white or white heat-stamped lettering on red and blue; multiblock red-, white-, and blue-painted doors to match body; car actually numbered "3428" on left; "RAILWAY / POST OFFICE" on right; brake wheel; operating plunger mechanism with unique rubberized mailman and mailbag; AAR trucks.

Top: Bronx Zoo examples 3376 (C) and 3376 (B). Be aware that white was the most common color for lettering on blue bodies; the example at left is 1969 production with yellow lettering. Second: 3386 Bronx Zoo and 6014 (B) Airex. Third: X6004 Baby Ruth (the example shown has improper bar-end trucks; typical production came with Scout trucks with magnetic couplers) and X6014 (B) Baby Ruth. Bottom: X6014 (C) Baby Ruth and 6014 (B) Bosco. E. Dougherty Collection.

	Gd	VG	Ex	LN

Note: The mailbag was magnetically attached to the mailman; the force of the activated plunger mechanism causes the mailbag to become dislodged and "tossed" through the open side door. The mailman and mailbag came in blue or gray; they were usually paired in a mixed color combination.

(A) Type IIb body (usually gray mold).

| | 30 | 75 | 105 | 130 |

(B) Type III body (usually gray mold).

| | 30 | 75 | 105 | 130 |

3434 POULTRY DISPATCH: 1959–60, 1964–66. 11¼" operating three-level stock car (commonly referred to as "chicken sweeper car"); brown-painted body with white heat-stamped lettering; unpainted gray sliding door with black heat-stamped lettering; brake wheel; operating plunger mechanism with rubberized man with broom; four-level figure plates (see Note below) with chickens; lighted; 1959–60 production with bar-end trucks, 1964–66 production with AAR trucks and operating couplers.

Note: The car body (same as 6434) is divided into three levels, but the figure plates have four levels. Earliest production came with a blue man with painted features; it was soon replaced by an unpainted gray man.

(A) 1959–60; slightly darker brown body.

| | 50 | 75 | 100 | 150 |

(B) 1964–66; slightly lighter brown body.

| | 50 | 75 | 100 | 150 |

3435 TRAVELING AQUARIUM: 1959–62. Unique operating boxcar; green-painted body with lettering described below; large "L" and clear wavelike windows integral to body mold; inside usually painted silver or black to control light reflection; brake wheel; illusion of swimming fish achieved through movement of continuous loop of decorated celluloid powered by a vibrator motor; lighted; on-off lever projects downward through frame; AAR trucks with operating couplers.

(A) Gold circle around large "L"; gold heat-stamped lettering with "TANK No. 1" and "TANK No. 2" designation.

| | 400 | 600 | 1000 | 1400 |

(B) Same as (A), except without gold circle around large "L".

| | 280 | 540 | 800 | 1100 |

(C) Gold heat-stamped lettering, but without gold circle around large "L" and without tank designations.

| | 150 | 240 | 300 | 450 |

(D) Most common version with yellow rubber-stamped lettering; no circle around "L" and without tank designations.

| | 100 | 175 | 250 | 300 |

Top: Two different versions of the 3424 Wabash boxcar with operating brakeman. The left car (B) has a medium blue body with white molded man. The car on the right (A) has a dark blue body with blue molded man. Second: 3428 (A) United States Mail and 3434 (B) poultry dispatch. Third: 3434 (A) poultry dispatch and 3484 Pennsylvania operating boxcar. Bottom: 3484-25 (B) A T & S F operating boxcar and 3494-1 (B) Pacemaker operating boxcar. L. Nuzzaci Collection.

Two versions of the 3435 traveling aquarium. The most common variation (D) is at right. Variation (B) on the left has gold heat-stamped lettering and "TANK No. 1" and "TANK No. 2" designation. *J. Algozzini Collection.*

	Gd	VG	Ex	LN

3454 AUTOMATIC MERCHANDISE CAR: 1946–47. 9¼" operating boxcar; most typically silver-painted body and metal doors with blue heat-stamped lettering; car actually numbered "3454" on left and "X3454" on right; PRR logo and technical data on right; brake wheel; frame with steps at the four corners; staple-end trucks with coil couplers.

Note: Car comes with six hard-plastic cubes marked "BABY RUTH" that resemble merchandise containers. Cubes are most common in brown, but also came in red and black; they are loaded into the car through a hinged roof hatch and tossed from a side door.

(A) Earliest 1946 production; red heat-stamped lettering; hinge pin for roof hatch *not* visible; extremely rare variation. **NRS**

(B) Same as (A), except common blue lettering.

	65	100	130	175

(C) 1947; common blue lettering; hinge pin for roof hatch visible at end of car body.

	65	100	130	175

3462 AUTOMATIC REFRIGERATED MILK CAR: 1947–48. 9¼" (short) operating milk car; white-painted body and roof hatch with black heat-stamped lettering; also numbered "RT3462" on right; circled-L Lionel logo; brake wheel; aluminum doors; frame with steps at the four corners attached to body by two large spring clips; unloading mechanism with rubberized man that delivers cans to platform through side doors; staple-end trucks with coil couplers.

Note: The 1947 model came with a brass-base unloading mechanism attached to the frame with only three flexible tabs (later models had four). Values listed include car, the necessary operating hardware, magnetic milk cans, and a basic white and green unloading platform. The 1947 production came with seven milk cans; later models had six.

(A) Early 1947; glossy cream body; the frame structure of the unloading platform is a matching glossy cream.

	35	55	80	105
(B) Typical cream body.	20	40	55	65
(C) White body.	20	40	55	70

X3464 A.T. & S.F.: 1949–52. 9¼" operating boxcar; orange-painted body with black heat-stamped lettering; car also numbered "63132"; Santa Fe logo on left and technical data on right; brake wheel; operating plunger mechanism with rubberized man; except for 1949 production, frame without steps; except for some 1952 production, staple-end trucks with magnetic couplers.

(A) 1949; brown-painted metal doors; frame with steps at the four corners.

	10	15	25	35

(B) 1950–51; chemically blackened metal doors.

	10	15	25	35

(C) 1952; black plastic doors; often with bar-end trucks.

	10	15	25	35

X3464 N Y C: 1949–52. 9¼" operating boxcar; tan-painted body with white heat-stamped lettering; car also numbered "159000"; New York Central System logo and technical data on right; brake wheel; operating plunger mechanism with rubberized man; except for 1949 production, frame without steps; except for some 1952 production, staple-end trucks with magnetic couplers.

(A) 1949–51; chemically blackened metal doors.

	10	15	25	35

(B) 1952; black plastic doors; often with bar-end trucks.

	10	15	25	35

3472 AUTOMATIC REFRIGERATED MILK CAR: 1949–53. 9¼" (short) operating milk car; white body and roof hatch with black heat-stamped lettering; also numbered "RT3472" on right; circled-L Lionel logo; brake wheel; frame with steps at the four corners attached to body by two large spring clips; unloading mechanism with rubberized man that delivers cans to platform through side doors; staple-end trucks with magnetic couplers into 1951, then bar-end trucks for balance of production.

Note: There are major mechanical and structural differences between the 1949 model and other examples. Values listed include car, the necessary operating hardware, six magnetic milk cans, and a basic white and green unloading platform.

(A) Early 1949; cream-painted body, aluminum doors, short roof hatch.

	20	35	50	70

(B) Later 1949; same as (A), except unpainted white body.

	20	35	50	70

(C) Most common production; unpainted cream body, plastic door and frame assembly, long roof hatch.

	15	30	45	60

A comparison of a 1946 merchandise car without a visible roof hatch pin (left) and a 1947 car with a visible roof hatch pin (right).

(D) Same as (C), except white body. Note that door and frame assembly and roof hatch often do not match body.

	Gd	VG	Ex	LN
	15	30	45	60

3474 WESTERN PACIFIC: 1952–53. 9¼" operating boxcar; silver-painted body with silver- and orange-painted plastic doors and black heat-stamped lettering; large two-part Western Pacific yellow feather decal and small "Rides Like a / Feather" decal; brake wheel; operating plunger mechanism with rubberized man; frame without steps; bar-end trucks.

	15	40	55	80

3482 AUTOMATIC REFRIGERATED MILK CAR: 1954–55. 9¼" (short) operating milk car; unpainted white body, roof hatch, and door and frame assembly with black heat-stamped lettering; circled-L Lionel logo; brake wheel; frame with steps at the four corners attached to body by slot and tab at one end and screw at other; new pneumatic plunger unloading mechanism with rubberized man that delivers cans to platform through side doors; bar-end trucks.

Note: Values listed include car, the necessary operating hardware, six magnetic milk cans, and a basic white and green unloading platform.

(A) Early 1954; usual large "3482" on left; "RT3472" on right.

	60	100	120	180

(B) Common example with "RT3482" on right.

	20	40	55	80

3484 PENNSYLVANIA: 1953. 6464-type Type I operating boxcar; Tuscan-painted body with white heat-stamped lettering; Tuscan-painted single-block doors; PRR logo on right; brake wheel; operating plunger

mechanism with rubberized man; bar-end trucks.

	15	35	50	80

3484-25 A T & S F: 1954, 1956. 6464-type operating boxcar; orange-painted body most typically with white lettering; orange-painted doors; car actually numbered "348425" on left and "X3484" on right; Santa Fe logo on left; brake wheel; operating plunger mechanism with rubberized man; bar-end trucks.

(A) Type I body with *black* heat-stamped lettering; single-block doors; rare.

	—	750	1000	1400

(B) Same as (A), except with common white heat-stamped lettering.

	30	60	100	130

(C) Type I body with white rubber-stamped lettering; single-block doors.

	30	60	100	130

(D) Same as (C), except with distinctly different glossy orange body.

	30	60	100	130

(E) Type IIa body with white heat-stamped lettering; either single or multiblock doors.

	30	60	100	130

(F) Same as (E), except with white rubber-stamped lettering.

	30	60	100	130

(G) Type IIb body with white heat-stamped lettering; multiblock doors.

	60	120	200	250

3494-1 PACEMAKER: 1955. 6464-type Type IIa operating boxcar; red and gray body with white rubber-stamped lettering; red (usually unpainted) single-block doors; car actually numbered "34941"; "NYC" on left and New York Central System logo (with a cedilla on second "S" of System) on right; brake wheel; operating plunger mechanism with rubberized man; bar-end trucks.

Note: The cedilla mark is most probably nothing more than a flaw in the rubber stamp.

(A) Gray- and red-painted body (usually white body mold).

	40	75	105	140

(B) Unpainted red body with gray-painted roof, ends, and lower half of side.

	40	75	105	140

3494-150 MISSOURI PACIFIC LINES: 1956. 6464-type Type IIb operating boxcar; unpainted gray body and blue-painted upper and lower side bands with white rubber-stamped lettering on blue and black rubber-stamped lettering on gray; unpainted yellow multiblock doors; car actually numbered "3494150" on right; stylized "Eagle", Missouri Pacific Lines seal and "NEW 3 54" on left, and "XME" on lower right; brake wheel; operating plunger mechanism with rubberized man; bar-end trucks.

Note: The left side "E" in "Eagle" on the 3494-150 is ⅝" high. See 6464-150 for comparison.

	55	90	120	170

3494-275 STATE OF MAINE: 1956–58. 6464-type Type IIb operating boxcar; unpainted royal blue body with white-painted center band and red-painted lower band; white heat-stamped lettering on royal blue and red, and black rubber-stamped lettering on white; unpainted royal multiblock door with red- and white-painted stripes to

CHRONOLOGY OF VARIATIONS—3462/3472/3482 MILK CAR

Model year			1947	1948	1949	1950	1951	1952–1953	1954	1955
Car number			3462		3472				3482	
Body	Color		Gloss white	Flat white or cream paint	White or eggshell plastic				White plastic	
	Doors		Aluminum		White or eggshell plastic				White plastic, notched opening	
	Hatch		Small, painted cream			Large, white or eggshell plastic			Large, white plastic	
	Miscellaneous		"RT 3462"		"RT 3472"					"RT 3482"
Mechanism	Type		1947, Type 1	1948, Type 2		1950, Type 3			1954, Type 4	
	Miscellaneous		Has slide	Swing plate has triangular hole in arm		L-shaped hole in arm, boss for can sweep			Large plunger, removable coil, large solenoid	
	Return		Hairpin spring			Small coil spring			Large coil spring	
	Material		Brass base	Nickel-plated steel or cadmium-plated steel						
Frame	Type		3462 side dents		3464 operating holes		3472 and 6472		3482 ribbed with cutouts	
	Miscellaneous		Has tab slots	No slots	Side dents	Door frame cutouts			Tab and screw mount	
Trucks	Design		Staple-end						Bar-end	
	Coupler		Coil		Magnetic, no tabs					
Misc.	Major variants		1947, 2 var.	1948	1949	1950–53			1954–55	
	Catalog price		$8.95	$9.95			$11.50	$10.50		

Operating boxcars manufactured from 1949 to 1953.
Top: X3464 (A) A.T. & S.F. with brown door and
X3464 (B) A.T. & S.F. with black door. Bottom:

X3464 (A) New York Central and 3474 Western
Pacific. R. Swanson Collection.

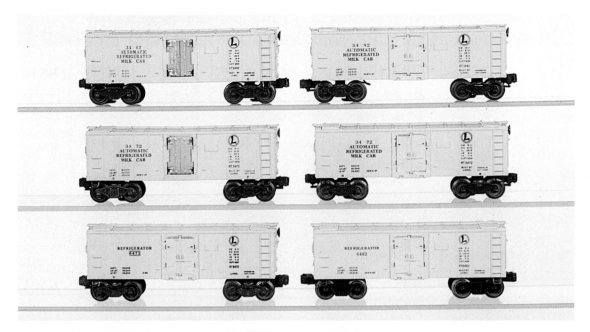

Top: Automatic refrigerated milk cars 3462 (B) and 3482 (B). Middle: Automatic refrigerated milk cars 3472 (A) and 3472 (C). Bottom: 6472 (A) refrigerator and 6482 refrigerator. These examples were the nonoperating versions of the above models. J. Algozzini Collection.

	Gd	VG	Ex	LN

match body (letters "OF" and "D" and "U" are heat-stamped on door sign boards); Bangor & Aroostook logo on right; brake wheel; operating plunger mechanism with rubberized man; bar-end trucks.

Note: See 6464-275 for other details.

(A) Earliest production; *only* "B.A.R." on left; "3494275" not present. **80 110 200 250**

(B) Most common example; "B.A.R. / 3494275" on left. **55 90 130 165**

3494-550 MONON: 1957–58. 6464 Type IIb operating boxcar; unpainted maroon body with white-painted upper band and white heat-stamped lettering on maroon and maroon heat-stamped "THE HOOSIER LINE" on white; unpainted maroon multiblock doors with white-painted upper stripe; car actually numbered "3494550"; brake wheel; operating plunger mechanism with rubberized man; bar-end trucks.

Note: Numerous examples show the progressive "fading" of "BLT 6-57 / BY LIONEL" as the heat-stamp tooling deteriorated. **125 225 400 550**

3494-625 SOO LINE: 1957–58. 6464 Type IIb operating boxcar; Tuscan-painted body with white heat-stamped lettering; Tuscan-painted multiblock doors; car actually numbered "3494625"; brake wheel; operating plunger mechanism with rubberized man; bar-end trucks.

(A) Tuscan-brown body. **115 210 400 525**

(B) Tuscan-red body. **115 210 400 525**

3530 ELECTRO MOBILE POWER: 1956–58. Operating GM Generator boxcar; unpainted blue body with white-painted stripe and blue and white heat-stamped lettering; sliding double doors; brake wheel; orange generator inside car and fuel tank (black or blue) on underframe; bar-end trucks.

Note: Each side of the car is molded differently. Opening a specific door completes the electrical circuit for the accompanying searchlight assembly through the simulated-wood pole and base; the pole has two wire leads that clip into the car roof and two other wire leads that run to the searchlight. There are two colors of pole-base units, blue or black. Cars usually come with a blue fuel tank and blue pole-base or a black fuel tank and black pole-base.

(A) White stripe extends through ladder detail on right; blue fuel tank and blue pole-base unit. **60 100 135 160**

(B) Same as (A), except black fuel tank and black pole-base unit. **70 110 150 175**

(C) White stripe ends at ladder detail on right; blue fuel tank and blue pole-base unit. **70 110 150 175**

(D) Same as (C), except black fuel tank and black pole-base unit. **60 100 135 160**

3619 HELICOPTER RECONNAISSANCE CAR: 1962–64. Operating military boxcar; unpainted yellow body with red and black heat-stamped lettering; two-part unpainted black roof; brake wheel; plunger-operated launch mechanism with red HO scale helicopter; AAR trucks usually with operating couplers.

Note: Each side of the car is molded differently.

(A) Light yellow body. **30 60 90 130**

	Gd	VG	Ex	LN
(B) Dark yellow body.	40	100	150	200

3656 LIONEL LINES: 1949–55. 9¼" (short) operating stock car from 3656 Operating Stockyard with Cattle Set; orange-painted body with heat-stamped lettering; circled-L Lionel logo; operating doors at the far ends (one side only) lower or raise when electrical contact is made or broken; fixed door integral to body mold on operating side and sliding door on other side; cattle move back and forth from car to corral by vibrator action; brake wheel; 1949 production with steps at the four corners; staple-end trucks with magnetic couplers into 1951, then bar-end trucks for balance of production.

Note: 1949 through mid-1950 versions of the cattle car had a die-cast sliding door, while later sliding doors were usually plastic. Values listed include car with a common version of corral, the necessary operating hardware, and nine black cattle. Many corral variations exist, however they can be categorized into two basic types: the 1949 model with fixed platform assembly and later versions with lift-out assembly. The very earliest 1949 production came with a very scarce corral that had a yellow-painted platform assembly and a small chain across the ramp opening.

(A) Early 1949; *black*-lettered car, metal sliding door; adhesive Armour emblem. **70 140 200 260**

(B) Typical 1949; white-lettered car, metal sliding door; adhesive Armour emblem.

35 50 80 110

(C) White-lettered car, metal sliding door.

25 50 75 100

(D) White-lettered car, plastic sliding door; later production typically had a much lighter coat of paint than earlier models.

25 50 75 100

3662 AUTOMATIC REFRIGERATED MILK CAR: 1955–60, 1964–66. Operating milk car in 1:48 scale; most typically unpainted white body with unpainted brown roof, roof hatch, ends, and doors; black heat-stamped lettering; circled-L Lionel logo; brake wheel; operating plunger mechanism with rubberized man that delivers cans to platform through side doors.

Note: The 3662 utilized a two-part molded body; the roof and ends were molded in one piece, and the sides were molded in another. Shades vary on the roof, with ends from Tuscan red to chocolate brown. Values listed include car, the necessary operating hardware, seven nonmagnetic milk cars, and a basic green and white unloading platform.

(A) White-painted body with "NEW 4-55"; bar-end trucks. **30 50 70 100**

(B) Typical unpainted white body with "NEW 4-55"; bar-end trucks into 1959, then AAR trucks with operating couplers. **30 50 70 100**

(C) 1964–66; typical unpainted white body but *without* "NEW 4-55"; AAR trucks with operating couplers.

30 50 70 100

3665 MINUTEMAN: 1961–64. Operating military boxcar; unpainted white body with red and blue heat-stamped lettering; two-part unpainted blue roof; brake wheel; plunger-operated launch mechanism with two-part rocket; AAR trucks usually with operating couplers.

Note: All rocket tips are blue; however, each rocket section comes in red or white, and parts are interchangeable. Also, each side of the car is molded differently.

(A) Common dark blue roof.

50 80 110 140

(B) Scarce light blue roof. **75 110 170 250**

(C) Very scarce body variation (3619 mold); a hole on one side above the "T" in "MINUTEMAN"; usually with light blue roof. **90 130 200 300**

3666 MINUTEMAN: Uncataloged, 1964. Operating military boxcar; unpainted white body with red and blue heat-stamped lettering; two-part unpainted light blue roof; brake wheel; plunger-operated cannon firing mechanism with olive cannon and four silver-painted 1¾" wood shells; AAR trucks typically with one fixed and one operating coupler.

Note: Each side of car is molded differently. The 3666 used the 3619 body mold; therefore, it came with a hole on one side above the "T" in "MINUTEMAN". Exclusive component of set 9820, an uncataloged outfit sold through Sears in 1964. (See *Greenberg's Guide to Lionel Trains, 1945–1969, Volume IV: Uncatalogued Sets.*)

170 350 500 750

3672 CORN PRODUCTS CO. –BOSCO: 1959–60. Operating milk car in 1:48 scale; yellow body with unpainted brown roof, roof hatch, ends, and doors; brown heat-stamped lettering; Bosco decal; brake wheel; operating plunger mechanism with rubberized man that delivers Bosco cans to platform through side doors; most typically with bar-end trucks.

Note: The 3672 (like 3662) utilized a two-part molded body; the roof and ends were molded in one piece, and the sides were molded in another. Values listed include car, the necessary operating hardware, seven nonmagnetic Bosco cans, and a unique yellow- and brown-painted unloading platform. Bosco cans are yellow and brown, with red rubber-stamped "BOSCO".

(A) Yellow-painted body.

120 265 430 600

(B) Unpainted yellow body.

110 250 425 575

3854 AUTOMATIC MERCHANDISE CAR: 1946–47. Operating boxcar (prewar design) in 1:48 scale; Tuscan-painted metal body with white heat-stamped lettering; chemically blackened metal doors; car actually numbered "3854" on left and "X3854" on right; PRR logo and technical data on right; brake wheel; frame with steps at the four corners; staple-end trucks with coil couplers.

Note: Car comes with six (usually brown) hard plastic cubes marked "BABY RUTH" that resemble

Top: 3494-150 Missouri Pacific operating boxcar and 3494-275 (B) State of Maine operating boxcar. Second: 3494-550 Monon operating boxcar and 3494-625 (A) Soo Line operating boxcar. Third: 3435 (D) traveling aquarium and 6445 Fort Knox gold reserve. Bottom: 3530 (D) Electro Mobile Power and 6530 firefighting instruction car. L. Nuzzaci Collection

3494-275 (A) State of Maine operating boxcar.

	Gd	VG	Ex	LN

merchandise containers; cubes are loaded into the car through a Tuscan-painted metal roof hatch tabbed into the body and tossed from a side door. Because of the length of the car, each truck was equipped with two sliding shoes (necessary to ensure contact with the RCS remote track).

	Gd	VG	Ex	LN
	200	400	600	800

X4454 BABY RUTH: 1946–49. 9¼" Electronic Control boxcar; light orange–painted body with black heat-stamped lettering; PRR logo and technical data on right; brake wheel; brown Electronic Control decal; frame with steps at the four corners and Electronic Control receiver on topside; staple-end trucks with coil couplers.

Top: 3665(A) Minuteman with rocket and 3619 (A) helicopter reconnaissance car. Bottom: 3672 (A) Bosco and 3662 (B) automatic refrigerated milk car.

The 3854 automatic merchandise car (left) was a prewar design in 1:48 scale. To show perspective, it has been coupled to X6454 (B) Southern Pacific from the 9¼-inch series.

	Gd	VG	Ex	LN
(A) 1946–early 1947 production; brown-painted metal doors.	80	140	200	275

(B) Late 1947–49; chemically blackened metal doors. Actual production most probably terminated by mid-1947.

	Gd	VG	Ex	LN
	60	115	175	210

X6004 BABY RUTH: 1950. 8½" nonopening double-door Type I boxcar; unpainted orange body with blue heat-stamped lettering; "Baby Ruth" in outlined lettering; PRR logo and technical data on left; Scout trucks with magnetic couplers.

	Gd	VG	Ex	LN
	4	6	8	12

6014 AIREX: Uncataloged, 1959. 8½" nonopening double-door Type I boxcar; unpainted red body with white and yellow heat-stamped lettering; Airex logo on right; AAR trucks with operating couplers; Lionel Service Manual designation 6014-100.

Note: Except for the number, the decorating format is the same as 6044 Airex.

	Gd	VG	Ex	LN
(A) Serif "1" in "6014"	.25	45	65	85
(B) Sans-serif "1" in "6014".	25	45	65	85

X6014 BABY RUTH: 1951–56. 8½" nonopening double-door Type I boxcar; unpainted body with heat-stamped lettering; "Baby Ruth" in solid lettering; PRR logo and technical data on left; staple-end trucks into 1952, then bar-end trucks for remainder of production.

	Gd	VG	Ex	LN
(A) Flat white body with black lettering.	5	7	9	11
(B) Glossy white body with black lettering.	5	7	9	11
(C) Red body with white lettering.	6	8	10	12

6014 BOSCO: 1958. 8½" nonopening double-door Type I boxcar; unpainted body with heat-stamped lettering PRR logo and technical data on left; AAR trucks with operating couplers.

Top: 6014 (A) and 6014 (C) Bosco cars. Second: 6014
Chun King and 6014 (K) Frisco. Third: 6014 (B)
Frisco (the example shown has bar-end trucks, which
was not the norm) and 6014 (H) Frisco. Note the

different shades of white; mid-1960s production was
distinctly whiter than 1957 production. Bottom: 6014
(B) Wix Filters and 6024 Nabisco Shredded Wheat. E.
Dougherty Collection.

6024 RCA Whirlpool and X6034 (A) Baby Ruth. E. Dougherty Collection.

Note: The 6014 Bosco shared the same by color suffix designation as 1957 production of 6014 Frisco.

(A) Red body with white lettering; Lionel Service Manual designation 6014-1.

5	8	11	14

(B) White body with black lettering; Lionel Service Manual designation 6014-60.

35	50	70	90

(C) Orange body with black lettering; Lionel Service Manual designation 6014-85.

5	8	11	14

6014 CHUN KING: Uncataloged, 1956. 8½" nonopening double-door Type I boxcar; unpainted red body with white rubber-stamped lettering; PRR logo and technical data on left; bar-end trucks. Exclusive component of set X-150, a promotional outfit marketed in 1956. (See

Greenberg's Guide to Lionel Trains, 1945–1969, Volume IV: Uncatalogued Sets.)

60	105	130	200

6014 FRISCO: 1957, 1963–69. 8½" nonopening double-door boxcar; unpainted body with heat-stamped lettering; AAR trucks that followed the normal sequence of changes found in the product line.

Note: Due to the length of time that the Frisco model was cataloged, it has the most variations of any 8½" boxcar. 1957 production had suffixes indicating color in the same way as the 6014 Bosco.

1957 Production:

(A) Type I red body with white lettering; Lionel Service Manual designation 6014-1.

4	6	8	10

	Gd	VG	Ex	LN

(B) Type I flat white body with black lettering; Lionel Service Manual designation 6014-60.

	4	6	8	10

(C) Type I orange body with dark blue lettering; Lionel Service Manual designation 6104-85.

	20	30	40	50

1963–69 Production:

All white examples have black lettering. Prior to 1969 they are designated as 6014-325 or 6014-335; however, a 6014-325 component box does *not* exist.

(D) Type I white body that is distinctly whiter than 1957 production.

	4	6	8	10

(E) Type I white body with coin slot.

	25	40	50	80

(F) Type IIa white body with coin slot.

	25	40	50	80

(G) Type IIb white body.

	4	6	8	10

(H) Type III white body.

	4	6	8	10

(I) Type III white body with coin slot.

	25	40	50	80

(J) 1969 production cataloged as 6014-410; Type III distinctly glossy white body.

	4	6	8	10

(K) 1969 production cataloged as 6014-85; Type III orange body with medium blue lettering.

	20	30	40	50

6014 WIX FILTERS: Uncataloged, 1959. 8½" nonopening double-door Type I boxcar; unpainted white body with red heat-stamped lettering; Wix logo on right; AAR trucks with operating couplers; Lionel Service Manual designation 6014-150. Exclusive component of set DX 837, an uncataloged outfit marketed in 1959. (See *Greenberg's Guide to Lionel Trains, 1945–1969, Volume IV: Uncatalogued Sets.*)

(A) Pure white body.

	85	125	170	280

(B) Cream body.

	80	120	160	260

6024 RCA WHIRLPOOL: Uncataloged, 1957–58. 8½" nonopening double-door Type I boxcar; unpainted red body with white heat-stamped lettering; PRR logo and technical data on left and RCA logo on right; AAR trucks with operating couplers; Lionel Service Manual designation 6024-60. Exclusive component of set X-589, an uncataloged outfit marketed in 1957. (See *Greenberg's Guide to Lionel Trains, 1945–1969, Volume IV: Uncatalogued Sets.*)

	30	50	70	90

6024 SHREDDED WHEAT: 1957. 8½" nonopening double-door Type I boxcar; unpainted orange body with black heat-stamped lettering; PRR logo and technical data on left and Nabisco logo on right; usually bar-end trucks but also AAR trucks with operating couplers.

	12	20	28	36

X6034 BABY RUTH: 1953–54. 8½" nonopening double-door Type I boxcar; unpainted orange body with blue heat-stamped lettering; "Baby Ruth" in solid lettering;

PRR logo and technical data on left; Scout trucks with magnetic couplers.

(A) As described above.

	5	9	14	20

(B) Very dark blue (almost black) lettering.

	5	9	14	20

6044 AIREX: Uncataloged, 1959–61. 8½" nonopening double-door Type I boxcar; unpainted blue body (shades vary dramatically) with white and yellow heat-stamped lettering; Airex logo on right; fixed coupler arch-bar trucks.

Note: Except for the number, the decorating format is the same as 6014 Airex.

(A) Distinctly different teal blue body with thick atypical orange lettering.

	40	70	100	125

(B) Distinctly different teal blue body with usual lettering.

	40	70	100	125

(C) Purplish dark blue body; very scarce.

	80	175	270	400

(D) Medium blue body; most common version.

	6	12	18	25

(6044-1X) McCALL'S-NESTLÉ's: Uncataloged, ca. 1961. 8½" nonopening double-door Type I boxcar; unpainted blue body with unique McCall's-Nestlé's miniature poster on *both* sides; truck type inconsequential, but usually with fixed coupler arch-bar trucks. See color photograph for additional details.

	450	700	900	1200

6050 LIBBY'S TOMATO JUICE: Uncataloged, 1963. 8½" nonopening double-door Type III boxcar with coin slot; unpainted white body with red and blue heat-stamped lettering and green heat-stamped stems on tomatoes; usually with fixed coupler arch-bar trucks. First issued with set 19263, Libby's promotional outfit from 1963. (See *Greenberg's Guide to Lionel Trains 1945–1969, Volume IV: Uncatalogued Sets.*) This car was the first use of the Type III body.

	18	30	45	65

6050 LIONEL SAVINGS BANK: 1961. 8½" nonopening double-door boxcar with coin slot; unpainted white body with green and red heat-stamped lettering; AAR trucks with operating couplers.

(A) Type I body with built date appearing as "BUILT BY / LIONEL".

	12	25	35	50

(B) Type I body with built date appearing as "BLT BY / LIONEL".

	12	25	35	50

(C) Same as (B), except Type IIa body.

	12	25	35	50

6050 SWIFT: 1962–63. 8½" nonopening double-door boxcar with coin slot; unpainted red body with white heat-stamped lettering; Swift's Premium logo on right; AAR trucks; two operating couplers in 1962, and usually one fixed and one operating coupler in 1963; Lionel Service Manual designation 6050-110.

(A) Type IIa dark red body.

	10	15	22	35

*Top: 6044 (B) Airex. Bottom: 6044 (D) Airex. R. Shanfeld
and R. Klumpp Collections.*

*The 6044-1X McCall's-Nestlé's boxcar was an early 1960s promotional item. We assume
from the artwork on the poster that both companies benefited from the promotion, with
the edge going to Nestlé's. This car was reportedly available through Grocerland, a Chicago-
area supermarket chain; we hope someone who was involved with the design or distribution can shed light on its background. Most unfortunately, fraudulent examples of the
poster have been reproduced; although they were done well with laser printer technology,
differences can be easily discerned in a side-by-side comparison. An original car has a
poster on each side that was attached by brown glue; this glue has dried with age, causing the posters to loosen and, in some instances, fall off.*

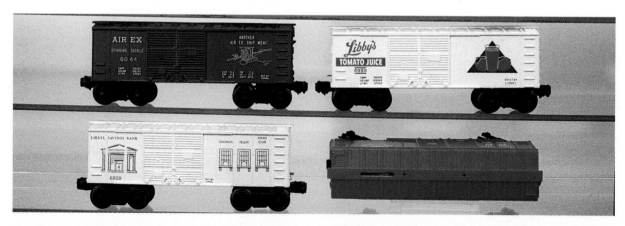

*Top: Scarce 6044 (C) Airex with dark blue body and 6050
Libby's tomato juice. Bottom: 6050 (B) Lionel savings* *bank and top view of 6050 (C) Swift with coin slot. E.
Dougherty Collection.*

6050 (B) Swift with Type II body and 6050 (D) Swift with Type III body. E. Dougherty Collection.

	Gd	VG	Ex	LN
(B) Type IIb light red body.	10	15	22	35

(C) Same as (B), except with two open holes in roof walk. Probably a factory error; the mounting holes needed to hold the superstructure for 3357 hydraulic platform maintenance car should have been plugged.

	10	15	25	40
(D) Type III light red body.	10	15	22	35

6352 PACIFIC FRUIT EXPRESS: 1955–57. Unique operating 6464-type Type IIb ice car; unpainted orange body with ice compartment door and roof hatch and unpainted light brown multiblock doors; body with black heat-stamped lettering; car actually numbered "63521"; Union Pacific logo to right of door and Southern Pacific logo on ice compartment door; brake wheel; bar-end trucks.

Note: The 6352 was available for separate sale, but it was originally issued as the companion to the 352 ice depot accessory. Values are for car only.

(A) Ice compartment door with *four* lines of rubber-stamped data.	45	80	110	150
(B) Ice compartment door with *three* lines of heat-stamped data.	60	100	140	210

6356 N Y C: 1954–55. 11¼" two-level stock car; yellow-painted body with black lettering; car actually numbered "63561"; New York Central logo on right; sliding doors; brake wheel; bar-end trucks.

	Gd	VG	Ex	LN
(A) Body with rubber-stamped lettering and large "BUILT BY / LIONEL".	25	55	80	110
(B) Body with heat-stamped lettering and large "BUILT BY / LIONEL".	12	25	35	50
(C) Body with heat-stamped lettering and small "BUILT BY / LIONEL".	12	25	35	50

6376 CIRCUS CAR: 1956–57. 11¼" two-level stock car; unpainted white body with red heat-stamped lettering and red-painted catwalk; large "LIONEL LINES" on left; sliding doors; brake wheel; bar-end trucks.

Note: Extreme caution advised if cleaning is necessary: the red tends to fade or run when wet.

	30	50	70	90

6428 UNITED STATES MAIL: 1960–61, 1965–66. 6464-type Type IV boxcar; red (including roof and ends)- white- and blue-painted body (gray body mold) with black heat-stamped lettering on white and white heat-stamped lettering on red and blue; multiblock red- white- and blue-painted doors to match body; car actually numbered "6428" on left; "RAILWAY / POST OFFICE" on right; brake wheel; AAR trucks.

Note: Except for the number, the body of 6428 had the identical decorating scheme as the operating 3428.

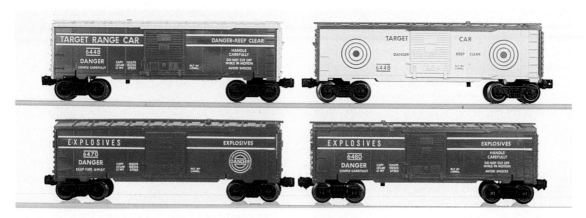

Top: 6448 (B) and 6448 (C) target range car. Observe the slots in the body side of the model at left. See 6470 listing for explanation of slots. Bottom: 6470 (B) and 6480 (B) explosives. Joe Algozzini Collection.

	Gd	VG	Ex	LN
(A) Glossy red body.	15	25	40	60
(B) Flat red body.	15	25	40	60

6434 POULTRY DISPATCH: 1958–59. 11¼" three-level stock car; red-painted body with white heat-stamped lettering; unpainted gray sliding door with black heat-stamped lettering; brake wheel; four-level figure plates with chickens; lighted; bar-end trucks.

Note: It appears there was a communication problem when the 6434 was produced; the car body is divided into three levels, but the figure plates have four levels! See 3434 entry for operating version of this car.

	40	60	80	100

6445 FORT KNOX GOLD RESERVE: 1961–63. Unique savings bank boxcar derived from 3435 tooling; silver-painted body with black heat-stamped lettering; coin slot in roof; clear windows integral to body mold; brake wheel; simulated bullion pile; AAR trucks with operating couplers.

	60	100	140	200

6448 TARGET RANGE CAR: 1961–64. Exploding 6464-type boxcar; unpainted body with heat-stamped lettering in combinations of white with red or red with white; end pieces screw-attached to frame; separate plain side, separate trigger side, and separate roof that are held together by molded hooks and a lock-pin that slides through the roof; frame with spring and trigger mechanism; AAR trucks with operating couplers.

Note: When loaded and properly assembled, the car "explodes" when hit by a rocket or missile fired from a military car or accessory. Many variations exist because parts are interchangeable. Similar cars are 6470 and 6480. See 6470 for explanation of "slots."

(A) Red roof and ends and white sides without slots.				
	10	20	30	45
(B) Same as (A), except sides with slots.				
	10	20	30	45
(C) White roof and ends and red sides without slots.				
	10	20	30	45
(D) Same as (C), except sides with slots.				
	10	20	30	45

X6454 A. T. & S. F.: 1948. 9¼" boxcar; orange-painted body with black heat-stamped lettering; brown-painted metal doors; car also numbered "63132"; Santa Fe logo on left and technical data on right; brake wheel; frame with steps at the four corners; staple-end trucks with magnetic couplers.

	15	28	40	55

X6454 BABY RUTH: 1948. 9¼" boxcar; orange-painted body with black heat-stamped lettering; brown-painted metal doors; PRR logo and technical data on right; brake wheel; frame with steps at the four corners; staple-end trucks with magnetic couplers.

	60	130	200	400

X6454 ERIE: 1949–52. 9¼" boxcar; brown-painted body with white heat-stamped lettering; car also numbered "81000"; Erie logo and technical data on right; brake wheel; except for 1949 production, frame without steps; except for some 1952 production, staple-end trucks with magnetic couplers.

(A) 1949–51; metal doors painted to match body.				
	20	35	50	75
(B) 1952; plastic doors painted to match body; often with bar-end trucks.				
	20	35	50	75

X6454 N Y C: 1948. 9¼" boxcar; painted body with heat-stamped lettering; all models with brown-painted metal doors; car also numbered "159000"; New York Central System logo and technical data on right; brake wheel; frame with steps at the four corners; staple-end trucks with magnetic couplers.

(A) Orange body with black lettering.				
	45	100	155	200
(B) Brown body with white lettering.				
	15	35	50	80
(C) Tan body with white lettering.				
	15	25	35	50

X6454 PENNSYLVANIA: 1949–52. 9¼" boxcar; Tuscan-painted body with white heat-stamped lettering; car also numbered "65400"; PRR logo and technical data on right; brake wheel; except for 1949 production, frame without steps; except for some 1952 production, staple-end trucks with magnetic couplers.

(A) 1949–51; metal doors painted to match body.				
	20	35	50	75
(B) 1952; plastic doors painted to match body; often with bar-end trucks.	20	35	50	75

X6454 SOUTHERN PACIFIC: 1949–52. 9¼" boxcar; brown-painted body with white heat-stamped lettering; car also numbered "96743"; Southern Pacific Lines logo and technical data on right; brake wheel; except for 1949 production, frame without steps; except for some 1952 production staple-end trucks with magnetic couplers.

(A) 1949; light brown body and early SP herald with large letters and break in outer circle between "R" and "N"; metal doors painted to match body; frame with steps at the four corners.	25	50	75	100
(B) 1950; same as (A), except late SP herald with small letters and frame without steps.				
	20	40	65	80
(C) 1951; red-brown–painted body and late SP herald with small letters; metal doors painted to match body.				
	15	30	50	75
(D) 1952; same as (C), except plastic doors painted to match body; often with bar-end trucks.				
	15	30	50	75

6464-1 WESTERN PACIFIC: 1953–54. 6464-series Type I (typically) boxcar; silver-painted body with heat-stamped lettering; silver-painted single-block doors; car actually num-

	Gd	VG	Ex	LN

bered "6464"; "W.P." on left; brake wheel; bar-end trucks.

(A) Preproduction body mold (referred to as Type Ia) with interior roof ribs; typical blue lettering.

| | 375 | 550 | 800 | 1100 |

(B) Type I body with *red* lettering; rare.

| | 450 | 900 | 1250 | 2200 |

(C) Same as (B), but with bright blue lettering.

| | 35 | 60 | 85 | 110 |

(D) Same as (B), but with medium blue lettering.

| | 35 | 60 | 85 | 110 |

(E) Same as (B), but with dark blue lettering.

| | 35 | 60 | 85 | 110 |

(F) Type IIa body with typical blue lettering; rare body mold variation.

| | 300 | 400 | 500 | 600 |

6464-25 GREAT NORTHERN: 1953–54. 6464-series Type I boxcar; orange-painted body with white heat-stamped lettering; orange-painted single-block doors; car actually numbered "6464"; "G.N." on left and Great Northern logo on right; brake wheel; bar-end trucks.

Note: Examples occasionally surface with a Great Northern decal placed over the heat-stamped Great Northern logo; these models are *not* factory production.

(A) Glossy orange body.

| | 35 | 65 | 90 | 110 |

(B) Flat orange body.

| | 35 | 65 | 90 | 110 |

6464-50 MINNEAPOLIS & ST LOUIS: 1953–56. 6464-series Type I (typically) boxcar; Tuscan-painted body with white heat-stamped lettering; Tuscan-painted single-block doors; car actually numbered "6464"; "M & ST L" on left and stylized The Peoria Gateway logo on right; brake wheel; bar-end trucks.

(A) Type I glossy Tuscan body.

| | 38 | 55 | 75 | 100 |

(B) Type I flat Tuscan body.

| | 38 | 55 | 75 | 100 |

(C) Type IIa flat Tuscan body; rare body mold variation.

| | 300 | 400 | 500 | 600 |

6464-75 ROCK ISLAND: 1953–54, 1969. 6464-series boxcar; green-painted body with gold heat-stamped lettering; green-painted doors; car actually numbered "6464"; "R.I." on left and Rock Island logo on right; brake wheel; bar-end trucks.

Note: See 6464-175 for identical decorating scheme.

(A) Type I glossy green body; single-block doors; "NEW 5-53".

| | 40 | 65 | 85 | 110 |

(B) Same as (A), except with flat green body.

| | 40 | 65 | 85 | 110 |

(C) 1969; Type IV body; multiblock doors; *without* "NEW 5-53".

| | 40 | 65 | 85 | 110 |

6464-100 WESTERN PACIFIC (blue feather): 1954. 6464-series Type IIa (typically) boxcar; orange-painted body with blue rubber-stamped feather and white rubber-stamped lettering; orange-painted single-block doors; car actually numbered "6464100"; blue Western Pacific logo on right; brake wheel; bar-end trucks.

Note: Even though the car is numbered with a -100 suffix, the correct component box is numbered "6464-250".

(A) Type I body; rare body mold variation.

| | | | | NRS |

(B) Type IIa body with large "W.P." and small "BUILT BY / LIONEL".

| | 350 | 600 | 830 | 1150 |

(C) Type IIa body with small "W.P." and large "BUILT BY / LIONEL".

| | 350 | 600 | 830 | 1150 |

6464-100 WESTERN PACIFIC (yellow feather): 1954–55. 6464-series boxcar; silver-painted body with yellow rubber-stamped feather and black rubber-stamped lettering; silver-painted single-block doors with yellow detail that meets feather; car actually numbered "6464100"; brake wheel; bar-end trucks.

Note: The large feather that decorates the car sides is designated short or long; however the difference in length between the two is less than ⅛".

(A) Type I body with short yellow feather.

| | 125 | 200 | 260 | 350 |

(B) Type IIa body with short yellow feather.

| | 60 | 90 | 125 | 165 |

(C) Type IIa body with long yellow feather.

| | 60 | 90 | 125 | 165 |

(D) Types IIa body with long yellow-orange feather.

| | 69 | 90 | 125 | 165 |

6464-125 PACEMAKER: 1954–56. 6464-series Type IIa boxcar; gray and red body with white lettering; most typically unpainted red single-block doors; car actually numbered "6464125"; "NYC" on left and New York Central System logo on right; brake wheel; bar-end trucks.

Note: Depending on how the car was masked for painting, the horizontal rivet detail across the top of the body may be red or gray. Some rubber-stamped examples have a cedilla mark, or "tail," under the second "S" in "SYSTEM"; however, this mark is most likely nothing more than a flaw in the rubber stamp.

(A) Gray- and red-painted body; rubber-stamped lettering.

| | 40 | 80 | 120 | 160 |

(B) Same as (A), except with cedilla mark.

| | 40 | 80 | 120 | 160 |

(C) Same as (A), except with heat-stamped lettering.

| | 40 | 80 | 120 | 160 |

(D) Unpainted red body with gray-painted roof, ends, and lower half of side; rubber-stamped lettering.

| | 40 | 80 | 120 | 160 |

(E) Same as (D), except with cedilla mark.

| | 40 | 80 | 120 | 160 |

(F) Same as (D), except with heat-stamped lettering.

| | 40 | 80 | 120 | 160 |

6464-150 MISSOURI PACIFIC: 1954–55, 1957. 6464-series boxcar; gray roof, ends, and center side band; blue upper and lower side bands; black rubber-stamped lettering on gray and white rubber-stamped lettering on blue; most typically solid yellow doors (single- or multi-block, painted or unpainted); actually numbered

A selection of 9¼-inch boxcars manufactured in 1948. Top: X6454 Baby Ruth and X6454 (A) orange N Y C.

Second: X6454 (B) brown N Y C and X6454 (C) tan N Y C. Bottom: X6454 A. T. & S. F. R. Swanson Collection.

More of the 6454 boxcars. Top: X6454 (A) Southern Pacific with early herald. Middle: X6454 (B) Southern Pacific (light brown) and X6454 (C) Southern Pacific

(red-brown). Bottom: X6454 (A) Erie and X6454 (A) Pennsylvania. R. Swanson Collection.

	Gd	VG	Ex	LN

"6464150" on opposite side of stylized "Eagle"; brake wheel; bar-end trucks.

Note: The 6464-150 Missouri Pacific has more collectible variations than any other car in the series. Because of the complexity of this boxcar, variations are grouped by their most common characteristics.

Group 1: Type IIa body; stylized "Eagle" on right side, with leading "E" ¾" high; no grooves; Missouri Pacific Lines seal in fourth panel; "NEW 3 54" on right; no "XME"; usually with gray-painted stripe on single-block doors.

(A) Unpainted royal blue body with gray-painted roof, ends, and center side band.

35 80 125 165

(B) Same as (B), except with unpainted navy blue body. 35 80 125 165

(C) Royal-painted body with gray-painted roof, ends, and center side band. 35 80 125 165

(D) Same as (C), except with navy-painted body.

30 80 125 165

(E) Navy-painted body with distinctly different glossy gray-painted roof, ends, and center side band.

30 80 125 165

Group 2: Type IIa body and same characteristics as Group 1, except with "NEW 3 54" on left and "XME" on lower right.

(F) Unpainted royal body with gray-painted roof, ends, and center side band. 35 80 125 165

(G) Same as (F), except with unpainted navy body.

35 80 125 165

(H) Unpainted gray body with royal-painted upper and lower side bands. 35 80 125 165

Group 3: Type IIa or IIb body *with* grooves; stylized "Eagle" on right side, with leading "E" ⅝" high; Missouri Pacific Lines seal in fourth panel except as noted; "NEW 3 54" on left; "XME" on lower right; solid yellow single-block doors (painted or unpainted).

(I) Type IIa unpainted royal body with gray-painted roof, ends, and center side band.

35 80 125 165

(J) Same as (I), except with Missouri Pacific Lines seal in fifth panel (first panel to left of door); very scarce variation. 500 900 1200 1800

(K) Same as (I), except with unpainted navy body.

35 80 125 165

(L) Same as (I), except with Type IIb body.

35 80 125 165

(M) Type IIa royal-painted body (usually white body mold) with gray-painted roof, ends, and center side band. 35 80 125 165

Group 4: Type IIb body; stylized "Eagle" on left side, with leading "E" ⅝" high; no grooves; Missouri Pacific Lines seal in fourth panel; "NEW 3 54" on left; "XME" on lower right, solid yellow multiblock doors.

(N) Unpainted gray body with royal-painted upper and lower side bands. 35 80 125 165

Group 5: Type IIb body; stylized "Eagle" on left side, with leading "E" ½" high; no grooves; distinctly smaller Missouri Pacific Lines seal in fourth panel; "NEW 3 54" on left; "XME" on lower right; solid yellow multiblock doors.

(O) Unpainted gray body with royal-painted upper and lower side bands. 35 80 125 165

(P) Royal-painted body with gray-painted roof, ends, and center side band. 35 80 125 165

6464-175 ROCK ISLAND: 1954–55. 6464-series Type I (typically) boxcar; silver-painted body with heat-stamped lettering; silver-painted single-block doors; car actually numbered "6464"; "R.I." on left and Rock Island logo on right; brake wheel; bar-end trucks.

Note: See 6464-75 for identical decorating scheme.

(A) Type I body with *black* lettering.

500 800 1100 1750

(B) Same as (A), with light blue lettering.

50 85 125 175

(C) Same as (A), with medium blue lettering.

50 85 125 175

(D) Type IIa body with medium blue lettering; rare body mold variation. 400 510 600 720

6464-200 PENNSYLVANIA: 1954–55, 1969. 6464-series boxcar; Tuscan-painted body with white heat-stamped lettering; Tuscan-painted doors; car actually numbered "6464"; PRR logo on right; brake wheel; bar-end trucks.

(A) Type I glossy Tuscan body; single-block doors; "NEW 5-53". 70 100 140 210

(B) Same as (A), except flat Tuscan body.

70 100 140 210

(C) Type IIa flat Tuscan body; single-block doors; "NEW 5-53". 70 100 140 210

(D) 1969; Type IV body; multiblock doors; *without* "NEW 5-53". 70 100 140 210

6464-225 SOUTHERN PACIFIC: 1954–56. 6464-series most typically Type IIa boxcar; black-painted body with white and yellow rubber-stamped lettering; black-painted single-block doors; car actually numbered "6464225"; white "S.P." and yellow Southern Pacific logo on left and yellow and red stylized "Overnight" arrow on right; brake wheel; bar-end trucks.

(A) Type I body; rare body mold variation.

500 900 1250 1800

(B) Type IIa semigloss black body.

50 75 100 150

(C) Type IIa flat black body.

50 75 100 150

6464-250 WESTERN PACIFIC: 1966. 6464-series most typically Type IV boxcar; orange-painted body with blue rubber-stamped feather and white rubber-stamped lettering; orange-painted multiblock doors; car actually numbered "6464250"; blue Western Pacific logo on right; brake wheel; AAR trucks.

	Gd	VG	Ex	LN

(A) Type III body; rare body mold variation.

	400	**500**	**600**	**700**

(B) Type IV light orange body.

	90	**150**	**200**	**275**

(C) Type IV medium orange body.

	90	**150**	**200**	**275**

(D) Same as (C), but distinctly different dark purple-blue feather.

	90	**150**	**200**	**275**

6464-275 STATE OF MAINE: 1955, 1957–59. 6464-series boxcar; blue roof, ends, and upper side band, with white center side and red lower side bands; white lettering on blue and red, and black lettering on white; multiblock door designed expressly for this model (letters "OF" and "D" and "U" are stamped on door sign boards; car actually numbered "6464275"; Bangor & Aroostook logo on right; brake wheel; Types IIa and IIb models with bar-end trucks, and Type III examples with AAR trucks.

Note: The 6464-275 has the most door variations of any car in the series; the one constant is that *all* are multiblock doors. Early 1955 production came with unpainted solid red doors, while later 1955 production usually came with unpainted white (ivory) doors with red- and royal-painted stripes.

Most 1957–59 examples came with unpainted royal or navy doors with red- and white-painted stripes. Some extraneous door color molds, such as maroon, were also used; out of necessity, these doors had to be painted all three matching colors.

As the introduction and charts mention, doors are easy to change and most do *not* warrant any premium; however, an exception is 1955 production with solid red State of Maine doors, which does bring a modest premium.

(A) Type IIa body *with* grooves; unpainted white (ivory) body with blue-painted roof, ends, and upper side band and red-painted lower side band; *all* lettering rubber-stamped; unpainted red doors with *rubber*-stamped lettering. **Note:** The shade of blue paint used in 1955 is unique to that year.

	55	**95**	**135**	**200**

(B) Type IIa body *with* grooves; unpainted royal blue body with white-painted center side band and red-painted lower side band; *all* lettering rubber-stamped; unpainted white (ivory) doors with royal blue– and red-painted stripes and *rubber*-stamped lettering. **Note:** The ivory shade of the doors is a poor match to the pure white paint used on the body.

	55	**95**	**135**	**200**

(C) Type IIa body *with* grooves; blue body mold painted *all* three colors (red, white, and blue); other details the same as (B).

	50	**75**	**100**	**125**

(D) Type IIb body; unpainted royal blue body with white-painted center side band and red-painted lower side band; black rubber-stamped lettering on white and white heat-stamped lettering on royal blue and red; usually unpainted royal blue doors with white- and red-painted stripes and *heat*-stamped lettering.

	50	**75**	**100**	**125**

(E) Same as (D), except with violet-blue body.

	50	**75**	**100**	**125**

(F) Type III body; blue body mold painted *all* three colors (red, white, and blue); black rubber-stamped lettering on white and white heat-stamped lettering on royal blue and red; most typically unpainted royal doors with white- and red-painted stripes and heat-stamped lettering.

	50	**75**	**100**	**125**

(G) Type III body; unpainted royal blue body with white-painted center side band and red-painted lower side band; other details the same as (F).

	50	**75**	**100**	**125**

6464-300 RUTLAND: 1955–56. 6464-series boxcar; most typically unpainted yellow body and dark green–painted roof, ends, and lower half of side with green lettering on yellow and yellow lettering on green; unpainted yellow doors (except split-door model); car actually numbered "6464300"; Rutland shield at upper right corner; brake wheel; bar-end trucks.

Note: 1955 production was rubber-stamped with the "R" in Rutland in the first panel, while 1956 production was heat-stamped with the "R" in Rutland in the second panel. Furthermore, 1955 models came with single-block doors, while 1956 examples usually came with multi-block doors.

Because of extremely high prices, the solid-shield model (B) and the split-door version (D) have been fraudulently post-factory altered. Consult expert opinion regarding authenticity before purchasing either of these variations.

(A) Very earliest production; Type IIa clear body mold painted *both* yellow and green; rubber-stamped lettering; rare.

	400	**500**	**600**	**700**

(B) Type IIa unpainted yellow body with glossy dark green–painted details; rubber-stamped lettering with solid-shield herald (the shield has a solid dark green background); rare.

	850	**1750**	**2500**	**3300**

(C) Same as (B), except with typical shield.

	40	**70**	**100**	**160**

(D) Type IIa unpainted yellow body with typical dark green–painted details; rubber-stamped lettering; single-block split-doors (bottom half of doors is dark green–painted); very scarce.

	400	**600**	**900**	**1300**

(E) Same as (D), except with usual unpainted doors; most common version.

	40	**70**	**100**	**160**

(F) Type IIa unpainted yellow body with typical dark green–painted details; heat-stamped lettering; scarce body mold variation.

	100	**200**	**300**	**450**

(G) Same as (F), except with usual Type IIb body mold; most common heat-stamped version.

	50	**100**	**150**	**200**

(H) Type IIb royal body mold painted *both* yellow and green; heat-stamped lettering; probably Lionel Service Department replacement body; very scarce.

	400	**500**	**600**	**700**

6464-325 BALTIMORE & OHIO / SENTINEL: 1956. 6464-series Type IIb boxcar; silver-painted body and aqua blue–painted lower band with navy blue heat-stamped

Top: 6464-1 (D) Western Pacific and 6464-25 (B) Great Northern. Second: 6464-50 (B) Minneapolis & St. Louis and 6464-75 (B) Rock Island. Third: 6464-100 (B) Western Pacific (yellow feather) and 6464-100 (C) Western Pacific (blue feather). Bottom: 6464-125 (B) Pacemaker and 6464-150 (A) Missouri Pacific. L. Nuzzaci Collection.

Top: Missouri Pacific variations 6464-150 (O) and 6464-150 (I). Second: 6464-225 (C) Southern Pacific and 6464-200 (B) Pennsylvania. Third: 6464-175 (A) Rock Island with scarce black lettering and 6464-250 (C) Western Pacific. Bottom: State of Maine variations 6464-275 (A) and 6464-275 (D). K. Rubright Collection.

Four versions of the 6464-300 Rutland boxcar. Top: Variation (C) at left is rubber-stamped, while variation (B) at right is heat-stamped. Note that the "R" in Rutland on all rubber-stamped examples is in the first panel.

Bottom: Variation (D) at left with split doors (bottom half is dark green–painted), and rare variation (B) at right with solid-shield herald (the shield has a solid dark green background). E. Dougherty Collection.

Top: 6464-325 (B) Baltimore & Ohio / Sentinel and 6464-350 (A) M-K-T. Middle: 6464-375 (A) Central of Georgia and 6464-400 (A) Baltimore & Ohio. Bottom:

6464-425 (A) New Haven and 6464-450 (A) Great Northern. L. Nuzzaci Collection.

	Gd	VG	Ex	LN

lettering on silver and white heat-stamped lettering on aqua blue; silver-painted most typically multiblock doors with aqua blue–painted lower stripe; car actually numbered "6464325"; B & O–Sentinel logo decal on right; brake wheel; bar-end trucks.

(A) Body with single-block doors. This door variation warrants a premium because the color combination is unique to the 6464-325.

	Gd	VG	Ex	LN
(A)	320	500	650	840

(B) Body with multiblock doors.

	280	450	605	780

6464-350 M-K-T (Missouri-Kansas-Texas): 1956. 6464-series Type IIb boxcar; Tuscan-painted body with white heat-stamped lettering; unpainted maroon or dark cherry multiblock doors; car actually numbered "6464350"; stylized "The Katy" on right; brake wheel; bar-end trucks.

	Gd	VG	Ex	LN
(A) Tuscan-red body.	115	205	290	400
(B) Tuscan-brown body.	115	205	290	400

6464-375 CENTRAL OF GEORGIA: 1956–57, 1966. 6464-series boxcar; most typically unpainted maroon body

	Gd	VG	Ex	LN

and silver-painted roof and oval with maroon or red heat-stamped lettering on silver and white heat-stamped lettering on maroon; silver-painted multiblock doors; car actually numbered "6464375"; "C.G." on left and Central of Georgia decal on right; brake wheel; 1956–57 models with bar-end trucks, and 1966 production with AAR trucks.

(A) Type IIb body with maroon and white lettering; "BLT 3-56 / BY LIONEL".

	Gd	VG	Ex	LN
	45	85	120	160

(B) Same as (A), except with red and white lettering.

	45	85	120	160

(C) Type IIb body with distinctly different silver gray–painted roof and oval; maroon and white lettering; "BLT 3-56 / BY LIONEL".

	45	85	120	160

(D) Type IV gray body mold painted *both* red and silver; red and white lettering; "BLT 3-56 / BY LIONEL"; rare.

	1000	1600	2200	2800

(E) Type IV body with maroon and white lettering; with only "BLT / BY LIONEL".

	45	85	120	160

(F) Same as (E), except with red and white lettering.

	45	85	120	160

6464-400 BALTIMORE & OHIO: 1956–57, 1969. 6464-series boxcar; blue body with silver-painted roof and orange-painted middle side slanted band with white heat-stamped lettering on blue and blue heat-stamped lettering on orange; blue (usually painted) multiblock doors with orange-painted stripe to match body; car actually numbered "6464400"; B & O–Timesaver decal on right; brake wheel; bar-end trucks.

(A) Type IIb unpainted medium blue body; "BLT 5-54 / BY LIONEL".

	40	75	110	150

(B) Same as (A), except with unpainted royal blue body.

	40	75	110	150

(C) Type IIb unpainted medium blue body; "BLT 2-56 / BY LIONEL".

	80	150	225	300

(D) Same as (C), except with unpainted royal blue body.

	80	150	225	300

(E) Type IIb unpainted royal blue body; "BLT 5-54 / BY LIONEL" on one side and "BLT 2-56 / BY LIONEL" on the other; very scarce.

	400	600	850	1100

(F) Type IV medium blue–painted body without any built date information.

	40	75	110	150

(G) Same as (F), except with distinctly different very dark blue lettering.

	40	75	110	150

(H) Same as (F), except with dark blue–painted body.

	40	75	110	150

6464-425 NEW HAVEN: 1956–58; cataloged in 1969 as 6464-425 but actually produced as black 6464-725. 6464-series boxcar; black body with white heat-stamped lettering; orange (painted or unpainted) multiblock doors; car actually numbered "6464425"; large N / H logo on left; brake wheel; bar-end trucks for 1956 and part of 1957 production, then AAR trucks for balance of production.

Note: The large "N" in "N / H" comes in two variations: the top right corner has a half or full serif (see the two photographs; the first shows the half-serif "N").

(A) Type IIa unpainted black body with half serif.

	30	50	75	90

(B) Same as (A), except with full serif.

	30	50	75	90

(C) Type IIa black-painted body with half serif.

	30	50	75	90

(D) Same as (C), except with full serif.

	30	50	75	90

(E) Type IIa distinctly different glossy black-painted body with half serif.

	30	50	75	90

(F) Type III black-painted body with full serif.

	30	50	75	90

6464-450 GREAT NORTHERN: 1956–57, 1966. 6464-series boxcar; olive-painted body and orange-painted middle side band with yellow heat-stamped lettering on olive and olive heat-stamped lettering on orange; yellow heat-stamped upper and lower stripes separate orange from olive; multiblock doors painted and heat-stamped to match body; car actually numbered "6464450"; "G.N." on left and Great Northern logo decal on right; brake wheel; 1957–58 examples with bar-end trucks and 1966 production with AAR trucks.

Note: Examples sometimes appear without the yellow stripes separating the orange and olive areas on the doors; these are considered factory errors.

(A) Type IIb body with "BLT 1-56 / BY LIONEL".

	60	100	135	175

(B) Type III body with "BLT 1-56 / BY LIONEL"; very scarce body mold variation.

	300	400	500	650

(C) Type IV dark olive body with only "BLT / BY LIONEL".

	60	100	135	175

(D) Same as (C), except with light olive body.

	60	100	135	175

6464-475 BOSTON AND MAINE: 1957–60, 1965–68. 6464-series boxcar; blue body with black and white heat-stamped lettering; unpainted black multiblock doors; car actually numbered "6464475"; small black "BM" on left and large, stylized black and white "BM" on right; brake wheel; bar-end trucks for most of 1957 production, then AAR trucks for all other examples.

Note: Models with complete built date are stamped "BLT 2-57 / BY LIONEL".

(A) Type IIb medium blue–painted body with complete built date.

	30	45	60	75

(B) Type IIb unpainted medium blue body with complete built date.

	30	45	60	75

(C) Type III medium blue–painted body with complete built date.

	30	45	60	75

(D) Type III unpainted medium blue body with complete built date.

	30	45	60	75

(E) Type IV unpainted medium blue body with complete built date.

	30	45	60	75

(F) Type IV unpainted dark blue body with complete built date.

	30	45	60	75

(G) Same as (F), except with only "BLT / BY LIONEL".

	30	45	60	75

	Gd	VG	Ex	LN

(H) Type IV medium blue–painted body (gray body mold) with complete built date.

	90	**120**	**160**	**200**

(I) Type IV dark blue-painted body (yellow or gray body mold) with only "BLT / BY LIONEL".

	50	**90**	**130**	**175**

(J) Type IV dark purple-blue–painted body (blue or gray body mold) with complete built date.

	90	**120**	**160**	**200**

6464-500 TIMKEN: 1957–59, 1969. 6464-series boxcar; yellow body with white-painted middle side band and charcoal gray heat-stamped lettering; yellow (painted or unpainted) multiblock doors with white-painted center stripe to match body; car actually numbered "6464500 TRB"; Roller Freight decal on right; brake wheel; most examples with bar-end trucks.

(A) Type IIb unpainted yellow body with "BLT 3-57 / BY LIONEL".

	60	**100**	**130**	**160**

(B) Same as (A), except with yellow-orange body.

	60	**100**	**130**	**160**

(C) Type IIb yellow-painted body (gray body mold) with "BLT 3-57 / BY LIONEL"; scarce.

	100	**150**	**210**	**300**

(D) Type III unpainted yellow body with "BLT 3-57 / BY LIONEL"; moderately scarce.

	80	**125**	**175**	**240**

(E) Type IV light yellow–painted body without any built date information.

	60	**100**	**130**	**160**

(F) Same as (E), except with medium yellow–painted body.

	60	**100**	**130**	**160**

6464-510 PACEMAKER: 1957–58. 6464-series Type IIb boxcar; pastel blue–painted body with black heat-stamped lettering; pastel yellow–painted multiblock doors; car actually numbered "6464510"; "NYC" on left and New York Central System logo on right; brake wheel; bar-end trucks.

Note: Except for the number, the lettering scheme on the 6464-510 is identical to the heat-stamped 6464-125. Exclusive component of outfit 1587S, known as the Girls' Set.

	300	**460**	**620**	**800**

6464-515 M-K-T: 1957–58. 6464-series Type IIb boxcar; pastel yellow–painted body with brown heat-stamped lettering; pastel blue–painted multiblock doors; car actually numbered "6464515"; stylized "The Katy" on right; brake wheel; bar-end trucks.

Note: Except for the number, the lettering scheme on the 6464-515 is identical to the 6464-350. Exclusive component of outfit 1587S, known as the Girls' Set.

	260	**430**	**590**	**750**

6464-525 MINNEAPOLIS & ST LOUIS: 1957–58, 1964–66. 6464-series boxcar; red-painted body with white heat-stamped lettering; most typically red-painted multiblock doors; car actually numbered "6464525"; large "M St L" on left and stylized The Peoria Gateway logo on right; brake wheel; early 1957 production with bar-end trucks, AAR trucks for balance of production.

	Gd	VG	Ex	LN
(A) Type IIb body.	**30**	**50**	**65**	**80**
(B) Type III body.	**30**	**50**	**65**	**80**
(C) Type IV body.	**30**	**50**	**65**	**80**

6464-650 RIO GRANDE: 1957–58, 1966. 6464-series boxcar; most typically unpainted yellow body with silver painted roof and lower band with black heat-stamped lettering; black heat-stamped stripe separates yellow and silver; yellow (usually unpainted) multiblock doors with silver-painted bottom separated by black heat-stamped stripe; car actually numbered "6464650"; "D & R G W" on left; brake wheel; 1957–58 examples with bar-end trucks and 1966 production with AAR trucks.

Note: Examples sometime surface without the black stripe separating the yellow and silver areas on either the body or the doors; these are considered factory errors.

(A) Type IIb body with "BLT 6-57 / BY LIONEL".

	50	**90**	**130**	**175**

(B) Type IV gray body mold painted *both* yellow and silver; yellow-painted doors match body; "BLT 6-57 / BY LIONEL"; unlike all other examples with a silver-painted roof, this model has a yellow-painted roof; rare.

	500	**750**	**1000**	**1500**

(C) Common Type IV body with only "BLT / BY LIONEL".

	50	**90**	**130**	**175**

6464-700 SANTA FE: 1961, 1966. 6464-series most typically Type IV boxcar; red-painted body with white heat-stamped lettering; red-painted multiblock doors; car actually numbered "6464-700"; large Santa Fe logo on left; brake wheel; AAR trucks.

(A) Type III body; rare body mold variation.

	400	**500**	**600**	**750**

(B) Type IV body.

	50	**90**	**130**	**175**

6464-725 NEW HAVEN: 1962–66, 1968; 1969 as a black model. 6464-series Type IV boxcar; orange-painted body (except variation D) with black heat-stamped lettering; unpainted black multiblock doors; car actually numbered "6464725"; large N / H logo with full serif on left; brake wheel; all orange examples with AAR trucks.

Note: Orange Picture box (orange body only) *always* erroneously marked "6464-735".

Lionel reissued the black New Haven (see 6464-425) in 1969; the consumer catalog (on page 8) pictured a Type IIb example from the mid-1950s that was numbered and identified in the text as 6464-425. However, the model produced was numbered 6464725 (same as the orange body) because the heat-stamp tooling had previously been changed from "425" to "725". To further confuse the issue, the correct Hagerstown or Hillside Checkerboard component box is marked 6464-425!

(A) Light orange body.	**35**	**55**	**70**	**110**
(B) Medium orange body.	**30**	**50**	**65**	**100**

(C) Same as (B), except with distinctly different high-gloss lettering.

	30	**50**	**65**	**100**

Top: 6464-475 (A) Boston and Maine and 6464-500 (C) Timken. Second: 6464-510 Pacemaker from Girls' Set and 6464-515 M-K-T from Girls' Set. Third: 6464-525 (A) Minneapolis & St. Louis and 6464-650 (A)

Rio Grande. Bottom: 6464-700 (B) Santa Fe (the example shown has improper bar-end trucks; typical production came with AAR trucks) and scarce black 6464-725 (D) New Haven. L. Nuzzaci Collection.

	Gd	VG	Ex	LN

(D) 1969; black-painted body with white heat-stamped lettering; orange (painted or unpainted) multiblock doors; bar-end trucks.

| | 80 | 175 | 250 | 350 |

6464-735 NEW HAVEN: Not manufactured. The consumer catalogs (sometimes) and the component box (always) identified the orange New Haven as 6464-735. See above entry.

6464-825 ALASKA RAILROAD: 1959–60. 6464-series boxcar; blue-painted body and yellow-painted upper stripe with navy heat-stamped lettering on yellow and yellow heat-stamped lettering on blue; blue-painted multiblock doors; car actually numbered "6464825"; Eskimo figure on left; brake wheel; AAR trucks.

Note: Madison Hardware in New York had numerous Alaska bodies but no blue-painted doors, so they often completed bodies with white or yellow doors. Also, fraudulent examples with a white stripe and/or white lettering are known to exist. Consult expert opinion before purchasing anything other than the norm.

(A) Type III body with yellow lettering.

| | 105 | 175 | 255 | 330 |

(B) Type III body with yellow-orange lettering.

| | 105 | 175 | 255 | 300 |

	Gd	VG	Ex	LN

(C) Type IV body with yellow lettering.

| | 150 | 200 | 300 | 400 |

(D) Type IV body with yellow-orange lettering.

| | 150 | 200 | 300 | 400 |

6464-900 NEW YORK CENTRAL: 1960–66. 6464-series most typically Type IV boxcar; jade green–painted body with white, black, and red heat-stamped lettering; jade green–painted multiblock doors; car actually numbered "6464900"; New York Central System logo on left; brake wheel; AAR trucks.

(A) Type III body; rare body mold variation.

| | 400 | 500 | 600 | 750 |

(B) Type IV light jade green body.

| | 50 | 85 | 120 | 150 |

(C) Same as (B), except with unpainted black multiblock doors. Though simple to duplicate, this is a legitimate variation, sometimes appearing in 1963. Valued slightly less than other models because of the availability of black doors.

| | 50 | 85 | 120 | 150 |

(D) Type IV dark jade green body.

| | 50 | 85 | 120 | 150 |

6464-1965 TRAIN COLLECTORS ASSOCIATION:

Top: 6464-725 (B) orange New Haven and 6464-825 (A) Alaska. Second: 6464-900 (B) New York Central. Third: 6468 (B) and (C) Baltimore & Ohio cars. Bottom: 6468-25 (C) New Haven and 6468-25 (B)

New Haven. Observe the opposite color of lettering on the examples. The model with the large white "N" is moderately scarce. L. Nuzzaci Collection.

	Gd	VG	Ex	LN

Uncataloged, 1965. 6464-series Type IV boxcar made for 1965 TCA (Train Collectors Association) national convention in Pittsburgh; blue-painted body with white heat-stamped lettering; blue-painted multiblock doors; brake wheel; AAR trucks.

	Gd	VG	Ex	LN
(A) White rubber-stamped "6464-1965" on underframe; 800 produced.	—	—	270	320
(B) White rubber-stamped "6464-1965X" on underframe; 74 produced.	—	—	280	350

6468 BALTIMORE & OHIO: 1953–55. Modified 6464-style double-door automobile boxcar; painted body with white heat-stamped lettering; special automobile car doors (not 6464 type) painted to match body; car actually numbered "6468"; "AUTOMOBILE" and B & O logo on right; brake wheel; bar-end trucks.

	Gd	VG	Ex	LN
(A) Glossy blue body.	20	40	60	80
(B) Flat blue body.	20	40	60	80
(C) Tuscan body.	140	215	320	410

6468-25 NEW HAVEN: 1956–58. Modified 6464-style double-door automobile boxcar; unpainted orange body with black and white heat-stamped lettering; special unpainted black automobile car doors (not 6464 type); car actually numbered "646825"; large N / H logo on left and "NEW HAVEN" and small "N H" on right; brake wheel; bar-end trucks.

Note: Examples routinely appear with Tuscan-painted doors, but they are *not* factory production. These models were post-factory completion of unfinished bodies and were available through Madison Hardware.

	Gd	VG	Ex	LN
(A) Large black "N" with full serif over large white "H"; black "NEW HAVEN" and white technical data.	25	45	60	80
(B) Same as (A), except large black "N" with half serif on top right corner.	25	45	60	80
(C) Large white "N" with half serif on top right corner over large black "H"; white "NEW HAVEN" and black technical data; moderately scarce.	120	150	220	300

6470 EXPLOSIVES: 1959–60. Exploding 6464-type boxcar; unpainted red body with white heat-stamped lettering; end pieces screw-attached to frame; separate plain side, separate trigger side, and separate roof that are held together by molded hooks and a lock-pin that slides through the roof; frame with spring and trigger mechanism; AAR trucks with operating couplers.

Note: When loaded and properly assembled, the car "explodes" when hit by a rocket or missile fired from

6464 TCA Specials

In 1967, as it had in other years, the Train Collectors Association asked Lionel to make a special car for its annual national convention. The TCA purchased a number of 6464-series Type IV boxcars and had them specially labeled. Each was rubber-stamped in white inside a white border "12Th T.C.A. / NATIONAL / CONVENTION / BALTIMORE, MD. / JUNE–1967" on the bottom of the underframe.

To convert these boxcars, one regular door was removed and placed inside. It was replaced by a special brass-plated door that covered the entire length of the door guides and included an enameled design with blue lettering and red highlights in a stylized circle. The elongated plated door was marked "TRAIN COLLECTORS ASSOCIATION ORGANIZED 1954 INCORPORATED 1957" and showed a railroad crossing signal lettered "NATIONAL CONVENTION / BALT. MD JUNE 67".

Unfortunately, a number of brass door reproductions have been made and installed on cars that have been rubber-stamped to appear as if they were 1967 convention cars. These fakes have been made too well in that they use real brass plates, whereas the originals were aluminum with a brass plating on one side, with decorations. One can look through the opposite door at the back side of the plate to determine authenticity: if it is solid brass, it is not genuine; original cars show brass streaks on the aluminum (A. Stewart comment).

A total of 601 boxcars (including a reported 6464-475 Boston and Maine prototype) were modified for the TCA order. In numerical sequence, the quantities produced are as follows:

6464-250	159
6464-375	100
6464-450	97
6464-475 prototype	1
6464-475	3
6464-525	7
6464-650	137
6464-700	92
6464-725	3
6464-900	2

Because of interchangeability, the 1967 TCA boxcars are virtually impossible to properly chronicle and value. However, we assume they are the most common Type IV models (see appropriate 6464 listing) and warrant about a $75 premium above the typical-production 6464-series item.

	Gd	VG	Ex	LN

a military car or accessory. It appears two sets of tooling were used to mold body sides; on some sides there are "slots" made by the tooling necessary to form the hooks that hold the side to the frame; on others, the tooling formed the hooks without making slots. See 6448 and 6480.

(A) Body sides without slots.

	12	28	40	55
(B) Body sides with slots.	12	28	40	55

6472 REFRIGERATOR: 1950–53. 9¼" (short) nonoperating milk car; unpainted white body and door and frame assembly (doors are functional) with black heat-stamped lettering; also numbered "RT6472" on right; circled-L Lionel logo; brake wheel; frame held to body by two large spring clips; staple-end trucks with magnetic couplers into 1951, then bar-end trucks for balance of production.

Note: This car was the nonoperating version of 3472.

(A) 1950; frame with steps at the four corners.

	18	28	38	50
(B) Frame without steps.	18	28	38	50

6473 HORSE TRANSPORT CAR: 1962–66, 1969. Modified 9¼" (short) stock car; unpainted yellow body with heat-stamped lettering; nonopening doors; horses bob in and out as car moves along track; horse heads (one pair brown and one pair white) mounted to a pivot arm, which acts as a balance beam. AAR trucks with operating couplers through mid-1963 and then usually one fixed and one operating coupler for the remainder of production.

(A) Light yellow body with maroon-brown lettering.

	10	20	28	40

(B) Light yellow body with red lettering.

	10	20	28	40

(C) Dark yellow body with maroon-brown lettering.

	10	20	28	40

(D) Dark yellow body with red lettering.

	10	20	28	40

6480 EXPLOSIVES: Uncataloged, 1961. Exploding 6464-type boxcar; same as 6470, except with fixed coupler arch-bar trucks. See 6470 and 6448.

(A) Body sides without slots.

	18	35	50	60

Top: Two versions of the 3656 Lionel Lines operating cattle car. Variation (A) at left and variation (D) at right. Unfortunately, the adhesive Armour emblem is missing from the black-lettered example on the left. Middle: 6656 (A) Lionel Lines and 6656 (C) Lionel Lines. Bottom: 6646 Lionel Lines and 6473 (B) horse transport car. J. Algozzini Collection.

Three variations of the 6672 Santa Fe refrigerator car. Top: Variation (B) and variation (D). Observe the black lettering and the absence of the circled-L Lionel logo on the example at right. Bottom: Scarce variation (A) with three lines of data to right of door. J. Algozzini Collection.

	Gd	VG	Ex	LN
(B) Body sides with slots.	18	35	50	60

6482 REFRIGERATOR: 1957. 9¼" (short) nonoperating milk car; unpainted white body and door and frame assembly (doors are functional) with black heat-stamped lettering; also numbered "RT6482" on right; circled-L Lionel logo; frame with steps at the four corners attached to body by slot and tab at one end and screw at other; AAR trucks with operating couplers.

Note: This car was the nonoperating version of 3482.

	Gd	VG	Ex	LN
	30	45	60	75

6530 FIREFIGHTING INSTRUCTION CAR: 1960–62. Unique boxcar derived from 3530 tooling; unpainted red body with white heat-stamped lettering; brake wheel; unpainted white sliding double doors; AAR trucks with operating couplers.

Note: Each side of the car is molded differently.

	Gd	VG	Ex	LN
	40	60	75	90

6556 M-K-T: 1958. 11¼" two-level stock car; red-painted body with white heat-stamped lettering; stylized "The Katy" on left; sliding doors; brake wheel; bar-end trucks.

| | Gd | VG | Ex | LN |

Note: Extreme caution advised if cleaning is necessary; the red is quite apt to fade when wet.

| | 70 | 150 | 240 | 400 |

5572 RAILWAY EXPRESS AGENCY: 1958–59; uncataloged 1963. Refrigerator car in 1:48 scale; green-painted body with gold heat-stamped lettering; REA logo decal on right; functional plug door; control panel with sliding cover; brake wheel; 1958–59 production typically with bar-end trucks, and 1963 model with AAR trucks and operating couplers.

Note: The roof and ends were molded in one piece, while the detailed bottom and sides were molded in another; this car utilized the tooling developed for 6672.

(A) Typical dark green body with 2400-series passenger trucks. A sometime component of outfit 1600 cataloged in 1958. Because this variation can easily be retrofitted with rear observation car trucks and magnetic couplers, it does not warrant any premium.

| | 45 | 75 | 100 | 125 |

(B) Typical dark green body with bar-end trucks.

| | 45 | 75 | 100 | 125 |

(C) 1963 reissue; light green body with AAR trucks.

| | 45 | 70 | 90 | 110 |

6646 LIONEL LINES: 1957. 9¼" (short) stock car; unpainted orange body with black heat-stamped lettering; circled-L Lionel logo; sliding doors that are usually a different shade of orange from that of the body; frame, with steps at the four corners; AAR trucks with operating couplers.

Note: In later years the short stock car tooling was modified to produce action cars 3376 and 3386, 3370, and 6473.

| | 12 | 25 | 35 | 48 |

6656 LIONEL LINES: 1950–53. 9¼" (short) stock car; usually bright yellow–painted body with black heat-stamped lettering; circled-L Lionel logo; sliding doors; brake wheel; earliest production with steps at the four corners; staple-end trucks with magnetic couplers into 1951, then bar-end trucks with magnetic couplers for balance of production.

(A) Very earliest production; adhesive Armour emblem on doors; bright yellow body; steps at the four corners.

| | 40 | 75 | 100 | 140 |

(B) 1949; same as (A), but without Armour emblem; steps at the four corners. | | 8 | 14 | 20 | 25 |

(C) Dark yellow body on frame without steps.

| | 8 | 14 | 20 | 25 |

6672 SANTA FE: 1954–56. Refrigerator car in 1:48 scale; unpainted white body and bottom with unpainted brown roof, ends, and doors; heat-stamped lettering; most examples with circled-L Lionel logo; functional plug door; control panel with sliding cover; brake wheel; bar-end trucks.

Note: The 6672 represented a new manufacturing technique whereby the roof and ends were molded in one piece, while the detailed bottom and sides were molded in another. Shades vary on the roof, with ends and the doors ranging from Tuscan red to chocolate brown.

(A) Earliest production; blue lettering with three lines of data to right of door; scarce.

| | 70 | 170 | 270 | 400 |

(B) Blue lettering with two lines of data to right of door. | | 25 | 50 | 70 | 90 |

(C) Black lettering with two lines of data to right of door. | | 25 | 50 | 70 | 90 |

(D) Same as (C), except without circled-L Lionel logo. | | 25 | 50 | 75 | 100 |

5

CABOOSES

Introduction by Roger Carp

Once upon a time, at the end of every freight train rode a caboose. No matter how long or how short the train, it hauled an "office on wheels" for its crew. This custom, which lasted into the 1980s, influenced toy train production. Put simply, every O or O27 gauge freight set marketed by Lionel had to include a caboose. This fact compelled the company to produce untold thousands of cabooses annually. It might, therefore, have been content to offer one or two elementary designs that could be added to every set.

To Lionel's credit, not to mention the delight of collectors and operators, it did far more. In addition to creating a basic design and mass-producing it with some noteworthy variations, engineers studied prototype cabooses to introduce new models that gave spark to the product line and enticed enthusiasts into buying more for their rosters. Different types of cabooses, along with the extra features and attractive decoration added to the basic model, brought excitement to a part of the line that might otherwise have remained mundane.

Of course, when World War II ended, sales personnel merely wanted to have a caboose, any caboose, to advertise. Engineers struggling to fulfill that wish scrutinized the models that had been in Lionel's O and O27 lines when federal restrictions had curtailed toy train production in 1942. There were several, all stamped sheet-metal cars with red- or brown-painted bodies lettered for Lionel Lines. The best of the older models (from the late 1930s) were the O gauge cabooses, the 2682 and its shorter cousin, the 2817. Both boasted shiny bodies, flattened cupolas, and fancy trim. The two models differed mainly in their couplers and trucks.

As nice as these tinplate cabooses were, two other designs towered over them in the early 1940s. The more celebrated was the 717, a scale-detailed model based on a New York Central Railroad prototype. This illuminated caboose, along with a twin that had tinplate trucks and automatic box couplers (the 2957), made their debut in 1940. Their 8¾-inch–long magnesium alloy bodies, painted Tuscan red and rubber-stamped white, featured

yellow marker lights and other plastic details. Then in 1941, as though to prove that the company never stood on its merits, Lionel introduced a second scale-detailed design. The 2757 captured the look of a Pennsylvania Railroad class N5 prototype. Painted Tuscan red with rubber-stamped white graphics, this superb caboose measured 7¾ inches in length. It boasted steps and a smokestack, red window frames, and frosted windows, not to mention interior lighting. The couplers and trucks on the 2757 were compatible with those on the 2957.

Which prewar caboose did Lionel decide to modify for the holiday season of 1945? Engineering personnel very likely sat down with sales executives and chose a middle ground. They rejected the older sheet-metal models as well as the most advanced scale-detailed one in favor of the 2757. In doing so, they followed the same course used with the first postwar boxcar and tank car. As an aside, the idea of updating the 2957 must have had some support because an all-but-identical car, assigned the number 2857, was shown in two top-of-the-line freight outfits and for separate sale in the 1946 catalog. No one knows if such a model was ever mass-produced.

After the war, Lionel started producing an updated version of the 2757 released as the 2457 in 1945. This illuminated model, painted brown or red and rubber-stamped white for the Pennsy, was loaded with such eye-catching details as painted window frames, celluloid window inserts, and a smokestack. The next year, Lionel expanded its roster with an O27 version that lacked interior lighting and other premium details. Also new in 1946 was the most desirable of the N5 cabooses, the 4457. It was equipped with the Electronic Control receiver that permitted it to function as part of the 4109WS Electronic Control Set.

Tinkering with the center-cupola N5 caboose was one way to expand the 1946 line. Another was to introduce a model based on a strikingly different prototype. Designers looked carefully at the kinds of cabooses found on railroads in the eastern United States until they came up with a winner. They brought out the 2419, a light gray work caboose whose injection-molded painted cab and toolboxes sat atop a die-cast metal frame. A deluxe dark gray version, numbered 2420, featured an operating searchlight that rotated. Both models were decorated for the Delaware, Lackawanna and Western Railroad and had an array of details, including a tall smokestack, wire handrails and steps, a ladder, two couplers, and two brakestands. On the Lionel Lines, as in real life, the work caboose worked in tandem with a rugged crane (the 2460), which also made its debut in 1946.

Appealing as the work caboose might have been, its form and function prevented it from complementing most sets. Lionel had to either stick with the tinplate N5 for regular freight outfits or turn to a similar design it could mass-produce at a lower cost. The answer appeared in 1947, when the company announced the first injection-molded cabooses. Two models, the 2257 and 2357, were based on a Southern Pacific Railroad prototype whose cupola was near the end of the car. The 2257 had no premium features (desirable variations feature a smokestack painted to match the body); the 2357 came with interior lighting, window inserts, and two couplers, ladders, and toolboxes.

In 1948 and 1949, Lionel revived memories of the heady days of the past by cataloging five new SP-type cabooses. Like one of the automobile manufacturers, it offered a model for every pocketbook. At one end of the spectrum was the 1007, an unpainted plastic caboose whose dearth of deluxe features made it right at home in inexpensive Scout sets. A step up, though it also lacked any notable details, was the 6257. A coat of paint and one or two brake wheels were all it could brag about. Next came the 6357. Painted red, maroon, or Tuscan red, it boasted interior lighting and sometimes a smokestack. Finally, there were the two deluxe models at the high end. The 6457 typically had a body painted Tuscan red, heat-stamped white graphics, illumination, two couplers and brake wheels, and a smokestack (most often die-cast). A special version of this caboose (the 4357) contained the equipment needed for it to replace the 4457 as part of the Electronic Control Set.

For most of the 1950s, Lionel maintained this broad range of conventional caboose models, though styles and numbers changed. Things stayed about the same in the middle, for example, with the 6257 and 6357 representing the best Lionel had to offer in O27. At the low end, shifts became apparent after 1952. Until then, the Scout caboose (the 1007 and 6007) represented the unpainted, bare-bones model. But Lionel discontinued the Scout line in 1953 and so began relying on two existing SP-type cabooses as its bottom-of-the-barrel models. The 6017 and 6037 came unpainted with one coupler and no deluxe features. The least-expensive O27 outfits contained one of these cars through 1954, when Lionel stopped producing the 6037. For the next three years, it relied on a Tuscan or red 6017 or a low-end work caboose to fill out the most basic sets.

No one could have quibbled if Lionel had elected to keep the 6457 as its premium caboose. In the early 1950s, this highly detailed, illuminated model surpassed any caboose put out by such competitors as Louis Marx and Company and The A. C. Gilbert Company. The fact that Lionel did delete the 6457 after 1952 and replaced it with an even more impressive O gauge model (the 6417 porthole caboose) testifies not only to the business acumen of its sales force but also to the talents of its engineering staff.

Executives believed that Lionel had to take the lead in developing realistic models of the latest locomotives and rolling stock for it to dominate the market and improve its product. The designers working under chief engineer Joseph Bonanno subscribed to the same credo and directed their skills to bringing out models of the highest caliber. To perceive the caboose as an afterthought, a set component that could be taken for granted, never occurred to them.

So, after introducing excellent models of conventional cabooses based on Pennsylvania Railroad and Southern Pacific prototypes in the 1940s, engineers introduced another style in 1953. They returned to the Pennsy for inspiration and concentrated on its N5c class of streamlined, turret-top "cabin cars." Right on schedule, they designed a model of this stately caboose, the 6417. First painted and lettered for the Pennsylvania, it soon was joined by another Tuscan red version decorated for Lionel Lines. In 1957, a sky blue model was packed with the pastel 1587S Lady Lionel (better knows as the Girls' Set). One-of-a-kind paint samples suggest that Lionel may have tried several colors (coral and turquoise among them) before settling on a bright shade of blue.

Among porthole cabooses, the 6417-50 Lehigh Valley deserves attention because it helped launch two key trends at Lionel. First, it broke with the tradition of conventional cabooses being red or brown (though a rare variation was painted Tuscan red). The regular-production model came painted gray with red heat-stamped lettering, which reflected the decision by sales executives to appeal to kids by marketing trains that were unmistakably toys.

The choice of colors for the 6417-50 wasn't capricious. Only available in the 2223W Big Haul Set, this caboose matched the 2321 Lackawanna F-M Train Master pulling the five-car train. Thus was begun a second trend, that of decorating rolling stock to resemble its motive power. The 6427 Virginian Railway porthole caboose and 6657 Denver and Rio Grande Western SP-type caboose belonged in this category, since both beautifully matched the locomotives that were included in their Super O outfits.

During the mid-1950s, Lionel's work caboose underwent the same minor "surgery" performed on its SP-type and porthole models. Of course, this happened only after the company mysteriously deleted the work caboose in 1951, the same year it deleted its crane. Fortunately for kids who loved work trains, the 6419 returned the next year. But notable alterations were performed on this diecast model in 1956. Designers modified the frame and cab to cut assembly costs and substituted a short smokestack. For the desirable 6419-100, they switched to the Norfolk and Western road name.

Lionel made a major modification to its work caboose in 1955, when it brought out one with a stamped sheet-metal frame. Decorated for the Lackawanna, the 6119 was equipped with an unpainted red cab and a single bin in place of the two toolboxes. In subsequent years, these plastic parts were orange, brown, or gray. Versions of the 6119 were packed with inexpensive O27 outfits.

As if Lionel's fleet wasn't sufficiently large and diverse, another style of conventional caboose made its debut in 1955. Designers decided against replicating a different center-cupola model as American Model Toys had done two years before with an O gauge caboose based on a Chesapeake and Ohio prototype. Neither did they offer the SP-type car in assorted road names as manufacturers of scale model trains typically did. Instead, they adapted another design and brought out a bay-window model. The 6517 featured a red-painted body with alcoves on each side rather than a cupola for crew members to monitor the train. Rubber-stamped white Lionel Lines graphics, interior lighting, twin couplers, and deluxe O27 passenger trucks highlighted this striking O gauge caboose.

Never again would Lionel be so adventurous with its cabooses. It chose, instead, to scale back its efforts and cut costs in the late 1950s and early 1960s. Unpainted SP-type models appeared at the bottom of the line (the 6047 and 6057), and the 6017 replaced the 6257 as the painted caboose in the middle. More road names appeared on low-end cabooses used as set components. For example, models came painted and lettered for the Boston and Maine, Chesapeake and Ohio, Minneapolis and St. Louis, and United States Navy in order to match the Alco diesels pulling their outfits. At the high end were the familiar 6357 SP-type (one decorated for the Santa Fe is the most valuable of all postwar cabooses) and 6437 porthole cars, along with an exciting newcomer. The 6557 had a liquid smoke unit that simulated a stove puffing away to warm a crew.

Lionel reduced the number and types of cabooses offered as the years passed in the 1960s. Low-end SP-type and work cabooses received little or sometimes no decoration so they could be produced at little cost for inexpensive uncataloged and promotional sets. At the opposite end, Lionel cataloged only a Pennsylvania Railroad porthole caboose (the 6437) and a Santa Fe work caboose (the 6130). Interestingly, some of the scarcest postwar caboose variations date from this time: the 6167 unmarked olive SP-type caboose, 6429 die-cast work caboose, and 6447 Pennsylvania porthole caboose.

Taken together, the variety of cabooses manufactured by Lionel attested once more to the ingenuity of its engineering staff. They managed to put five prototypical designs into production between 1945 and 1955. Furthermore, all or some versions of each caboose featured premium details and interior illumination. Having these different designs at their disposal, salesmen and designers could easily expand the line to satisfy children and hobbyists alike.

That's exactly what they did from the late 1950s through the 1960s. In place of new designs came a rainbow of colors and an array of road names on the O27 gauge SP-type and work cabooses. The assortment of cabooses available was nothing short of amazing. One Super O model even emitted whiffs of smoke from its stack, and another carried medical technicians and equipment to handle any emergencies along the route. Admittedly, Lionel never added an animated figure to a caboose as Gilbert did for its S gauge American Flyer line. Still, what Lionel did achieve is impressive. No wonder its cabooses, which might have become forgotten elements of freight outfits, command increasing attention from postwar enthusiasts.

TINPLATE N5-TYPE CABOOSES

The postwar tinplate caboose was cataloged as 2457 for O gauge, 2472 for O27 gauge, and 4457 for the Electronic Control Set. Except for premium details, all models were basically the same and shared a common lettering scheme. The O gauge 2457 was lighted and included every premium detail available except for the Electronic Control Set receiver and decals. By contrast, the 2472 was stripped to bare bones, with end rails and ladders as the only details.

WORK CABOOSES

Lionel manufactured two types of work cabooses: one with a die-cast frame and the other with a sheet-metal frame. At a quick glance, the types look similar, but in reality they are as different as day and night. The only part they have in common is the cab of the 1956 model of 6419 and that of all 6119 types.

From 1946, when the work caboose made its debut, through 1955, all models used basically the same parts and had a cab attached to the frame with four screws. In 1956 Lionel designers made modifications to reduce costs. They added molded projections (tabs) to the cab, which interlocked with two slots in the new frame casting.

All pre-1956 models used a *tall* die-cast smokestack that made the roof susceptible to cracking if handled or packed improperly. All 1956 models used a *short* smokestack that had been developed for the bay-window caboose.

The road name and number on all D. L. & W. 2419, 2420, 6419, 6420, and 6429 work caboose cabs were heat-stamped in black and overscored and underscored. All frames were lettered "LIONEL LINES"; sans-serif versions were rubber-stamped, while serif examples generally were heat-stamped. The casting for the frame was reinforced in 1947 with the addition of six small squares that are visible on the underside.

Lionel introduced the 6119 work caboose in 1955. This family of cabooses used a stamped sheet-metal frame similar to that found on the 6111 and 6121 flatcars, but without the railing at one end. The frame was properly slotted to accept both a cab and a tool tray with tabs. A flexible extrusion at the tray end was included on the underside of the frame to secure the cab and tray once they were in place.

All frames include steps at the four corners and are embossed on the underside in four lines: "MADE IN / U.S. OF AMERICA / THE LIONEL CORPORATION / NEW YORK, N.Y." The embossing stamp deteriorated with age and showed progressive stages of visibility. Frames from the 1950s were usually painted. As a cost-saving measure, painted frames were replaced in the 1960s with chemically blackened versions, which in turn were replaced by chemically treated frames that appeared bronze in color.

The name "LIONEL" was usually stamped on the sides of frames; all sans-serif examples were heat-stamped, while serif versions were either heat-stamped (earlier production) or rubber-stamped (later production). Unlettered frames started to appear in 1965 and became the norm for the remainder of work caboose production.

Another noticeable change involved the scribed wood slats on the cab; they were present below the rectangular plate for logos and lettering on all early models. Sometime in 1966 designers enlarged the rectangular plate and deleted the slats and also added another small rectangular surface or builder's plate to the immediate left of the logo and lettering rectangle.

Cataloged production models came with a short smokestack. The road name and number on all 6119 D. L. & W. work caboose cabs were heat-stamped and overscored and underscored. Be aware that frames are easily and often switched. Truck and coupler modifications followed the normal progression, as did other parts of the product line.

SP-TYPE CABOOSES

The quest for realism and detail in postwar trains led to Lionel's expanded use of injection-molded plastic bodies. The company first used injection-molding for the 2452 gondola in 1945 and then the 2454 boxcar and 2465 double-dome tank car in 1946. Lionel management was quite pleased with the lower production and assembly costs associated with this technology and set out to use it for cabooses.

The 2257 model, a version with no deluxe features for O27 gauge, was 1947 production; in 1948 Lionel introduced the magnetic coupler for the O27 line and renumbered all O27 gauge rolling stock with 6000-series numbers to reflect the intended coupler change. It is not uncommon, however, to find O27 items from the 1948 line with 6000-series numbers and coil couplers; there were always overlaps of discontinued parts, especially during a year of major transition.

There are at least eight different SP-type caboose

frames. All cabooses manufactured prior to 1957 were attached to the appropriate frame with two screws. The pre-1957 frames are basically two types: those for deluxe lighted models and those for unlighted models. The lighted frames included necessary holes for battery boxes, wires, and a lamp socket. In mid-1957 Lionel introduced the tab frame with end rails that eliminated the need for screws. Most tab frames were chemically blackened, but some examples, usually from the later 1950s, were painted black. In 1963 the introduction of a galvanized tab frame without end rails further reduced costs on bottom-end cabooses.

Typically, SP-type cabooses came with heat-stamped markings, but these markings differed. Cabooses with the SP or the circled-L logo, because of the asymmetrical shape of the body, required a separate left-side and right-side heat-stamp plate to keep the graphics in the same place on each side of the car. This process is known as *one-way lettering*. On low-end cabooses, such as the 1007 and 6017, or models lacking the SP and circled-L logos, a single heat-stamp plate was decorated both sides of the car. This process, which saved on tooling costs and production time, is known as *reversible lettering* because each side of the caboose is the exact opposite of the other. In the heat-stamping, each side of the car received its markings in a separate step. Since the two sides were not stamped simultaneously, a car could be found with one side blank, which was nothing more than a simple manufacturing error.

N5C PORTHOLE-TYPE CABOOSES

Lionel first cataloged its version of the porthole caboose in 1953. Designers modeled it on the class N5c streamlined, turret-top cabin car developed by the Pennsylvania Railroad. All body shells were molded plastic, either black or clear, and included the mold number "6417-4". Bodies were painted the intended color and decorated with heat-stamped markings. All Pennsylvania road name cabooses included the stylized built date: "BLT 2-53 N5C / LIONEL / L". Lionel Lines models were stamped "BLT 11-53 / LIONEL / L"; Lehigh Valley examples were marked "BLT 6-54 / LIONEL / L". All 6417 and 6427 models were equipped with bar-end trucks, while the 6437 and 6447 came with AAR trucks.

BAY-WINDOW CABOOSES

The handsome bay-window-style caboose debuted in 1955; it was a top-of-the-line O gauge item. A window shade (a shaped piece of thick black paper) was inserted between the body of the caboose and the window shell at the bay area. The use of shades was not consistent; mint examples have been observed without them. All models were painted, decorated with white rubber-stamped lettering, and fitted with die-cast O27 gauge passenger trucks.

SP-TYPE CABOOSE CHARACTERISTICS

Compiled by Paul V. Ambrose

The following chart completely re-identifies all the SP caboose body types; it also corrects past errors and provides new data. However, because it would be a herculean task, we have not at this time associated a specific body type(s) with any of the SP caboose listings. With further research and collector input, we hope to identify specific types in future editions.

Mold Variations

Former Designation	1	2	1A	2A	Not Defined				All 3s			4
New Designation	1A	1B	2A	2B	3A	3B	4A	4B	4C	4D	4E	5
Characteristics												
Ladder slots	yes	yes	yes	yes	yes	yes	no	no	no	no	no	yes
Frames around front- and rear-facing cupola windows	no	no	no	no	no	no	no	no	no	no	no	yes
Reinforced roofline below side-facing cupola windows	no	no	no	no	yes	yes	yes	yes	yes	yes	yes	yes
Step construction	thin	thin	thin	thin	thin	thin	thin	thin	thin	thin	thin	thick
Catwalk overhang supports	no	no	no	no	no	no	no	no	no	no	no	yes
Catwalk board opposite cupola	none	none	none	none	tall	short	none	none	none	none	none	none
Stack plug: flat, recessed (rec.), or raised rim (RR)	RR	RR	RR	RR	rec.	rec.	flat	flat	flat	flat	RR	rec.
Reinforced stack plug (interior)	yes	yes	yes	yes	yes	yes	no	no	no	no	yes	no
Wedges (roof panel 4)	no	no	no	no	no	no	no	no	yes	yes	yes	no
Cupola roof railing: curved, high short (HS), low long (LL), low short (LS)	HS	HS	HS	HS	HS	HS	LS	LL	LL	LL	LL	curved
Extra rivet (each end) above door	no	no	no	no	yes	yes	yes	yes	yes	yes	yes	yes
Side rivet detail below windows 2 and 4	8	8	4	4	8	8	8	8	4	8	8	4
Detail near grab iron at front left corner: 2 rivets with rivet touching, 2 rivets with space 3 rivets	touch	space	touch	space	space	space	space	space	space	space	space	3 rivets
Roof panels in panel 2 (adjacent to catwalk) showing faint repair lines	no	no	no	no	no	no	yes	yes	yes	yes	yes	no

Note: The new Type 4C has unique detail on the inside of the roof: Instead of a channel, the interior roof is flat and has "PART NO 2357-3" handscribed into the mold.

From *Greenberg's Guide to Lionel Trains, 1945–1969, Vol. VII*

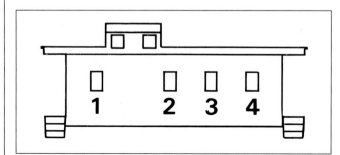

Vertical rivets below side windows 3 and 4
- Eight rivets: Types 1A, 1B, 3A, 3B, 4A, 4B, 4D, 4E
- Four rivets: Types 2A, 2B, 4C, 5

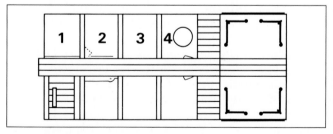

SP-style caboose roof details
Note that a raised board is present in the center portion of the catwalk in roof panel 1 for Types 3A and 3B. Also observe the faint repair lines in panel 2, which are present on all Type 4 examples, and the wedge detail in panel 4, which appears on types 4C, 4D, and 4E.

Top: 1007 (A) and (B) Lionel Lines. Note the raised board on catwalk ½ inch from the right end. Bottom: 4357 (B) Lionel SP *from the Electronic Control Set. This example also includes the raised board on the catwalk. R. Swanson Collection.*

	Gd	VG	Ex	LN

1007 LIONEL LINES: 1948–52. SP-type; unpainted body with white heat-stamped reversible lettering; black-painted or chemically blackened frame; no deluxe features; Scout trucks with one Scout coupler.

	Gd	VG	Ex	LN
(A) Red body; common.	3	5	8	10
(B) Red body, mold includes raised center board on catwalk; scarce.	20	40	75	100
(C) Tuscan body; very scarce.	100	225	350	500

2257 LIONEL-SP: 1947. SP-type; various painted bodies, typically with white heat-stamped lettering; no deluxe features; black-painted frame with two brake wheels usually mounted on the inside of the railing towards the body; staple-end trucks with one coil coupler; considered O27 gauge.

	Gd	VG	Ex	LN
(A) Red body; no deluxe features; common.	5	7	10	12
(B) Red-orange body; no deluxe features; common.	5	7	10	12
(C) Red-orange body and matching plastic smokestack; other features inconsequential; very scarce.	100	175	300	400
(D) Same as (C), but with atypical rubber-stamped lettering; rare.	150	225	350	500
(E) Tuscan body and matching plastic smokestack; other features inconsequential; very scarce.	100	175	300	400

	Gd	VG	Ex	LN
(F) Same as (E), but with atypical rubber-stamped lettering; rare.	150	225	350	500

2357 LIONEL-SP: 1947–48. SP-type; various painted bodies, typically with white heat-stamped lettering; plastic smokestack painted to match body; lighted; window shell; ladders; black-painted frame with battery boxes and two brake wheels (earliest production had brake wheels mounted on the inside of the railing towards the body, but soon these moved to outside of railing, due to interference with mounting body to frame); staple-end trucks with two coil couplers.

	Gd	VG	Ex	LN
(A) Tuscan body and smokestack; most common.	15	20	30	35
(B) Same as (A), but with atypical rubber-stamped lettering; rare.	150	225	350	500
(C) Red body and smokestack; no deluxe features; very scarce.	115	175	275	400
(D) Red body and smokestack; deluxe features inconsequential; atypical rubber-stamped lettering; rare.	150	225	350	500
(E) Tile red body; no smokestack; usually with battery boxes and ladders; one coupler; scarce.	40	75	150	200
(F) Tile red body; no smokestack or ladders; usually without battery boxes; one coupler; underframe rubber-stamped "6357"; scarce.	40	75	150	200

All the cabooses in this picture are named Lionel and include SP. Top: 2257 (A) and very scarce 2257 (E) with matching plastic smokestack. Middle: 2357 (A) and very scarce 2357 (C) with matching plastic smokestack. Bottom: Scarce tile red examples 2357 (E) and 2357 (F). R. Swanson Collection.

	Gd	VG	Ex	LN

2419 D. L. & W. (Delaware, Lackawanna and Western): 1946-47. Work caboose; light gray-painted toolboxes and cab with black heat-stamped lettering; tall smokestack; two brakestands; handrails; steps; ladder; light gray-painted die-cast frame with black heat-stamped serif lettering; frame casting reinforced in 1947 with the addition of six small squares on the underside; staple-end trucks with two coil couplers.

	20	30	45	60

2420 D. L. & W.: 1946–47. Work caboose with searchlight; dark gray-painted toolboxes and cab with black heat-stamped lettering; tall smokestack; two brakestands; handrails; steps; ladder; typically dark gray-painted die-cast frame with black lettering; frame casting reinforced in 1947 with the addition of six small squares on the underside; staple-end trucks with two coil couplers.

(A) Light gray frame with rubber-stamped sans-serif lettering; very scarce. **100 150 225 325**

(B) Light gray frame with rubber-stamped serif lettering; very scarce. **100 150 225 325**

(C) Dark gray frame with rubber-stamped sans-serif lettering. **40 70 100 120**

(D) Dark gray frame with heat-stamped serif lettering. **40 70 100 120**

(2457) 477618 PENNSYLVANIA: 1945–47. Tinplate caboose; semigloss painted bodies with white rubber-stamped lettering; caboose actually numbered "477618";

all with "EASTERN DIV." except as noted; window frames and celluloid window inserts; smokestack; black-painted frame with steps at the four corners; lighted; battery box; plastic air pump; end rails with ladder; brakestand at each end; underside of frame usually rubber-stamped "2457". There are numerous wheel, axle, collector roller, and coupler variations, but all examples came with staple-end trucks and coil coupler(s). Most variations with pierced front and rear cupola windows.

(A) Brown body and smokestack with red window frames; off-center lettering, probably a 1941 or 1942 reject used to meet the extraordinary demand for sets in 1945. **35 60 100 150**

(B) Same as (A), except properly centered lettering. **35 60 100 150**

(C) Red body and smokestack with red window frames. **15 22 30 40**

(D) Red body and smokestack with black window frames. **15 22 30 40**

(E) Red body and smokestack with black window frames, but without "EASTERN DIV." **15 22 30 40**

(F) Same as (E), but with black smokestack. **15 22 30 40**

(2472) 477618 PENNSYLVANIA: 1946–47. Tinplate caboose; semigloss red-painted body with white rubber-stamped lettering; most versions with unpierced front

Seven D. L. & W. work cabooses. Top: 2419, 2420, and box for red 6119 shown on second shelf. Notice both the size of the box, which was downsized in 1955 to eliminate the full wraparound liner of previous years, and the high smokestacks on the 2419 and 2420

models. Second: 6119 and 6119-25 D. L. & W. and box. All 6119 caboose boxes were further downsized in 1956. Third: 6119-50 and 6119-75 and box. Bottom: 6119-100 and Orange Picture box. R. Shanfeld Collection.

	Gd	VG	Ex	LN

and rear cupola windows; caboose actually numbered "477618" (the same as 2457); black-painted frame typically without steps; end rails with ladder; not lighted and lacks all other premium details offered on 2457; underside of frame usually rubber-stamped "2472"; staple-end trucks with one coil coupler. There are numerous wheel, axle, and coupler variations.

(A) Body with "EASTERN DIV."

	Gd	VG	Ex	LN
	10	15	25	30

(B) Body without "EASTERN DIV."

	10	15	25	30

(C) Same as (B), but pierced front and rear cupola windows (possible depletion of inventory of 2457 bodies).

	12	15	25	30

4357 LIONEL-SP: 1948–49. SP-type; Tuscan-painted body with white heat-stamped lettering; SP logo; blue-and-white Electronic Control decals; smokestack; lighted; window shell; ladders; black-painted frame with battery boxes, two brake wheels, and Electronic Control receiver; staple-end trucks with two coil couplers.

	Gd	VG	Ex	LN

(A) Matching plastic smokestack.

	55	90	165	250

(B) Black die-cast smokestack.

	55	90	165	250

4457 PENNSYLVANIA: 1946–47. Tinplate caboose; semigloss red-painted body and smokestack with black window frames; underside of frame rubber-stamped "4457"; lettering and other premium details are the same as 2457, with the addition of an Electronic Control receiver and blue-and-white Electronic Control decals; staple-end trucks with two coil couplers.

	45	80	165	225

6007 LIONEL LINES: 1950. SP-type; unpainted red body with white heat-stamped reversible lettering; no deluxe features; chemically blackened frame; Scout trucks with one magnetic coupler.

	3	6	9	12

6017 LIONEL LINES: 1951–62. SP-type; various bodies, with white heat-stamped reversible lettering; no

Four different tinplate N5-type cabooses. Top: 2457 (D) and (E). Observe that the example on the right does not have "EASTERN DIV." or the extra step that was spot-welded onto the top frame step. Bottom: 2457 (A) and (B). The left caboose is the better-documented variation that has "PENNSYLVANIA" lettering *noticeably offset to the left. A photo of this caboose appears on page 14 of the 1946 advance catalog. The right caboose has the lettering more nearly centered. The off-centered lettering body is probably a 1941 or 1942 reject used to meet the extraordinary demand for sets in 1945. R. Swanson Collection.*

	Gd	VG	Ex	LN

deluxe features, but some early models did include one brake wheel; pre-1957 production attached to frame with screws, and later production exclusively with tab frame; 1951 models with staple-end trucks and one magnetic coupler, 1952–56 examples with bar-end trucks and one magnetic coupler, and 1957 and all later production with tab frame and AAR trucks with one operating coupler.

Note: The body molds for 1951–57 examples were unpainted because 6017 was the bottom end of the line. However, by 1958 it had become a better caboose, due in part to the demise of the 6257, and was regularly painted; unpainted "low-end" cabooses were introduced as 6047 and 6057. Painted bodies varied from Tuscan to maroon to shades of tile red. To complicate matters further, this caboose utilized so many mold variations and underlying colors of plastic that it is nearly impossible to place them in exact chronological order. When applied to plastic of different colors, identical paint will cast different hues.

(A) Unpainted red body. A red 6017 with bar-end trucks was typical production in the early 1950s; red was supplanted by Tuscan in the mid-1950s, only to reappear in 1957–58 with a different body type and a tab frame with AAR trucks.

	Gd	VG	Ex	LN
	3	6	10	15

(B) Unpainted Tuscan body; mid-1950s production, usually with bar-end trucks.   **2   4   6   8**

(C) Glossy Tuscan-painted body (usually on orange body mold); scarce.   **50   75   150   200**

(D) Semigloss Tuscan-painted body (usually on orange body mold).   **15   40   70   100**

(E) Maroon-painted body.   **3   6   10   15**

(F) Light tile red-painted body.   **3   6   10   15**

(G) Dark tile red-painted body.   **3   6   10   15**

(H) Brown-painted body; the most common color for the late 1950s and early 1960s production.   **2   4   6   8**

6017 LIONEL: 1956. SP-type; unpainted shiny maroon body with white heat-stamped reversible lettering that is completely different from 6017 LIONEL LINES; no deluxe features; chemically blackened frame; bar-end

Note that the 6017 cabooses shown here are listed under the entry with Lionel Lines. Top: 6017 (F) and (B). Bottom: Two shade variations of 6017 (H). Brown was the most common color for models produced in the late 1950s and early 1960s. R. Shanfeld Collection.

	Gd	VG	Ex	LN

trucks with one coupler. A moderately scarce variation that has not aroused much collector interest.

	15	30	40	75

6017(-)50 UNITED STATES MARINE CORPS: 1958. SP-type; dark blue-painted body with white heat-stamped reversible lettering; actually numbered "601750"; no deluxe features; chemically blackened tab frame; AAR trucks with one operating coupler.

	20	30	55	75

6017(-85) LIONEL LINES: 1958. SP-type; light gray-painted body with black heat-stamped reversible lettering; numbered only "6017"; no deluxe features; chemically blackened tab frame; AAR trucks with one operating coupler.

	20	35	50	80

6017(-100) BOSTON and MAINE: 1959, 1962, 1965–66. SP-type; various shades of blue-painted bodies with white heat-stamped one-way lettering and stylized B M logo; numbered only "6017"; no deluxe features; chemically blackened tab frame; AAR trucks with one operating coupler.

(A) Dark purple-blue body; very scarce.

	250	450	600	900

(B) Glossy medium blue body.

	10	25	40	50

(C) Semigloss medium blue body.

	10	25	40	50

(D) Semigloss light blue body.

	10	25	40	50

6017(-185) A. T. & S. F.: 1959–60. SP-type; light gray-painted body with red or maroon heat-stamped reversible lettering; numbered only "6017"; no deluxe features; chemically blackened tab frame; AAR trucks with one operating coupler.

	10	20	35	50

6017(-200) UNITED STATES NAVY: 1960. SP-type;

	Gd	VG	Ex	LN

light blue–painted body with white heat-stamped reversible lettering and Navy logo; numbered only "6017"; no deluxe features; chemically blackened tab frame; AAR truck with one operating coupler.

	35	50	85	125

6017(-235) A. T. & S. F.: 1962. SP-type; red-painted body with white heat-stamped reversible lettering; numbered only "6017"; no deluxe features; chemically blackened tab frame; AAR trucks with one operating coupler.

	25	35	50	65

6027 ALASKA RAILROAD: 1959. SP-type; dark blue–painted body with yellow heat-stamped one-way lettering and Eskimo figure; no deluxe features; chemically blackened tab frame; AAR trucks with one operating coupler.

	25	45	80	100

6037 LIONEL LINES: 1952–54. SP-type; unpainted bodies with white heat-stamped reversible lettering; no deluxe features; chemically blackened frame; Scout trucks with one magnetic coupler.

(A) Tuscan body; common.	2	4	6	8
(B) Red body; scarce.	15	25	45	65

6047 LIONEL LINES: 1962. SP-type; unpainted red body with white heat-stamped reversible lettering; no deluxe features; chemically blackened tab frame; archbar trucks with one fixed coupler; also featured in 1959–61 advance catalog sets and uncataloged sets of the era.

(A) Coral-pink body.	15	25	45	65
(B) Medium red body.	2	4	6	8

6057 LIONEL LINES: 1959–62, 1969. SP-type; typically unpainted red body with white heat-stamped reversible lettering; no deluxe features; chemically blackened tab frame; AAR trucks with one operating coupler.

(A) Earliest production, red-painted body.

	20	40	70	100

Top: 6017-50 United States Marine Corps and 6017-85 gray Lionel Lines. Second: 6017-100 (C) Boston and Maine and rare dark blue 6017-100 (A) Boston and Maine. Third: Two 6017-185 A. T. & S. F. cabooses. At left, painted black body; at right, painted red body. Note the color of the underlying plastic where the paint is worn. Bottom: 6017-235 A. T. & S. F. and 6017-200 United States Navy. R. Shanfeld Collection.

	Gd	VG	Ex	LN
(B) Coral-pink body.	15	25	45	65
(C) Medium red body.	3	6	10	15

6057(-50) LIONEL LINES: 1962. SP-type; unpainted orange body with black heat-stamped reversible lettering; no deluxe features; chemically blackened tab frame; AAR trucks with one operating coupler.

	12	15	25	40

6058 CHESAPEAKE and OHIO: 1961. SP-type; dark yellow–painted body with dark blue heat-stamped reversible lettering; no deluxe features; chemically blackened tab frame; AAR trucks with one operating coupler.

	15	25	45	65

6059 M & St L (Minneapolis & St. Louis): 1961–69. SP-type; various bodies with white heat-stamped one-way lettering; no deluxe features; chemically blackened tab frame; AAR trucks usually with one operating coupler (however, 1963–64 versions, cataloged as 6059-50, often came with one fixed and one operating coupler).

(A) Earliest production, red-painted gray body; scarce.

	8	10	16	25

	Gd	VG	Ex	LN
(B) Unpainted medium red body.				
	4	6	8	10
(C) Unpainted dark red body.				
	4	6	8	10
(D) Unpainted maroon body.				
	6	9	12	15

(6059-50): See 6059.

(6067) UNMARKED: Uncataloged, 1961–62. SP-type; various unpainted bodies with no lettering; no deluxe features; chemically blackened tab frame; usually with arch-bar trucks and one fixed coupler.

Note: This caboose came on a frame with end rails. See (6167) unmarked.

	Gd	VG	Ex	LN
(A) Red body.	2	4	6	8
(B) Yellow body; moderately scarce.				
	10	15	25	40
(C) Brown body; scarce.	15	25	40	60

6119 D. L. & W.: 1955–56. Work caboose; unpainted red tool tray and cab with white heat-stamped lettering; short smokestack; black-painted frame with white heat

6027 Alaska Railroad and 6037 Lionel Lines. R. Shanfeld Collection.

6047 Lionel Lines.

6057 Lionel Lines.

6057-50 Lionel Lines.

6058 Chesapeake and Ohio.

Minneapolis and St. Louis examples 6059 (B) and (C).

	Gd	VG	Ex	LN

stamped serif lettering; bar-end trucks with one coupler.

	10	15	25	45

6119(-)25 D. L. & W.: 1956. Work caboose; unpainted orange tool tray and cab with black heat-stamped lettering; actually numbered "611925"; short smokestack; orange-painted frame (part no. 6119-29) with black heat-stamped serif lettering; bar-end trucks with one coupler

	10	15	30	50

6119(-50) D. L. & W.: 1956. Work caboose; unpainted brown tool tray and cab with white heat-stamped lettering; short smokestack; brown-painted frame with white heat-stamped serif lettering; bar-end trucks with one coupler.

	15	25	55	70

6119(-75) D. L. & W.: 1957. Work caboose; unpainted gray tool tray and cab with black heat-stamped lettering; short smokestack; light gray-painted frame typically with black heat-stamped sans-serif lettering; bar-end trucks with one coupler.

(A) Common frame as described above.

	12	15	35	45

(B) Very scarce variation with closely spaced, black rubber-stamped serif lettering on frame.

	100	150	250	325

	Gd	VG	Ex	LN

6119(-100) D. L. & W.: 1957–66, 1969. Work caboose, also cataloged in 1964 and listed in the Lionel Service Manual with a -110 suffix; unpainted gray tool tray and typically unpainted red cab with white heat-stamped lettering; short smokestack; typically black-painted or chemically blackened frame with lettering variations; 1957 issues with bar-end trucks and one coupler, later issues with AAR trucks and usually one operating coupler. Followed the normal progression of truck and coupler modifications, as did other items in the product line.

(A) Black-painted frame with white heat-stamped serif lettering; bar-end trucks.

	12	15	25	40

(B) Black-painted frame with white heat-stamped sans-serif lettering; bar-end or AAR trucks.

	12	15	25	40

(C) Chemically blackened frame with white rubber-stamped serif lettering; AAR trucks.

	12	15	25	40

(D) Ca. 1964; very scarce variation with red-painted red cab; frame lettering inconsequential; AAR trucks. Many work cabooses that are dated to 1963–64 appear with one fixed and one operating coupler.

	40	75	125	175

(E) Early 1966; scarce variation; cab still with wood slats below the logo and lettering rectangle, but with a builder's plate heat-stamped "BUILT BY / LIONEL";

	Gd	VG	Ex	LN

chemically blackened or treated unlettered frame; AAR trucks. **40 75 125 175**

(F) Late 1966; scarce; cab with enlarged logo and lettering rectangle and a builder's plate heat-stamped "BUILT BY / LIONEL"; chemically blackened or treated unlettered frame; AAR trucks. **40 75 125 175**

(G) 1969 set component with gray tool tray and pale red cab with white heat-stamped Santa Fe logo; chemically blackened or treated unlettered frame; AAR trucks; cab (same as late 6130) with enlarged logo and lettering rectangle and blank builder's plate. This odd assembly was a desperate attempt by Lionel to deplete any and all parts inventory. **12 15 25 35**

6119(-110): See 6119(-100).

(6119-125) UNNUMBERED: Uncataloged, 1964. Work caboose; unpainted olive tool tray and cab with white heat-stamped markings; cab with first-aid–type cross, and tool tray with "RESCUE / UNIT" and cross; short smokestack; chemically blackened frame with white rubber-stamped serif lettering; AAR trucks with one operating coupler. **60 100 140 250**

(6120) UNMARKED: Uncataloged 1961–63. Work caboose; unpainted yellow tool tray and cab; no smokestack; black-painted or chemically blackened frame; arch-bar trucks with one fixed coupler. An advance catalog and low-end uncataloged set component. **7 15 25 35**

6130 A T S F (Santa Fe): 1961, 1965–69. Work caboose; red tool tray and cab with white heat-stamped lettering; cab with Santa Fe logo and tool tray with "6130", "ATSF", and "BUILT BY / LIONEL"; short smokestack; typically black frame; AAR trucks with varying coupler combinations; followed the normal progression of truck and coupler modifications as did other parts of the product line

(A) Early 1960s production; red-painted tool tray and cab; black-painted frame with white rubber-stamped serif lettering; one operating coupler. **10 20 30 50**

(B) Same as (A), except with red-orange-painted tool tray and cab. **10 20 30 50**

(C) Same as (A), but with a chemically blackened unlettered frame. **10 20 30 50**

(D) Early 1966; very scarce variation; tool tray and cab painted true red; cab with wood slats below the logo and lettering rectangle but with a blank builder's plate; chemically blackened unlettered frame; usually with one fixed and one operating coupler. **40 75 125 175**

(E) Late 1966 and after production; *unpainted* pale red tool tray and cab; cab with enlarged logo and lettering rectangle and builder's plate; chemically blackened or treated unlettered frame; usually with one fixed and one operating coupler. **15 25 45 60**

6167 LIONEL LINES: 1963–64. SP-type; typically unpainted red body with white heat-stamped reversible lettering; no deluxe features; galvanized tab frame; AAR

trucks with coupler combinations as noted below; the galvanized tab frame was introduced in 1963 and did *not* include end rails.

(A) Common version with either two fixed couplers or one fixed and one operating coupler. **3 6 9 12**

(B) Lionel Service Manual and catalog listing as 6167-100 with one operating coupler. **3 6 9 12**

(C) Lionel Service Manual listing as 6167-150 with one fixed coupler. **3 6 9 12**

(D) Red-painted body; coupler features inconsequential; very scarce. **40 75 125 175**

(6167) UNMARKED: 1963–64. SP-type; various unpainted bodies with no lettering; no deluxe features; galvanized tab frame; AAR or arch-bar trucks with coupler combinations noted below; the galvanized tab frame was introduced in 1963 and did *not* include end rails.

(A) Red body with one fixed coupler; Lionel Service Manual and catalog listing as 6167-25. **3 6 10 14**

(B) Red body with one fixed and one operating coupler; Lionel Service Manual and catalog listing as 6167-125. **3 6 10 14**

(C) Yellow body with one fixed coupler; Lionel Service Manual and catalog listing as 6167-50. **10 15 25 40**

(D) Olive body; uncataloged set component; very scarce. **125 225 350 500**

(E) Brown body; uncataloged set component; scarce. See also (6067). **15 25 40 60**

(6167-25): See (6167) UNMARKED.
(6167-50): See (6167) UNMARKED.

6167(-85) UNION PACIFIC: Uncataloged, 1963–66; cataloged 1969. SP-type; unpainted yellow body with black heat-stamped reversible lettering; numbered only "6167"; no deluxe features; galvanized tab frame or chemically blackened tab frame; varying truck and coupler combinations. First issued with set 19263, a Libby's promotional outfit from 1963. (See *Greenberg's Guide to Lionel Trains 1945–1969, Volume IV: Uncatalogued Sets.*) **10 15 30 40**

(6167-100): See 6167 LIONEL LINES.
(6167-125): See (6167) UNMARKED.
(6167-150): See 6167 LIONEL LINES.

6219 C & O (Chesapeake and Ohio): 1960. Work caboose; dark blue–painted tool tray and cab with yellow heat-stamped lettering; short smokestack; black-painted frame with yellow rubber-stamped serif lettering; AAR trucks with one operating coupler. **25 35 75 90**

The 6257, cataloged 1948–56 and 1963-64, was an unlighted model that was a grade above the 6017. Regular

6130 (A) Santa Fe and 6219 Chesapeake and Ohio. R. Shanfeld Collection. Other work cabooses are shown on page 162.

Top: 6167 (A) Lionel Lines and unmarked 6167 (A). Bottom: Unmarked 6167 (C), and 6167-85 Union Pacific. R. Shanfeld Collection.

	Gd	VG	Ex	LN

production did not include a window shell, smokestack, battery boxes, or ladders. Most examples did, however, come with one brake wheel at the cupola end, though the application of brake wheels was not consistent; early production often included two brake wheels, while some mid-1950s and all 1960s items came without any. The 6257 listings below are classified by lettering, as are the 6357 listings (see the photograph for illustrations of all types). Types I and II lettering are one-way, which means separate left-side and right-side heat-stamp plates were required.

	Gd	VG	Ex	LN

Types III and IV lettering are reversible, which means the same plate was used to decorate both sides of the caboose.

6257 (Type I lettering) LIONEL-SP: 1948–52. SP-type; various painted bodies with white heat-stamped lettering; SP logo; no deluxe features; black-painted frame usually with two brake wheels or chemically blackened frame usually with one brake wheel; pre-1952 examples with staple-end trucks and one magnetic coupler; 1952 production had bar-end trucks and one magnetic coupler.

Top: Very scarce unmarked 6167 (D) olive body, and unmarked 6067 (C). Observe that the brown caboose on the right came on a frame with end rails. Bottom: Unmarked 6067 (A), and unmarked 6167 (A). The example at right does not include end rails. R. Gladsen Collection.

	Gd	VG	Ex	LN

(A) Dark tile red body and matching plastic smokestack; usually with battery boxes; very scarce.

	125	225	350	500
(B) Red body.	3	6	8	11
(C) Red-orange body.	3	6	8	11
(D) Tile red body.	3	6	8	11

6257X (Type I lettering) LIONEL-SP: 1948. SP-type; tile red-painted body with white heat-stamped lettering; SP logo; no deluxe features; black-painted frame with two brake wheels; staple-end trucks with two magnetic couplers.

Note: Since the caboose body and frame are identical to early 6257 production (see above listing), it must be obtained with the proper box (Early Classic numbered "6257X") to warrant values listed.

	12	15	30	35

6257 (Type II lettering) LIONEL–Circled-L: 1953–55. SP-type; various bodies with white heat-stamped lettering; circled-L Lionel logo; no deluxe features; chemically blackened frame usually with one brake wheel; bar-end trucks with one coupler; usually designated 6257-25.

(A) Red-painted body.	6	12	25	30
(B) Dark red-painted body.	6	12	25	30
(C) Tile red-painted body.	6	12	25	30
(D) Unpainted red body.	4	6	9	12

6257 (Type III lettering) LIONEL: 1956. SP-type; unpainted red body with white heat-stamped reversible lettering; no deluxe features; chemically blackened frame usually with one brake wheel; bar-end trucks with one coupler; usually designated 6257-50.

(A) "6257" at left.	5	8	15	20
(B) "6257" at right.	5	8	15	20

6257 (Type IV lettering) LIONEL LINES: 1963–64. SP-type; unpainted red body with white heat-stamped reversible lettering; die-cast smokestack; chemically blackened tab frame; AAR trucks with one operating coupler; usually listed in the consumer catalog as 6257-100.

	7	10	18	25

The 6357, cataloged 1948–61, was a medium-grade lighted model with a window shell, but it did not come equipped with battery boxes or ladders. Most examples came with one brake wheel at the cupola end and one magnetic coupler. Pre-1952 production did not include a smokestack; however, after the 6457 was discontinued in 1952, the 6357 was to become the top-of-the-line SP-type caboose so a smokestack was added. The 6357 listings below are classified by lettering. Types I and II lettering are one-way, which means separate left-side and right-side heat-stamp plates were required. Type III lettering is reversible, which means the same plate was used to decorate both sides of the caboose.

6357 (Type I lettering) LIONEL-SP: 1948–53. SP-type; various painted bodies with white heat-stamped lettering; SP logo; lighted; window shell; frame with one brake wheel; pre-1952 examples with staple-end trucks and one magnetic coupler, and 1952–53 production with bar-end trucks and one magnetic coupler.

(A) Semigloss tile red body; no smokestack.

	6	10	18	25

(B) Tile red body; no smokestack.

	6	10	18	25

(C) Tuscan body (shades vary); black die-cast smokestack.

	6	10	18	25

(D) Maroon body (shades vary); black die-cast smokestack.

	6	10	18	25

6357 (Type II lettering) LIONEL–Circled-L: 1953–56. SP-type; painted bodies with white heat-stamped lettering; circled-L Lionel logo; smokestack; lighted, window shell; chemically blackened frame with one brake wheel; bar-end trucks with one coupler; usually designated 6357-25.

(A) Maroon body (shades vary); black die-cast smokestack.

	6	12	18	30

(B) Tuscan body (shades vary); black die-cast smokestack.

	6	12	18	30

(C) Maroon body and matching painted die-cast smokestack; very scarce.

	125	225	350	500

6357 (Type III lettering) LIONEL: 1957–61. SP-type; maroon-painted body with white heat-stamped reversible

---

6257 SP-TYPE CABOOSE LETTERING

Chart by Paul V. Ambrose

Type I. SP below cupola window. All examples lettered "LIONEL".

Type II. Circled-L Lionel logo below cupola window. All examples lettered "LIONEL".

Type III. Nothing below cupola window. All examples lettered "LIONEL" regardless of whether "6257" at left or at right.

Type IV. Nothing below cupola window. All examples lettered "LIONEL LINES".

6257X (Type I lettering) Lionel SP.

6257 (D) (Type II lettering) Lionel circled-L emblem.

6257 (A) (Type III lettering) Lionel, and 6257 (Type IV lettering) Lionel Lines.

6357 (A) Lionel (Type I lettering) Lionel SP. Note the absence of a smokestack.

6357 (C) (Type I lettering) Lionel SP.

Here are two examples of the 6357 with Type III lettering. Unlike Types I and II, Type III lettering is reversible, as shown by the position of the "6357" on the models above.

	Gd	VG	Ex	LN

lettering; smokestack; lighted; window shell; chemically blackened frame with one brake wheel; bar-end trucks with one coupler into 1959, then AAR trucks with one operating coupler.

	Gd	VG	Ex	LN
(A) "6357" at left.	6	15	20	35
(B) "6357" at right.	6	15	20	35

6357(-50) A. T. & S. F.: 1960. SP-type; red-painted body with white heat-stamped reversible lettering; numbered only "6357"; smokestack; lighted, window shell; chemically blackened frame with one brake wheel; AAR trucks with one operating coupler; component of 2555W Father and Son outfit.

	Gd	VG	Ex	LN

Note: Examine this item carefully; it *must* be numbered "6357". Unscrupulous sellers have added smokestacks to 6017-235 Santa Fe bodies and mounted the bogus cabs on lighted chassis in hopes of passing them off as very scarce variations. Caution advised; study the picture of a legitimate item shown here. An original box (Orange Perforated numbered "6357-50") adds a substantial premium. **320 450 900 1200**

(6417) 536417 PENNSYLVANIA: 1953–57. N5c porthole; Tuscan-painted body with white heat-stamped lettering; actually numbered "536417"; lighted; window shell; bar-end trucks.

(A) With "NEW YORK ZONE" centered under the car number. **10 15 35 45**

(B) Without "NEW YORK ZONE"; scarce. **100 150 230 350**

(6417-25) 64173 LIONEL LINES: 1954. N5c porthole; Tuscan-painted body with white heat-stamped lettering; actually numbered "64173"; lighted; window shell; bar-end trucks. **15 25 40 60**

(6417-50) 641751 LEHIGH VALLEY: 1954. N5c porthole; typically gray-painted body with red heat-stamped lettering; actually numbered "641751"; lighted; window shell; bar-end trucks.

(A) Gray-painted body. **50 65 140 175**

(B) Tuscan-painted body on a black mold with white heat-stamped lettering; rare variation, possibly a factory error. **350 600 1000 1500**

6419 (pre-1956 model) D. L. & W.: 1948–50, 1952–55. Work caboose; light gray–painted toolboxes and cab with black heat-stamped lettering; tall smokestack; two brake stands; handrails; steps, ladder; light gray–painted die-cast frame with black heat-stamped serif lettering; 1948–50 with staple-end trucks and two magnetic couplers, and 1952–55 with bar-end trucks and two magnetic couplers. **15 25 40 50**

6419(-25) D. L. & W.: 1954–55. Work caboose; same information as 6419 (pre-1956 model), except with bar-end trucks exclusively and one coupler. **13 20 30 40**

6419(-50) (1956 model) D. L. & W.: 1956–57. Work caboose; unpainted light gray toolboxes and modified cab with tabs and black heat-stamped lettering; short smokestack; two brake wheels; handrails; steps; ladder; light gray–painted modified die-cast frame with black heat-stamped lettering; bar-end trucks attached with truck clips with two couplers. **15 25 50 65**

6419(-75) (1956 model) D. L. & W.: 1956. Work caboose; same information as 6419(-50), except with one coupler. **15 25 50 65**

(6419-100) 576419 N & W (Norfolk and Western): 1957–58. Work caboose; unpainted light gray toolboxes and modified cab with tabs and black heat-stamped lettering; cab stamped "N & W / 576419"; short smokestack; two brakestands; handrails; steps; ladder; light gray–painted modified die-cast frame with black heat-stamped serif lettering; bar-end trucks attached with truck clips usually with two couplers. **45 75 135 200**

6420 D. L. & W.: 1948–50. Work caboose with searchlight; dark gray–painted toolboxes and cab with black heat-stamped lettering; tall smokestack; two brakestands; handrails; steps; ladder; dark gray–painted die-cast frame with black lettering; staple-end trucks with two magnetic couplers.

(A) Frame with rubber-stamped sans-serif lettering. **35 65 105 175**

(B) Frame with heat-stamped serif lettering. **35 165 105 175**

(6427) 64273 LIONEL LINES: 1954–60. N5c porthole; Tuscan-painted body with white heat-stamped lettering; actually numbered "64273"; lighted; window shell; bar-end trucks with one coupler. **12 15 30 45**

6427(-60) VIRGINIAN: 1958. N5c porthole; dark blue–painted body with yellow heat-stamped lettering; "BLT 8-58 / BY LIONEL" on left and "6427" on right; lighted; window shell; bar-end trucks with one coupler. **115 150 315 450**

(6427-500) 576427 PENNSYLVANIA: 1957–58. N5c porthole; sky blue–painted body with white heat-stamped lettering; actually numbered "576427"; lighted; window

6357 SP-TYPE CABOOSE LETTERING

Chart by Paul V. Ambrose

Type I. SP below cupola window. All examples named "LIONEL".

Type II. Circled-L logo below cupola window. All examples named "LIONEL".

Type III. Nothing below cupola window. All examples named "LIONEL" regardless of whether "6357" at left or at right.

Top: 6357-50 A. T. & S. F. from the famous "over and under" set, and Tuscan 6457 (A) Lionel with matching plastic smokestack. Second: Maroon 6457 (D) Lionel (note the example has one bar-end, and one staple-end truck and Tuscan 6457 (C) Lionel with die-cast smokestack. Third: Two shades of the 6557 smoking caboose. Bottom: Scarce 6657 (B) Denver and Rio Grande Western without ladder slots, and 6657 (A) with ladder slots. R. Shanfeld Collection.

	Gd	VG	Ex	LN

shell; bar-end trucks with one coupler; exclusive component of the Girls' Set.   **125   200   350   525**

6429 D. L. & W.: 1963. Work caboose; light gray–painted toolboxes and modified cab with tabs and black heat-stamped lettering; short smokestack; two brakestands; handrails; steps; ladder; light gray-painted modified die-cast frame with black heat-stamped lettering; AAR trucks usually with two operating couplers; component of one Super O outfit only.

Note: Gray is the most common body mold color for the 6429 cab; however, red molds and yellow molds have also been verified.   **125   200   310   425**

6437 PENNSYLVANIA: 1961–68. N5c porthole; Tuscan-painted body with white heat-stamped lettering; lighted; window shell; AAR trucks usually with one operating

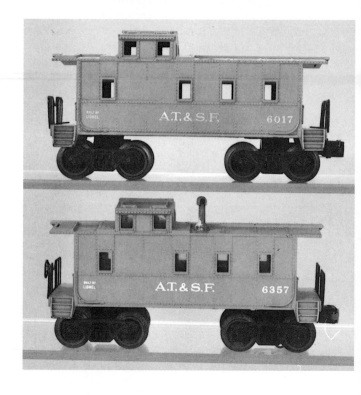

Look closely at the number on these two cabooses. The 6017-235 on the top is common, but the 6357-50 on the bottom is scarce and valuable. Unscrupulous sellers have added smokestacks to 6017-235 bodies and sold them as very scarce variations. K. Rubright Collection.

Top: 6417 (A) Pennsylvania with "NEW YORK ZONE" and scarce 6417 (B) without "NEW YORK ZONE." Bottom: 6417-25 Lionel Lines and 6427 Lionel Lines. R. Shanfeld Collection.

Top: 6417-50 (A) gray Lehigh Valley and rare Tuscan 6417-50 (B) Lehigh Valley. Middle: 6427-60 Virginian (erroneously shown with two couplers), and 6427-500 Pennsylvania from the Girls' Set. Bottom: 6437 Pennsylvania, and 6447 Pennsylvania. Notice that these caboose numbers came with AAR trucks, and the 6447 was nonilluminated. R. Shanfeld Collection.

	Gd	VG	Ex	LN

coupler; followed the normal progression of box, truck, and coupler modifications as did other items in the line.

| | 15 | 22 | 30 | 45 |

6447 PENNSYLVANIA: 1963. N5c porthole; Tuscan-painted body with white heat-stamped lettering; *not* lighted; window shell; AAR trucks with one operating coupler; component of one Super O outfit only.

| | 125 | 200 | 350 | 525 |

6457 LIONEL: 1949–52. SP-type; various painted bodies with white heat-stamped lettering; circled-L logo; smokestack; lighted; window shell; ladders; black-painted frame with battery boxes and two brake wheels; pre-1952 examples with staple-end trucks and two magnetic couplers, and 1952 production with bar-end trucks and two magnetic couplers.

(A) Tuscan body with matching plastic smokestack.

| | 15 | 20 | 32 | 50 |

Top: 6419 (B) D. L. & W. with high smokestack and 6419-50 (A) D. L. & W. with low smokestack. Middle: 6419-100 N & W (cab stamped "576419") and 6420 D. L. & W. Bottom:

Scarce 6429 D. L. & W. from 1963 with factory-correct AAR trucks. R. Shanfeld Collection. Other work cabooses are shown on page 156.

	Gd	VG	Ex	LN
(B) Tuscan body with matching die-cast smokestack.	12	15	25	35
(C) Tuscan body with black die-cast smokestack.	12	15	25	35
(D) Maroon body with black die-cast smokestack.	12	15	25	35

6517 LIONEL LINES: 1955–59. Bay-window; red-painted body with white rubber-stamped lettering; lighted; small smokestack; ladders; window shell; window shades; O27 gauge passenger trucks.

	Gd	VG	Ex	LN
(A) Early production with "BLT 12-55" and "LIONEL" underscored.	30	50	80	100
(B) Later production, no underscoring.	20	40	60	75
(C) Distinctly different darker red body; no underscoring.	30	50	75	90

(6517-75) C301 ERIE: 1966. Bay-window; red-painted body with white rubber-stamped lettering; actually numbered "C301"; lighted; small smokestack; ladders; window shell; window shades; O27 gauge passenger trucks; underframe is usually rubber-stamped "6517-75 / LIONEL". Shown in 1966 accessory catalog, but not featured in consumer catalog.

	Gd	VG	Ex	LN
(A) Medium red body.	180	250	465	525
(B) Dark red body.	180	250	465	525

6517/1966 TCA (Train Collectors Association): 1966. Bay-window; orange-painted body with white rubber-stamped lettering; lighted; small smokestack; ladders; window shell; window shades; O27 gauge passenger trucks. Uniquely decorated with TCA logo for Santa Monica, California, national convention. Alan Stewart reports that 700 models were produced; the first 500 were painted red by mistake and had to be repainted orange.

Gd	VG	Ex	LN
90	125	200	300

6557 LIONEL: 1958–59. SP-type with liquid smoke unit; various painted bodies with white heat-stamped reversible lettering; lighted; window shell; chemically blackened frame usually with one brake wheel; bar-end trucks with one coupler.

	Gd	VG	Ex	LN
(A) Tuscan body with number on left.	85	150	250	325
(B) Distinctly darker Tuscan body with number on left.	85	150	250	325
(C) Brown body with number on right; very scarce.	240	350	575	800

6657 RIO GRANDE: 1957–58. SP-type; predominantly yellow-painted body, sides with silver-painted lower stripe and silver-painted roof and ends; three black side-detail stripes with black heat-stamped one-way lettering and stylized Denver and Rio Grande Western decal; smokestack; lighted; window shell; chemically blackened frame usually with one brake wheel; bar-end trucks with one coupler.

Top: 6517 (A) Lionel Lines with underscoring at right and 6517 (B) Lionel Lines without underscoring. Bottom: 6517-75 (A) Erie and 6517-1966 TCA. R. Shanfeld Collection.

Top: 6814 (B) Lionel Rescue Unit and an unnumbered rescue unit that appears in our listings as (6119-125).

Bottom: 6814 (A) Lionel and 6824 U. S. M. C. Rescue Units. R. Shanfeld Collection.

	Gd	VG	Ex	LN
(A) Body with ladder slots.	50	75	150	200
(B) Body without ladder slots; very scarce.	100	150	300	400

6814 RESCUE / UNIT: 1959–61. Work caboose, commonly referred to as First-Aid Medical Car; white-painted tool tray and cab with red heat-stamped markings; cab with cross, and tray with "RESCUE / UNIT", cross, and "6814"; short smokestack; white control panel; figure; two stretchers; oxygen tank unit; light gray-painted frame with black heat-stamped serif lettering; AAR trucks with one operating coupler.

(A) As described above.

	Gd	VG	Ex	LN
	35	50	115	175

(B) Tool tray and cab as described, except *without* control panel, figure, stretchers, and oxygen tank unit; black-painted or chemically blackened frame with white heat-stamped sans-serif lettering; an uncataloged set component.

	Gd	VG	Ex	LN
	30	40	100	125

6824 RESCUE / UNIT and U. S. M. C.: 1960. Work caboose, commonly referred to as First-Aid Medical Car; olive-painted tool tray and cab with white heat-stamped markings; cab with cross, and tray with "RESCUE / UNIT", cross, and "6824"; short smokestack; olive-painted control panel; figure; two stretchers; oxygen tank unit; olive-painted frame with white rubber-stamped "U. S. M. C." lettering; AAR trucks with one operating coupler.

	Gd	VG	Ex	LN
	60	90	175	250

477618: See (2457), (2472).
576419: See (6419-100).
576427: See (6427-500).

6

CRANES AND SEARCHLIGHT CARS

Introduction by Roger Carp

The cranes and searchlight cars cataloged during the postwar period exemplify Lionel's quest to achieve a balance between realism and imagination in its toy trains. Throughout the company's history, designers sought to bring out models that captured the look of actual locomotives and rolling stock while entertaining children. Few items struck a perfect balance, of course, although engines came very close. Operating cars and accessories that featured special visual effects or involved manual dexterity when used also seemed to neatly combine accurate replication and play value. That's the reason kids have always prized cranes and searchlight cars, and collectors find they never lose their charm.

Engineers at Lionel recognized the sales potential of cranes and searchlight cars long before the postwar era. They introduced a Standard gauge crane (the 219) in 1926 and an O gauge version (the 810) four years later. Searchlight cars made their debut in both lines in 1931, with the Standard gauge 220 and 520 and the O gauge 820. These cars were great fun to play with as part of the work trains offered during the 1930s. However, contemporary tin lithography technology prevented Lionel from offering scale replicas of prototype rolling stock. Acknowledging this point or, more likely, preferring to produce toys, designers decorated these prewar pieces in lively colors that pleased the eye yet were far from accurate.

Models cataloged in the years immediately preceding World War II served as starting points for Lionel's production when the conflict ended. Determined to bring out rolling stock for both the O and O27 gauge lines, sales and engineering executives closely examined all the cars at hand. In the case of cranes and searchlight cars, they adopted different strategies, as attested by the items that were eventually mass-produced. With cranes, Lionel modified an existing car for the O27 line while pressing on with the development of a new model in the larger gauge. As for a searchlight car, decision-makers rejected all pre-

war pieces. They evidently preferred to wait until designers could finish work on something entirely new.

Lionel's first postwar cranes gave credence to the promise in the 1945 catalog of "Sensational surprises on the way for 1946." First came the 2560 crane, which was cataloged as part of the O27 line through the next year. This 7½-inch–long sheet-metal model represented a modified version of a small O gauge predecessor, the 2660. The example depicted in the 1946 and 1947 catalogs, decorated for the Pennsylvania Railroad and featuring a brown cab with a red roof, looked more impressive than the regular-production crane. Somehow the 2560, with its tiny yellow and red cab planted on a plain metal frame painted black, lacked the impressive bulk of the "big hooks" typically found on real railroads. This crane had the equipment to do its job, but fell flat when it came to image. It was a toy, and boys wanted something more realistic in the late 1940s.

Luckily for them, Lionel's engineers were already working on a model that would dazzle O gaugers for the next four years. Capitalizing on the promise of injection-molded thermoplastics, they designed a realistic model of the Bucyrus Erie crane used on many American railroads. On the 2460 they attached a large, detailed plastic cab to an 8⅜-inch–long die-cast frame painted black and heat-stamped white. A newly designed injection-molded boom dominated the car and seemed to outstretch the Bakelite one used on the 2560. This spectacular model rode on six-wheel trucks that were similar to the deluxe trucks installed on the top-of-the-line 2426W tender and 2625 *Irvington* heavyweight passenger cars. The 2460 captured the feel of prototype cranes and offered kids hours of play.

Without a doubt, the O gauge crane made its companion look antiquated and puny. Why did Lionel go to the trouble of cataloging the 2560? One logical response is that production supervisors had an abundance of parts left from before the war that they wanted to deplete. More likely, sales personnel felt compelled to assemble the broadest line possible for O27 gauge, even if that meant making new parts for items like the 2560, which essentially was a prewar carryover. Regardless of Lionel's motive, its O gauge crane won the sweepstakes as a superbly realistic model loaded with play value. Its cab rotated, and two round cranks raised and lowered the boom and the block and tackle. Kids could pick up other cars, not to mention die-cast vehicles, lead figures, and anything else in reach. The most desirable versions of the 2460 are the early ones with a light or dark gray cab.

Meanwhile, decisions had been made about a searchlight car to go with the crane. Instead of reviving a prewar model, the executives who planned the product line turned for ideas to Frank Pettit, the development engineer working at the company's factory in Hillside, New Jersey. He cleverly installed a small floodlight on the new work caboose so Lionel could claim to have updated its searchlight car with the 2420, first cataloged in 1946 as a companion to the 2460.

There was no reason to stop there. Lionel desired something more for its line, and the engineering staff wanted to keep on tinkering. So they began with the die-cast depressed-center frame that had been developed for the 2461 transformer car. At one end of the gray frame they mounted a floodlight; in the center they installed an on-off switch hidden by a plastic generator. Operators activated this switch via a section of remote-control track. A magnet in the track made contact with a metal strip attached to the bottom of the car, thus turning the light on or off. Now they had something!

The finished model, the 6520, entered the line in 1949 and was an immediate success. The searchlight didn't rotate, but the bracket holding it could be maneuvered from one side to the other. The car worked beautifully with the 2460 crane to clear any wrecks that might occur at night on O gauge layouts. Operators still enjoy using the 6520 with their cranes. Collectors, however, pay more attention to the generator than they do to the floodlight. They treasure cars having original green generators. Buyers must beware of frauds, as reproductions are plentiful.

With a crane and a searchlight car highlighting the O gauge line, Lionel reacted with the unexpected. In 1950, an illustration in the black-and-white advance catalog indicated that Lionel planned to add a radio-controlled crane (the 4460) to the Electronic Control Set. This never materialized, and the path-breaking outfit was dropped from the line a year later. A second inexplicable change occurred in 1951: Lionel failed to catalog a crane at all. The reason for deleting what surely was a steady seller remains a mystery. Maybe shortages of materials caused by the Korean War were to blame.

Regardless of what happened in 1951, Lionel did bring back its Bucyrus Erie crane the next year. But the 6460, as it was known, was missing the premium six-wheel trucks that had distinguished the 2460. To save money, Lionel substituted four-wheel trucks. The new crane boasted a new die-cast frame as well as minor alterations to the heat-stamped lettering on its black cab. This model

might have been disappointing; the improved searchlight car for 1952 was not. The 3520 featured a rotating light that was activated in the same manner as the discontinued 6520. As the car traveled, its floodlight revolved as tiny rubber "feet" on the bottom of its housing were electrically vibrated within a circular driving-coil assembly.

Apparently never satisfied with their efforts, engineers brought out another version of the searchlight car in 1954. They modified the vibrating mechanism rotating the floodlight so it was powered by electricity from the track and turned continuously. Consequently, Lionel eliminated the on-off switch from the new 3620. Examples equipped with original orange plastic searchlight caps, whether left unpainted or painted gray, are highly desired. Again, however, the presence of reproductions means that a collector should exercise caution before buying a model with one of these scarce parts.

Content with the searchlight car, designers turned their attention back to the crane in 1955. The new 6560, though still a handsome model, lacked some of the detail and heft of its predecessors. Most telling, the heavy die-cast frame was gone, replaced by a black plastic one. One year before, Lionel had experimented with painting the cab red. For the 6560, it modified the cab (typically left unpainted) to include an integral-molded smokestack. Scarce variations came molded in red-orange or black, common ones in red. Slight changes to the lettering and cranks were reported in the late 1950s and through the 1960s.

Except for one year (1965), the 6560 was cataloged without interruption from 1955 until the demise of the Lionel train line in 1969. Apparently unable to improve the crane, engineers went back to work on the searchlight car and brought out a new design in 1956 with the 3650. Once again, their ingenuity was astonishing. They added play value to the searchlight car by enabling operators to remove the floodlight from the frame and place it several inches away to illuminate a different area. The key was a cable of wire mounted in the center of the car where the large generator formerly had been. To maintain realism, a small gray plastic generator was installed at the end opposite the light.

The 3650 extension searchlight car stayed in the line through 1959. This gap took 2 years to fill. Then in 1961 the final searchlight car of the postwar era was announced. The 6822 traded the depressed-center frame for a nondescript unpainted red flatcar body. On top of the chassis, factory workers secured a gray or black plastic superstructure with room for a searchlight assembly and a blue rubberized male figure. At some point, they mistakenly attached it to a few bodies being used for the 6828 flatcar with P & H crane. In the process they created the scarcest of all searchlight car variations.

The correct model, known as the 6822 night crew searchlight car, remained a part of the product line all the way through 1969. It certainly looked different from earlier cars and perhaps resembled a prototype car more closely than any other Lionel searchlight car. Still, the salient point is that its floodlight lacked mobility, which deprived the 6822 of much play value.

The questionable design of this searchlight car suggests that the struggle to survive in the 1960s was forcing Lionel to take measures that disrupted the delicate balance between realism and imagination. Cranes, fortunately, were another story. They managed to maintain that balance despite having details removed and costs cut. Both types of cars shed light on how marketing goals could align and conflict with engineering considerations to influence the toy trains manufactured by Lionel during the postwar decades.

CRANES

Lionel cataloged cranes every postwar year except 1951, yet had only four stock numbers. The earliest model was a prewar carryover, the sheet-metal 2560. The second postwar crane, cataloged as 2460, was a superlative copy of a Bucyrus Erie model, with a die-cast frame and six-wheel trucks. In 1952 Lionel replaced it with the similar 6460 model, which used less-expensive four-wheel trucks with magnetic couplers.

The company instituted major cost reductions in 1955 with the 6560 series. The cab was attached through three slots (instead of with six screws), the die-cast frame was replaced by a plastic one, and cabs and frames typically were unpainted. The Bucyrus Erie crane was cataloged as 6560 through the remainder of the postwar era; it followed the same box, truck, and coupler modifications as did other items in the line.

All 2460, 6460, and 6560 cranes included technical data on the frame that often appears as "WT-375, 000-2-18NH". However, the hyphens before and after the "2" were removed from the heat-stamp plate after 1946 production. Therefore, 1946 production of gray-cab cranes included all three hyphens, while later-issue black-cab 2460 cranes included only one.

Another change was made in 1952, when the 6460 was issued. Early examples apparently came with either all three hyphens or only one after "WT". By contrast, 1954 black issues and the red-cab 6460-25 typically came without any hyphens; the 6560 cranes introduced in 1955 routinely came with all three. The terminology used in the listings is described as follows:

three hyphens: WT-375,000-2-18NH
one hyphen: WT-375,000 2 18NH
no hyphens: WT 375,000 2 18NH.

Be aware that most crane parts are readily interchangeable within a series, and this creates the possibility for many potential variations. All crane cabs, except 2560, included heat-stamped lettering and were named "BUCYRUS ERIE"; all red and black cabs were lettered in white, while gray cabs were lettered in black. All frames, except that of 2560, were heat-stamped with white lettering.

The Bucyrus Erie crane was loaded with play value. Besides the rotating cab, it featured a boom and a hook that were functioning parts. A die-cast handwheel or crank capped each of these assemblies. Pre-1958 examples of this part were cast with four symmetrical openings; sometime in 1958 the tooling was modified to plug the openings, so most post-1958 cranes came with revised solid cranks.

The crane hook on 2560, 2460, and 6460 models was turned 90 degrees from the plane of the pulley. The 6560 series introduced the revised hook, aligned with the plane. Metal trucks were the norm through 1957; they gave way to AAR trucks for 1958 and all future production.

SEARCHLIGHT CARS

The first postwar example of a searchlight car made its debut in 1949 as number 6250. Four more models filled out the series. All but one of these five models used a depressed-center die-cast frame; the last release, 6822, came with a molded plastic flatcar body. Die-cast frames were painted gray and decorated with black rubber-stamped lettering, "LIONEL LINES" appearing in either serif or sans-serif style. The item number, except for 6822, appeared on either side of the road name. The 6822 was lettered only "LIONEL", with the number "6822" typically appearing on the left side of "LIONEL".

The 6520 model had what would be considered a stationary searchlight, but the bracket to which the searchlight housing was attached could be turned manually about 90 degrees to the left or right. Many of the same parts were in the first three releases, especially the plastic generator (diesel motor housing, as listed in the Lionel Service Manual). Be aware that it is easy to switch generators from one car to another. Furthermore, soldering and unsoldering a single wire are all that is necessary to change searchlight housings. Because of these tangibles, many potential variations are possible.

The introduction of the 3520 with a rotating searchlight in 1952 required a new searchlight assembly. Lionel developed a driving-coil assembly, a metal housing base, and a plastic searchlight housing, commonly referred to as a searchlight cap. The principle of operation is as follows: the searchlight housing (cap) was attached to the housing-base assembly, which sat freely on the driving-coil assembly. The driving-coil assembly held the lamp and functioned as a vibrator mechanism to rotate the base. Most housings were unpainted gray plastic (shades vary), and most bases were bright aluminum. However, some very early issues utilized a chemically blackened base. Also, early housing bases, whether chemically blackened or bright aluminum, came with eight air circulation holes, instead of the usual four. Variations of searchlight caps and housing bases are shown in the color photograph accompanying the 3520 and 3620 listings.

An easily detachable part, such as a searchlight housing or housing base, allows for many potential

	Gd	VG	Ex	LN

variations, and these parts *are* often switched by collectors and dealers.

2460 BUCYRUS ERIE: 1946–50. Crane; "LIONEL LINES" in single arch on painted cab; black-painted die-cast frame with white heat-stamped lettering; early-issue cord was white, then routinely changed to black; six-wheel trucks with coil couplers.

Note: Gray cabs were 1946 production.

	Gd	VG	Ex	LN
(A) Dark gray cab; three hyphens.	75	100	200	250
(B) Light gray cab; three hyphens.	75	100	200	250
(C) Black cab; thin number on frame; one hyphen.	35	50	75	100
(D) Black cab; thick number on frame; one hyphen.	35	50	75	100

2560 LIONEL LINES: 1946–47. Crane; continuation of prewar 2660, with modifications; glossy or flat black-painted frame with steps at the four corners; light yellow-painted cab with red-painted roof; raised "LIONEL CRANE" molded on both sides of unpainted boom; typically white cord; black rubber-stamped lettering with "L" in circle above rear crank and "LIONEL / LINES / 2560" on rear of cab; staple-end trucks with coil couplers.

	Gd	VG	Ex	LN
(A) Green boom.	20	40	55	100
(B) Brown boom.	20	40	55	100
(C) Black boom.	20	40	55	100

3520 LIONEL LINES: 1952–53. Rotating searchlight; similar to 6250 but with a frame modification for a rotating searchlight with a vibrator mechanism; gray-painted die-cast frame with black rubber-stamped lettering; remote-control on-off mechanism; steps at four corners; brake stand opposite searchlight; orange generator; usually bar-end trucks.

Note: A chemically blackened or bright aluminum assembly with eight holes is scarcer than bright aluminum with four holes.

	Gd	VG	Ex	LN
(A) Frame with serif lettering.	60	100	150	200
(B) Frame with sans-serif lettering.	30	40	58	75

3620 LIONEL LINES: 1954–56. Rotating searchlight; similar to 3250, but without the remote-control on-off mechanism; searchlight revolves continuously in conjunction with electrical power. Gray-painted die-cast frame with black rubber-stamped sans-serif lettering; steps at four corners; brake stand opposite searchlight; orange generator; bar-end trucks.

Note: The searchlight housing (cap) comes in four collectible variations:
(a) unpainted gray plastic
(b) unpainted orange plastic
(c) gray-painted orange plastic
(d) gray-painted gray plastic.
Page 20 of the 1954 consumer catalog actually shows

Top: 2560 (A) crane with green boom. Middle: 2560 (B) with brown boom and 2560 (E) with black boom. Bottom: The two major versions of the early postwar production of the Bucyrus Erie crane. Gray 2460 (B), and black 2460 (C). E. Dougherty Collection.

	Gd	VG	Ex	LN

the 3620 with an orange cap. Be aware that gray paint is often removed from an orange cap to create the visually appealing orange cap with orange generator combination. Also, the orange cap has been reproduced. Because of two sizes of frame lettering and four distinctly different searchlight caps, there are eight possible 3620 variations.

(A) Frame with thin lettering and cap (a).

	25	35	45	70

(B) Frame with thin lettering and cap (b).

	50	100	140	200

(C) Frame with thin lettering and cap (c).

	80	125	160	250

(D) Frame with thin lettering and cap (d).

	25	35	45	70

(E) Frame with thick lettering and cap (a).

	25	35	45	70

(F) Frame with thick lettering and cap (b).

	50	100	140	200

(G) Frame with thick lettering and cap (c).

	80	125	160	250

(H) Frame with thick lettering and cap (d).

	25	35	45	70

3620X LIONEL LINES: 1955. Rotating searchlight; this model is identical to 3620, except it was assembled with old inventory of 3520 frames with black rubber-stamped sans-serif lettering; frame actually numbered "3520". The item does not warrant any premium because the variation is easily duplicated.

	25	35	45	70

3650 LIONEL LINES: 1956–59. Extension searchlight; gray-painted die-cast frame with black rubber-stamped sans-serif lettering; special hole added to frame for crank storage; steps at four corners; two brakestands; small unpainted gray generator; typically unpainted gray plastic searchlight cap with red magnetic base; steel plate attached to frame by bent tabs; red reel with green wire and black oxidized die-cast crank (spool handle, according to the Lionel Service Manual); bar-end trucks.

(A) Light gray frame.	40	50	68	90
(B) Dark gray frame.	65	80	140	175
(C) Distinctly different olive-gray frame.				
	80	100	150	225

6460 BUCYRUS ERIE: 1952–54. Crane; "LIONEL / LINES" on black-painted cab; black-painted die-cast frame with white heat-stamped lettering; four-wheel (typically bar-end) trucks.

(A) Frame with thick lettering and three hyphens.

	20	40	60	80

(B) Frame with thin lettering and one hyphen.

	20	40	60	80

(C) Frame with thin lettering and no hyphens.

	20	40	60	80

6460(-25) BUCYRUS ERIE: 1954. Crane; same information as 6460, except red-painted cab (-25 was the suffix

Typical 3620 frame with thin lettering and orange generator, but atypical (preproduction) tan searchlight cap. R. Shanfeld Collection.

	Gd	VG	Ex	LN

for red); frame with thin lettering and no hyphens.

	40	60	95	120

6520 LIONEL LINES: 1949–51. Stationary searchlight; gray-painted die-cast frame with black rubber-stamped serif lettering; remote-control on-off mechanism; steps at four corners; brakestand opposite searchlight; generator typically one of three production colors; die-cast searchlight housing in three variations; staple-end trucks.

Note: Be advised that it is easy to switch generators and searchlight housings from one car to another.

Generator variations:
Gray: preproduction; rare.
Tan: preproduction; rare.
Green: scarce.
Maroon: less common.
Orange: most common.

Searchlight housing variations:
Smooth glossy black: very scarce.
Smooth glossy gray: less common.
Crinkle flat gray: most common.

(A) Gray generator; searchlight housing inconsequential (the value of each variation of this item is based on the generator).

				NRS

(B) Tan generator; searchlight housing inconsequential.

	200	350	500	700

(C) Green generator with black searchlight housing.

	150	175	300	375

(D) Green generator with either gray searchlight housing.

	140	160	250	325

(E) Maroon generator with either gray searchlight housing.

	25	40	60	85

(F) Orange generator with either gray searchlight housing.

	25	40	60	85

6560 BUCYRUS ERIE: 1955–64, 1966–69. Crane; redesigned in 1955 to use a less-expensive molded plastic instead of a die-cast frame; the cab, routinely unpainted, was modified to include an integral-molded smokestack and was fastened through three slots to cab-plate assembly instead of with six screws; "LIONEL / LINES" on two lines on cab; unpainted black frame with white heat-stamped lettering and three hyphens; truck type mentioned with specific entries below.

Note: Some 1963–64 production was designated

Top: 3520 (B) with chemically blackened searchlight housing and 3620 (A). Second: 3650 (A) extension search-light and 6520 (E) searchlight. Third: 6520 (F) and scarce 6520 (D) with green generator. Bottom: 6822 (A) and 6822 (B). E. Dougherty Collection.

Top: 6460-25 Bucyrus Erie crane with red cab and 6460 (B). Second: 6560 (A) with red-orange cab (this example usually came on a unique unlettered frame) and 6560 (E). Third: 6560 (H) and 6560 (I) with scarce dark-blue frame. Bottom: 6560 (C) and 6560 (D). E. Dougherty Collection.

Top: 6560 (F) without "6560" on frame. Bottom: 6560 (J) with the frame rubber-stamped only "6560".

	Gd	VG	Ex	LN

6560-50 and typically came with one fixed and one operating coupler.

(A) Early 1955 production with a strikingly different red-orange cab on a unique unlettered plastic frame identified with mold number 2460-5; the Lionel Service Manual states that the first several thousand 6560 cranes were assembled using bar-end trucks, which were mounted with ⁴⁄₃₂" x ⁷⁄₃₂" binding head screws and spacer rings.

	60	100	175	250

(B) Very scarce variation with red cab that is painted red; bar-end trucks mounted with binding head screws; unlike the frame with variation (A), this example usually included typical heat-stamping on frame but *without* 6560.

	65	150	200	300

(C) Black cab with smokestack (not typical production); possible Lionel Service Department replacement part or cab used for late production of the 282 gantry crane.

	75	100	175	250

(D) Gray cab; open cranks; bar-end trucks.

	40	50	85	120

(E) Red cab; open cranks; bar-end trucks.

	20	30	45	75

(F) Moderately scarce variation with typical heat-stamping on frame, except *without* "6560"; red cab; open cranks; bar-end trucks.

	40	50	85	120

(G) Red cab; open cranks; AAR trucks.

	20	30	45	75

(H) Red cab; solid cranks; AAR trucks.

	20	30	45	75

(I) Hagerstown crane with dark-blue frame; red cab; open cranks; varying truck and coupler combinations. Instead of chemically blackened, some late-1960s production used chemically treated cranks and hooks that appeared to be bronze.

	40	50	95	120

	Gd	VG	Ex	LN

(J) Red cab; solid cranks; varying truck and coupler combinations; *only* data on frame is white rubber-stamped "6560". Most probably early MPC production that utilized leftover postwar parts.

	40	50	95	120

6560(-)25 BUCYRUS ERIE: 1956. Crane; same information as 6560; red cab; open cranks; bar-end trucks; typical heat-stamping on frame except number appears as "656025".

	45	65	110	140

6822 LIONEL: 1961–69. Night crew searchlight; unpainted red flat car body (shades vary) with white heat-stamped lettering; brake wheel; plastic superstructure with searchlight assembly; blue male figure, usually with painted face; AAR trucks with either two operating or one fixed and one operating coupler.

(A) Gray superstructure with black searchlight cap.

	20	30	45	70

(B) Black superstructure with gray searchlight cap.

	20	30	45	70

(C) Very scarce variation numbered "6828". Color of superstructure and searchlight cap inconsequential.

	500	750	1200	1500

6560-25 Bucyrus Erie crane. E. Dougherty Collection.

7

FLATCARS

by Alan Stewart

Lionel did not have the chroniclers of their production in mind when they introduced new products, so they took basic parts and made them into many different items that don't necessarily fit neatly into any one category. This makes organizing a book, or even a chapter, about Lionel trains a bit of a challenge. For example, the 6461 flatcar with transformer and the 6520 searchlight car are both built on the same die-cast depressed-center frame. Should they be classified together in the same section, in different sections of the same chapter, or in different chapters? In the end, the author and editor have to decide what seems best, based on user preferences and past experience.

Each chapter in this new, substantially revised edition has been carefully prepared with one aim in mind: to provide collectors with the most accurate and complete information possible, presented in a form most convenient for the reader. Other chapters offer listings in one numerical sequence. However, because of the complex nature of Lionel's flatcar production, some broad categories are useful. The listings of this chapter have been extensively reorganized from past editions to bring two of the highly collectible flatcar frame types together under single subheadings:

the 6100 series and
the 6511 series.

The highly collectible 6100-series 8-inch stamped metal flatcars share a common stamping with the 6119-type work caboose frames. Just add a second end railing and presto! A whole new product line! With only three different loads but a variety of frame paint color and frame lettering style and color, these rival the 6014s in variation count. A whole string of 6100-series cars on your shelf is certainly as colorful as the 6014s, and you don't have to stand as close to see the differences!

There are "only" 30 different 6464 boxcar numbers listed in Chapter 4, with at least one collection containing more than 300 of these cars, each one different in at least one detail that knowledgeable collectors can objectively agree upon. This chapter lists at least 70 different numbers just for the 10-inch molded plastic flatcars of the 6511 series. With mold changes to accommodate different loads and functions over the years, with color changes and variations in the loads, there's no telling how many variations there may be of the 6511 series alone! But daunting as the task may seem, we are, with the help of a legion of dedicated contributors, pressing on with the quest for a "complete" enumeration. If you liked 6464 variations, you are going to love what's in store for you here!

Certainly the die-cast depressed-center frame cars and the interesting variations of the 6519 Allis Chalmers car frame could likewise be grouped. But, like stock and refrigerator cars, these are sufficiently unique and not so numerous that they are better left to appear wherever they fall in the numerical sequence of flatcars. If you become frustrated with the necessary interruption in numerical sequence that grouping according to frame type brings, remember that there is no such interruption in the handy index at the back of this book. A quick check there takes you directly to the page listing the car number you seek.

Note: Today we use "flatcar," but Lionel never did. It was always "flat car"! Also, to help verify Lionel models and legitimate variations within the complex category of flatcars, this chapter includes information on boxes and part numbers where appropriate.

As you browse through this book, you will note the comments and observations of a great many people. Without such input over the years, this extensive an array of variations could never have been assembled. Yet no claim of completeness can be made since new reports continue to trickle in, over a quarter-century after the last "real Lionel" piece was made. If you are interested enough to study these fascinating flatcars in detail, you too may discover yet another unrecorded variation we can add to future editions. If so, a note addressed to Kalmbach Publishing Co. describing your observations will be greatly appreciated.

Lionel usually put the catalog number once on each side of their flatcars, as they did with almost every other item of rolling stock or power unit they produced. But this was not always the case. Some later uncataloged flatcars made for low-priced sets had no decoration at all or just had "LIONEL" on each side. Even some cataloged cars, such as the 6500 flatcar with airplane and the entire series of 6111 tin flatcars, had no number. Where this occurs, the flatcar is listed by its catalog number if there is one, or by the number appearing in the pages of the Lionel Service Manual. If no number can be found in either place, the item is listed and described at the end of this chapter under the imaginative title "UNNUMBERED FLATCARS." Also under this heading you will find a brief description of all unnumbered flatcars, cross-referring to their catalog numbers so you can go to the normal listing.

Note also that the titles of each item may not correspond to the name on the original box or even to every catalog listing. Lionel was not particularly consistent in these titles, so we have tried to use the title given in the consumer catalog for the first year the item appeared.

In these listings, the use of the term "frame" is different from the usage in other chapters of this book, due to the special construction of flatcars. Here it refers to that lower portion that constitutes the "body" of a flatcar, as opposed to the superstructure.

Cautionary Note:

Reported market prices listed in this chapter require original loads where applicable. Reproductions of automobiles, boats, helicopters, pipes, satellites, rockets, and many other loads exist. New load and component reproductions continue to appear.

Another feature to watch for is the color of unpainted plastic items. Some plastics change color over the years, especially with exposure to ultraviolet light. This can come from being displayed in a store window or on a collector's shelf with fluorescent lighting! In 1959, Lionel apparently used a batch of white plastic that fairly quickly turned a light caramel color. In this chapter the white automobile that appears on 6414 and 6424 flatcars is a potential victim. (Other well-known examples are the 57 AEC switcher, 6014-150 Wix boxcar, and 3366 operating circus car.) Other molded-in colors, and especially paint colors, can also be faded by exposure. You can usually detect this by looking at interior or underside areas and noting any difference in color or shade.

For their valuable contributions to the revision of this chapter, special thanks go to Joe Algozzini, Ken Coates, Don Corrigan, Newton Derby, Terral Klaassen, Ken Parks, Walt Pear, Buz Ray, Jim Sattler, and Mark Stephens.

1877 GENERAL FLATCAR WITH SIX HORSES: 1959–62. Molded brown plastic frame with AAR or arch-bar trucks riveted to it. Frame rails have "1877" on the left and "BUILT BY LIONEL" on the right in yellow heat-stamped sans-serif letters. Wire truss rod each side simulating frame support. Car may have both operating couplers, only one, or have both fixed couplers, depending on the value of the set in which it was included; fixed couplers tend to be found on the arch-bar trucks. Came with ten molded maroon fence sections—two long side rails with vertical slots to hold the eight cross sections; all fence sections are easy to remove—and lose! Load is six Plasticville horses—two white, two tan and brown, and two black; original horses marked with "BB" logo (Bachmann Bros.) on belly.

Note: Separate-sale cars and some in sets came in a Perforated Picture box. Watch for reproduction horses and fence sections.   **30   50   80   100**

1887 GENERAL FLATCAR WITH SIX HORSES: Uncataloged, 1959. Frame details same as 1877 except for the number. Should have molded yellow fence sections instead of the maroon color included with 1877. This car came with uncataloged Sears set 9666 and with a nearly identical set packaged in a display-style box. These two sets are commonly referred to as Halloween sets because of the orange-red, black, and gold colors of their General-style locomotive.

Note: Since this is a fairly rare car, watch especially for a number change. Reproduction fence sections are practically indistinguishable from the originals. Should have same horses as 1877. **80   130   180   230**

2411 FLATCAR: 1946–48. Die-cast metal frame painted medium gray with rubber-stamped "LIONEL LINES" in black serif lettering. There is no number on the sides; instead, the "2411" is rubber-stamped once in black on the frame underside, although several apparently original cars have been observed without this stamp. Car should have a wheelstand and two wire railings at each end and include eight blackened metal stakes as well as the proper load. Staple-end trucks with coil couplers are attached to metal plates that tab under the step plate on one end and are secured with a screw on the other.

Note: Since the same frame was used to produce the 2419 and 2420 work cabooses, marks on the frame underside indicate where tooling changes were made to provide screw holes for these cars. In fact, the 2419-2 part number molded in raised letters on the frame underside indicates that the 2419 was the initial design in the series. One example observed has the screw holes still molded in for 2419, but also has the stake holes open and was made and stamped as a 2411! The same car with magnetic couplers became 6411, starting with one O27 gauge set in 1948. Watch for missing or broken steps and reproduction stakes and load.

(A) 1946. Known as the "BIG INCH" in the catalog, had load of three blackened metal pipes. Since this is the most desirable load, the pipes have been closely reproduced. Original pipes are pressed metal with lengthwise markings inside. Observed reproductions are machined and have smooth interior surfaces. Staple-end trucks. As with most molded parts, it was necessary to use ejector

Top: Two versions of the General flatcar with six horses; 1877 with brown fences and 1887 with yellow fences. Both have archbar trucks and truss rod frame supports. Middle: 2411 (B) flatcar with three large unstained logs, and 2411 (A) with three

blackened metal pipes. Both have the common serif lettering. Bottom: 2461 (C) transformer car with unlettered frame, probably earliest production, and 2461 (B). R. Shanfeld Collection.

	Gd	VG	Ex	LN

pins to push the 2419-2 frame out of its mold. These pins left the six ¼"-diameter circles on the underside; three on each side, with the center two offset and the end pairs exactly opposite each other. The metal above these pins must not have been sufficiently thick and the pins may have caused some distortion in the deck of the car, because shortly after production began, the area around the pins was thickened. This change appears as a rectangular pad with the ¼" ejector pin mark on its surface. The same change appears on 2419 and 2420 frames and serves only to distinguish early from later 1946 production. There is no difference in value.   **50   70   90   125**

(B) 1947–48. Load became three ⅝"-diameter x 7" unstained wood logs. Number stamped on frame underside may have thinner strokes. Staple-end trucks.

15   25   30   45

(C) Same as (B), but sans-serif lettering. K. Coates Collection.   **NRS**

2461 TRANSFORMER CAR: 1947–48. Die-cast metal depressed-center frame painted medium gray. Usually has black rubber-stamped "2461 LIONEL LINES 2461" in serif lettering on each lower frame rail. Two steps and a brakestand each end of car. Staple-end trucks. Load is a plastic transformer model molded in two halves, painted red or black and then glued together. It attaches to the frame with two screws that thread into square brass nuts trapped in pockets between halves of the mold. Also sandwiched in at the top are the bases of two long and two

short insulators. Very early models used TS-70 horseshoe washers in addition to glue to retain these insulators, but they were soon omitted. Unfortunately, these insulators are easily broken, and of course they have been reproduced.

Note: Prices listed for Excellent and Like New require original unbroken insulators. Broken, replaced, or repaired insulators reduce condition to Very Good, regardless of condition of rest of car. Replacement insulators have a straight mounting shank rather than the collar that traps them between mold halves on the originals. To see it, remove the transformer and look inside. Original white insulators have yellowed somewhat with age, while the replacements are new-looking. Watch for broken brake-wheel stands and steps, in addition to reproduction transformers and insulators. The prototype car for this Lionel model was pictured in the November 1940 issue of Lionel's *Model Builder* magazine (R. LaVoie and T. Rollo comments).

(A) 1946. Has red-painted transformer with a white transformer car decal on sides near the top. Within the "C" in "Car" is the circled Lionel "L". Occasionally this car has a decal on only one side, but this is most likely a factory error or a case where one decal flaked off, as they often do.   **40   65   110   140**

(B) 1947. Has black-painted transformer, and the decal is almost always on one side only. Very rare to find a black transformer with decals on both sides.

35   50   75   100

(C) 1946. This unusual variation has no lettering on the side frames at all. Instead, "2461" is rubber-stamped

Gd   VG   Ex   LN   **Gd   VG   Ex   LN**

at the bottom of one of the honeycomb wells on the under- side of the depressed center. This car most often has a red transformer, and it was probably initial production. Note that it's easy to switch transformers.   **NRS**

3309 TURBO MISSILE LAUNCHING CAR: 1963–64. Also see 3349 turbo missile firing car. Molded red plastic depressed-center frame unpainted and unlettered with blue molded launch mechanism and, sometimes, a blue molded missile rack with spare missile. "Turbo missile" refers to a molded white plastic wheel-shaped flying disk with red center launched by a spring mechanism. Came with two fixed couplers, or one fixed and one operating coupler, and AAR trucks, arch-bar trucks, or a combina- tion of the two. The truck and coupler information men- tioned here differentiates this car from 3349, which came with AAR trucks and operating couplers at both ends (S. Bradley comment).

Note: This car was not cataloged for separate sale but is shown as part of sets 11321 in 1963 and 11440 in 1964. It has also appeared in several uncataloged sets. No box marked for the 3309 has yet appeared, but there are three versions of the 3309-5 instruction sheet, all dated 7-62.

(A) Light red body (R. Royer comment).

25	**40**	**60**	**85**

(B) Same as (A) but distinctly different cherry red body (R. Royer comment). **25   40   60   85**

(C) Same as (A) but distinctly different teal blue launcher (R. Royer and J. Breslin comments).

35	**50**	**70**	**100**

(D) Rare molded olive drab frame unpainted, oth- erwise as described. Usually found with one operating and one fixed coupler. Available only as part of several uncataloged military sets.

100	**225**	**325**	**450**

3349 TURBO MISSILE FIRING CAR: 1962–65. See also 3309 turbo missile launching car. Although 3349 was repeatedly illustrated in Lionel's catalogs with a number on the side, regular-production items came without num- bering or lettering. I. D. Smith comments that the die- cast frame 3650 and the plastic frame 3349 share the same frame mold, with neither having a molded-in part number. Comes with AAR trucks with two operating cou- plers; this and the fact that it always included a spare missile rack with missile are all that distinguish it from 3309 described previously.

Top: 3309 turbo missile launching car with usual red frame and with rare olive drab molded frame. The latter car is shown with spare missile and rack, but it typically came without these. Second: 3349 turbo missile firing car, identical to 3309 but has spare missile, two operating couplers, and a slightly different name! 3361 (D) log dump car with sans-serif lettering. Third: 3361 (A) with larger serif lettering. 3362 with log load, which was cataloged and boxed as 3364 operating log dump car. Bottom: 3362 helium tank unloading car with correct load for this number. 3409 operating helicopter launching car, the economy version of 3419. R. Shanfeld Collection.

	Gd	VG	Ex	LN

Note: Set 11385 from the 1963 catalog lists this car as 3349-100, the only such listing for a dash number. Significance of the -100 is unknown, since a new example of this set is shown in *Greenberg's Guide to Lionel Trains, 1945–1969, Volume III: Sets,* where it is described as a common 3349. The box is pictured and it appears standard. One would think this a Lionel catalog error except for one curious fact. There are three different versions of the 3349-8 instruction sheet, all dated 7-62. But a 3349-105 sheet dated 4-63 has also been reliably reported.

(A) Light red body (P. Catalano comment).

	25	40	60	85

(B) Dark red body.

	25	40	60	85

3361 LOG DUMP CAR: 1955–59. Frame is molded medium gray plastic with black rubber-stamped lettering. Number on frame is 336155, a combination of the catalog number 3361 and the year of introduction, 1955. Load is five stained wooden logs each 7/16"-diameter x 45/8". Bar-end trucks are attached to a metal channel that runs the length of the car and holds the operating mechanism. Unlike the earlier 3451 and 3461 operating lumber cars that dumped in one motion, 3361 has a ratcheting dump mechanism. Each press of the unload button on the remote-control track section controller tilts the dump rack a little more until, after several presses, the logs roll off and the rack falls back into place.

Note: Separate-sale cars came in larger boxes marked "3361" only and included a liner and an unloading bin. Cars that came with a set typically were packed in a smaller box marked "3361X", box part no. 3361-28, without the bin, which was packed separately in the set box. Note that this bin, while still having the molded-in 160 number, is about 8½" long and is made of somewhat flexible injection-molded plastic. It was new for 1955 and replaced the rigid 7"-long Bakelite bin that had been produced since before World War II.

(A) Has "LIONEL LINES" with thick (7/32") serif letters, "336155" on right in large serif numbers and car dimensions to left in sans-serif lettering. Drive gear for operating mechanism is white plastic (T. Rollo and R. Hutchinson comments).

	20	30	45	60

(B) Same as (A), but drive gear is black plastic. J. Sattler and R. Brezak Collections.

	20	30	45	60

(C) Has "LIONEL LINES" with lighter serif letters than (A), "336155" moved to the left and dimension data to right. Drive gear is black plastic. K. Koehler, L. Backus, and M. Ocilka Collections.

	20	30	45	60

(D) Has "LIONEL LINES" in thinner (1/8") sans-serif letters with car number to the right and dimensions on the left. Frame mold is darker gray, and the drive gear is usually medium orange plastic. J. Sattler and L. Backus Collections.

	20	30	45	60

3362 HELIUM TANK UNLOADING CAR: 1961–63. Dark green molded plastic frame with rubber-stamped "LIONEL LINES 3362" in white serif lettering; sans-serif data lines. A metal channel runs the length of the car's underside and provides attachment for the early AAR trucks (each with operating coupler) and the dump mechanism. Unlike the earlier 3361, which had a ratcheting dump mechanism that reset after the dump cycle, 3362 dumps in one quick, spring-powered move and must be manually reset. The trigger is a plunger much like that used to actuate the couplers of this era. It holds the spring-loaded dump rack closed until pulled away by the same magnetic track section that operates the couplers. Load is three silver-painted wood tanks that have been reproduced.

Note: Although not cataloged as a helium tank unloading car after 1963, the same car, with the same number, was cataloged starting in 1965 as 3364 operating log dump car and in 1969 as "3362 and 3364 operating dump car." Included instruction sheet 3362-15 dated 6-61. See entries for 3364 and 3362/3364 below.

	12	27	42	60

3362/3364 OPERATING DUMP CAR: 1969. Same car as 3362 described above, but load is only two of the wood simulated helium tanks. The car lacked any markings and was packaged in a unique double-numbered box. Trucks usually are the late AAR design, with one operating and one fixed coupler.

Note: Since the lettering on 3362 was rubber-stamped, this variation could be made by simply wiping off the lettering on a standard car. Consequently, the value is primarily in the original double-numbered Hagerstown Checkerboard box, which is required for a Like New price. Included instruction sheet 3362-15 dated 6-61. Car does not fit in its box and must be angled with trucks displaced to their extremes in opposite directions to squeeze in.

	12	25	35	50

3364 OPERATING LOG DUMP CAR: 1965–66, 1968. Car is identical to 3362 described above, but load is three wood logs (called poles in the instruction sheet) stained brown, each 5/8"-diameter x 6". Lionel never produced a car numbered 3364, but they did package the 3362 with the three-log load in an Orange Picture box labeled "No. 3364 / LIONEL / LOG / UNLOADING CAR"; this box is much harder to find than the box marked for 3362. Car has AAR trucks with one fixed and one operating coupler, but may be found with two operating couplers.

Note: Included instruction sheet 3364-10 dated 4/65 and a 1-165 warranty card. Since the value of this car is primarily in the box, that item is required for a Like New price.

	12	25	35	50

3451 OPERATING LUMBER CAR: 1946–48. Frame is black-painted die-cast metal, and the tilting platform is blackened stamped steel. Has one die-cast brakestand, four tilting stakes, and four removable stakes. White "3451 LIONEL LINES 3451" on each side of frame rail may be rubber-stamped or heat-stamped. Staple-end trucks of either type. Load is five natural wood logs, each 7/16"-diameter x approximately 45/8".

Gd   VG   Ex   LN

(A) 1946 version has the three shaft retainers for the tilt tray fastened with round-head drive screws. There is a nickel-sized hole in the frame near the center with three small scallops jutting inward around the edge 120 degrees apart. This version always came with rubber-stamped lettering, which is often faint or obliterated. Staple-end trucks with no stake marks on the underside where the coupler head attaches to the truck.

12   25   35   50

(B) For 1947 the frame casting was changed. A 1¼" hole, about half-dollar size, with no scallops, replaced the nickel-sized hole. Bosses were added around the drive screw hole tops. Tilt stake shaft-retainer clips fit over these bosses, which were rolled like a rivet to retain the clips. However, the drive screw holes remained open. Early versions retained the rubber-stamped lettering. Staple-end trucks with stake marks on the underside where the coupler head attaches to the truck.

12   25   35   50

(C) Late 1947 and all 1948. Same as (B) but white heat-stamped lettering. Sometime in this period Lionel introduced the two box sizes for 3451; a large separate-sale box with liner when the 160 bin was included, and a smaller box with no liner for use in sets where the 160 bin was packed elsewhere in the set box. This latter box is known without the "X" (as in 3451X) used later and with a rubber-stamped "X" on the box ends only. All three of these boxes have "San Francisco" on them.

12   25   35   50

3461 OPERATING LUMBER CAR: 1949–55. Construction identical to 3451 described above, except trucks changed to magnetic couplers and number changed accordingly. Other changes noted in variation listings.

Note: Since the 3361 plastic-frame log dump car debuted in 1955, it is likely 1954 was the last year of production for 3461 and it was cataloged the next year just to help dealers dispose of existing stock. It is unclear whether 3461 continued in black for 1954 or was completely replaced by the green frame 3461-25.

(A) Early 1949 with 1¼" hole in frame and drive screw holes completely filled. Has very rare white sans-serif

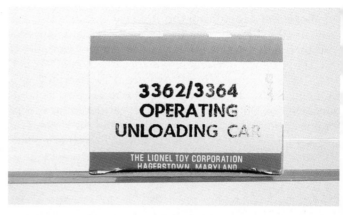

Hagerstown Checkerboard box containing unmarked 3362/3364 operating dump car.

Gd   VG   Ex   LN

rubber-stamped lettering, possibly because the heat-stamp tooling was not ready in time. Staple-end trucks. Load is the same five natural wood logs used on 3451. H. Lovelock Collection.   **NRS**

(B) 1949–53. Same as (A), except white sans-serif heat-stamped lettering. Trucks changed from staple-end to bar-end trucks during this period. Load remained same as (A). This is the most common version of 3461. As with 3451, there were two box sizes; a large one with 160 bin and liner and a 3461X without the bin or liner.

10   25   35   50

(C) For 1954 and possibly before, the frame was changed a final time to decrease the 1¼" hole to 1¹⁄₁₆" diameter. The purpose of this hole remains unknown. Frame color is shown in the 1954 catalog in both black and green, and the -25 on the number does not appear at all in the catalog, only on the box for the green color car. The tilting platform remained blackened steel. Whether a black frame with the 1¹⁄₁₆" hole exists is unknown. Even if it does, it may prove only that the hole size changed prior to 1954. As in previous years two box sizes were used: one marked "3461-25" for the large separate-sale box with 160 bin and liner, and the other labeled "3461-25X" for the small box included only with sets. Bar-end

Top: 3461 (A) operating lumber car with rubber-stamped lettering, and 3451 (C) with heat-stamped lettering. Bottom: 3461 (C) in green with heat-stamped lettering, and first use of stained logs, and 3451 (A) with rubber-stamped lettering.

| | Gd | VG | Ex | LN | | | Gd | VG | Ex | LN |

trucks. The load, for the first time, was stained brown logs rather than the natural wood color used previously. This became the standard log color for 1954 and later.

15   30   45   60

6100-SERIES 8-INCH STAMPED-STEEL FLATCARS

In determining catalog numbers and correct loads, we have made extensive reference to the Lionel Service Manual as well as reports from collectors, especially in the listings that follow. Since the blackened-steel racks were identical for log and pipe cars, even Lionel may have switched loads as supply and demand dictated. Actually, all the Service Manual tells us is that 6111 was a log car, 6121 a pipe car, 6121-60 a yellow pipe car, and there was a 6121-87 frame of unspecified color. 6111 was cataloged in 1955–1957 while 6121 appeared in 1956–1957 and 6151 in 1958 only.

Frames

Introduced in 1955, this series of 8-inch stamped-steel flatcars shared a common stamping with the 6119 series of work cabooses that debuted the same year (see Chapter 5). Presence or absence of one end rail and variations in frame-hole patterns to accommodate caboose or flatcar superstructures are all that distinguished the two stampings. Yet the little flatcar disappeared after 1958, while the work caboose continued through the end in 1969. During the flatcar's four years, many paint colors were available.

Trucks

Early production probably used stock left from 1954, as some of these cars with metal bar-end trucks have no uncoupler tabs. Coupler tabs were introduced in 1955 to facilitate manual uncoupling. These tabs occur on most 6100-series flatcars until 1957, when the AAR design took their place. Axle design on the AAR trucks has some notable variation that might be useful in dating but has not yet been sufficiently documented. All reported examples have two operating couplers for all years.

Paint

Although quite robust (being steel stampings), these cars were always painted and tended to chip or scratch easily. Like the work cabooses, they had a step at each corner. The slightest bend in a step, as from swiveling the truck too far, caused the paint to crack and flake off. Even cars new in the box show up with minor defects from handling or poor paint adhesion. Lionel solved this problem on later work caboose frames by applying a black oxide finish, a type of rust resistant surface finish that doesn't flake or chip, though it can be scratched. But for the painted flatcars, perfection is difficult to find, which only adds to the challenge and fun of collecting. Numerous colors were used, and since color photographs don't show the shades well, some attempt is made to describe the colors in the listings.

Lettering

Not one of these 6100-series flatcars ever had the catalog number applied; only the name "LIONEL" is centered on the frame in serif or sans-serif lettering, black or white, heat-stamped or rubber-stamped. This was not Lionel's usual practice and makes documentation quite a challenge. It appears that the first two or so years of production used heat-stamped lettering, while toward the last, and certainly for all of 1958 (when only 6151 was cataloged), all "LIONEL" lettering was rubber-stamped. Evidently three heat-stamp dies were used, as this type of lettering appears very exactly in three different lengths. Measuring across the bottom, from the left-most edge to the right-most edge of the "L"s in "LIONEL", the two lengths for serif letters are 2 inches exactly and 2¹⁄₁₆ inches. For the sans-serif letters, always heat-stamped, the length is 2⅛ inches with no variation. The rubber-stamped lettering, applied with a more flexible tool, is 2 1/8 inches +/- 1/32 inches or so, sometimes varying the whole tolerance on opposite sides of the same car.

Loads

Only three logs or three pipes were provided where appropriate. Replacement logs and pipes came in sets of five, and these are listed in the Lionel Service Manual, leading some to the belief that this is the proper quantity for the car. But since this is an inexpensive car, it only got three when provided to the customer. Logs, always brown-stained, were usually the standard ⁷⁄₁₆-inch–diameter x 4⅝ inches. However, several examples have ½-inch–diameter x 5⅝-inch logs that may well be correct. The pipes are the standard silvery colored thin plastic 6511-24.

Boxes

Fortunately, these flatcars appeared in a period when most items were still individually boxed. Thus the printed content helps identify intended loads. Unfortunately, these boxes are quite hard to find—their survival rate is even worse than that of their contents. A modest premium should be allowed for the original box, depending on its condition. Of course, being inexpensive cars, these often came unboxed in inexpensive sets where items nestled in the set box liner. Boxes for 6111-75 and 6111-110 log cars are known, but strangely, none for plain 6111. Boxes for the pipe car are 6121, 6121-25, 6121-60, and 6121-85. The suffixes probably indicate color, but Lionel's scheme for this, if they had one, has not been deciphered.

6100 VARIATIONS

(A) Medium lemon yellow, black 2" heat-stamped serif lettering, metal bar-end trucks with tabs. Reported with log load in 6111-75 box. F. S. Davis Collection.

5   10   15   20

	Gd	VG	Ex	LN

(B) Medium lemon yellow, black sans-serif letters, AAR trucks. Reported with log load in 6111-110 box. F. S. Davis Collection. **5 10 15 20**

(C) Medium lemon yellow, white 2¹⁄₁₆" heat-stamped serif letters. Load unknown. Very rare. J. Algozzini Collection. **NRS**

(D) Light mustard yellow. Might also be called cream yellow, black rubber-stamped serif letters, AAR trucks. Load unknown. **5 10 15 20**

(E) Peach color, similar to color used to paint hands and face on Lionel's painted figures. Black rubber-stamped serif letters, AAR trucks. Load is three ½"-diameter logs, but it came new in 6121 box, which is supposed to be for a pipe car. Very rare color. A. Stewart Collection. **NRS**

(F) Fire engine red, white 2¹⁄₁₆" heat-stamped serif letters, bar-end trucks with tabs. Reported with three pipes in 6121 box. F. S. Davis Collection. **5 10 15 20**

(G) Bright red, more glossy, slightly more orange than fire engine red. Frequently has "orange peel" look to paint on car underside, although rest of car is all right. White 2¹⁄₁₆" heat-stamped serif letters, AAR trucks. Came in 6121-85 box with three pipes. A. Stewart Collection. **5 10 15 20**

(H) Bright red, white rubber-stamped serif letters, AAR trucks. Reported with three pipes in 6121-85 box. F. S. Davis Collection. **5 10 15 20**

(I) Bright red, white heat-stamped sans-serif letters, AAR trucks. Reported with three pipes in a 6121-85 box. F. S. Davis Collection. **5 10 15 20**

(J) Blood red, a very dark, muddy red. White rubber-stamped serif letters, AAR trucks. One Like New example found with three standard logs but load unverified. A fairly scarce color. **10 20 30 50**

(K) Light gray, like the normal tray on a 6119 work caboose. White 2¹⁄₁₆" heat-stamped serif letters, bar-end

trucks without tabs. A second example has one tab and one no-tab truck. Both examples came in 6121 box with three pipes. A. Stewart Collection. **5 10 15 20**

(L) Light gray, white 2¹⁄₁₆" heat-stamped serif letters, AAR trucks. New example found with three standard logs but no box, so load unverified. **5 10 15 20**

(M) Light gray, white heat-stamped sans-serif letters, AAR trucks. Load unknown. **5 10 15 20**

Note: The following listings are all "dark gray," though several shades have been reported. In sunlight, they appear as entirely different colors! There are even shades of the same basic variation, all described as they occur.

(N) Basic dark gray like the frame on the dark gray version of 3650 searchlight extension car. White 2" heat-stamped serif letters, AAR trucks. Load unknown. **5 10 15 20**

(O) Dark gray, white sans-serif letters, AAR trucks. Load is three pipes and came in 6121-85 box. A. Stewart Collection. **5 10 15 20**

(P) Battleship gray; noticeably darker than dark gray with a hint of blue in it. Two shades observed, both with white 2¹⁄₁₆" white serif letters and AAR trucks. Load unknown. **5 10 15 20**

(Q) Drab gray; about the same degree of darkness as battleship gray, but has a hint of olive in it. White 2" serif letters, AAR trucks. Load unknown. **5 10 15 20**

(R) Drab gray, white sans-serif letters, AAR trucks. Load unknown. **5 10 15 20**

(S) Gunmetal gray, the darkest of them all with a bit more gloss than the other shades. White 2¹⁄₁₆" serif letters, AAR trucks. Load unknown. **5 10 15 20**

6151 FLATCAR WITH RANGE PATROL TRUCK: 1958. Same car as 6100 series described above, always

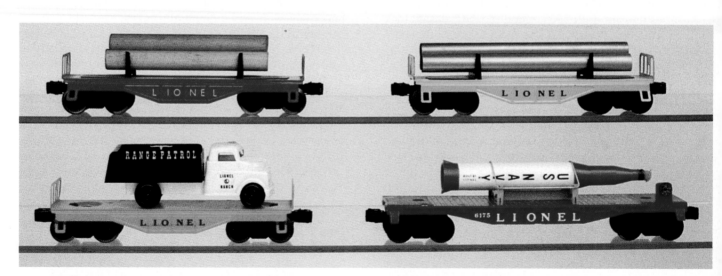

Top: 6111 (I), cataloged as 6111 with logs but 6121 when load was three pipes, and 6121 (A) with three silvery gray plastic pipes. Bottom: 6151 (A) flatcar with range patrol truck, and 6175 (A) *rocket car. Note sponge tip on rocket still intact, rare even on otherwise brand-new rockets. R. Shanfeld and R. Gladsen Collections.*

Flatcars of the 6100 series, shown with original boxes. Top: Versions (A) and (B). Middle: Versions (F) and (S). Bottom: Versions (G) and (I). F. S. Davis Collection.

	Gd	VG	Ex	LN

with black rubber-stamped "LIONEL" on each side in serif letters. Holes for the two load racks remained, but the racks were absent on this car. Flatcar trucks are AAR design with two operating couplers. Load should be a white molded truck chassis with black molded "box" or rear superstructure. Truck cab doors have black heat-stamped lettering and box has white heat-stamped lettering with longhorn emblem. Pyro made entire truck for Lionel, and no variations have been reported. One 6418-9 elastic band held the truck to the flatcar. **Note:** Unlike the 6100 series above, this car seems always to be individually boxed. There are at least five variations of this box, but space does not permit that discussion.

(A) Vivid yellowish orange frame. J. Sattler and H. Degano Collections. **40 80 120 150**

(B) Bright lemon yellow frame. T. Budniak and J. Bratspis Collections. **40 80 120 150**

(C) Yellowish cream frame (C. Weber observation). **40 80 120 150**

Note: This concludes coverage of the 6100 series.

6361 TIMBER TRANSPORT CAR: 1960–61, 1964–66, and 1968–69. Dark green molded frame usually with white rubber-stamped serif lettering but later unlettered. AAR trucks (usually with two operating couplers) riveted to steel channel underframe. This channel attaches to the plastic frame with a tab at one end and a screw at the other. Load is three sections of real tree branches, complete with bark, retained on the car by two chains and a spring.

	Gd	VG	Ex	LN

Note: In 1960, for the first time in many years, there was no log-unloading car in the Lionel line. The plastic frame of 3361, now discontinued, was modified slightly to become 6361. For this year only, the same steel underframe used on 6362 railway truck car was used for 6361. It contained only the two pilot holes, two holes for the truck rivets, and the screw hole. In 1961, the plastic frame was again modified to produce 3362 helium tank unloading car. So the changes to accommodate the dump trigger appear in 6361 as well, and the steel underframe, common to both cars, was likewise modified. Instruction sheet 6361-16 was included to show how the components of the load went together (R. Gluckman observation).

(A) 1960 only, with early AAR trucks, dull white rubber-stamped lettering, blackened timber chains, solid underframe. J. Sattler, R. LaVoie, and J. Algozzini Collections. **25 50 70 90**

(B) Post-1960 production with modified frame and underframe. Usually found with late AAR trucks. **25 50 70 90**

(C) Last production for 1968–69 same as (B), except has a lighter green molded frame, late AAR trucks, no lettering, and blackened timber chains (also reported with gold-color chains but authenticity not verified). Came in a Hagerstown Checkerboard box marked "6361/TIMBER CAR" (R. LaVoie comments). G. Halverson and N. Ritschel Collections. **40 80 110 150**

6362 RAILWAY TRUCK CAR: 1955–57. With only slight modification, the gray molded plastic frame for

	Gd	**VG**	**Ex**	**LN**

3361 operating lumber car became the orange molded frame for this car. It even used the same steel underframe, with the mechanism mounting and wiring holes removed. Bar-end trucks, with and without tab couplers, clip to this channel. Load is three basic 479-1 Lionel bar-end trucks without coupler plate or mounting stud.

Note: These trucks were packaged individually and cataloged for separate sale as replacement accessories all three years 6362 was produced.

(A) Translucent orange molded frame with black rubber-stamped lettering. Data lines are sans-serif but "LIONEL LINES" is in tall serif lettering. Found with and without tab couplers. J. Kotil and J. Sattler Collections.

	20	40	60	75

(B) Same as (A), except "LIONEL LINES" is sans-serif in noticeably shorter letters. J. Kotil and D. Mitarotonda Collections.

	20	40	60	75

(C) Same as (A), except frame is "faded" opaque orange, similar in shade to the cab and tray on 6119-25 work caboose. S. Bradley Collection.

	85	120	150	180

	Gd	**VG**	**Ex**	**LN**

6401 FLATCAR: 1965. Gray molded 1877-3 frame completely unadorned and undecorated. Usually found with AAR trucks with one operating and one fixed coupler. However, over the years, the same frame also came with arch-bar trucks, all fixed couplers, or a mixture of all the above. No load.

Note: Listed (but not illustrated) only at the very bottom of page 14 in the 1965 catalog. There it says, "[p]erfect for carrying cars, crates and accessories." This same flatcar came with various loads in several sets in the 1960s and thus is quite common. Very uncommon and highly collectible is the minuscule Orange Picture box made especially for 6401. It is worth many times the price of its contents. Price shown is for the flatcar alone. Add a very substantial premium for the original box, depending on condition.

(A) Common version molded in light gray plastic. G. Halverson, R. LaVoie, and W. Triezenberg Collections.

	2	5	8	12

(B) Also known with a decidedly darker gray molded frame. A. Stewart Collection.

	2	5	8	12

Top: 6362 (A) railway truck car and 6362 (B) with sans-serif lettering. Second: 6402 (B) with unusual boat load, shown only in 1969 set 11730; 6401 (B) flatcar and two views of its rare tiny separate-sale box. Third: 6406 (B) flatcar with single auto, shown *with "premium" automobile but should have gray-bumper version; 6402 (A) with usual load on darker gray flatcar. Bottom: 6404 (A) flatcar with single auto; 6406 flatcar with single auto as actually found in uncataloged set 19142-100.*

	Gd	**VG**	**Ex**	**LN**

6402 FLATCAR WITH CABLE REELS: 1962 advance catalog; 1964–66 and 1969. Same as 6401 but with various loads. Listed but not illustrated at the very bottom of page 13 in the 1964 catalog with no load and the very words that describe 6401 in its 1965 listing. Since set usage confirms 6402 as a load-carrying car, and 6401 is known in a box with no room for a load, the two numbers are considered confirmed as listed. Set 11500 in 1964 lists this component as 6402-50, but no reported difference has been ascribed to the -50. When load is two empty LIONEL cable reels, a 6402-5 long elastic band that hooks over the tiny projections in the center of each end of the frame secures them to the car. Only the 1969 set 11730 shows 6402 with a load (a blue hull 6801-75 boat) other than cable reels.

Note: This basic flatcar was also used extensively in low-budget uncataloged sets, many of which are shown and described in *Greenberg's Guide to Lionel Trains, 1945–1969, Volume IV: Uncatalogued Sets*. In these applications, other loads such as automobiles of various colors, a tank, jeep with cannon, and so forth, were used, but the Lionel number for these, if different, is not known. See 6406 listing and "Unnumbered Flatcars" at the end of this chapter.

(A) Load is two molded orange or light gray empty reels. **6 12 18 25**

(B) As shown in 1969 set 11730 only, load is a blue hull 6801-75 boat. **25 45 65 80**

(C) Same as (A), but frame is molded in brown, or maroonish brown, same as 1877 but with no lettering or truss rods. **6 12 18 25**

6404 FLATCAR WITH SINGLE AUTO: Uncataloged. Black molded 1877-3 frame with "6404" on the left in sans-serif numerals and "BUILT BY LIONEL" on the right in serif letters, all heat-stamped in white. Has wire truss rods and almost always arch-bar trucks with fixed couplers.

Note: Never cataloged and, strictly speaking, never shown. However, in the 1960 advance catalog, set 1109 includes a 6511-series flatcar with a single automobile load. In the 9-61 supplement to the Lionel Service Manual, 6404 is listed with a 6404-30 auto (maroon). Refer to *Greenberg's Guide to Lionel Trains, 1945–1969, Volume III: Sets* for further details and note that the picture there shows a yellow automobile while the text mentions a brown one. At any rate, it is generally accepted that 6404 was distributed with this and probably other uncataloged sets. It is actually quite hard to find. Even harder to find, if it exists at all, is a molded maroon automobile, although a "mahogany" color has been observed. More likely the load was usually a gray-bumper automobile from the regular line. See the sidebar on Lionel automobiles in this chapter. We are still looking for information from the 1960 Merchants' Green Stamp catalog to see if 6404 might have been included in one of their sets. This was the first Lionel item to come with an automobile having unplated gray bumpers (J. Algozzini

	Gd	**VG**	**Ex**	**LN**

comment). D. Fleming and Vaughn Collections. In the following listings, the price for common color automobiles (red and yellow) is primarily for the flatcar, while the price with uncommon automobile colors reflects primarily the value of the automobile. Note also there is scant documentation that all the colors listed were distributed that way by Lionel. One of the rarer colors has been found on 6402 gray cars in low-budget uncataloged sets. Also see 6406.

(A) Load is a molded red original automobile with gray bumpers. **20 35 50 75**

(B) Same as (A), but automobile is molded in one of the shades of yellow. **25 50 75 125**

(C) Same as (A), but automobile is molded in dark brown. **50 100 150 200**

(D) Same as (A), but automobile is molded in kelly green. **100 150 200 250**

(E) Same as (A), but truss rods eliminated and frame has late AAR trucks with operating couplers. Load is a mauve (pale bluish purple) molded automobile with gray bumpers. Possibly from Merchants' Green Stamp set, but no evidence yet specifically linking it to this set. Reader comments invited (J. Sattler comment). **NRS**

6405 FLATCAR WITH PIGGY-BACK VAN: 1961. Same as 1877 except frame rails are heat-stamped "6405" on the left in sans-serif numerals instead of the serif "1877". Trucks are usually early AAR with two operating couplers.

Note: Not listed for separate sale and shown only with set 1642 in 1961, which came with unboxed components. Nevertheless, 6405 is not difficult to find in its own Orange Picture box. The Lionel Service Manual shows the load as a 6405-150 trailer. All reported examples have trailer version (I) with or without the CJ sign (see sidebar on Lionel Trailer Vans). Note that the version with a drilled hole for coupling to a Midgetoy tractor would not be an appropriate load for 6405. The need for this hole did not arise until four years after 6405 was discontinued. Be alert for reproduction trailers, pony wheels, and rubber wheels. J. Sattler Collection.

12 25 40 55

6406 FLATCAR WITH SINGLE AUTO: 1961 advance catalog. Not listed in any Lionel catalog but shown as part of set 1123 in the 1961 advance catalog. One of three sets that year designed for the mass toy market (rather than whatever other market Lionel thought all the rest of its sets were designed for!). In the catalog picture, the number is shown on the frame rail. No such example has yet been reported. The Lionel Service Manual shows a unique 6406-3 part no. for the frame and 6406-30 for an "Auto (yellow)". Fixed coupler arch-bar trucks, part no. 561-1, are specified.

Note: *In Greenberg's Guide to Lionel Trains, 1945–1969, Volume III: Sets,* outfit 1123 is reported to include either a maroon or gray unmarked flatcar with fixed-coupler arch-bar trucks and a gray-bumper automobile. These flatcars would be indistinguishable from 6402 (C)

Gd   VG   Ex   LN

or 6401 except perhaps for the trucks. Only a yellow auto with gray bumpers can be documented as a proper load. Refer to entries 6402 and 6404.

(A) Gray flatcar frame with fixed-coupler arch-bar trucks. Load is any shade molded yellow original automobile. D. Morris Collection.   **35   55   85   110**

(B) Same as (A), except frame is molded maroonish brown, same color as 1877. A. LaRue, J. Divi, and R. Dupstet Collections.   **35   55   85   110**

6411 FLATCAR: 1948–50. Same as 2411, except has magnetic coupler trucks and "6411" rubber-stamped on the frame underside. Load is three brown-stained wood logs ⅝"-diameter x 7".

Note: 1948 was a coupler transition year for Lionel; the electromagnetic (coil) couplers were still produced for O gauge sets and all the separate-sale rolling stock, but the new magnetic couplers were being introduced in O27 sets. This transition occasioned the number shift from 2400 series for coil couplers to 6400 series for the magnetic. Set 1449WS featured the only appearance of 6411 that year.

(A) 1948 version with staple-end coil coupler trucks. An easily made variation that has been reliably reported as original. Obviously an example of using up stock. I. D. Smith and S. Carlson Collections.
11   20   30   45

(B) 1948–50 versions with intended staple-end magnetic coupler trucks. I. D. Smith, L. Steur, and Schmaus Collections.   **11   20   30   45**

(C) Same as (B), but a distinctly darker gray. Same color variation can be seen on 6419 and 6420 work caboose frames.   **11   20   30   45**

(D) Same as (B), but sans-serif lettering. A. Stewart Collection.   **NRS**

6413 MERCURY CAPSULE CARRYING CAR: 1962–63. Blue molded plastic frame with no molded-in part number. Uncharacteristic for Lionel; only the usual Lionel information is molded in raised letters on one underside frame rail. White sans-serif lettering is heat-stamped along each side of the car. Mounting pads for brake wheels are molded in at each end, but 6413 always came without them. This frame was initially used in 1958 on the 6519 Allis Chalmers car.

Note: When packaging was changed with introduction of the Orange Perforated boxes in 1959, Lionel thought they could save money by minimizing box size. For rolling stock, this could be done by turning the trucks "backwards," so the couplers were underneath the car. Unfortunately for the 6544 missile firing trail car, this left the brakestands right against the end of the box. With their long lever arms, the brakestands frequently cracked their plastic mounting tabs before the car even made it to a dealer's shelf. By the time 6413 was introduced, Lionel had gotten the word and simply left off the brake wheels.

Above: 6405 flatcar with piggy-back van showing truss rods and AAR trucks on flatcar and unused sign slots on van.

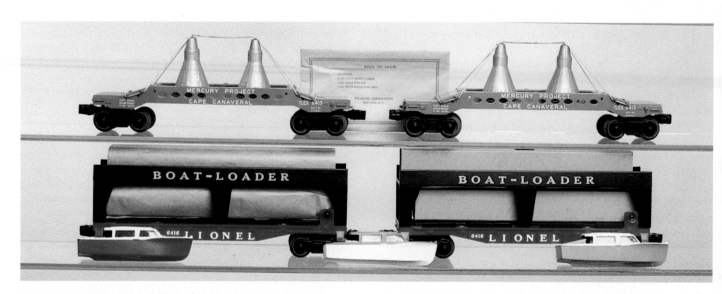

Top: Usual medium blue 6413 (A) Mercury capsule carrying car. Unusual 6413 (B) with teal blue molded frame. Shown between the cars is the envelope containing small parts and an instruction sheet that came with each car. Bottom: 6416 four-boat transport car with usual plain waxy paper wrap for boats. Early production with paperboard sleeves for the boats. Boat shown in center is correct. Boats on left and right were made from the same mold by the same supplier but probably were never supplied originally by Lionel in these colors.

	Gd	VG	Ex	LN

Two blackened-metal plates fit crosswise in the frame and are held in place by tabbing into the oval holes along each side rail. Round holes in these plates retain the base of the two silvery gray molded Mercury capsules. A music-wire bar bridges the tops of the two capsules, hooking into a small hole in each nose cone. Elastic bands are retained at each end of the bar and stretch over short "wings" on the frame sides to complete the installation. On new cars in their Orange Picture boxes, the 6413-6 wire bar, 6418-9 elastic bands, and a 6413-8 instruction sheet dated 6-62 are packaged in a 6413-9 manila envelope labeled "ASSEM. NO. 6413-10". Trucks are AAR-style, usually with two operating couplers. Very hard to find intact (M. Ocilka comment).

Reproductions of the capsules, wire bar, and elastic bands are available. Excellent and better condition requires all original components.

(A) Most common molded medium blue frame, usually with two operating couplers. G. Wilson Collection.
70 110 140 175

(B) Quite rare aquamarine or faded-looking greenish blue molded frame, usually with one operating and one fixed coupler. G. Wilson Collection. **NRS**

6418 MACHINERY CAR: 1955–57. Has die-cast metal frame painted medium gray with a brakestand staked on at each end. Molded into the underside of the frame is the usual Lionel information, along with a blank plaque or the number 6418. Equipped with two bar-end metal trucks at each end clipped to a mounting plate that is attached to the frame with a screw so it can swivel. Listed in the catalog for O gauge only, because the center of the car will not clear the motor housing when trying to negotiate the curved portion of O27 switches. Inner trucks have no coupler plate, while the end trucks have magnetic couplers with or without tabs. Load is two simulated bridge girders as specified in the listings, attached with two 6418-9 elastic bands. Only two girders are listed in Lionel Service Manual: 6418-14 bridge side (black) and 6418-21 (red).

Note: When 6418 was introduced in 1955, it was the only flatcar to use this huge new frame and the car number was molded into the bottom. With the introduction of 6518 transformer car in 1956, Lionel needed to use the same frame for both cars. So the 6418 number was removed, leaving a blank plaque on the underside of the frame thereafter, and the car number was put on the respective load. Note also that to mount the transformer on 6518, two holes had to be drilled in the frame that were not required for 6418. A 6418 with these holes has been made from a 6518, since Lionel seldom drilled holes it did not need. The bridge sides (girders) were the same as those on the 214 plate girder bridge. Loads are easily switched but only the unnumbered girder is correct for a car with a 6418 number on the bottom, and only a numbered girder is correct for a 6418 with a blank plaque. The loads described below show all reported girder variations. Any of them could possibly have come with the frames shown, but it is doubtful all of them actually did!

(A) Frame with 6418 molded into the underside. Load is two black molded girders with "LIONEL" in raised letters with the top surface of the letters heat-stamped in white. B. McLeavy Collection. **45 75 100 125**

(B) Same as (A), except load is two orange molded girders with no coloring on the raised "LIONEL". R. Spivock Collection. **45 75 100 125**

(C) Same as (B), except orange molded girder is painted light gray. **45 75 100 125**

(D) Same as (B), except "LIONEL" is heat-stamped in white on the raised surface of the letters on the orange girders. **45 75 100 125**

(E) Same as (B), except "LIONEL" is outlined in black on the orange girders. **45 75 100 125**

(F) Same as (B), except black molded girders with the USS logo on the left and "U.S. STEEL", all in raised letters outlined in white. There is no "6418".
45 75 100 125

(G) Frame has blank plaque on its underside instead of "6418". Load is two black molded girders same as (E), but "6418" is added in raised numerals on the lower right. All raised lettering outlined in white except "6418", which remains black. **45 75 100 125**

(H) Same as (G), except "6418" is also heat-stamped white on the top surface. **45 75 100 125**

(I) Same as (H), except girders are molded a pinkish orange and the "U.S. STEEL", logo, and number are outlined in black. **45 75 100 125**

6461 TRANSFORMER CAR: 1949–50. Same as 2461(B), except for number and staple-end trucks with magnetic couplers. **25 40 75 100**

6511-SERIES FLATCARS

Lionel had two separate molds for the 6511-series flatcar frame, as it did for the 6464 boxcar. Unlike the 6464s, the products of each of these two molds included a distinctive molded-in part number. Introduced in 1953 was the mold that put part number 6511-2 on the underside of each frame, with the exception of the helicopter and satellite launcher cars. This was the only 10-inch plastic flatcar frame until 1956, when a proliferation of uses for the frame dictated increased capacity. Lionel then built a second mold, with the part number 6424-11 molded into the underside of every frame it produced. No car produced exclusively before 1956 has a part number other than 6511-2. With many exceptions, cars produced in 1956 through 1969 may be found with frames from either mold. The exceptions and the reason for them are mentioned in the detailed listings.

Mold 6424-11 originally had provision for thirteen stake holes, but only two were actually open on flatcars produced in 1956 and 1957. The 6803 series of flatcars with military units, introduced in 1958, needed more flatcar capacity with stake holes to accommodate the axle retainers that hold the military units in place. So the

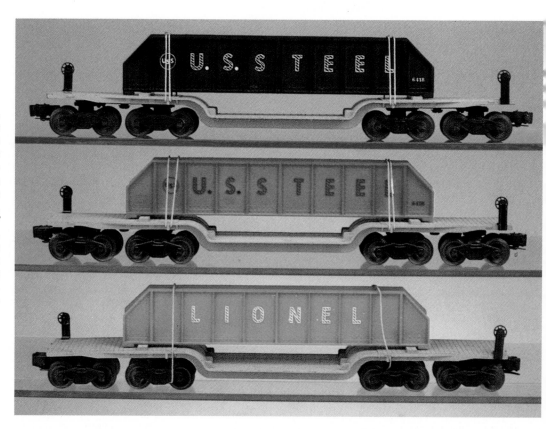

Top: 6418 (H) machinery car. This and the version below should have a blank plaque on the frame underside where the 6418 number was in 1955 production. Middle: 6418 (I) with harder-to-find pinkish orange girders. Bottom: 6418 (D), which should have "6418" molded in frame underside. This is from 1955 production only. Correct girder retention is shown on examples above; this shows how not to do it! R. Shanfeld and R. Gladsen Collections.

6424-11 mold was reworked to open all thirteen stake holes. The fourteenth hole by the brakestand was never put in 6424-11 as it had been in 6511-2. After Lionel used mold 6424-11 to produce the 6469 liquefied-gas tank car in 1963, sales volume was most likely so low that two molds were no longer necessary. Since 6424-11 at that point was configured with open end slots for the bulkheads, it was retired for the duration of the "real Lionel."

Through the courtesy of Lionel Trains Inc., we were able to inspect and photograph the two molds. They are called four-slide molds because the two sides and two ends move (besides the normal separation of the top and bottom halves). When the top and bottom halves of the mold are closing, preparatory to the injection of the liquid plastic, cams move the side and end portions of the mold into place.

To make changes in the mold, such as the major one in 1958 that filled in the slots on each end where the truck mounting plates had been secured, an insert is made and installed in the mold. This leaves slight marks in the finished product. Examine any of the 10-inch cars that have their trucks riveted to the frame, and you will see where these two slots in each end were filled in. As we shall see in the 6805 listing, more than one insert could be used to fill in the ends!

Lionel made many changes to the two molds over the years, and the changes left their distinctive marks on the frames produced. Describing and explaining these changes is too complex and lengthy for this volume. For our

purposes, it is enough to note in the listings any major changes required to produce that car.

Lionel produced several variations of the helicopter and satellite car. Since a new mold bottom half was necessary to accommodate the launch mechanism, all variations have the part number 3419-30 molded into their underside. Note the complete absence of detail on this bottom. You can satisfy yourself that only the 6511-2 mold was used to produce 3419-30 frames by examining the back side of the brakestand and the simulated chain and linkage detail leading from the brake wheel on the frame side. Frames made from the 6424-11 mold differ markedly in these and other areas.

For some unknown reason, the four vertical frame reinforcements in the center of the car on each side were extended about 1/16 inch only in mold 6424-11 between 1961 and 1963. As a result, on several cars there are four bumps on the "fish belly" portion of the side rail lower edges. The listings that follow refer to them as "lower frame-rail projections." The mold was subsequently restored to the normal configuration.

Another interesting detail common to this series is that each car usually has the catalog number only once on each side. In the beginning, when metal trucks were used, this number appeared only to the right of "LIONEL". When the change was made to plastic trucks, this number was moved to the left of "LIONEL". Being a frugal company, Lionel used up existing stock. So a few cars with plastic trucks can be found with the number still on

	Gd	VG	Ex	LN

the right. These are very collectible variations. Only one example of a car that properly came with metal trucks but has the number on the left is known—6805. Of course some cars spanned the transition from metal to plastic trucks and they can be found both ways! Number 6264 is one example. Alas, as is true of most rules, this one has a major exception: all four of the olive-painted military flatcars (3429, 3820, 6640, and 6651) came with plastic trucks but have the number on the right!

3330 FLATCAR WITH OPERATING SUBMARINE IN KIT FORM: 1960–62.

Medium blue molded 6511-2 frame unpainted with white heat-stamped "3330 LIONEL" in serif lettering each side. Probably because of the unique blue mold color, only mold 6511-2 was used for all the submarine cars. There is no apparent mechanical reason the 6424-11 mold was not also used. Has early AAR trucks with operating couplers riveted directly to frame. Load is an unassembled, rubber band–powered submarine in medium gray unpainted plastic. Near the top on each side in black heat-stamped sans-serif lettering appears "U.S. NAVY 3830".

Note: The submarine has two main halves, and the kit of parts was packaged in a clear plastic bag sandwiched between the halves. As originally packaged, the whole kit was held together by rubber bands and placed on the flatcar, which was then slid into its Orange Perforated box. Also included is a copy of one of the two versions of 3330-107 instruction sheet dated 8-60. Submarine must be unassembled and have all the bits and pieces, including the tiny capsule of glue, for Like New price. Also note that the unassembled submarine was available for separate sale in a unique box numbered 3330-100, pictured and described in *Greenberg's Guide to Lionel Trains, 1945–1969, Volume VI: Accessories*. The submarine and all its parts except the glue capsule have been reproduced. **60   100   150   200**

3409 OPERATING HELICOPTER LAUNCHING CAR: 1961 advance catalog only.

Shown but not listed as part of set 1124, one of three designed for the mass toy market and not included in the regular consumer catalog. May also have come with other uncataloged sets. Frame is molded light blue plastic with "3409 LIONEL" heat-stamped in white serif letters on each side rail. This was Lionel's most cost-reduced helicopter car, with two fixed coupler arch-bar trucks and only a manual release for launching the helicopter. Mechanism housing is bright plated steel, as is the manual release lever. Note that the mechanism for the manual release cars is different from cars with remote-control launching capability. There is no reset lever and no bottom plate for remote-control release. Winder is small (1⅜"-diameter) black plastic. Load is a Type II helicopter (see sidebar for helicopter types). Frame underside has part no. 3419-30 molded in raised numerals, which is common to all helicopter and satellite launching cars. No box known for this item.

Note: Reproduction helicopters are readily available.

Prices shown for Excellent and Like New require original unbroken helicopter. A fairly scarce car (R. Shanfeld comments).   **45   90   125   190**

3410 HELICOPTER LAUNCHING CAR: 1961–63.

Cataloged only in lower-priced sets, not as a separate-sale item. Identical to 3409 above except "3410 LIONEL" on each side and trucks are early AAR, usually with both operating couplers. Load can be a Type II, VII, or VIII helicopter (see sidebar for helicopter types). A fairly scarce car, although more common than 3409. An original Orange Picture box printed especially for this car is known.

40   80   120   160

3413 MERCURY CAPSULE LAUNCHING CAR: 1962–64.

Red molded 6511-2 frame with only "LIONEL" heat-stamped in white serif letters on each frame rail. Catalog number does not appear anywhere on car. Although available, flatcars from the 6424-11 mold were not used because the stake holes required for attaching the unpainted gray superstructure were not in that mold at the time. Trucks are early AAR, usually with two operating couplers. Red molded rocket launcher housing contains a powerful spring, released by a plunger beneath the car similar to the coupler operating disk. The spring is concealed inside the launch cylinder, which must be compressed manually to cock the firing mechanism. To fit into its original box, the mechanism had to be cocked. Since there is no "safety" lock, the mechanism often released during handling, with unfortunate consequences for the box. Load is a white rocket with red tail and a gray Mercury capsule nose cone. The thin plastic tube body of the rocket is fairly brittle and will crack if flexed too much. Light and darker shades of blue are found in the star insignia on the rocket. A flimsy cloth parachute with wood risers is attached to the nose cone and is packaged inside the rocket barrel. In operation, the rocket is launched by a remote-control track section. At the apogee of flight, the Mercury capsule is supposed to separate, dragging the parachute out of the rocket body so it can deploy and return the capsule gently to the ground while the rest of the rocket crashes. Try this, if at all, with a reproduction rocket and parachute.

Note: Watch for broken railings on the superstructure, a cracked rocket barrel, and missing parts. All original parts must be present and intact for Excellent and Like New prices.

(A) Dark gray superstructure.

65   110   145   175

(B) Light gray superstructure.

65   110   145   175

3419 OPERATING HELICOPTER LAUNCHING CAR: 1959–65.

Has 3419-30 frame molded in various shades of blue with "3419 LIONEL" heat-stamped in white serif letters on each side frame rail. AAR trucks, usually with both operating couplers. For 1959 only, the winder was just over 2" in diameter. Thereafter, the diameter

3330-100 operating submarine kit in separate-sale box. 3330 flatcar with operating submarine in kit form shown just as it came out of the original box except trucks were turned to operating position. R. Shanfeld Collection.

	Gd	VG	Ex	LN

was reduced to 1⅜". Also in 1959 there were two levers protruding through the deck of the flatcar; a long reset lever and a short manual release lever. The latter was stamped as part of the hinged plate on the mechanism bottom that moves in response to a remote-control track section magnet for remote launching. Pressing this lever did the same thing the magnet would do: push the hinged plate down and launch the helicopter. To wind the spring again, the operator must press the reset lever, bringing a pawl back up in contact with the ratchet stops molded into the underside of the winder. On some 1959 cars, the operating mechanism is made of blackened metal instead of the usual bright plated metal. The reset lever also can be found this way. Occasionally a bright reset lever will appear with a blackened mechanism. Cars with blackened mechanisms are somewhat hard to find. All helicopter cars had a molded black tail stand that holds the tail of the helicopter in place for transport and launch. This just snaps into two holes that were used for stakes in other frames made from this same mold.

Note: Watch for broken "ears" on the tailstand, which has been reproduced. Also check for broken steps, cracked side frames and a properly operating mechanism on the car. When 3419 was redesigned for 1960, the manual release lever was reshaped and bent 90 degrees, so it sticks out to the side just below the frame rail, instead of up through the car floor. This undoubtedly simplified assembly. However, there must have been leftovers from 1959, since the instruction sheet for 1960 notes that some cars may have the manual release lever protruding through the car floor. The key element of value on most of these flatcars is the helicopter load. Except for unusual colors, the cars themselves are one of the most plentiful in Lionelville.

(A) Original version was probably the one with blackened mechanism, including the reset lever. Has large winder and manual release lever in the car floor; the frame is molded dark royal blue, which is a more vibrant dark blue than navy blue, which is a duller or muddier dark blue. Load is a Type I helicopter (see sidebar for helicopter types). This car also can be found with a blackened mechanism but a bright plated reset lever, another distinct variation to some. **45 80 120 160**

(B) Same as (A), but the mechanism is bright plated, including the reset lever. Most common version of the large winder car. **40 75 110 150**

(C) Redesigned version for 1960 with small (1⅜"-diameter) winder and manual release lever protruding out below the frame rail instead of through the car floor. Some may have been made with the release lever still up through the floor, but these would be easy to make from a 1959 frame and 1960 mechanism, just as Lionel probably did originally, so this is not listed as a variation. Frame is same molded royal blue as (A), but load is a Type II helicopter. **45 80 120 160**

(D) Same as (C), but frame is molded light blue, same as used on 3409 and 3410. Not a common color. **45 80 120 160**

(E) Same as (C), but frame is molded in aqua blue, a lighter, paler color than (C). Quite a rare color. J. Sattler Collection. **NRS**

(F) Same as (E), but darker, nearly purple molded frame. C. Rohlfing Collection. **50 90 130 175**

3429 U.S.M.C. OPERATING HELICOPTER LAUNCHING CAR: 1960. Cataloged only as part of set 1805, the Land-Sea-and Air Gift Pack, but known to be included in at least one uncataloged military set. Car is same as version (E) of 3419, but the royal blue molded frame is painted olive drab. Black molded frames under the olive drab paint also have been reliably reported. White heat-stamped "BUILT BY/LIONEL U. S. M. C. 3429" on frame side rails. Like the other painted military flatcars, this contradicts the rule of number left with plastic trucks. Has AAR trucks, both with operating coupler.

Note: A very rare flatcar but virtually worthless without the authentic Type V helicopter that came only with this car. **200 325 465 600**

3460 FLATCAR WITH TRAILERS: 1955–57. Came only with 460 Piggy Back Transportation Set, where it was packaged in the box liner with no separate car box. Cataloged as a replacement item in 1955 only, but no box has yet surfaced to authenticate that it was available separately. Red molded 6511-2 plastic frame with "LIONEL

Top: 3413 (A) Mercury capsule car with dark gray superstructure and 3413 (B) with lighter gray superstructure. Second: 3410 helicopter launching car with Type VII helicopter from 1963 set 11341; 3419 (C) with Type II helicopter. Third: 3419 (D) with Type II helicopter and 3419 (F) with Type II helicopter. Note absence of reset lever and underside release flap, which is not correct for 3419.

Bottom: 3419 (A), erroneously shown with a Type VII helicopter; only Type I is correct for this car (note black reset and release levers). 3419 (D) earliest production with launch lever still protruding up through floor—shown erroneously with Type I helicopter, which is correct only for 3419 (A) or (B). R. Shanfeld Collection.

3460" heat-stamped in white serif lettering on frame side rails. A stamped steel black-pained two-piece rack mounts to the flatcar deck to retain the two-trailer load. Bar-end trucks with or without tab couplers clip to stamped metal plates that tab into two slots molded in each end of the frame. The same screw that attaches the rack to the car floor threads into the other end of each truck plate for a nice assembly economy. Accessory 460 was cataloged through 1957, but evidently was not a good seller, so it is doubtful it was manufactured more than one year, accounting for use of only the 6511-2 car frame. Load is two Type I or Type II trailers (see sidebar on Lionel trailer vans).

Note: 3460 is a Lionel anomaly, since it has an operating car number but no operating features. The identical flatcar was introduced for separate sale in 1956 as 6430. The "FRUEHAUF" signs and the van roofs are

	Gd	VG	Ex	LN

frequently missing. All the pieces must be present and original for a Like New price.

(A) Vans have "FRUEHAUF" signs with black lettering on a bright background. Somewhat harder to find and probably earliest production.

	22	45	65	90

(B) Vans have "FRUEHAUF" signs with black background and bright lettering.

	22	45	65	90

3470 AERIAL TARGET LAUNCHING CAR: 1962–64. Usually has dark navy blue molded 6511-2 frame with no number or lettering. This mold was used exclusively because it contained the stake holes needed for the superstructure. Rather than change the mold just for this car, Lionel stamped a large hole in the frame after molding to accommodate the fan assembly, as well as two

LIONEL HELICOPTER TYPES

Orphaned helicopter launching cars abound, so the main component of value is the *original helicopter itself*. This was one of Lionel's most popular cars of the period, lasting 7 years in the catalog during a time of waning interest in trains, with many new items lasting only a year or two. During its life designers made several changes in the helicopter to reduce cost, improve operation, and provide a different appearance. Because of the fragility of the original and the abundance of orphaned cars, the helicopters, both the O and HO models, have been reproduced.

All original O gauge helicopters molded in gray with a separate snap-in tail have "BUILT BY / LIONEL" molded in raised letters on the left side of the tail skid. Later yellow molded O gauge helicopters with integral tail have "BLT BY / LIONEL" on the right side of the skid. Since the tail skid is the most fragile part of the model, and because Lionel Trains Inc. (LTI) has enforced its trademark diligently, you can be pretty sure the car you are buying has an original load if this lettering is present. But beware of a missing tail rotor blade or a broken tail skid.

Although Lionel also used the gray O gauge helicopter as a load on one HO car, the company made a much smaller molded red helicopter for that line; it also appeared in the O gauge 3619 reconnaissance helicopter car. This helicopter came with and without the "BUILT BY / LIONEL", which is on the right side of the integral tail when it appears. Fortunately, many of the reproductions of the HO helicopter are yellow, and both red and yellow reproductions use a different or a considerably altered mold. Lionel made only red molded HO helicopters. None of the originals of any size was painted.

Reproductions of the snap-in tail on the gray O gauge helicopter are available, so it is possible to find an original with a reproduction tail. Since the damaged tail is very difficult to remove, there are usually signs of a struggle, in addition to the absence of the "BUILT BY / LIONEL", to alert you. A damaged or broken tail or a damaged front bubble is fatal to the value of any of these helicopters. Damaged blades or landing skids can usually be replaced with an original part. A helicopter with a damaged bubble but a good snap-in tail is worth acquiring to salvage the tail. Sometimes the bubble is intact but is cloudy because of mold growing on the inner surface. If you remove the shaft and landing skid so you can get inside with a Q-tip, a bit of bathroom cleaner can work wonders.

There were variations in the color of the snap-in tail. Most are yellowish translucent, while some are a whitish clear translucent or yellow opaque. It may be that the yellowish translucent started out white and changed with age, but several examples that have been

on display still have whitish clear tails—so Lionel probably used two different batches of plastic. Translucent tails occur most often on the operating helicopters and the helicopter that came with 6820, while the opaque yellow tail most often appears with the 6819. Since these models all used the same basic parts, it is easy to make the body of a nonoperating model into an operating helicopter and vice versa. Thus no particular value is associated with any tail variation.

After all this, we are finally ready to list the helicopter variations. They are identified by a Roman numeral for ease of reference in the flatcar descriptions.

Type I. Made in 1959 only. Original operating design with two rotor blades, each 6⅞ inches long including the tip pods. Rotor shaft about 2³⁄₁₆ inches long to accommodate both blades and the spring that allowed them to be positioned together for transport and at 90 degrees for flight. Blades are always black and are not the same as those used on the helicopters for 6819 and 6820. The top blade presses onto the shaft, while the bottom blade is free to rotate on the shaft. The facing hubs have half-circle "steps" that allow the top blade to drive the lower blade when they are in the 90-degree position. The spring keeps the blades engaged in this position. While the blade for 6819 and 6820 helicopters is similar to the bottom 3419 blade, it lacks the step and usually comes in brown. Decoration for the gray molded helicopter body consists of a black heat-stamped door detail and a dark blue "NAVY" heat-stamped mid-body on each side. They do not have a tiny square hole in the middle of the boom underside that was added in 1960 to secure the missile rack for 6820. Double-rotor helicopters have appeared with white and clear molded blades, but these are of dubious authenticity since MPC/LTI made various color blades from the same original mold and there are no markings on the blades of any period.

Type II. On 1960's operating model, the blade mechanism was greatly simplified. One 5¼-inch rotor pressed directly on a shortened 1⅝-inch shaft, eliminating the spacers, spring, and one rotor. This design continued for the operating helicopters for the rest of production. The two-color decoration carried over and remained as long as gray "NAVY" operating helicopters were produced. For 1960, Lionel added a square hole to the underside of the boom to secure the missile rack on 6820 helicopters. This hole remained on all subsequent gray molded models through the end of production. Some 1959 bodies were most likely carried over, since there are examples of the single-rotor helicopter without this hole.

Type III. 1959–60. Nonoperating helicopter that came with 6819. Same gray molded body and decoration as described in Type I. Usually, but not always, found with opaque yellow molded tail. Has unique 6⅞-inch–long rotor with tip pods like the lower blade on Type I, but without the stepped hub. Blade available in black or brown with the latter the more common color. The 6819 flatcar that carried this load was offered in both 1959 and 1960, so the helicopter can be found with and without the small square hole in the underside of the boom.

Type IV. Probably 1960 or later. Nonoperating model same as Type III, but without the heat-stamped decoration. Enough examples have been observed to conclude that this was probably a cost-reduced version, perhaps for a low-budget uncataloged set. Watch closely though, since many reproduction helicopters lack the decoration too.

Type V. 1960 only. Operating model same as Type II, except "USMC" in black replaces the blue "NAVY". Although this was the load for a 1960-only 3429 flatcar, examples have been observed with and without the small square hole in the boom underside. This would indicate that some 1959 gray bodies were carried over to 1960. One of the rarest of the Lionel helicopters.

Type VI. 1960–61. Nonoperating model same as Type III, except red molded missile rack added to boom. Rack has a tab to lock it in the small square hole in the boom underside that was added for this purpose in 1960. This helicopter variation came only on 6820 aerial missile transport car. Rack carried two white plastic air-to-air missiles. Often referred to as "Little John" missiles, but no Lionel reference to this name has been found. These were basically 44-40 missiles that came with such cars as 6544 missile firing car and 6844 missile carrying car. Two modifications were made: There was no weight inside the missile, and a molded red tail cone was added. Original tail cones have a small blind hole in the center that reproductions so far do not have. The weight inside an original 44-40 missile is nearly impossible to remove without destroying the plastic, so some fakes have been made using original tail cones in 44-40 missiles. These can be detected by their added weight. The need for new missiles arises because of the unfortunate tendency of the tail cone to split the missile's side between the fins. Watch for a cracked or broken missile rack as well. Missiles are held in place by friction; if pushed in too far, they crack the rack.

Type VII. Operating model for 1962 and later was completely redesigned to further reduce cost. The rotor, shaft, skid, and bubble were unchanged from Type II, but a new mold produced an unpainted yellow body with three window openings on each side and an integral tail rotor. No decoration of any kind was used. Unfortunately the tail rotor, although slightly stronger, was still far too fragile for a toy doomed to repeated crash landings. Now there was not even a service part that could save a broken tail, a condition that renders the helicopter virtually worthless. Instead of "BUILT BY / LIONEL" on the left side as on the snap-in tail of the gray helicopters, the integral tail on the yellow models has "BLT BY / LIONEL" on the right side in raised letters. This or Type VIII below are the only correct helicopters for 419 Lionel Heliport.

Type VIII. 1962 or later. Operating model same as Type VII, but with a redesigned tail rotor for increased strength. The lower blade of the tail rotor increased to about three times its initial thickness, and it connects to the lower part of the tail skid. Unfortunately the top blade is as thin and vulnerable as ever and is usually missing on these models. Evidently a late mold change, and examples with an intact tail and upper blade rival the USMC helicopter for rarity.

Type IX. 1962–64. Operating model in HO scale that made it into the O gauge line as a load for 3619 reconnaissance helicopter car. Just a miniaturized version of Type VII, this red molded helicopter was constructed in the identical manner, including an integral tail. Early versions had no markings whatever to identify them as Lionel products. Like its O gauge counterpart, this helicopter was unpainted and completely undecorated. Fortunately, the reproductions use a different or altered mold and are usually yellow. If you are buying an item that included this unmarked helicopter, compare it with a yellow reproduction. If the mold features are identical, it is a reproduction. There is some speculation that this version came only with HO cars and Type X below came only with 3619. Since helicopters are so easily switched, this will probably never be conclusively established, but it is considered unlikely. The HO helicopter appeared in that line a year or two before its use with 3619, so Lionel probably corrected its oversight and produced Type X below for both applications. In any event, Type X likely is the "correct" load for 3619.

Type X. 1962–64. Operating model in HO scale identical to Type IX, except "BUILT BY / LIONEL" has been added in raised lettering molded into the right side of the tail. This version is most likely the correct helicopter for 3619.

3419 (A) operating helicopter launching car with correct Type I helicopter. Note the blackened mechanism and launch lever but a plated reset lever. This is a transition between 3419 (A)

and (B). 3429 U.S.M.C. operating helicopter launching car with correct Type V helicopter. Note "USMC" replaces "NAVY" on side.

rectangular slots, one at each end of the car, to attach the superstructure. To remove the superstructure, a tab at the brakewheel end is released. AAR trucks, usually with two operating couplers but some, probably from low-budget uncataloged sets, have one fixed coupler. The superstructure is a one-piece white molded shell that contains the entire mechanism, consisting of a battery holder, a squirrel cage blower with its motor, and a molded plastic nozzle piece in varying colors. Power comes from two D-cell flashlight batteries connected in series. Between the two batteries and extending through the top of the shell is a red switch that operates by separating the batteries when turned parallel to the car and allows them to come together, turning on the blower, when the handles are crosswise to the shell. Sans-serif lettering on the sides of the shell is heat-stamped, usually in bright red.

The car came with a small envelope, marked "ASSEM. NO. 3470-20" that contained four 3470-12 target balloons and an instruction sheet. Original balloons have target rings printed in two places with the Lionel "L" in the center. Unfortunately, these soften and deteriorate with age so, even when new, they are found in a gooey heap and can no longer be used. Reproductions are available. In operation, 3470 makes use of the Coanda Effect to keep an inflated balloon hovering an inch or so above the basket, even with the train moving at express speed. When the car is at rest with the blower off, the balloon rests in the basket. If the train is moved with the blower off, the balloon soon blows away. Play value comes from trying to hit the balloon with one of the missile launchers Lionel supplied. They usually came in an Orange Picture box of the period but also have been observed in a 1966 Cellophane-front

box issued to deplete old inventory (J. Diggle and S. Bradley comments).

(A) Usual dark blue flatcar and blower has a clear plastic nozzle. J. Sattler Collection.

	Gd	VG	Ex	LN
	30	50	75	100

(B) Same as (A), but a red plastic nozzle. J. Diggle Collection.

	40	60	90	120

(C) Same as (A), but a light gray plastic nozzle. J. Diggle Collection.

	30	50	75	100

(D) Same as (A), but a black plastic nozzle. G. Pardue Collection. **NRS**

(E) May have any blower nozzle color, but 6511-2 frame is light blue, similar to 3409 and 3410 operating helicopter car frames. Believed to date from 1963. S. Blotner and G. Pardue Collections.

	150	225	350	475

(F) May have any blower nozzle color, usual dark blue frame, but superstructure lettering is heat-stamped maroon instead of the usual bright red. R. Shanfeld Collection. **NRS**

3509 SATELLITE LAUNCHING CAR: 1961–62. Like the 3409 manually operated helicopter car, the 3509 was not listed for separate sale but appeared in some lower-priced cataloged and uncataloged sets. It used the same 3419-30 mold as the helicopter cars, but with two changes. The frame color is dark green, and the mold was revised to provide a short rectangular tab in the center of the deck toward the end away from the brake wheel. To this tab is glued the gray molded antenna console, which cannot be removed without breaking the tab. A light or slightly darker yellow molded plastic antenna (reproductions

6430 (B) shown here with Type II vans, which are incorrect for this car, but shows similarity to 3460 (van turned to show

FRUEHAUF signs and removable roof); 3460 (B) with correct placement of vans.

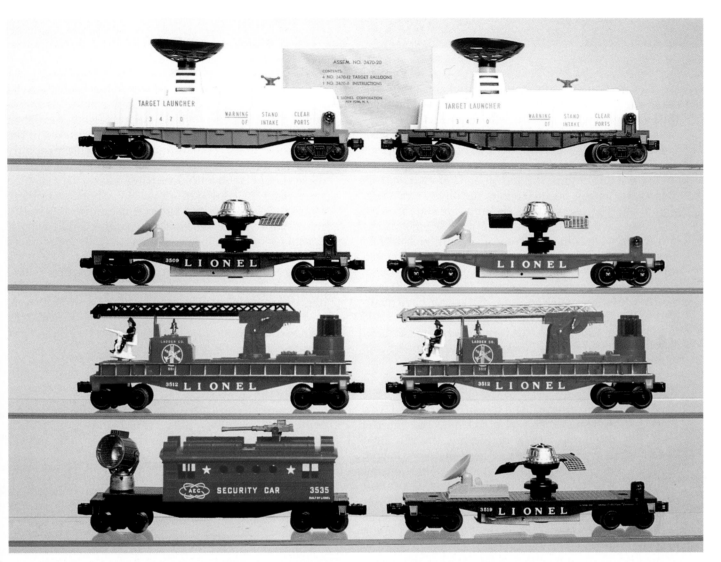

Top: 3460 (E) aerial target launching car with rare light blue frame (reddish nozzle is obscured by basket); 3470 (C) with usual dark navy blue frame. Shown between cars is the 3470-20 envelope containing balloons and instruction sheet that came with each car. Second: 3509 satellite launching car (budget version of 3519) and 3510 (the lowest budget version of 3519 possible).

Third: 3512 (A) operating fireman and ladder car with black-painted extension ladder, and 3512 (B) with bright plated extension ladder. Note row of three nozzles behind fireman, usually missing. Bottom: 3535 operating security car with rotating searchlight, and 3519 operating satellite launching car.

| | Gd | VG | Ex | LN |

available) presses into a swiveling ball socket in the console. The mechanism is the same as for the helicopter cars of this period, always bright-plated with a small-diameter winder. But the winder on the satellite cars has a longer "neck" to accommodate the centering pin of the satellite. As with the helicopter cars, the mechanism differs substantially between the manual-release and the remote-control cars. See 3409 for details. Heat-stamped "3509 LIONEL" in white serif lettering on frame. The car is equipped with AAR trucks and two operating couplers or one fixed and one operating; its load is a two-piece black molded satellite. The top part is vacuum metalized with a chrome finish attached to the bottom with a spring clip in early production and later heat-staked. Bottom half has solar panel "wings" with two distinct shapes—a

smoothly curved shape (early) and an angled shape. They are decorated with white heat-stamped simulated solar panel grids. First made for the HO line and assigned part no. 0333-100, this satellite appears better proportioned for the O gauge line. Reproduction satellites are available, but lack the detail and quality of the original.

Note: Shown with a blue frame in the 1961 catalog, but never observed in this color. Less common than the 3519 remote-control version. **22   45   60   90**

3510 SATELLITE LAUNCHING CAR: 1962. Advance catalog only, as a component of set 11011. Usual 3419-30 frame, this time molded in bright red with only "LIONEL" heat-stamped in white serif letters on the side rails. The catalog number does not appear anywhere on the car.

LIONEL TRAILER VANS

Several trailer variations exist, and since they just sit on the flatcar, trailers are easy to switch. Moreover the side signs, when present, attach with tabs, so they too are easy to switch. Mold colors for the vans are dark green, light gray, white, and yellow, in order of appearance over the years.

In the accompanying listings, *dual rear wheels* means two wheels on each end of the single axle. *Sign slots* mean the two vertical rectangular slots in each side used for mounting a sign. *Pony wheels* means the simulated wheels on the front of the trailer that fold down for support when the tractor is detached and fold up out of the way when a tractor is coupled. This one-piece simulated set of pony wheels is blackened die-cast metal, while reproductions and MPC reruns are available in black molded plastic. A leaf spring twist-riveted to the trailer underside holds it in either of its two positions. The usual color is black for this spring, but copper examples are known.

Note that only very late production had any provision for attaching a tractor to these vans. When 6431 appeared in 1966, it was just a late 6430 packaged with a die-cast Midgetoy tractor painted bright red. For the tractor to attach to Lionel's plastic van, the van mold had to be changed to include a ¼-inch–diameter hole in the floor. This hole is molded and appears in the front "triangle" of simulated bracing just ahead of a raised rectangular area with a ¹⁄₁₆-inch–diameter hole common to all Lionel vans. Note that the molded hole does not contact the raised area behind it. Evidently, Lionel had some leftover yellow molded trailers that they wished to use up. Since they could not be coupled with the tractor, Lionel made a fixture and drilled in the ¼-inch hole. The fixture allowed the drill to contact the raised area, and the hole is slightly rearward of the molded hole's position. No yellow van has been observed with a molded hole, and all examples show clear evidence of having been drilled. All white vans furnished with 6431 have a molded hole precisely centered in the triangular area. The sign slots were most probably removed when the tractor coupling hole was done, so there should be no authentic white vans with a molded coupling hole and sign slots. No yellow vans have appeared without sign slots. A premium is usually charged for yellow vans with the trailer coupling hole, but this is not justified since the load from the common 6405 could be modified without detection.

Signs for Cooper-Jarrett Inc. are hereafter called CJ signs. They come in four versions: (1) aluminum background with a light copper color arrow and circle and black printing on each; (2) same, but a darker orange copper color; (3) black background with the light copper color arrow and circle, but the city names are aluminum color; and (4) same, but darker orange copper color. These signs came in pairs, so the arrow always points to the front of the van. New examples have been observed with the signs on backward, but they always point to the same end of the van. If the signs on each side point to opposite ends of the van, it is an indication of tampering.

All Lionel vans have four ¼-inch–diameter blind holes, arranged at corners of an approximate square, molded into the trailer underside. These were for use with the forklift on 460 Piggy Back Transportation Set, but remained throughout production. Vans were available as the load for 460 and as 460-150, a set of two trailers in a separate-sale box. Along the bottom edge of each trailer side are two small projections, one near the center and the other just forward of the wheel. When supplied for use with 460, these each had a dab of red

	Gd	VG	Ex	LN

Has two arch-bar trucks, both with fixed couplers, otherwise identical to 3509. No box exists for this car (P. Catalano comment).

Note: Less common than 3509. Of interest are a few cars that were never assembled. They have the correct trucks but nothing else, and the tab meant to retain the console is intact. These are desirable only to the variation collector and are NRS items. **40   90   155   200**

3512 OPERATING FIREMAN AND LADDER CAR: 1959–61. Red molded 6424-11 frame with "3512 LIONEL" heat-stamped in white serif letters on frame rails. Special AAR trucks with operating couplers. No brake wheel was installed because it would interfere with one of the side ladders. Frame 6511-2 could have been used, as it was for similar cars 3540 and 3545, but here the stake holes were not used, as they were on the other cars, so 6511-2 with all but two of the holes filled in presented a better appearance. Red molded superstructure with a heat-stamped emblem and lettering in white on each side, including the catalog number 3512. The drive belt used the turning axles of the truck (wheels are pressed on the axle, unlike standard trucks) to power the car's action. A geared wheel, a long arm, and a rack and pinion arrangement cause the fireman to oscillate while a hidden slotted hood rotates around the lamp to create the flashing illusion. There are two ladders on top, arranged as an extension ladder with a clever but extremely cheap and paint and served as spotting marks to assist the fork-lift operator in engaging the proper pair of holes in the trailer bottom. They remained throughout production, but were only painted on green trailers.

Type I. Dark green molded van with removable roof, dual rear wheels, and sign slots. This version has two metalized (like embossed foil) signs with adhesive backing that stick on at the front. Top center says "FRUEHAUF / Dura Van", and the lower right corner (left if you are looking at it head on) says "FRUE-HAUF". In this version, the signs have a silvery background with raised black letters. Side signs say "LIONEL TRAINS" in black sans-serif letters on an aluminum background. Tiny red dots of paint adorn the lower side frame projections. The red paint is often worn off or has been removed by owners who do not know its purpose.

Type II. Same as Type I, but "FRUEHAUF" signs have black background with raised letters in a silvery color. Some of these signs have poorly defined lettering that is hard to read, and the sign looks mostly black.

Type III. Van and roof color change to light gray and sign changes to CJ sign (1). Otherwise, same as Type II, including "FRUEHAUF" signs but no red spotting marks.

Type IV. Same as Type III, except the supply of "FRUEHAUF" signs was exhausted, so this version has neither one on the front.

Type V. Same as Type IV, except CJ sign (2). Several examples of this version observed with a

copper-color pony wheel spring clip not observed on any other version.

Type VI. Same as Type IV, except CJ sign (3) or (4) and usual black spring clip.

Type VII. Same as Type IV, except no signs and single rear wheels. "Economy" version made for 6440.

Type VIII. Van and roof color changes to white. CJ sign (3) or (4) with usual duals and black spring clip. Most often found as a load for 6810.

Type IX. Van and roof color changes to yellow. Single rear wheels, roof glued in place. This is the normal load for 6405. Example observed new in box with CJ sign (2), but more often found with slots but no signs.

Type X. Type IX is also found with a hole drilled in to couple with the Midgetoy tractor. Since Lionel went to the trouble of revising the mold to eliminate the sign slots for white 6431 trailers, it seems unlikely they would put signs on the leftover 6405 yellow trailers they probably drilled to use up. However, several collectors display these with various CJ signs as if they were original, so who knows? May have single or dual rear wheels.

Type XI. Mold changed to remove sign slots and add hole in floor for coupling to Midgetoy tractor. The white color and duals are restored, and the roof is glued in place. One of these vans was also included, along with the Midgetoy tractor, in uncataloged 461 platform with truck and trailer.

	Gd	VG	Ex	LN

fragile mechanism for raising and extending the ladders.

Note: This was quite an investment for Lionel, since twenty-six of the thirty-eight serviceable parts listed in the Lionel Service Manual are unique to this car. It was far too fragile and intricate for children, and its survival rate is low. Unless it is new in the box, chances of finding one that is not broken, incomplete, or adorned with reproduction parts is slim. Even new in the box, 3512, along with 3540 and 3545, suffered from a material incompatibility problem that caused the drive belt to "melt." If the car is new, traces of this part can still be seen clinging to the axles. Not the first time Lionel had this problem: 38 pumping water towers and 65 handcars come to mind.

In used 3512s, the inner ladder is usually missing

altogether, and the extension arrangement surely is. It's an absolute wonder how Lionel ever got this thing together in production, but it works splendidly when it's all there. This is a car that requires extreme care prior to purchase. First to go are the three tiny "nozzles" on a rack behind the fireman. The side ladders (from the 394 rotary beacon) are usually missing, and one or more of the fragile "hooks" that retain them are frequently broken, as are the "ears" that hold the extension ladder just behind the fireman. If you have one of these cars, especially the silver ladder version, all intact and original, you have a rare bird indeed.

(A) Version with black extension ladder.

30   60   95   120

	Gd	VG	Ex	LN

(B) Less common version with silver extension ladder. J. Sattler Collection.

	40	**80**	**125**	**180**

3519 OPERATING SATELLITE LAUNCHING CAR: 1961–64. Shown in the 1961 catalog with blue and red frames, but known only with a dark green molded 3419-30 frame. Side rails have "3519 LIONEL" in heat-stamped white serif letters. Early AAR trucks with operating couplers. Mechanism is the more complex version with a reset lever and a bottom plate for launching over a remote-control track section. An extension from this plate jutting out under the side frame rail allows for manual launching if desired. See 3509 for details on the load and superstructure, which are identical on this car.

	20	**30**	**55**	**80**

3535 OPERATING SECURITY CAR WITH ROTATING SEARCHLIGHT: 1960–61. Black molded 6511-2 frame with no decoration or lettering whatever. Once again, lack of stake holes made the 6424-11 frame unsuitable. All examples observed still have the unique holes in the frame, including one in the center for the lamp, required for 3540 introduced a year earlier. AAR trucks with operating couplers. The truck under the searchlight end is special, having a pickup roller and a ground spring. Lionel's patented Vibrotor mechanism powers the bright-plated holder and gray molded searchlight, all borrowed from 3620 searchlight car. A steel plate shock mounted to the car frame supports the searchlight assembly. With wires coming from the pickup roller, the lamp, and the Vibrotor, a junction point was needed to facilitate production. So a copper strip was riveted to the plastic frame to provide one! It's hidden by the red molded superstructure, a modified cab from the 520 electric locomotive last produced in 1957. Decoration, including the 3535 catalog number, is applied to each cab side with white heat-stamping. Slots were added to the frame so the cab could snap in place with no fastener required. A gray molded twin gun borrowed from the military truck used on 6804 and 6809 is held to the cab roof by a unique red molded swivel bracket.

Note: Critical parts are the gun, bracket, and searchlight assembly, all of which are available as reproductions.

	35	**80**	**125**	**150**

3540 OPERATING RADAR SCANNING SCOPE CAR: 1959–60. Bright red molded 6511-2 frame with "3540 LIONEL" in heat-stamped white serif letters on the side frames. Lionel did not use mold 6424-11 since side stake holes are required to attach 3540's superstructure, and only two were then available in that mold. Designers added three special holes to the frame: one in the center for a lamp socket, a larger one at the brakewheel end for the antenna socket, and a small hole for the lamp wire. These holes remained in frames used for 3535 and others. A medium gray molded superstructure snaps into the stake holes at each end, while two alignment tabs fit in the center stake holes. Two simulated control panels borrowed from the 44 mobile missile launcher tab into slots on each side of the superstructure. They are printed in black on thin clear plastic and are easily dislodged and lost. Seated at the radar screen is a molded blue man with painted face and hands. He observes a translucent green screen with black target grid and white sweep and target traces that is backlit with the frame-mounted lamp. The same dual dish antenna used on the 465 sound dispatching station snaps into a socket behind the operator. On the other end of the superstructure, a black molded radar antenna with silver-painted grid rotates when the car is moving. Special AAR trucks with operating couplers are required. At the brakewheel end is a roller pickup and a ground spring. Beneath the radar screen is a truck with a drive disk that turns the antenna through a connecting shaft. Larger-diameter axles are used, and the wheels are pressed on, so they are not free to rotate independently as in a normal truck. Axles have a special finish to better grip the O-ring that looped around the two truck axles and the drive disk. This same mechanism was used in 3512 and 3545. Unfortunately, a material incompatibility problem resulted in the O-ring "melting" on all three cars. Residue of the ring can be seen clinging to the axles on brand-new cars.

Note: Critical items are the very fragile radar screen (especially the tiny "horn"), the operator, the yellow antenna and post, and the control panels. All are available as reproductions.

	35	**85**	**135**	**180**

3545 OPERATING TV MONITOR CAR: 1961–62. Except for colors and add-ons, this car is identical to 3540 described above. The 6511-2 frame is molded black, this time with "3545 LIONEL" heat-stamped in white serif letters on the frame sides. Slots and holes added to the frame for 3535 and 3540 remain. Since the lamp to backlight the console screen was eliminated on this car, there was no need for a pickup roller. So the brakewheel end truck is a normal AAR design with operating coupler. Instead of the twin antenna, 3545 has a simulated bank of floodlights behind the operator. Base and floodlights are yellow molded plastic, while the snap-on reflector is the same mold color painted silver. The radar antenna on 3540 gives way to a molded yellow simulated TV camera on 3545, complete with a second 50-84 crewman identical to the console operator. Unlike the radar antenna, which fastens tightly to its shaft and rotates constantly, the TV camera sits loosely on the shaft. An off-center weight is hidden in the camera housing below the operator's seat; this, with the slight friction between the shaft and housing, causes the camera to "pan" back and forth. Darker medium blue molded plastic is used for the superstructure. Replacing the radar screen in the console is a white TV screen with black printing. On this the operator views a clear track ahead with a Santa Fe passenger train approaching on a parallel track. Since it sits loosely on the shaft, the TV camera will fall off if the car is tipped over in handling or by derailment. Only a slender pin holds the crewman in his seat, and it is

	Gd	VG	Ex	LN

easily broken. Because of the tight fit of the crewman to his seat, it is likely this pin was often broken in production. Brand-new cars have been observed in this condition. Other critical items are the floodlight and the two control panel inserts. See 3540 description for additional details. **50 110 170 225**

3820 U.S.M.C. OPERATING SUBMARINE CAR: 1960–62. Cataloged only as a set component and never for separate sale. It debuted in the Land-Sea-and Air Gift Pack in 1960 and appeared in sets 1810 in 1961 and 13028 in 1962. Also known in at least one uncataloged military set. Black molded 6511-2 frame painted olive drab. White heat-stamped sans-serif lettering, but "3820" appears on the right in serif numerals. Like the other olive-painted flatcars, this violates the usual practice of putting the number on the left on cars with plastic trucks. Frames from mold 6424-11 could not be used because the wire retainers for the submarine require stake holes for their attachment. The car has AAR trucks, usually with operating couplers, but the uncataloged version may have one fixed coupler; its load is a factory-assembled gray molded submarine with heat-stamped "U.S. NAVY 3830" in sans-serif lettering on each side.

Note: This is identical to the load for 3830. No special submarine was made for the Marines. All the parts and the submarine have been reproduced.
  60 120 190 250

3830 OPERATING SUBMARINE CAR: 1960–63. Most common of the submarine cars, this version used a blue molded 6511-2 frame heat-stamped "3830 LIONEL" on each side frame rail. Otherwise the car and its load are identical to 3820 described above.
  50 85 120 150

6175 ROCKET CAR: 1958–61. Red or black molded frame with each color available in 6511-2 or 6424-11 molds with heat-stamped "6175 LIONEL" in white on the frame side rails. Early AAR trucks with two operating couplers. Load is a rocket model with thin white plastic tube body heat-stamped in blue with "BUILT BY / LIONEL" and "U S NAVY". Nose and tail are molded red plastic. At the tip is a sponge pad secured with a metal compression ring. On original rockets, even brand new, this pad is decomposed or missing. It is the same rocket supplied with the 175 rocket launcher. One 6418-9 elastic band holds the rocket in place on a medium gray molded rack that snaps into the flatcar's stake pockets.

Note: Watch for reproduction rack, rocket, rocket nose, and elastic band. Also, the thin rocket main body is brittle and tends to crack.

(A) Red molded 6511-2 frame. G. Pardue Collection
  25 50 70 100
(B) Black molded 6511-2 frame. J. Sattler Collection.
  25 50 70 100
(C) Red molded 6424-11 frame (M. Ocilka comment).
  25 50 70 100
(D) Black molded 6424-11 frame. M. Ocilka Collection.
  25 50 70 100

6262 WHEEL CAR: 1956–57. White heat-stamped serif lettering on frame side rails. Gray molded superstructure with slots to hold eight sets of Lionel wheels and axles, although the car probably was furnished with only six sets. All catalog pictures show six sets, and, where described, the words say six sets. It would be unlike Lionel to furnish more than was advertised. Wheel sets were secured for shipping with a rubber band, long since deteriorated on new examples observed, which did contain only six.

Note: Since the wheel sets are easily lost, many sellers

Top: 3540 operating radar scanning scope car and 3545 operating TV monitor car. Bottom: 3820 U.S.M.C. operating submarine car (note correct submarine is same as used on 3830) and 3830 operating submarine car.

	Gd	VG	Ex	LN

make sure there are eight. Look at every detail of yours if you have a set of eight. Chances are at least two will have a detail difference.

(A) Red molded 6511-2 frame. Considered early 1956 production and most often found in set 1549 headed by 1615 switcher. Bar-end trucks with tab couplers. This car could have been made using 6424-11 frames, and black cars could have used 6511-2 frames; neither has been reported. T. Rollo Collection. **160   300   450   700**

(B) Black molded 6424-11 frame with "LIONEL 6262", Bar-end trucks with tab couplers. Considered later 1956 production. M. Ocilka Collection.
30   50   65   80

(C) Same as (B), except AAR trucks. Considered early 1957 production using up frames with the number on the right. Although quite collectible, there is no price premium, since this car is easily made by switching trucks, just as Lionel did originally. G. Wilson Collection.
30   50   65   80

(D) Same as (C), except "6262 LIONEL" with the catalog number switched to the left. Considered later 1957 production. L. Harold Collection.
30   50   65   80

6264 LUMBER CAR: 1957–58. Red molded 6511-2 frame with white heat-stamped serif lettering on the side rails. Three light brown molded lumber racks attached to the stake holes in the frame. Since 6424-11 frames never had a stake hole next to the brakestand, that frame could not be used. Lionel made the car for the 264 operating forklift platform and packaged it in the box liner. This accessory continued in the catalog through 1960, but the separate-sale car disappeared after 1958 and is fairly hard to find in an original separate-sale box. A second edition of the 264 instruction sheet notes that the blackened metal side stakes on this car are to be installed with the flat side toward the car center. Load is twelve 264-11 timbers. For the separate-sale car, these and eight 2411-4 posts were packaged in a small manila envelope with black printing, part no. 6264-8. Hardwood lumber, side stakes, and the lumber racks have been reproduced. Add a substantial premium for the separate-sale box, depending on condition.

(A) Although plastic AAR trucks were introduced in 1957, the most common version of 6264 is found with bar-end trucks, with or without tab couplers. Catalog number is on the right of "LIONEL". Trucks clip to stamped-metal plates that each attach to the car frame with two tabs and a recessed flat-head Phillips screw. J. Sattler and M. Sokol Collections. **20   40   55   70**

(B) By the time the last 6264s were produced, the 6511-2 mold had been extensively revised to close the end slots and add recesses for riveting the trucks directly to the frame. The countersunk screw holes had also been removed. This version is much less common and has "6264 LIONEL" with AAR trucks. It probably did not originally come in a separate-sale box; only with 264. G. Wilson and F. Davis Collections. **20   40   55   70**

6311 FLATCAR WITH PIPES: 1955. Reddish brown molded 6511-2 frame with heat-stamped "LIONEL 6311" in white on the side rails. Mold 6424-11 had not been built when this car made its brief appearance. Included in several lower-priced sets and shown in the back of the catalog as being separately available only on special order. Has its own Middle Classic box. Load is three standard plastic pipes held in place by only six of the 2411-4 black-ened metal posts, rather than the thirteen included with 6511. This car was evidently replaced by 6121 in 1956. Bar-end trucks with operating couplers can be found with or without the tabs introduced in 1955. Blackened stamped-metal plates with two tabs secure the trucks to the frame. Pipes and stakes have been reproduced.
15   25   40   70

6343 BARREL RAMP CAR: 1961–62. Red molded 6424-11 frame with lower frame rail projections (see introduction to 6511-series cars for explanation). Has heat-stamped "6343 LIONEL" in white serif lettering on each side rail. Either mold could have been used, but a slot and a screw hole had to be added to accommodate the light gray molded superstructure, and 6424-11 got the nod. AAR trucks, usually with two operating couplers. Load is six stained brown barrels, same as used with 362 barrel loader and other items.

Note: Watch for cracked or broken railing on original superstructure and for reproduction barrels and superstructure. **15   25   40   60**

6407 FLATCAR WITH MISSILE AND REMOVABLE MERCURY CAPSULE: 1963. Red molded 6511-2 frame with only "LIONEL" heat-stamped on each frame rail in white serif letters. Lionel could not use mold 6424-11 because of the need for stake holes to attach the gray molded 6801-64 cradle that holds the missile. AAR trucks, with one fixed and one operating coupler.

Note: This same unnumbered flatcar, except perhaps for the trucks, was used for 6408 and 6501. Of most interest is the load, a gigantic (by Lionel standards) missile with two-piece removable Mercury capsule. Sterling Plastics, a major manufacturer of school supplies at the time, made the rocket for Lionel. It started life as a pencil case and came in a clear plastic package, along with a ruler and assorted school supplies. The dark blue molded "capsule" was press-fitted into the white molded rocket body and contained a pencil sharpener. Removing the capsule opened the body for pencil storage. Twisting the capsule with respect to its base allowed it to come apart for emptying the pencil shavings. Sterling also sold the Mercury capsule pencil sharpener separately, molded in a variety of colors. The rocket body had the word "ASTRONAUT" arrayed vertically on its side with other markings. Red molded tail fins snapped into a broad groove in the semi-flexible polypropylene molded body. This body material has an oily finish when molded and must be specially treated to accept decoration. Even then, the printing does not adhere well and is easy to scratch or rub off. Sterling's name and trademark were

Top: 6175 (D) rocket car with sponge tip on rocket discolored but still there; 6262 (A) wheel car with rare red frame. Second: 6262 (B) wheel car with usual black frame, and 6264 (A) lumber car. Third: 6264 (B) lumber car and envelope of parts that probably came only with version (A) of this car; 6311 flatcar with pipes showing correct three-pipe load and only six stakes. Bottom: 6343 barrel ramp car (note frame rail extensions always present on this car) and 6361 (B) timber transport car.

molded in raised lettering on the capsule base and on the angled surface just below the tail fins.

When Lionel contracted for these rockets as a flatcar load, they did not want to pay for the pencil sharpener (if they had, they certainly would have advertised this feature!) or have "ASTRONAUT" on the side. Otherwise, the pencil case and the Lionel load are identical. Probably by mistake or for their own convenience, Sterling shipped some rockets to Lionel with the pencil sharpener installed. New Lionel examples with this feature have been reported by several reliable sources. For separate sale, 6407 came in its own Orange Picture box, which is quite rare. When included in sets of the period, it was usually unboxed.

Since they are rare and valuable, the rocket and nose cone have been reproduced. Original tooling was purchased from Sterling, which removed its name and logo prior to sale. So reproduction capsules can be identified by the lack of the Sterling data on the base. The rocket body lacks this identification on the angled surface just below the tail fins. But reproduction rockets can be identified at a glance an easier way; unlike originals, the red

color from the tail fins "bleeds" into the white of reproduction rockets over time. They were made sufficiently long ago that this is evident on all examples recently observed. As to capsules, dark blue with and without the sharpener, and always with the Sterling data, are considered original. Beyond that, buyer beware. J. Sattler and R. Shanfeld Collections.

Gd	VG	Ex	LN
125	300	475	650

6408 FLATCAR WITH PIPES: 1963. Shown only in set 11351 in the 1963 catalog and not listed for separate sale. Red molded 6511-2 frame with only "LIONEL" heat-stamped in white serif letters on each frame rail. Same frame and lettering as 6407 and 6501. AAR trucks with one fixed and one operating coupler. No number is found on production cars, although the catalog picture shows one. Probably also distributed with uncataloged sets. Load is five standard silvery gray plastic pipes secured to the frame with a rubber band. Car is listed in the 5-63 supplement to the Lionel Service Manual as 6408-25. Like most in this series, 6408 had a brake wheel.

	Gd	VG	Ex	LN

Note: Reproduction pipes have thicker walls than originals and are not as silvery. **10 20 30 40**

6409-25 FLATCAR WITH PIPES: 1963. Cost-reduced version of 6408 with no brake wheel and two fixed couplers on the AAR trucks. Load is only three standard pipes, secured to the frame with a rubber band. Shown only in set 11311 in the 1963 catalog. Both this listing and the Lionel Service Manual designate 6409-25 as the car number. No number is actually on the car. Probably appeared in some uncataloged sets as well. G. Halverson and Schreiner Collections (S. Bradley comment).
10 20 30 40

6414 EVANS AUTO TRANSPORT CAR: 1955–66. Red molded frame with heat-stamped white serif lettering. Two-piece stamped-metal superstructure assembled with tabs and attached to the frame with four tabs through the stake holes. Painted black prior to assembly and usually has white rubber-stamped "AUTO - LOADER" in the middle and the Evans logo at each end. When production began, this superstructure had well-defined antiskid detail on the decks along the tire paths. This stamping die detail was not maintained and became fainter as time went on. By the end, it had worn smooth or been removed. Load is always four automobiles in various colors. See the sidebar regarding these automobiles and the variation listings for more details on individual flatcars and their load.

Note: Prices for Excellent and Like New condition require the presence of four original undamaged Lionel automobiles in more common varieties; subtract 20 to 25 percent for each missing automobile. Add a premium for the original paperboard automobile wrappers and the original box, depending on condition. Reproduction cars are readily available, some with the Lionel name and data. All but the LTI reruns from the original molds have one fatal defect discussed in the sidebar. The LTI models are clearly marked in the mold. Variations listed below include the most common load. Unusual automobile colors, if authentic, will add substantially to the values shown.

(A) Darker red 6511-2 frame with the number right, from 1955–57. Bar-end trucks attached to blackened stamped-metal truck mounting plates. Load is four premium automobiles (see sidebar), almost always in red, green, yellow, and white. Red automobile color closely matches the flatcar frame color. When new, the two automobiles

6407 flatcar with missile and removable Mercury capsule with original rocket and capsule. Note sharp definition of red tail-fin band and rocket body. Red "bleeds" into white rocket body on all reproductions to date.

on each deck came packaged in a paperboard carrier.
40 70 100 125

(B) Same as (A), except the number 6414 is on the left side and AAR trucks, both with operating couplers, are riveted directly to the frame. This dates to 1958–63, and the paperboard carriers for the automobiles were eliminated. Also found with two red and two yellow automobiles instead of four colors. R. LaVoie and C. Rohlfing Collections.
40 70 100 125

(C) Same as (B), except 6424-11 frame. Note the introductory explanation of how Lionel reworked mold 6424-11 for 1958. **40 70 100 125**

(D) Same as (B) or (C), except sometimes found with one fixed and one operating coupler. Load is four cheapie automobiles as explained in the sidebar. Dates to 1961 and is known in a rare Orange Picture box printed "6414-85" for the car number. The box and automobiles are the main elements of value. J. Sattler and J. Algozzini Collections. **300 450 600 750**

(E) Same as (B), except frame is a lighter red and load is four lighter red cars with gray bumpers. Car color closely matches the flatcar frame color. Probably dates to 1964–66. R. Hutchinson Collection.
50 75 175 300

(F) Same as (E), except load is four lemon yellow cars with gray bumpers. **150 275 450 650**

(G) Same as (E), except load is four mustard yellow cars with gray bumpers. L. Savage Collection.
150 275 450 650

(H) Same as (E), except load is four chocolate brown cars with gray bumpers. J. Sattler and J. Algozzini Collections. **300 500 750 1000**

(I) Same as (E), except load is four kelly green cars with gray bumpers. J. Sattler Collection.
400 700 950 1400

(J) Same as (E), except light red frame is lettered only "LIONEL" in the usual heat-stamped white serif letters, with no number 6414. Late open journal AAR trucks, with one operating and one fixed coupler. Replacing the white rubber-stamped lettering found on most auto racks is a black background decal with yellow sans-serif "6414 AUTO LOADER" letters. There is only one Evans logo, on the right end of the decal. No antiskid detail on either top or bottom deck. This car was made by Lionel for Glen Uhl, then a Lionel Service Station owner in Akron, Ohio, and a Lionel stockholder. It first appeared at the 1970 Train Collectors Association national convention in Chicago and sold for $6. Reportedly, only 200 were made. A reproduction decal closely matching the original has been available for many years, but this car is difficult to fake convincingly because of the other detail variations. Load is four light red cars, closely matching the flatcar frame color, with gray bumpers.
50 100 200 300

6416 FOUR BOAT TRANSPORT CAR: 1961–63. Except for lettering and load, this car is identical to 6414 Evans auto transport car. Darker red 6511-2 frame with

Lionel's production of their 1955 Ford model, spread over more than a decade, probably exceeded Ford's production of the prototype! Unfortunately, a photograph doesn't capture the many interesting colors and shades. Top: Far left and right, the "cheapie" autos with wheels molded into the shell are shown as HO racing cars in the only two colors used. Left to right between them are a medium yellow premium auto with chrome bumpers, a lemon yellow gray-bumper car, another lemon yellow gray-bumper car to show contrast in bumper color to white premium auto—with chrome removed from darker gray plastic beneath. Second: Four red autos with subtle shade differences. First and third have chrome bumpers, while the other two are gray-bumper autos. Third:

White autos are known only in the premium variety, never as gray-bumper or "cheapie" versions. Here are three shades with the left auto turning a caramel color as described in the sidebar. The pink auto is the only painted version with separate wheels reported as original. The example shown is from the collection of M. Rini, the original owner. Fourth: 6414 (I); photo does not capture the bright kelly green color of the autos. A reproduction car (top) is about 1/16 inch shorter than the original (bottom). Bottom: Rare "true blue" and common red premium autos are shown on an unmarked red flatcar that was probably never made by Lionel as shown. 6424 (A) twin auto car with typical color premium autos. R. Shanfeld Collection.

heat-stamped "6416 LIONEL" in white serif letters. Frame 6424-11 could have been used, but no examples have yet been reported. Black-painted superstructure includes antiskid detail and has "BOAT - LOADER" in rubber-stamped white serif letters. AAR trucks with operating couplers. Load is four cabin cruiser–type boats with white-painted hulls, blue-painted cabin, brown-painted interior piece, and a clear molded window insert. In early production the two boats on each deck were packaged in special paperboard sleeves. Later, a "tube" of paper wrap of that period surrounded the two boats on each deck. When found today, this boat packaging is usually missing.

Note: Athearn made these boats for Lionel. Athearn used the same boat as a load on one of their HO scale flatcars, as did Lionel; they also sold a set of four boats packaged in an HO box. Athearn later reran these boats in the original colors and other colors as well, most notably with

red hulls and white cabins. These were also available in sets of four. Most likely the three major boat parts were molded in a "family" mold that produced all three parts at once. Originals are molded in black and painted their separate colors. Had they been from separate molds, each part could have been molded in the finish color, eliminating the paint operation. At any rate, original boats almost certainly had only white hulls with blue cabins. The interior piece is painted brown, and originals usually have varying degrees of black still showing along their unseen outer sides. Later versions seem to be uniformly brown in these areas. Unfortunately, the boat must be disassembled to check this, and it is not a very reliable test, since original and rerun parts are interchangeable. Red hull versions are also painted red over black, and they make nice conversation pieces. To be sure, they were made from the same mold by the same vendor as the originals, but it is highly doubtful they originally

LIONEL AUTOMOBILES

Body Shell

Lionel's catalog text announcing the new 6414 for 1955 says: "[F]our removable precision scale model Ford autos." Precision scale they weren't, but these automobiles do resemble 1955 Ford two-door sedans. As originally produced, they consist of five molded plastic pieces, four rubber wheels, and two steel axles. A body shell molded in colored plastic is the main component. Only one supposedly original painted example has ever been reported. All the rest have the finish color molded in. Six long "legs" of plastic are molded into the shell interior—three at the front and three at the back. The two on the car center line are oriented parallel to the ends of the car and attach the frame. The other four are oriented parallel to the car sides and are centered inboard of each wheel well. Each of these four has a notch in the end for retaining an axle.

The Test

The key feature of the body shell is that it measures 4⁵⁄16 inches from the tip of the front fender above the headlight to the tip of the rear fender above the taillight—not the taillight lens, which extends farther rearward, but the tip of the fender above it. Reproductions have been made with an original as a master, and fortunately the mold-maker did not allow for shrinkage. As a result, all known reproductions are about ⅛ inch shorter than the original. This is the best way to tell an original from a reproduction. Mark this distance along the edge of a 3-inch x 5-inch card and keep it in your train meet kit. New LTI reruns of this shell are made from the original mold and are the same length as the originals. They are clearly marked with LTI data on the bottom. It is not possible to put new body shells undetectably on old bottoms for reasons we'll discuss later.

Frame

Next is the black molded "frame," or bottom plastic piece. Details of the car workings, such as drive shaft, frame members, transmission, and so forth are molded in raised relief. At the very front, reading with the front of the car pointing up, is "MADE IN / U.S. OF AMERICA". At the other end, reading with the rear of the car pointing up, is "THE LIONEL CORPORATION / NEW YORK NEW YORK". Lionel's circled-L logo is on the gas tank, oriented to read like the front lettering. This lettering also appeared on reproduction cars available from New York's Madison Hardware in the 1970s and later. Other reproductions omitted the Lionel data when LTI started enforcing its trademark. At the front and back of the top (car inside) side of the frame appear two sets of parallel tabs, like a thumb and forefinger. They engage the mating tabs on the body shell. Glue bonds the frame and shell more or less permanently. Disassembling the car requires breaking at least one of the tabs. You can detect the repair with close examination if your suspicions are aroused.

Window Insert

A clear molded plastic insert fits inside the body shell to provide windows. Two "legs" of this part rest on the frame to hold the windows in place, but sometimes glue was used too, possibly as a production aid.

Bumpers

A front and rear bumper in various colors are the final molded plastic parts. Initially, they were vacuum metalized to provide a chrome finish, so the underlying plastic color did not matter. Dark gray, clear, orange, and white have been reported as underlying colors. As a cost-reduction measure, Lionel eliminated this metalizing step in later years and molded the bumpers in light gray. Most collectors consider automobiles with chrome bumpers and a window insert "premium." Both bumpers are molded so they can be trapped between the body shell and the frame. If broken, they cannot be replaced without at least partially separating shell and frame, creating the problem we mentioned previously.

Wheels and Axles

In production, wheel and axle assemblies were installed before the shell and frame were bonded. But wheels can be removed by pressing out the axle. Molded tabs or legs from the body shell retain the axle with the slender sides of notches. These can be broken, allowing the axle to float around on one or both sides, depending on the extent of damage. This is another condition that is virtually impossible to repair without breaking the shell-to-frame tabs. Reproduction wheels observed have a larger hub and different appearance than originals.

Colors

By far the most common colors for premium automobiles are red, white, green, and yellow. For gray-bumper cars, red is most common, with lemon yellow a distant second. But what makes the Lionel automobile so interesting—and collectible—are the not-so-common colors and the color shades. There are quite a few of these, but one in particular may be the result of an inferior batch of plastic. About 1959, Lionel molded a number of items, including the automobile, in a white plastic that fairly quickly turned a caramel color. Exposure to ultraviolet light, as in a display window or from fluorescent light, may have exacerbated this change. Other examples with the same problem are the 57 AEC switcher, the 6014-150 Wix boxcar, and the 3366 operating circus car. It's usually possible to detect the changed color by examining the inside color or the bottom edges, where exposure would be different. However, some caramel color examples are so uniform, and somewhat darker, that they appear to be an original plastic color.

Here's a summary of Lionel automobile colors:

Red: Premium cars are a darker red; gray-bumper cars a noticeably lighter red. There are shade differences in both, but this is the basic distinction.

Yellow: Premium cars are a medium yellow. Gray-bumper cars are known in a much brighter lemon yellow (most common) and a darker mustard yellow. This makes a total of three distinct shades of yellow that are commonly recognized.

Green: Premium cars are a dull bluish green. Some have called them turquoise, but that is a bluer, more vivid color than the typical green premium automobile. Gray-bumper cars are known in a bright kelly green, a most collectible and expensive color.

White: Premium cars are various shades of white, as described above. Gray-bumper cars are not known in any shade of white.

Caramel: May be a color change, and definitely is if it appears blotchy or if much whiter plastic is visible on the inside or in protected areas. But several uniform examples have been observed that are original—or the color transformation is remarkably complete. All observed examples are premium cars.

Yellowish Cream: May be the same color change as described for caramel, but the examples observed are uniform and no shade difference on the bottom edges or inside is apparent, so they are most likely all right.

Brown: Lionel molded a chocolate brown only for later gray-bumper automobiles; a very rare and expensive color.

Blue: A medium true blue occurs on a few premium automobiles, and they command a truly premium price.

Mahogany: A sort of maroonish brown similar to 1877's color has been observed on a gray-bumper car.

Mauve: A pale bluish purple has been reliably reported in a gray-bumper car. May be same as the blue mentioned above, since no one has reported a side-by-side comparison.

Only one painted car with separate wheels has been reported and it may well be "real." But with modern equipment and the skill of some painters, great caution should be exercised in the purchase of a painted car.

Packaging

For the first two or three years, Lionel wrapped the two automobiles on each deck in a thin paperboard carrier with slots punched out for the wheels to fit through. When the automobiles were in place, the wrap was glued closed. It held them well for shipment, but almost has to be ripped apart to release them. As a result, it is hard to find the automobiles in their original carrier. This same two-automobile carrier is found on early 6424 flatcars and in the separate-sale 6414-25 four automobiles, which came in a Middle Classic box. Only premium autos are found in this carrier. It probably disappeared at the same time gray-bumper cars were introduced, but this has not been definitely established. Thereafter, the automobiles were just set in place on the flatcar, which was then put in its outer box. Over the years, 6414 came in five distinctly different boxes: Middle Classic, 1955; Late Classic, 1956–58; Orange Perforated, 1959–60; Orange Picture, 1961–65; and Cellophane-front "window box," 1966.

Cheapie Automobiles

Lionel's final cost reductions produced a series of cars collectively known as "cheapie" automobiles. These were offshoots of an outsized HO scale executive inspection car and a race car set that used the shell of the O gauge automobile mounted on an HO motorized rail car chassis. To accomplish this, the shell mold had to be changed to remove the interior "legs" used to attach the frame and wheels. Two bulkheads took their place—one crosswise between the front wheel positions, the other at the rear wheel positions. For this reason, and because the regular rubber wheels could no longer be attached and the car looked odd with no wheels at all, the wheel wells were filled in to produce simulated wheels. In addition, a hole was necessary through each side at the lower rear corner of the door outline so the shell could just snap onto the chassis. Other additions were a frosted window insert so the works were hidden, heat-stamped white walls on the simulated tires, and a black racing number on each door. The race car was almost complete. The final touch was to glue light gray-bumpers front and rear, since there was no longer a frame to hold these parts in place. This all happened for 0068 executive inspection car and 6100 auto raceway in 1961. For 1962, Lionel used the Tri-ang Scalextric slot cars, and the executive inspection car is shown with a racing number on its side! For quick inspections, no doubt!

There were probably twelve mold cavities producing Lionel auto shells, and each had the cavity number molded into the roof's underside in raised relief. With a strong light, a magnifying glass, and great patience, these numbers are visible through the side windows on most cars. Cavities 1, 4, 6, 7, 9, 10, and 11 were observed in a small sample. Apparently, only cavities 1 and 4 acquired the filled-in wheels; it was done in two steps. First, just the simulated wheels were added. The six legs for frame and wheel attachment remained. Both red and yellow shells were molded, and these are the classic cheapie automobiles. Color shades were the same as the corresponding color premium cars. Just the shells were used; there were no decoration, no window insert, no frame, and no bumpers. Cost reduction on this car could go no further.

Then Lionel modified the mold again to remove the six legs and add the two bulkheads. Shells were again molded in the same red and yellow, always found only from cavity 1 or 4. These automobiles were otherwise just like the previous run with nothing but the bare-bones shell.

Finally, a hole was added in each door and the decoration was applied. The racing number "1" always appears on the red car and the number "7" on the yellow car, although at least one example of a yellow shell painted red and then decorated has been observed. No undecorated shells have been reported with the side holes, and no decorated shells have turned up without these side holes. All decorated shells have both a racing number and white walls. They have been found with and without frosted window inserts and with and without light gray-bumpers. Plain or with add-ons, they are much less common than completely undecorated shells.

When found as a load on 6414, there are usually two red and two yellow cheapie cars. Perhaps the most desirable load would be one of each color with the bulkhead interior and one of each with the legs. But since only the color is visible when the car is on the shelf or layout, this is of little import. Decorated cars always have the bulkhead interior, since they are undoubtedly leftover race car shells.

To summarize, there are twelve cheapie shell variations. Cavities 1 and 4 with legs in red and yellow from each cavity makes four, the same with the bulkhead interior makes eight, and the same with decoration makes twelve. Painted shells, add-on bumpers, and frosted window insert do not count.

After 1961, mold cavities 1 and 4 returned to their prior configuration and all subsequent production went back to rubber wheels, a clear window insert, and light gray-bumpers. Although cataloged for 12 years, slow sales and large inventories probably meant 6414 was not produced every year during this period. Only a 1961 vintage darker red 6414 with AAR trucks and the number on the left would be correct for the cheapie automobiles.

came on a 6416. Add a generous premium for original paper-board boat packaging.   **80   150   200   250**

6424 TWIN AUTO CAR: 1956–59. This is the flatcar for which Lionel made the 6424-11 mold, but the company also used the earlier 6511-2 frame for the 6424. Black molded frame with heat-stamped number and "LIONEL" in white serif letters. Number may be left or right, and trucks are as shown in the listings. Frame was originally built for truck plates, but was changed to direct mounted trucks for 1958. Superstructure is a two-piece metal stamping painted black, the same as that used on 6430 except for the center section. Metal truck versions have the superstructure attached with the same screws that hold the truck plates. Plastic truck versions have the superstructure riveted to the frame. Load is usually two of the more common premium cars (see sidebar on Lionel automobiles), but some interesting variations are also found. If you have a rare color automobile, it shows up much better on a 6424 than on a 6414. This flatcar can be found packaged in boxes numbered 6424, 6424-60, 6424-85, and 6424-110. Red molded flatcars have surfaced but all actually observed have been fakes.

(A) 1956–57 vintage with 6424-11 frame and bar-end trucks with two operating couplers, found with and without tabs. Uses truck-mounting plates, and the 6424 number is on the right.   **16   30   42   65**

(B) Probably late 1957 to early 1958 version same as (A), except AAR trucks are riveted to the truck-mounting plates. Number still on right.   **16   30   42   65**

Variations of 6414 Evans auto transport car, cataloged for 12 consecutive years. Top: 6414 (A) with four most common premium auto colors (this is the most common version); 6414 (B) with same common autos. Second: 6414 (E) with four gray-bumper autos molded in red closely matching lighter red flatcar frame color; 6414 (D) with "cheapie" autos in the only two colors known.

Third: 6414 (D) again, but note "bulkhead" construction on overturned auto (this was the version used for HO slot and inspection cars). 6414 (G) with four gray-bumper cars in mustard yellow. Bottom: 6414 (F) with four gray-bumper cars in lemon yellow; 6414 (H) with four rare gray-bumper cars in chocolate brown. R. Shanfeld Collection.

	Gd	VG	Ex	LN

(C) 1958 and later version with 6511-2 frame, number on left and AAR trucks with two operating couplers riveted directly to the frame. Slots at each end of the car, used to attach the truck-mounting plates, have been closed. Separate rivets attach the superstructure to the frame. This car has been observed brand new in 6424-60 and 6424-85 Classic boxes, both having a red and a white premium car in a paperboard sleeve.

	16	30	42	65

(D) Same as (C), except special version of 6424-11 frame. When Lionel modified the 6424-11 frame for 1958, it was a major revision that not only replaced truck plates by direct mounted plastic trucks but made a frame suitable for the 6805 atomic energy disposal car. When the two slots in each end that held the truck-mounting plates were closed, the mold inserts that did the job provided two bumps at each end to serve as rail stops for 6805. Also included in the change were four slots in the frame for clips to secure 6805's two container-mounting rails. Collectors have dubbed them "6805 slots." Thus, any car molded in 1958 in the 6424-11 mold while it was configured for 6805 got that car's special features. The 6424 was such a car. So this variation has the "6805 slots" that remained in the mold as long as the "real" Lionel used it, and it has the rail stops that later were eliminated. Quite a hard variation to find and easily overlooked, it has been found in a 6424-110 Orange Picture box.

	80	130	185	260

(E) Same as (D), except the rail stops have been eliminated. A new mold insert filled in the truck-mounting plate slots so they were flush with the deck and included the antiskid markings. But the 6805 slots remained. One example of this car has no superstructure, and it appears that none was ever installed. A. Stewart Collection.

	80	130	185	260

6430 COOPER-JARRETT VAN CAR: 1956–58. Molded red frame with heat-stamped car number (right or left) and "LIONEL" in white serif letters. Trucks, always with two operating couplers, are metal bar-end (with or without tabs) or AAR types. Load is always two molded plastic trailers, or "vans," usually with a removable roof (see the sidebar on Lionel trailer vans). Vans are retained to the flatcar by a two-piece metal rack, the same as on 3460.

(A) Darker red molded 6511-2 frame with car number on the right. Trucks clipped to stamped-metal truck plates. Same screws attach rack to car and retain truck plates. Some 1957 production may be found with AAR trucks attached to metal truck plates. Load is two vans, Type II, III, IV, V, or VI. J. Sattler Collection.

	20	40	60	80

(B) Darker red molded 6511-2 frame revised to accept AAR trucks riveted directly to it. Separate rivets attach rack to frame. Number moves to left of "LIONEL." Load is two vans, Type VI or VII.

	20	40	60	80

(C) Same as (B), except lighter red molded 6511-2 frame. Load is two vans, Type X (rare) or XI (most

common). This and versions (D) and (E) were most likely all distributed as components of 6431.

	20	40	60	80

(D) Same as (C), except 6424-11 frame.

	20	40	60	80

(E) Same as (D), except frame rail extensions on 6424-11 frame. A. Stewart Collection.

	20	40	60	80

6431 PIGGY-BACK CAR WITH TRAILER TRUCKS AND TRACTOR: 1966. Identical to 6430 versions (C), (D), and (E), except packaged in a special Cellophane-front box with a die-cast Midgetoy tractor painted bright red. Inside of tractor roof has "MIDGE TOY / ROCKFORD ILL. / U. S. A. / PAT. / 2775847" cast in raised letters. Wheels and axles evidently assembled to tractor prior to painting, as they usually show overspray.

Note: The 6431 number is found only on the box ends, so the box is required for Like New or better. Watch for incorrect versions of 6430 flatcar and incorrect or reproduction trailers.

	80	160	250	300

6440 TWIN PIGGY-BACK VAN CAR: 1961–63. A cost-reduced version of 6430, this car had no metal rack to retain the vans. Lionel Service Manual shows no elastic bands, so retention was by rubber bands or just gravity. Darker red molded 6511-2 frame with heat-stamped "6440 LIONEL" in white serif letters. AAR trucks riveted directly to frame. Usually found with two operating couplers, but also known with one fixed coupler. Load is two Type VII gray vans (see sidebar on Lionel trailer vans). Packaged in an Orange Picture box marked "No. 6440 / FLAT CAR / WITH PIGGY-BACK VANS".

	25	60	95	125

6467 MISCELLANEOUS CAR: 1956. Red molded 6511-2 frame with heat-stamped "LIONEL 6467" in serif letters. Frame 6424-11 could not be used due to the need for stake holes. Bar-end trucks with tab couplers clipped to special blackened stamped steel truck-mounting plates. The two end tabs on these plates are higher than normal so they can clamp the end of the black molded bulkhead in place. One bulkhead at each end of car, each with a brake wheel. With the normal brake wheel in its usual spot, there are three brake wheels on 6467. The angle brace on the bulkhead latches into a stake hole. Four 2411-4 posts are centered between the bulkheads. No load was furnished with this car.

	18	35	50	80

6469 LIQUEFIED GAS TANK CAR: 1963. Lighter orange-red molded 6424-11 frame with frame rail extensions and 6805 slots (see the introduction to 6500-series flatcars). Only "LIONEL" in white serif letters is heat-stamped on the side rails; "6469" appears on each side of the load. Basically the same car as 6467, but with some interesting differences. By 1963 Lionel had revised the 6424-11 mold to open the stake holes. Designers eliminated the truck-mounting plates, so there was nothing to

To left: 6424 (C) twin auto car shown with two premium autos in two of the four most common colors. Although the left auto appears blue, it is actually green with a slightly bluish tint. To right:

6424 (D) with the other two most common premium auto colors. Note the "bumps" at each end of the flatcar just below the auto's rear bumpers.

	Gd	VG	Ex	LN

hold the rear of the bulkheads in place except glue, which is what they used. Bulkheads are identical to those used on 6467; note that the end slots on the frame are open to accommodate them. AAR trucks, one or both of which has operating couplers, are riveted directly to the frame. The load is a simulated tank made out of a cardboard tube. Glossy white paper with black printing and an Erie emblem is wrapped and glued around the tube. Stamped-steel end caps are painted white and crimped in place. This load has been reproduced and appears quite close to the original, except some versions leave the end caps unpainted. M. Ocilka Collection.

Note: Beware of reproduction bulkheads and of 6467 and 6477 miscellaneous cars masquerading as this car.

	55	**100**	**150**	**225**

6477 MISCELLANEOUS CAR WITH PIPES: 1957–58. This car was identical to 6467 described above, except that it had a different number and was cataloged through Lionel's transition from metal to plastic trucks. It always kept the 6511-2 frame and special stamped-steel truck plates. Load is five standard silvery gray plastic pipes.

(A) Bar-end metal trucks found with and without tabs on the couplers, number on right. J. Sattler and R. LaVoie Collections.

	15	**40**	**65**	**90**

(B) Plastic AAR trucks riveted to the truck plate, number on right. R. Pauli Collection.

	15	**40**	**65**	**90**

(C) Same as (B), but number moved to the left of "LIONEL".

	15	**40**	**65**	**90**

6500 BEECHCRAFT BONANZA TRANSPORT CAR: 1962. Black molded 6511-2 frame with only "LIONEL" heat-stamped in white serif letters on the side rails. One of the few Lionel cars not identified with the catalog number anywhere on the frame or load, although the airplane number is molded into its belly. Undoubtedly an economy measure, allowing use of one heat-stamp for 6500, 6501, and 6502. AAR trucks with operating couplers are riveted directly to frame. Load is a scarce and fragile red and white model of a Beechcraft Bonanza secured to frame with a 6418-9 elastic band. Load is by far the major component of value. Reproduction parts as well as the entire airplane are available. The propeller in particular is

frequently broken. Packaged in an Orange Picture box.

Note: Original propellers turn freely and are not removable, while a reproduction propeller in an original airplane usually will not turn or can be easily pulled out. This was basically a reissue of 6800-60 airplane with four rivets in each wing instead of the three in 6800 wings. Also, the aircraft registration number N2742B is heat-stamped on one wing while the fuselage has "BONANZA" on each side. Yellow and black 6800-60 aircraft have no decoration at all. Quite a rare situation in which the later product was actually an improvement on the earlier issue.

(A) Plane has red upper surfaces on wings and fuselage, white lower surfaces and propeller. White lettering.

	280	**410**	**540**	**700**

(B) Colors reversed with white upper and red lower surfaces and propeller. Lettering is red. This is the harder to find of two scarce items.

	350	**500**	**650**	**850**

6501 SOLID FUEL MOTORBOAT CAR: 1962–63. Red molded 6511-2 frame with only "LIONEL" heat-stamped in white serif letters on side rails. Catalog number does not appear on car or load. AAR trucks with operating couplers riveted directly to frame. Load is a white hulled boat with brown deck. Boat rests on a gray molded cradle pressed into the flatcar's stake holes. A 6418-9 elastic band secures the boat to the cradle. New 6501s were packaged in an Orange Picture box with an instruction sheet and approximately forty fuel pellets sealed in a foil packet. Add a premium for these items if found with a less than new car. Fuel pellets are sodium bicarbonate.

To prepare for launch, the jet nozzle is removed from its housing at the rear of the hull bottom. Warm tap water is poured into the housing, which connects to a small tank in the hull. Then four or five fuel pellets are popped into the housing, and the nozzle is quickly reinstalled. Holding a thumb over the nozzle, the boat is shaken several times and placed into the water. Enough gas is expelled through the nozzle to propel the boat about 10 feet, according to Lionel's instructions. J. Sattler Collection.

	55	**85**	**120**	**150**

6502 STEEL GIRDER TRANSPORT CAR: 1962 consumer and 1963 advance catalogs. Shown only as a

Top: 6430 (A) Cooper-Jarrett van car shown with two Type V vans. Same 6430 (A) but with two Type IV vans. See sidebar on Lionel trailer vans for details. Second: 6430 (B) with two Type VIII vans showing versions (3) and (4) of the CJ (Cooper-Jarrett) signs. Note that the arrows on these signs always point to the front of the van. Third: 6431 as originally packaged in

Cellophane-front box with Midge Toy tractor. Only the box bore the 6431 number. Flatcar is 6430 (D) with two Type XI vans. Note absence of sign slots on sides. Bottom: 6440 twin piggy-back van transport car with two Type VII vans unique to this car; 6461 transformer car with decaled side of transformer shown. R. Shanfeld Collection.

component of sets 11201 (1962) and 11415 (1963 advance catalog). Never listed for separate sale. Although a 6424-11 frame could have been used, all reported examples are on the 6511-2 frame with fixed couplers. The brake wheel was retained on many examples reported, which is unusual for a very low-budget car. No catalog number on car or load. Only "LIONEL" is heat-stamped on the side rails in white serif letters in most cases. Load is easily switched, but should be an orange molded "LIONEL" girder with no decoration and unused rivet holes along its bottom edge. Lionel Service Manual has two listings for this car; a page dated 10-62 for 6502 and 5-63 for 6502-50. Both specify an orange girder, dummy coupler trucks, and a 6418-9 elastic band to secure the load. Only the 10-62 page lists a brake wheel. We assume the 6502-2 body shown for 6502 is black, while the 5-63 listing specifies a 3330-3 frame (blue).

(A) Black molded 6511-2 frame as described with

	Gd	VG	Ex	LN

arch-bar trucks. This is the color shown in the 1962 catalog. J. Bratspis Collection.

	20	40	50	80

(B) Same as (A), except red flatcar. No documentation for this color, but car exists and this may well be its correct number. Note that the trucks differentiate this car from 6409-25.

	20	40	50	80

(C) Blue molded 6511-2 frame (various shades) with fixed coupler AAR trucks but no brake wheel or "LIONEL" lettering. Just the most basic flatcar. This is probably the 6502-50, with the -50 signifying deletion of the lettering and brake wheel or perhaps the different color. J. Sattler Collection.

	20	40	50	80

6511 PIPE CAR: 1953–56. New for 1953, the first of what would become the largest variety of cars of one basic type in Lionel's history. All 6511s bear the original 6511-2 mold number in raised numerals on the underside. Although provision was made for fourteen stake

Top: 6467 miscellaneous car that came with four stakes (not shown) but no load; 6469 liquefied gas tank car. Note absence of a number on frame and frame-rail extensions. (See introduction to 6511-series flatcars for details.) Second: 6477 (C) miscellaneous car with pipes (correct load is four silvery gray plastic pipes); 6500 (A) Beechcraft Bonanza transport car with slightly more common red over white colors. "Bonanza" marking just forward of tail is hidden by wing. Third: 6500 (B) considered rarer version in white over red colors. Note absence of number on 6500 flatcar frames. 6501 solid fuel motorboat car shown with original sealed packet of fuel pellets. Bottom: 6502 (C) steel girder transport car. This unlettered version with no brake wheel probably carried Lionel designation 6502-50. 6502 (A) in black with "LIONEL" and brake wheel (wrong side shown). R. Shanfeld Collection.

holes, only thirteen were open initially. Frame side rails all have "LIONEL 6511" heat-stamped in white serif letters. Bar-end trucks are clipped to truck-mounting plates that tab through end slots in the car frame and are held at the other end by a screw. Initially, these plates were blackened die-cast metal with plenty of detail. Rivet detail was included on the visible top part of the tabs. Structural rib detail on the plastic flatcar bottom was continued in the die-casting. These cars are noticeably heavier than the standard 6511 series car and hold the rails well. Thirteen 2411-4 side posts were contained in a small manila envelope, part no. 6511-17, included with each car. An illustration on the envelope shows how to install the posts in the stake holes. Load is five standard silvery gray plastic pipes. Pipes and stakes have been reproduced for this car.

(A) Black molded frame painted a dull brick red,

	Gd	VG	Ex	LN
die-cast truck plates. C. Rohlfing, R. LaVoie, and F. Hazekamp Collections.	10	20	40	60

(B) Same as (A), but painted dark red, a darker, truer, and somewhat brighter red than (A). F. Hazekamp Collection.

	10	20	40	60

(C) Same as (B), but truck plates changed to blackened stamped steel with no detail.

	10	20	40	60

(D) Same as (C), but a light chocolate brown molded frame unpainted. This car sometimes appears with a very glossy finish. J. Sattler and F. Hazekamp Collections.

	10	20	40	60

(E) Same as (C), but a reddish brown molded frame unpainted. T. Klaassen Collection.

	10	20	40	60

6512 CHERRY PICKER CAR: 1962–63. Black molded 6511-2 frame with only "LIONEL" heat-stamped in white

| | Gd | VG | Ex | LN |

serif letters on the side rails. No catalog number any-where on car. AAR trucks with operating couplers riveted directly to frame. Lionel could have used frame 6424-11 but would have had to cut two special holes in the frame for the ladder base—so they selected 6511-2. They adapted the mechanism and ladders from the 3512 fireman and ladder car, changing the ladder base from red to gray and adding a small pin that projects through a curved slot in the frame. Its purpose is to limit the swing of the ladder to only a few degrees either side of center, preventing the weight of the astronaut's cage from tipping over the car. If the ladder base swings freely, this pin is broken. A silvery gray molded rubber astronaut figure with painted face occupies an orange molded cage at the end of the extension ladder. He stands on a platform that can swivel, so when viewed from the side, he can appear or disappear. Extending to the side of the cage is an arm molded as part of the astronaut's platform. When the cage is maneuvered near the Mercury capsule atop 3413's rocket in launch position, this lever contacts the capsule and the astronaut appears. As the cage is withdrawn, he disappears. With a vivid imagination, you can pretend he entered the capsule. Holding the cage to the ladder is an orange molded plastic bracket with two pins that suspend the cage. This bracket latches into the extension ladder and is often broken or missing. A very fragile car that bears close inspection prior to purchase. Most of the critical parts have been reproduced. **35   70   105   150**

6630 MISSILE LAUNCHING CAR: 1961 advance catalog. This is a cost-reduced version of 6650 and is shown as part of set 1125. However, it is known as a part of several uncataloged sets as well. Although 6650 is known on both 6424-11 and 6511-2 frames, this car has been reported on only a black molded 6511-2 frame. Heat-stamped "6630 LIONEL" in white serif letters on the side rails. Brake wheel is omitted. Arch-bar trucks with fixed couplers rivet directly to the frame. Launching mechanism and rocket are as described in the 6650 listing.
30   70   105   140

6640 U.S.M.C. MISSILE LAUNCHING CAR: 1960. Not cataloged for separate sale and shown only as part of 1805 Land-Sea-and Air Gift Pack. Although 6650 is found on both 6511-2 and 6424-11 frames, this car has been reported on only 6511-2 painted olive drab. Heat-stamped sans-serif lettering in white on the side rails with the number on the right. AAR trucks with operating couplers riveted directly to frame. Launching mechanism is same as 6650, except usual blue molded base is molded olive drab for this car. See 6650 listing for description of mechanism and missile. No separate box was made for this rare car. **85   150   225   300**

6650 I.R.B.M. MISSILE LAUNCHING CAR: 1959–63. Red molded frame with heat-stamped "6650 LIONEL" in white serif letters on the side rails. AAR trucks with operating couplers are riveted directly to frame. Blue molded

superstructure base with black molded launch ramp. Simulated counterweight in base contains a rubber diaphragm intended to slow the elevation of the ramp to firing position. Over the years, this diaphragm usually has hardened so the mechanism no longer operates properly. Normally, the operator lowers the ramp by depressing a metal lever extending at the upper side of the base. This compresses a spring above the diaphragm and cocks the launch mechanism. The operator must also cock the missile firing mechanism, contained in the ramp, by moving its metal tab rearward. After cocking, the missile is placed in position so the slot in its tail engages the metal tab. A wire link connects the base's elevating mechanism to the ramp's launch lever. Pressing the blue molded firing button releases the ramp elevating mechanism. The spring, whose action is retarded by the diaphragm, slowly raises the ramp. When 30 to 45 degrees of elevation is reached, the wire link trips the firing mechanism and launches the missile. Load is a two-stage 6650-80 missile, whose main sections are pressed together. They can be separated by gentle twisting and pulling so that red or white colors can be mixed or matched. Only an all-red missile was never originally produced by Lionel, although it's easy to make one. The nose section has a blue molded rubber tip (also known in red) intended to minimize impact damage. Reproduction missiles are readily available and have thicker fins than originals.

(A) Frame mold is 6424-11. M. Ocilka and C. Rohlfing Collections. **25   45   60   85**

(B) Frame mold is 6511-2. J. Sattler and J. Algozzini Collections. **25   45   60   85**

6651 SHELL LAUNCHING CAR: Uncataloged, 1964–65. Made only for uncataloged military sets but available separately for many years from the original Madison Hardware in New York. Two 6651-10 instruction sheets are known for this car, one dated 8/64 and the other 8/65. These furnished the car's official name. Basically a 6650 with a huge cannon replacing the ramp mechanism. Only reported with a 6511-2 frame painted olive drab. Heat-stamped sans-serif lettering in white on side rails with number right. AAR trucks with operating couplers riveted directly to frame. Superstructure base is same olive drab molded part as used on 6640. Olive drab molded cannon mechanism is unique, but operates like 6650 except it launches a 5/16"-diameter x 1⅞"-long wood shell painted silver. Lionel introduced three cannons about 1964; 347 and 3666 for the Sears 9820 military outfit and this car for other uncataloged sets. All fired a silver-painted wood shell, but each had a unique size. Shells usually missing and have been reproduced, but who can tell? Apparently only one shell came with the car—the instruction sheets indicate that, for multiple firings, additional 6651-8 shells were available at 50 cents for a set of four. D. McCarthy and J. Sattler Collections.
60   110   160   225

6660 BOOM CAR: 1958. Red molded frame with heat stamped "6660 LIONEL" in white serif letters. AAR trucks

Top: 6502 (B) steel girder transport car. This color flatcar is known with and without "LIONEL" on the frame rails and with and without a brake wheel. 6511 (D) pipe car shown with original envelope containing thirteen side posts. Second: 6511 (B) painted dark red; 6512 cherry picker car. Third: 6518 (A) transformer car. Compare transformer with 6461, noting side plaques added for lettering. Bottom: 6519 (A) Allis Chalmers car with usual darker orange molded frame; 6519 (C) in rare "faded" orange mold color. R. Shanfeld Collection.

	Gd	VG	Ex	LN

with operating couplers riveted directly to frame. Blackened stamped-steel crane base that attaches to frame stake holes with tabs. Contains two outriggers that can be manually moved in and out and swiveled up and down. Long and short molded yellow booms attach to a blackened stamped steel housing swivel mounted atop the base. Housing has two silver cranks: one moves the hook up and down, the other raises or lowers the booms, which are connected by a wire link. Uses a standard crane hook.

(A) Frame mold is 6424-11.

	Gd	VG	Ex	LN
	30	55	80	120

(B) Frame mold is 6511-2.

	Gd	VG	Ex	LN
	30	55	80	120

6670 DERRICK CAR: 1959–60. Cost-reduced version of 6660 with the base and outriggers deleted. Red molded frame with heat-stamped serif letters in white. AAR trucks with two operating couplers riveted directly to frame. Same boom-and-hook mechanism as 6660, but swivel mounted directly to frame instead of to steel outrigger base. Required addition of a mounting hole in the frame. This car was introduced well into the plastic-truck era, when car numbers had been moved to the left, yet it is found with the number on right! Most likely an error in initial setup of the heat-stamp die.

(A) Darker red molded 6511-2 frame with "LIONEL

6670". L. Savage, J. Algozzini, and D. Fleming Collections.

	Gd	VG	Ex	LN
	20	50	70	100

(B) Same as (A), except 6424-11 frame. F. S. Davis Collection.

	Gd	VG	Ex	LN
	20	50	70	100

(C) Darker red molded 6511-2 frame with number corrected to left of "LIONEL".

	Gd	VG	Ex	LN
	20	50	70	100

(D) Same as (C), with 6424-11 frame.

	Gd	VG	Ex	LN
	20	50	70	100

(E) Brighter molded red 6424-11 frame with number left. D. Fleming and D. Miller Collections.

	Gd	VG	Ex	LN
	20	50	70	100

6800 AIRPLANE CAR: 1957–60. Red molded frame with car number and "LIONEL" heat-stamped in white serif letters on the side rails. Load is a yellow and black model of a Beechcraft Bonanza airplane with retractable landing gear and folding wings. Molded into the fuselage bottom in raised lettering is "NO. 6800-60 AIRPLANE / THE LIONEL CORPORATION / NEW YORK, N.Y. / MADE IN U.S. OF AMERICA". A mold insert was used for the number, so it is on a plaque raised above the surrounding surface. Airplanes are easily switched, and wings are removable so variations can be created. Original versions have black upper surfaces on both wings

Top: 6630 missile launching car, a cost-reduced version of 6650; 6640 U.S.M.C. missile launching car with one side of frame unlettered (factory error). Bottom: 6640 with correct frame lettering; 6650 I.R.B.M. missile launching car. All launchers used the same missile, which can be found in red over white, all white, and white over red. An all-red missile can be assembled but has never been reported as original. R. Shanfeld Collection.

	Gd	VG	Ex	LN

and fuselage with yellow lower surfaces and a yellow propeller or the exact reverse. There was no applied lettering on 6800 as there was on the later 6500 airplane. Two distinctly different shades of yellow were used: lighter lemon yellow and darker orange-yellow. Three rivets hold each wing upper and lower half together, compared to four on the red and white 6500 airplanes. The airplane was available for separate sale in a special Late Classic box marked "No. 6800-60 / AIRPLANE". Airplane has been reproduced, and most delete the Lionel data, but early reproductions were a close copy, including the lettering. Also watch for original and reproduction parts mixed on the same airplane (P. Ambrose and I. D. Smith comments).

(A) 1957 production with 6424-11 frame, number right and bar-end trucks clipped to blackened stamped-steel truck-mounting plates.

	75	125	175	240

(B) Frame 6424-11 changed for 1958 to accept AAR trucks riveted directly to it. Number moved left of "LIONEL". T. Klaassen Collection.

	75	125	175	240

(C) Frame 6511-2 with number right but AAR trucks riveted directly to frame. J. Letterese Collection.

	75	125	175	240

(D) Same as (C), but number corrected to left of "LIONEL". T. Klaassen Collection.

	75	125	175	240

6801 BOAT CAR: 1957–60. Red molded frame with heat-stamped "LIONEL" and car number in white serif letters. Two operating couplers. Gray molded cradle to hold the load presses into stake holes in frame. Load is an unpainted two-color boat with clear plastic windshield, secured to cradle by a 6418-9 elastic band. First issue has a white hull and brown deck, with no markings whatever to identify it as a Lionel product. Next came a yellow hull with white deck. On the floor of the cockpit in raised letters is "NO. 6801-60 BOAT / MADE IN U.S. OF AMERICA" on the right side of the simulated motor cover and "THE LIONEL CORPORATION / NEW YORK, N.Y." on the left. Last was a blue-hull boat with the same white deck and lettering. Brown-deck version was available for separate sale in a Late Classic box. This is the reproduction most difficult to distinguish. Compare size of motor cover and top of seat backs with a known original for easiest identification. A blue- or yellow-hull boat without the Lionel identification is a reproduction. Boats are easy to switch, but only the brown-deck version seems to appear in original separate-sale boxes, cataloged only in 1957–58. With the flatcar, this color usually comes in a 6801 box. Yellow-hull boats with flatcar were packaged as 6801-50 and blue hulls as 6801-75, based on observation of brand-new examples. But Lionel did what was expedient at the time, so there were deviations. There is no hard-and-fast rule for the correct flatcar for each boat color, but generally the brown-deck boat would be on the metal-truck flatcar and perhaps a transition flatcar. Colored-hull boats would be on the plastic-truck flatcars.

(A) 1957 production has 6511-2 frame with bar-end trucks clipped to blackened stamped steel truck plates. Car number is right of "LIONEL". Mold 6424-11 could not be used in 1957 because the stake holes along the edges had not yet been opened, so there was no place to attach the boat cradle. R. Gluckman Collection.

	45	75	110	140

	Gd	VG	Ex	LN

(B) Frame 6511-2 modified to accept AAR trucks riveted directly to it. Number moved to left of "LIONEL". T. Klaassen Collection.   **45   75   110   140**

(C) Same as (B), except frame is 6424-11, which had been revised for 1958 to add more stake holes.
45   75   110   140

6802 FLATCAR WITH TWO U.S. STEEL GIRDERS:
1958–59. Red molded frame heat-stamped "6802 LIONEL" in white serif letters. AAR trucks with two operating couplers riveted directly to frame. Load is two black molded U.S. Steel girders with top surface of raised lettering heat-stamped in white, secured to frame with 6418-9 elastic band. See 6418 listing for discussion of Lionel girder loads. Girders should have number 6418 at lower right; it can be black or highlighted in white.

(A) Frame is 6424-11. J. Sattler Collection.
12   25   30   40

(B) Frame is 6511-2. R. Pauli Collection.
12   25   30   40

GENERAL NOTE FOR 6803, 6804, 6806, 6807, 6808, and 6809 FLATCARS

Pyro Plastics made the loads for these flatcars for Lionel; the company sold the same toys and others of similar design under their own brand. Pyro's line included the same gray color molded for Lionel as well as their own olive drab. Fortunately or not, depending on your view, the original molds survived and have been used for reproductions. Through the extensive efforts of the TCA Standards Committee, the rerun parts are usually marked, although obscurely. For example, on trucks with swiveling operator's seat (machine guns, radar antenna, searchlight, or speakers), look on the underside of the seat in a good light. Reproductions have a molded raised letter (usually "M"), while originals have a number. Because of the fragility of these toys, it is rare to find an intact original load. Often an original vehicle has the seat and bracket replaced. Look closely for parts that have been broken and glued.

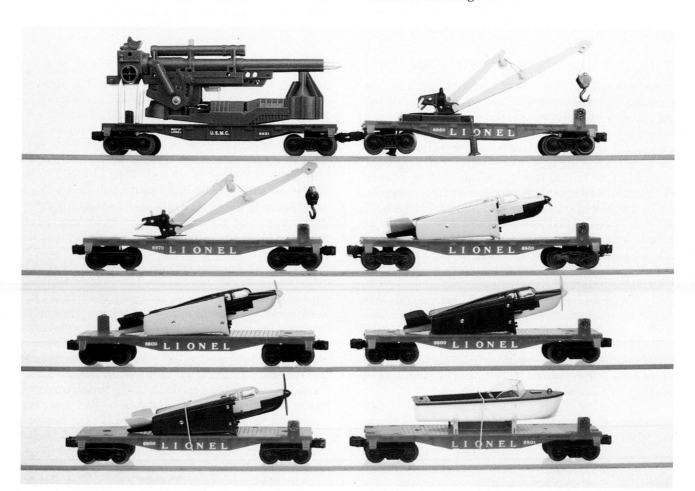

Top: Uncataloged 6651 shell launching car; 6660 (A) boom car with metal crane base containing movable outriggers. Second: 6670 (C) derrick car, a lower-cost version that replaced 6660; 6800 (A) airplane car with correct yellow over black airplane (note three rivets in wing; there were four in 6500). No lettering was used on 6800 airplane. Third: 6800 (B) with black over yellow airplane but yellow upper wing surfaces. This is probably not an original Lionel combination. 6800 (B) with correct black over yellow color combination. Bottom: 6800 (B) with wing color that probably did not come originally from Lionel on this color fuselage. 6801 (A) but with AAR trucks, probably late 1957 or early 1958 production. Boat is first version with no lettering on cabin floor. R. Shanfeld Collection.

	Gd	VG	Ex	LN

A molded black axle retainer that presses (and is usually glued) into the flatcar's stake holes holds the wheeled vehicles to the flatcar. A 6418-9 elastic band secures the DKW "DUCK" on 6807 and the tracked vehicles (which have hidden wheels). Wheeled vehicles, except the DKW, have a white heat-stamped emblem and "U.S.M.C." on each door. In addition, the van has "U.S. NAVY" and the caduceus emblem on the box.

All flatcars have red molded frames with heat-stamped "LIONEL" and the car number to the left in white serif letters. AAR trucks with two operating couplers are riveted directly to the frame. For a Like New price, the loads must be intact and original with no evidence of broken and glued parts.

6803 MARINE CORPS TANK AND SOUND TRUCK CAR: 1958–59. See general note preceding. Load is a tank with swiveling turret and a truck with swiveling loudspeakers.
  (A) Frame is 6511-2. J. Algozzini Collection.

	70	140	205	280

  (B) Frame is 6424-11. J. Sattler Collection.

	70	140	205	280

6804 MARINE CORPS ANTIAIRCRAFT AND SOUND TRUCK CAR: 1958–59. See general note preceding 6803. Load is a truck with swiveling twin antiaircraft guns and a truck with swiveling loudspeakers.
  (A) Frame is 6511-2. J. Algozzini Collection.

	70	140	205	280

  (B) Frame is 6424-11. J. Sattler Collection.

	70	140	205	280

6805 ATOMIC ENERGY DISPOSAL CAR: 1958–59. Red molded 6424-11 frame with heat-stamped "6805 LIONEL" in white serif letters. One bar-end metal truck with pickup roller and the other with special brass eyelet in the truck's swivel stop tab. Trucks attach directly to frame with clips, rather than the rivets used for plastic trucks. A unique item in many respects, this is the only known flatcar in the 6511 series with metal trucks and the car number left of "LIONEL" and the only example of metal trucks mounted directly to the frame. It is also the only known instance of a metal truck providing an electrical ground through a wire soldered to the brass eyelet mentioned above.

This car required a major change to the 6424-11 mold. End slots that held the truck plates were filled in by means of mold inserts that produced two "bumps" to serve as retainers and end stops for the two Super O rails attached to the deck. When 6805 production ended, another set of inserts removed these bumps from the mold. The deck acquired four slots for clips to hold the rails and provide electrical contact. These slots remained in the mold at least into the MPC era. For convenience, they are known as "6805 slots." Of course with the mounting slots for truck plates gone, the frame also had to be modified to allow direct attachment of the trucks. Mold

6511-2 also got the conversion for direct mounted trucks but never got the end stops or 6805 holes, so a 6511-2 frame never appears on this car.

The load is two simulated radioactive waste containers heat-stamped "DANGER" in red and "RADIOACTIVE / WASTE" in black. Containers are molded black and painted a light gray or a yellowish cream. Snapped inside is a translucent red molded base and light filter containing a special 402-300 flashing lamp. Electrical contacts are arranged so that the containers can be clipped to the rails with the printing facing two different ways. Note that MPC reissued these containers but they were unpainted gray plastic and had "RADIOACTIVE / WASTE" in slightly smaller letters. Frequently one or more of the "handles" molded at the top of the containers is missing or has been glued.
  (A) Black molded containers painted light gray.

	35	80	125	170

  (B) Black molded containers painted yellowish cream.

	35	80	125	170

6806 MARINE CORPS RADAR AND MEDICAL TRUCK CAR: 1958–59. See general note preceding 6803. Load is a truck with swiveling radar antenna and a medical van.
  (A) Frame is 6511-2. J. Algozzini Collection.

	70	125	175	225

  (B) Frame is 6424-11. T. Klaassen Collection.

	70	125	175	225

6807 MARINE CORPS "DUCK" CAR: 1958–59. See general note preceding 6803. Load is a model of amphibious DKW that actually floats.
  (A) Frame is 6511-2. G. Wilson Collection.

	60	100	150	200

  (B) Frame is 6424-11. L. Savage Collection.

	60	100	150	200

6808 MARINE CORPS TWO GUN TANK AND SEARCHLIGHT TRUCK CAR: 1958–59. See general note preceding 6803. Load is a tank with swiveling twin antiaircraft guns and a truck with swiveling searchlight.
  (A) Frame is 6511-2. J. Algozzini Collection.

	100	175	250	350

  (B) Frame is 6424-11. T. Klaassen Collection.

	100	175	250	350

6809 MARINE CORPS ANTIAIRCRAFT AND MEDICAL TRUCK CAR: 1958–59. See general note preceding 6803. Load is a truck with swiveling twin antiaircraft guns and a medical van.
  (A) Frame is 6511-2. J. Algozzini and F. Cordone Collections.

	85	155	210	300

  (B) Frame is 6424-11. T. Klaassen Collection.

	85	155	210	300

6810 FLATCAR WITH COOPER-JARRETT VAN: 1958. Red molded frame with heat-stamped "6810

Top: 6801 (B) boat car with blue-hull boat in usual shade of blue; 6801 (C) with teal blue hull—a shade of blue sometimes attributed to aging but found on other blue molded Lionel items of this era. Second: 6801 (B) with yellow-hull boat showing correct method of securing boat to cradle with single furnished elastic band. 214 plate girder bridge showing girder modified in 1956 for 6418 machinery car and also used on 6802. Third:

6802 (A) flatcar with two U.S. Steel girders that was supposed to show girder with molded "6418", but unfortunately the wrong one was selected; 6802 (A) identical car and load. Both show a 1955 girder, which is not correct for this 1958–1959 car. Bottom: 6803 (A) Marine Corps tank and sound truck car; 6804 (B) Marine Corps antiaircraft and sound truck car. R. Shanfeld and R. Gladsen Collections.

	Gd	VG	Ex	LN

LIONEL" in white serif letters. AAR trucks with two operating couplers riveted directly to frame. Load is a white trailer van with Cooper-Jarrett signs. Signs have black background with bright printing and a light or dark copper arrow with black printing. See sidebar on Lionel's trailer vans in this chapter.

(A) Frame mold is 6511-2. K. Coates Collection.

	18	**35**	**45**	**60**

(B) Frame mold is 6424-11. A. Stewart Collection.

	18	**35**	**45**	**60**

6812 TRACK MAINTENANCE CAR: 1959–61. Red molded 6511-2 or 6424-11 frame with heat-stamped "6812 LIONEL" in white serif letters. AAR trucks with two operating couplers riveted directly to frame. No load but car has a superstructure with three main parts: base, maintenance platform, and a metal elevating screw with plastic

crank handle. All three plastic parts were molded in five distinct colors: black, gray, dark yellow, lemon yellow, and cream. Since the parts are interchangeable, there are forty-five possible different combinations. The variations below are those reliably reported and generally accepted as the only ways these cars were produced. Crank handle color almost always matches platform color. When new, a small manila envelope labeled "PART No. 6812-40" was included. It contained one of the two-man crew and two connecting wires. The second 3562-62 crew member came mounted on the base. A T-shaped projection on the platform retained the envelope's blue molded man. Both figures had painted hands and face. Although not documented, it appears any superstructure color could appear on either frame. If not, it could easily be made, so no frame mold numbers are mentioned in the listings. Turning the crank raises or lowers the platform. A rib prevents rotation of the platform.

	Gd	VG	Ex	LN

Continuous counterclockwise rotation of the crank raises the platform until it can be removed. Platform rails are very fragile, as is the crank handle.

Note: Watch for broken railings and reproduction figures, platform, and crank. Intact original parts are required for Excellent or better price.

(A) Matching cream superstructure parts, generally considered hardest to find variation. J. Sattler Collection.

45   100   175   250

(B) Matching dark yellow superstructure parts. J. Algozzini Collection. **30   70   125   150**

(C) Matching lemon yellow superstructure parts. P. Iurilli Collection. **18   55   90   125**

(D) Matching black superstructure parts. T. Klaassen Collection. **18   55   90   125**

(E) Matching gray superstructure parts. R. Shanfeld Collection. **18   55   90   125**

(F) Black base, gray platform and crank handle. J. Algozzini Collection. **18   55   90   125**

	Gd	VG	Ex	LN

(G) Gray base, black platform and crank handle. J. Sattler Collection. **18   55   90   125**

6816 FLATCAR WITH ALLIS CHALMERS TRACTOR DOZER: 1959–60. Red or black molded frame with heat-stamped "6816 LIONEL" in white serif letters. AAR trucks with two operating couplers riveted directly to frame. Load is an orange molded model of an Allis Chalmers bulldozer retained with a 6418-9 elastic band. There are six variations of the load as follows:

(1) All plastic pieces molded in dark orange, heat-stamped "ALLIS CHALMERS" in white on seat back, only "TORQUE CONVERTER" emblem heat-stamped on seat sides in black, raised surface of "ALLIS CHALMERS" hood lettering heat-stamped in black, longer rear hitch with three open holes.

(2) Same, except no heat-stamp on hood letters.

(3) Same as (2), except "HD 16 DIESEL" added in black above torque converter emblem on seat sides.

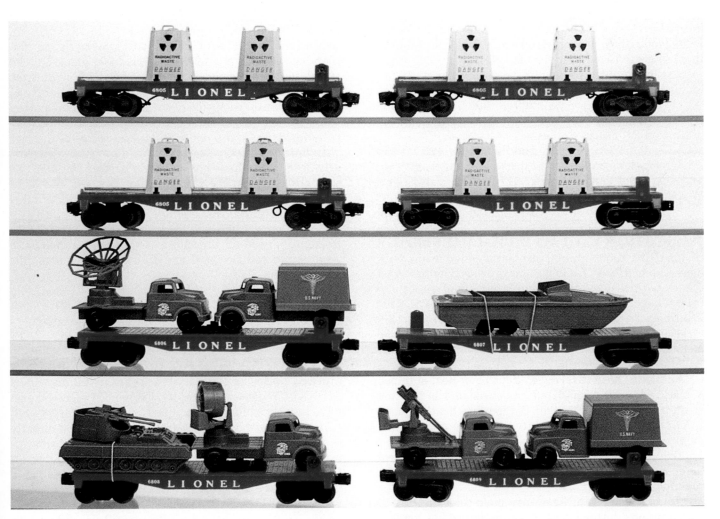

Top: 6805 (A) Atomic Energy disposal car with light gray–painted canisters; 6805 (B) with yellowish cream–painted canisters. Second: 6805 (A) identical to car above it; an example of a fake 6805 made from a 6469 frame. Note absence of wiring and no rail stops molded into flatcar frame. Also note frame-rail extensions. (See intro-duction to 6500-series flatcars for details.) Third: 6806 (B) Marine Corps radar and medical truck car; 6807 (A) Marine Corps "duck" car. Bottom: 6808 (A) Marine Corps two gun tank and searchlight truck car; 6809 (A) Marine Corps antiaircraft and medical truck car. R. Shanfeld and R. Gladsen Collections.

	Gd	**VG**	**Ex**	**LN**

(4) Same as (3), except rear hitch shortened and holes filled in.

(5) Same as (4), except seat back lettering changed to black.

(6) Same as (5), except all plastic pieces molded in light "faded" orange color. This and version (1) are hardest to find.

Since the loads are easy to interchange, no specific version is assigned to a particular flatcar, although new versions of the black flat are often found with version (6) bulldozer, indicating that black was later production for the flatcar as well. Separate-sale packaging for the bulldozer was made for Allis Chalmers' promotional use in a unique striped box and for Lionel distribution in an Orange Picture box (*See Greenberg's Guide to Lionel Trains, 1945–1969, Volume VI: Accessories*). A very desirable and fragile collectible, this load demands close scrutiny prior to purchase. Watch for broken or repaired blade control hydraulic struts, exhaust stack, and air cleaner stack. Listings below include any of the bulldozers in versions (2), (3), (4), and (5). Add a substantial premium for versions (1) or (6) and for the original Perforated Picture box, depending on condition. A perfect original bulldozer is required for Like New price.

(A) Red molded 6511-2 frame with version (2), (3), (4), or (5) load. T. Klaassen Collection.

	200	**300**	**420**	**550**

(B) Red molded 6424-11 frame with version (2), (3), (4), or (5) load. M. Ocilka Collection.

	200	**320**	**420**	**550**

(C) Black molded 6424-11 frame with any load. Very scarce and not known with a 6511-2 mold in this color. Wirtz and M. Ocilka Collections.

	300	**750**	**1500**	**2500**

6817 FLATCAR WITH ALLIS CHALMERS MOTOR SCRAPER: 1959–60. Red or black molded frame with heat-stamped "6817 LIONEL" in white serif letters. AAR trucks with two operating couplers riveted directly to frame. Load is a darker orange molded model of an Allis Chalmers tractor and scraper retained with a 6418-9 elastic band. There are two basic versions of this load as follows:

(1) Early version with raised surface of "ALLIS CHALMERS" hood lettering on the tractor heat-stamped in black, wire frame simulated windshield and an inverted U-shape molded into the grill. Scraper has heat-stamped "ALLIS CHALMERS" in white along the main frame member on each side.

(2) All heat-stamped decoration removed, grill changed to remove inverted U-shape, and windshield deleted. Most common version.

Some variation in the orange mold color appears in both versions, but not nearly as pronounced as version (6) of the bulldozer.

Separate-sale packaging for the scraper was made for Allis Chalmers' promotional use in a unique striped box and for Lionel distribution in a plain white box with the

6817-100 number and Lionel data stamped only on the end flaps (See *Greenberg's Guide to Lionel Trains, 1945–1969, Volume VI: Accessories*). A very desirable and fragile collectable, this load demands close scrutiny prior to purchase. Watch for broken or repaired exhaust stack and tractor-to-scraper attach pin. On the scraper, look for missing or broken hydraulic cylinders linking the frame to the hopper and missing interior pieces. Listings below include a version (2) scraper. Add a substantial premium for version (1) and for the original Perforated Picture box, depending on condition. A perfect original scraper is required for Like New price.

(A) Red molded 6511-2 frame with version (2) load. T. Klaassen Collection.

	200	**320**	**425**	**550**

(B) Red molded 6424-11 frame with version (2) load. J. Sattler Collection.

	200	**320**	**425**	**550**

(C) Black molded 6424-11 frame with any load. This color never reported with 6511-2 frame.

	500	**1250**	**2000**	**3500**

6818 FLATCAR WITH TRANSFORMER: 1958. Red molded frame with heat-stamped "6818 LIONEL" in white serif letters. AAR trucks with two operating couplers riveted directly to frame. Load is a black molded simulated transformer, same as used on 6518 with three exceptions. First, Lionel changed the mold slightly to add two nibs on each side of the inner base. This helped align the transformer to the same black molded axle retainer used on the 6803, 6804, etc. series of flatcars with military vehicle loads. This retainer had been cleverly designed to have not only axle holders but also two side clips to grip the transformer. Second, the 6518 number on the lower plaque became 6818. Here, Lionel missed a potential cost savings, since 6818 appears on both the flatcar frame and the load. Third, the two square brass nuts used for attaching the transformer to 6518 were eliminated. See 2461 and 6518 for additional details and cautions.

(A) Frame mold is 6511-2. J. Sattler Collection.

	25	**45**	**60**	**75**

(B) Frame mold is 6424-11. R. LaVoie Collection.

	25	**45**	**60**	**75**

6819 FLATCAR WITH HELICOPTER: 1959–60. Red molded 6424-11 frame with heat-stamped "6819 LIONEL" in white serif letters. Frame 6511-2 could also have been used but no example has ever been reported. AAR trucks with two operating couplers riveted directly to frame. Load is Type III or IV nonoperating helicopter secured with a 6418-9 elastic band (see sidebar on Lionel helicopters).

(A) Darker red molded 6424-11 frame with either load version. T. Klaassen Collection.

	25	**50**	**70**	**95**

(B) Lighter red molded 6424-11 frame with frame rail extensions and either load version. See introduction to 6511-series flatcars for frame mold variations. T. Klaassen Collection.

	25	**50**	**70**	**95**

Top: 6810 (B) flatcar with Cooper-Jarrett van shown with a Type VIII van with CJ (Cooper-Jarrett) sign (4). See sidebar on Lionel trailer vans for details. Top right, 6812 (D) track maintenance car with matching components except crank handle. Second: 6812 (B) and 6812 (C) except nonmatching crank handle. Third: 6812 (E)

and 6812 (A). Bottom: 6816 (C) flatcar with Allis Chalmers tractor dozer shown with dozer variation (6). Note missing hydraulic control struts to blade, a common problem with these fragile models. To right, 6816 (A) shown with dozer variation (E) with perfect struts. R. Shanfeld Collection.

	Gd	VG	Ex	LN

6820 AERIAL MISSILE TRANSPORT CAR: 1960–61. Usually black molded 6424-11 frame, always with center rail extensions, painted semigloss medium blue. See introduction to 6511-series flatcars for details on center rail extensions. Heat-stamped "6820 LIONEL" in white serif letters. AAR trucks with operating couplers riveted directly to frame. Load is a Type VI helicopter with two missiles attached (see sidebar on Lionel helicopters). Came unboxed with set 1633 in 1960 and component boxed as a separate-sale item. Original intact helicopter with correct missiles and tail cones must be present for Like New price. Add a significant premium for the original Perforated Picture box, depending on condition. J. Bratspis Collection.

	80	**150**	**255**	**360**

6821 FLATCAR WITH CRATES: 1959–60. Red molded frame with heat-stamped "6821 LIONEL" in white serif letters. AAR trucks with two operating couplers riveted directly to frame. Load is a tan molded simulated cargo piece 8" long, secured to flatcar by a 6418-9 elastic band. Load is the superstructure from 3444 animated gondola, except there is no heat-stamped lettering, and the holes for the on-off switch and mounting screws have been filled in. Note that a 4½" portion of this structure was used as a load for a Lionel HO gondola and is not a correct load for 6821.

(A) Frame mold is 6511-2. C. Rohlfing and T. Klaassen Collections. | **20** | **28** | **35** | **45**

(B) Frame mold is 6424-11. D. Alcorn and M. Ocilka Collections. | **20** | **28** | **35** | **45**

Top: *6817 (A) flatcar with Allis Chalmers motor scraper shown with scraper variation (2); 6818 (A) flatcar with transformer. Second: 6819 (A) flatcar with helicopter shown with Type IV nonoperating helicopter (see sidebar on Lionel helicopter types for details); 6820 aerial missile transport car. Third: 6821 (A) flatcar with crates; 6823 (B) flatcar with I.R.B.M. missiles. Compare missile* rack positions on this and following example. Missing fourteenth stake hole on 6424-11 mold affected missile packaging on some variations. Bottom: *6823 (A) showing normal missile rack placement; 6826 flatcar with Christmas trees. Note use of both stakes and an elastic band to retain load. Probably at least the stakes were eliminated for 1960 production. R. Shanfeld Collection.*

6823 FLATCAR WITH I.R.B.M. MISSILES: 1959–60. Red molded frame with heat-stamped "6823 LIONEL" in white serif letters. AAR trucks with two operating couplers riveted directly to frame. Load is two 6650-80 two-section missiles, each secured to a 6801-64 gray molded cradle by a 6418-9 elastic band (see 6650 listing). All examples reported have both missiles in matching colors: all white, red over white, or white over red. An all-red missile is easily made, but has never been reliably reported as original. Cradle is same as that on 6801 boat car and is secured to flatcar frame by pressing into stake holes. Two cradles are required for 6823; since the stake hole by brakestand was never put into 6424-11 mold, there was a problem when frames from this mold were used. Lionel solved it by cutting off the "leg" of the cradle that would go into the missing hole, so the cradle is retained in only three places.

Note: Watch for reproduction missiles and cradles. All original parts are required for Like New price.

	Gd	VG	Ex	LN
(A) Frame mold is 6511-2. K. Koehler Collection.				
	25	45	60	75
(B) Frame mold is 6424-11. T. Klaassen Collection.				
	25	45	60	75

6825 FLATCAR WITH ARCH TRESTLE BRIDGE: 1959–62. Red molded frame with heat-stamped car number and "LIONEL" in white serif letters. AAR trucks with two operating couplers riveted directly to frame. Load is a gray or black molded plastic trestle bridge from Lionel's HO line, secured to the flatcar by a 6418-9 elastic band. Bridge has been reproduced without usual 0110-18 part number and Lionel data molded in raised letters on the underside.

(A) Frame mold is 6511-2 with car number left of "LIONEL". Either color bridge. D. Alcorn Collection.

15 30 50 65

(B) Frame mold is 6424-11 with car number right of "LIONEL". Either color bridge. G. Halverson, R.

Top: 6825 (A) flatcar with arch trestle bridge with black bridge from Lionel's HO line; 6825 (C) with same bridge in gray.

	Gd	VG	Ex	LN

Gluckman, F. Cordone, and F. Cieri Collections.

| | 15 | 30 | 50 | 65 |

(C) Same as (B), except car number corrected to left of "LIONEL". T. Klaassen Collection.

| | 15 | 30 | 50 | 65 |

6826 FLATCAR WITH CHRISTMAS TREES: 1959–60. Red molded 6511-2 frame with heat-stamped "6823 LIONEL" in white serif letters. AAR trucks with two operating couplers riveted directly to frame. There have been no reports of a 6424-11 frame, which could have been used. Load is a small bundle of simulated Christmas trees that deteriorate easily and usually are missing altogether. These reportedly came from weeds growing near the Lionel factory in New Jersey. Reproductions allegedly have been harvested from the same source. According to the Lionel Service Manual, these trees were held on the flatcar by four standard metal stakes, but examples have been observed with a 6418-9 elastic band. Perhaps they came both ways, as the 1959 catalog shows both stakes and bands, while the sole picture in the 1960 catalog (set 1635WS) shows no retainer at all! Reader reports of brand-new 6826s are requested.

| | 50 | 90 | 145 | 200 |

6827 HARNISCHFEGER POWER SHOVEL CAR: 1960–63. Black molded 6424-11 frame with lower rail extensions (see introduction to 6511-series flatcars). Heat-stamped "6827 LIONEL" in white serif letters. AAR trucks with two operating couplers riveted directly to frame. Load is a very detailed black and yellow molded plastic model of a P&H power shovel that came new as a kit. A special box in P&H, rather than Lionel, colors contained the kit, which was packaged with the flatcar in a larger Orange Picture box. For 1960 only, kit was cataloged for separate sale as 6827-100. This and the companion 6828 crane are among Lionel's most fragile loads. Unless this item is still new in the box, pieces are almost certain to be missing, so brand-new, unassembled kits warrant a substantial premium.

Note: Originally came with booklet, "P & H: The Story of a Trademark," and an unusual undated 6827-113 instruction sheet on white paper with a large yellow image of the power shovel overprinted with usual black ink. An illustration showing assembly of the model has the cab printed in yellow as well. On these sheets, Lionel's Service Department has a Chestnut Street address. Later production omits the booklet and the yellow printing on the instruction

sheet, and shows the service department on Hoffman Place. Reproductions of this intricate model have not yet appeared, although selected reproduction parts are available.

(A) Cab of model molded in light yellow. R. Davis Collection.

| | 65 | 100 | 140 | 200 |

(B) Cab of model molded in distinctly darker yellow. H. Klump Collection.

| | 65 | 100 | 140 | 200 |

6828 HARNISCHFEGER MOBILE CONSTRUCTION CRANE CAR: 1960–63, 1966. Usually black molded 6424-11 frame with lower rail extensions (see introduction to 6511-series flatcars). Heat-stamped "6828 LIONEL" in white serif letters. AAR trucks with two operating couplers riveted directly to frame. Load is a very detailed black and yellow molded plastic model of a P&H construction crane that came new as a kit. Every part was unique except the 6560-13 hook. A special box in P&H, rather than Lionel, colors contained the kit, which was packaged with the flatcar in a larger Orange Picture box—except in 1966 when a Cellophane-front box took its place. For 1960 only, kit was cataloged for separate sale as 6828-100. This and the companion 6827 power shovel are among Lionel's most fragile loads. Unless it's still new in the box, pieces are almost certain to be missing, so brand-new, unassembled kits warrant a substantial premium.

See note under 6827.

(A) Cab of model molded in light yellow.

| | 80 | 130 | 180 | 240 |

(B) Cab of model molded in a distinctly darker yellow.

| | 90 | 140 | 190 | 250 |

(C) Extremely rare flatcar frame same as described except molded in red. 1966 vintage came new in a hard-to-find Cellophane-front box. Most 1966 examples in this packaging are on black flatcars. Either color load. R. Shanfeld Collection. **NRS**

6830 SUBMARINE CAR: 1960–61. Medium blue molded 6511-2 frame heat-stamped "6830 LIONEL" in white serif letters. AAR trucks with two operating couplers riveted directly to frame. Load is a factory assembled nonoperating submarine model molded in gray. Parts are same as 3830 except operating mechanism omitted. Heat-stamped on each side just below the conning tower is "U.S. NAVY 6830" in black sans-serif letters. Submarine is held to the flatcar by two wire retainers that anchor into the stake holes and slide into grooves along the base

Gd VG Ex LN

Gd VG Ex LN

of the model. The entire submarine and all its parts are available as reproductions. A few examples of this car have been found on red 6424-11 frames painted blue and heat-stamped with standard 6830 lettering. They are configured for 6805, including the rail end caps, but with only two stake holes instead of the 13 found on 6805. Since they lack stake holes for the wire retainers that hold the submarine, they are nonfunctional and were likely prototypes. **50 90 120 150**

6844 MISSILE CARRYING CAR: 1959–60. Usually black molded 6424-11 frame heat-stamped "6844 LIONEL" in white serif lettering. AAR trucks with two operating couplers riveted directly to frame. Load is six white molded 44-40 missiles with a weight inside. Removable missiles slip onto pins molded into gray superstructure, which is riveted to frame.

Note: Pins tend to break because the missiles give plenty of leverage, so this part has been reproduced. Reproduction missiles also available and are slightly shorter than originals.

(A) Black molded frame without lower frame rail extensions (see introduction to Lionel 6511-series flatcars). M. Ocilka and I. D. Smith Collections.
20 40 60 85

(B) Black molded frame with lower frame rail extensions. **20 40 60 85**

(C) Rare red molded frame without lower frame rail extensions. Superstructure on this car is molded a creamy gray noticeably different than standard 6844s. Because of

this version's rarity, forgeries have been tried, but the heat-stamped number is difficult to align properly. Competent appraisal is recommended prior to purchase. G. Halverson Collection. **300 500 650 1000**

Note: This concludes the 6511 series listings.

6518 TRANSFORMER CAR: 1956–58. Frame is identical to 6418 (F), except two holes are drilled for screws to retain the transformer. Load is a transformer as described for 2461, except this one is molded black rather than painted and two plaques have been added to each side. "6518" is heat-stamped in white on the lower plaque while "LIONEL / TRANSFORMER / CAR" appears on the upper. Insulators are a more translucent white than used on 2461 (see 2461 and 6418 for more details and cautions).

(A) As described above. **45 80 115 120**

(B) Same but frame slightly darker semigloss gray instead of the usual flat gray. A. Eggenberger Collection. **45 80 115 150**

6519 ALLIS CHALMERS CAR: 1958–61. New for 1958 with a unique orange molded "hump-up" frame but no molded part number. At each end is a metal brakestand riveted to a slender plastic projection from the frame. This mounting proved to be very fragile, and the brake wheels were finally removed for later uses of this frame. However, all 6519s have them, and more often than not, at least one is broken. Blue heat-stamped lettering and the Allis Chalmers emblem appear on each side rail. AAR

Top: 6828 (C) Harnischfeger mobile construction crane car showing separate box for crane and envelope of small parts. Boxed crane and flatcar were packaged in a larger conventional Lionel box. 6828 (A) showing fully assembled crane. Bottom: 6827 (B) Harnischfeger power shovel car as it was packaged in the box shown at rear. 6827 (A) showing fully assembled power shovel. As with 6828, the boxed shovel and flatcar were packaged in a larger conventional Lionel box. R. Shanfeld, H. Klump, and R. Gladsen Collections.

	Gd	VG	Ex	LN

trucks with operating couplers are riveted directly to the frame. Load is a gray molded model of what the 1958 catalog calls a "condenser and heat exchanger." It is molded in two halves that glue together. One tab at the center on each side locks the load to the frame. Thin wire "tie downs" at each end hook into the condenser, with the ends resting in holes at the edge of the frame.

Note: Carefully examine the underside where the brakestands rivet on for signs of cracking. Like New or better requires both brakestands and no sign of cracking. Store and transport this car carefully, since any force applied to the long lever arm of either brakestand will make short work of the mounting tab.

(A) Darker orange molded frame, darker blue lettering. R. Gluckman Collection.

	35	60	75	100

(B) Medium orange molded frame, lighter blue lettering. R. Gluckman Collection.

	35	60	75	100

(C) Distinctly different "faded" orange base (similar to 6119-25 work caboose cab). Most difficult version to find. T. Klaassen Collection.   **40   80   110   150**

6544 MISSILE FIRING CAR: 1960–64. Same frame as 6519 but molded in blue (see 6519 for caution on brakestands). Heat-stamped side rail lettering in white. AAR trucks with two operating couplers riveted directly to frame. Gray molded superstructure with four rocket-launching positions controlled sequentially by a reddish molded thumb wheel. Heat-stamped graphics in black or white on simulated control panel. This superstructure was used on 448 Missile Firing Range Set, but there were no graphics on that control panel. This is not correct for 6544. Superstructure just snaps on and off by tabs under the frame rails and is easy to switch. Load is four small weighted 44-40 rockets packaged in a manila envelope. There is room on the superstructure for four rockets stored on end, with four more in launch position, though only four were furnished with the car. Reproduction rockets are readily available, but are slightly shorter than originals.

Note: Car came new in a Perforated Picture box so short that the trucks had to be turned with their couplers in to fit. This left the brake wheels right against the box end, so even brand-new pieces can have these fragile parts cracked or broken off. An example with perfect brakestands is quite rare and commands a substantial premium. Like New requires both brakestands, with no evidence of cracked or repaired mounting tabs.

(A) Control panel has heat-stamped graphics in white. R. Shanfeld Collection.   **45   80   110   170**

(B) Control panel has heat-stamped graphics in black. Not rare but much harder to find than (A). R. Shanfeld Collection.   **175   300   415   600**

6561 CABLE CAR: 1953–56. Same die-cast depressed-center frame built for 2461 transformer car with a slight modification to adapt it for holding two Lionel cable reels. Gray-painted frame (shades vary slightly) with rubber-stamped "6561 LIONEL LINES 6561" in black serif letters on the side rails. Bar-end trucks with operating couplers attach to truck-mounting plates as with 2461. Load is two molded plastic reels wound with a single layer of .072"-diameter aluminum wire. Frame modified from 2461 by adding a hole and slot in the hatch cover detail at each end of the load. These slots retain eyelets crimped on each end of an elastic cord that stretches over the reels to hold them in place. This cord has been reproduced. Only orange or gray molded reels with the aluminum wire are a correct original load, although any color Lionel or MPC cable reel will fit (G. Wilson and B. Myles comments).

Top: 6830 submarine car with nonoperating submarine and unnumbered (factory error) 6844 missile carrying car. Bottom: Black 6844 (A) missile carrying car and red 6844 (B) missile carrying car. R. Shanfeld Collection.

6544 (A) missile firing car with white-lettered console and 6544 (B) with black-lettered console. R. Shanfeld Collection.

6561 (A) cable car with gray reels and 6561 (C) cable car with light orange reels. R. Shanfeld Collection.

	Gd	VG	Ex	LN

(A) Light orange molded plastic reels, more common version. 20 45 65 90

(B) Darker orange molded plastic reels. J. Sattler Collection. 20 45 65 90

(C) Gray molded plastic reels, only slightly harder to find than orange. J. Sattler Collection. 20 45 75 100

UNNUMBERED FLATCARS

(A) Gray molded 1877-3 frame completely undecorated with no truss rod, same as 6401. AAR trucks with one fixed and one operating coupler riveted directly to frame. Load is a moss green molded military tank with matching one-piece molded wheel and axle sets. Load secured to flatcar by an elastic band. A well known component of Sears Military Set 9820 from 1964 (see *Greenberg's Guide to Lionel Trains, Volume IV: Uncatalogued Sets*). Payton Products supplied the model tank; the company sold the same item and many others through dime stores and other toy outlets of the day. Besides the tank, Lionel bought the toy soldiers for the Sears and other sets, along with a jeep and cannon for another uncataloged set, from Payton. Reproduction tanks, some apparently made from the original mold, are prevalent but the color is olive drab or mottled, not the authentic moss green. Originals have the letter "Q" molded inside the turret, on the tank underside, or both as do original Payton olive drab versions. The swivel turret just snaps on and can be removed with care. Original tank in the proper moss green is the only element of value. **NRS**

(B) Same as (A), but load is a moss green molded jeep pulling a matching cannon. Same source as discussed in (A). Secured to flatcar by a unique elastic band made of the same material yet several times longer than 6418-9. Came as a component of uncataloged set 19434 and probably others. Color is the key to originality, and originality is the only element of value. **NRS**

(C) Same as (A), but load is unusual color gray-bumper automobile model. See 6404. The usual red and yellow cars probably came with cataloged sets, while unusual colors, such as chocolate brown and kelly green, are known components of low-budget uncataloged sets. An original scarce color automobile is the only element of value. **NRS**

(D) Brownish maroon molded frame, otherwise same as 6401 but with two fixed couplers or one fixed and one operating coupler, was also used in uncataloged sets. May have had no load or carried an empty cable reel or a gray-bumper automobile of any color. This color frame never reliably reported with a military load. 5 10 15 20

10-inch Frames Molded in Various Colors

(E) Red molded 6511-2 frame lettered only "LIONEL" in white. AAR trucks with one fixed and one operating coupler. See 6407 and 6408.

(F) Same as (E), but two fixed couplers. See 6409-25.

(G) Red molded 6511-2 frame lettered only "LIONEL" in white. Arch-bar trucks with two fixed couplers, no brake wheel. See 3510.

6801 (B) with uncataloged jeep and cannon that came with uncataloged set 19434 shown above it. Huge elastic band shown was used to hold both pieces to flatcar. 6801 (A) with military tank from Sears 9820 Military Train Set shown above it. Note correct moss

green color of both loads. These items, as well as the military figures also included in both sets, were made for Lionel by Payton Plastics, which sold the same toys and many others molded in olive drab. An example of their packaging is shown in the center.

(H) Red molded 6511-2 frame lettered only "LIONEL" in white. AAR trucks with two operating couplers. See 6501.

(I) Black molded 6511-2 frame lettered only "LIONEL" in white. Arch-bar trucks with two fixed couplers, no brake wheel. See 6502.

(J) Black molded 6511-2 frame lettered only "LIONEL" in white. AAR trucks with two operating couplers. See 6500.

(K) Blue molded 6511-2 frame with no lettering at all. AAR or arch-bar trucks with two fixed couplers. No brake wheel. See 6502.

8

GONDOLAS

Introduction by Roger Carp

The gondolas cataloged during the postwar era are generally among the simplest models Lionel produced. And why not? After all, these freight cars amount to little more than trays on wheels! Besides, the children using the O and O27 gauge gondolas didn't need much to prod their imaginations on how to enjoy them. They instinctively knew that the cars could be filled with almost anything at hand: blocks, marbles, stones, Lincoln Logs, plastic vehicles, and sticks. Simple models loaded with play value definitely pleased Lionel's management, and they made sure virtually every freight outfit included a gondola.

Collectors who take a close look at gondolas discover that the story is a bit more complex. Models did change over the years, as new frames were developed and features were added or deleted. From the earliest postwar model evolved two families of gondolas, differentiated by their length. And the longer of them eventually became the basis of operating gondolas with some fascinating and humorous animated features. For Lionel enthusiasts, therefore, the gondola proves to be far more interesting and desirable than many initially think.

The history of this freight car began at the end of World War II, as Lionel's engineering and sales staffs scrambled to bring out trains for the upcoming holiday season. Since many of the items released in 1945 represented modified prewar models, the company might logically have updated one of the O or O27 gauge gondolas available through 1942. The possible choices weren't unsatisfactory either. The 2812 and 2812X were attractively painted, stamped sheet-metal cars, as was the slightly smaller 2652. All, however, looked like toys and seemed old-fashioned when viewed alongside the scale detailed freight cars developed for the 700 series that was cataloged from 1940 to 1942. So there was good reason not to revive one of the prewar gondolas.

Responding to the demand for a train set, engineers managed to produce a brand-new gondola, the 2452. How they were able to finish this project so rapidly can't be determined. Maybe plans to design a scale gondola that

would fit with the 716 hopper, for example, were under way before war forced Lionel to curtail them. To be sure, the new gondola lacked the size and intricate detail of the 700-series cars. It measured only 8 inches long, whereas the 714 boxcar and 716 hopper were 10½ inches long. Compared to those classic models, it unquestionably fell short.

All the same, the 2452 made an impressive addition to the line. Above all, it showed how successfully Lionel could use the latest injection-molding technology. Its plastic body, mounted on a metal frame with steps, had integrally molded grab irons and ribs. Painted black, the gondola had graphics for the Pennsylvania Railroad and assorted car data heat-stamped in white. The earliest versions came packed with a set of small barrels that opened. Without a doubt, the new model had the most realistic appearance of any Lionel gondola manufactured until that time and fit in with the other freight cars available right after the war.

The 8-inch gondola underwent various changes, major and minor, between 1946 and 1949. First, a version without brake wheels and barrels entered the line and lasted through 1947. Also in 1946, the frame was altered somewhat for the 4452. That gondola had to be modified to accommodate the Electronic Control unit necessary for it to function as part of the 4109WS Electronic Control Set. Then in 1948, a model with Lionel's new magnetic couplers made its debut as the 6452. It also came without brake wheels or barrels.

That same year witnessed the arrival of the first Scout gondola, the 1002. Generally speaking, it came with a black or blue unpainted plastic body lettered for Lionel. Scarce variations boasted silver, yellow, or red bodies. This short gondola gained fame in 1950, when numbers of them were shipped to dealers as part of a special display demonstrating the virtues of Magnetraction. A locomotive pulled fourteen gondolas and a caboose around a layout and into a large tunnel, where they disappeared. Unknown to the crowds watching, the train descended into a loop of track before reappearing at the other end of the tunnel. This trick, as retailers never hesitated to point out, wouldn't have been possible without the power of Magnetraction to pull long trains.

Having relegated the 8-inch gondola to the bottom of the line in 1948, Lionel pressed its engineering staff to come out with a high-quality model for the upper end. They answered with an outstanding gondola that, at 9⁹⁄₁₆ inches in length, certainly wouldn't be mistaken for the 2452 or its progeny. The 6462 instantly became a vital element of the product line, being cataloged through 1958 and appearing in the vast majority of freight outfits being offered. When introduced, it featured a plastic body on a metal frame with steps at the four corners and a brake wheel on each side. Designers initially specified that the body be painted black with New York Central Railroad graphics and car data heat-stamped in white. A red-painted version made its debut in 1950. Six unstained wood drums came with these early versions, although before many years passed smaller ones stained a dark brown were substituted.

Lionel must have been satisfied with the 6462 because it was cataloged in many sets and advertised as a separate-sale item. Obvious as well as subtle changes took place during the model's years of production. For example, the steps and brake wheels were removed to lower costs. Similarly, factory workers stopped painting the black and red cars sometime in the mid-1950s. And drums weren't included in models sold with less-expensive sets. Even though many variations have been observed, none is particularly valuable, which explains why most collectors overlook the 6462.

To entice operators into buying more of these cars, Lionel needed to diversify them. The company could have increased the number of road names on the 6462, but this would have required new heat-stamps. Simpler and faster was offering the gondola in more colors. A green-painted version appeared in 1954, and a pink one with blue lettering brightened up the pastel 1587S Girls' Set three years later. But these two variations didn't exhaust Lionel's efforts. One-of-a-kind paint samples indicate that it also considered yellow, mint green, bright blue, coral, turquoise, and gray.

Another technique for broadening the appeal of gondolas involved animation. Here, the wood drums often packed with the gondolas proved important. First, in 1952, came the 362 barrel loader, which used vibration to tip over small drums and then send them up a ramp. At the top, they rolled into a waiting gondola. Was there a way barrels could be unloaded from a freight car? Engineers sat down at their drawing boards and devised the 3562 Atchison, Topeka & Santa Fe barrel car for the 1954 line. This operating gondola depended on remote control to send drums vibrating up a metal trough to the end of the car, where a rubber figure appeared to push them into a plastic bin. All variations of the 3562 used a new body style that differed in noticeable ways from the 6462s.

The notion of modifying a long gondola to work with an operating accessory also led to the introduction of the 6342 New York Central gondola in 1956. The ramp installed in this car enabled the metal pipes dropped into it by the 342 culvert loader to roll to the opposite end.

The 6342 was an integral part of that accessory's operation and so was packed with it rather than being offered for separate sale. Also, when the 345 culvert unloading station came out in 1957, a 6342 gondola was included with it.

In 1956, Lionel came up with a twist on its red New York Central gondola. Unpainted black and red cars were given a new number (6562) and load. Instead of wood drums they transported four red plastic canisters. The same new load was used with the latest short gondola, the 6112, which replaced the 6012.

For 1957, the whimsical 3444 animated cop and hobo car headlined. Inside a red gondola body (lettered for the Erie Railroad), engineers installed a continuous band of 16mm film looped around a pair of spools. To the film they attached the figures of a railroad police officer and a tramp. A motor concealed beneath some plastic crates in the gondola powered sprockets on the spools. Flicking a switch on the car got the film moving, so the cop appeared to chase the hobo. Kids and their parents loved the animation and marveled at the ingenuity of Lionel's designers.

The last major changes to the postwar gondola appeared in 1959. Lionel brought out its final long models. Gone was the metal frame; trucks were riveted directly to the body. Consumers chose between a black unpainted New York Central car with three cable reels (the 6062) or a blue one with three canisters (the 6162). A variation of the latter featured an unpainted yellow body and three white or red canisters. Lettered for the Alaska Railroad, it was part of set 1611, marking Alaska's entrance into the Union.

Also in 1959, Lionel eliminated the metal frame on its short model and added half an inch to its body. The unpainted 6042, available in black or blue plastic lettered in white for Lionel, had a detailed undercarriage and molded-on brake wheel. It came with two red or white canisters, though one version had a cable reel.

The end of the postwar era saw Lionel's gondolas fade into obscurity. The 6142 superseded the 6042 in 1963, and black, blue, and green versions came with a pair of canisters or cable reels. These gondolas appeared in many uncataloged outfits, as did some unpainted blue and green versions that had no lettering of any kind. In particular, an unmarked olive drab 8½-inch–long gondola has become highly collectible. Even when deprived of decoration and detail, a Lionel car can be a prize.

1002 LIONEL: 1948–52. Short gondola; typically unpainted body with white heat-stamped lettering. There are two categories of the 1002. The first was an exclusive component of Scout sets; it came with Scout trucks and couplers and was never offered for separate sale.

(A) Unpainted blue body (shades vary).

| | 6 | 9 | 12 | 15 |

(B) Unpainted black body.

| | 5 | 7 | 10 | 12 |

In 1950 Lionel produced a special train and display for dealers to allow them to demonstrate the pulling power

All postwar gondolas can be designated as either short (8 inches long) or long (9⁹/₁₆ inches). Top: 1002 (C) Lionel and 1002 (A) Lionel (erroneously shown with magnetic couplers). Second: 1002 (E) Lionel and 1002 (D) Lionel. Third: 6002 NYC (erroneously shown with a barrel load) and 6162-60 Alaska (erroneously shown with one extra red canister). Fourth: 6462 (B) NYC and red 6462 (D) NYC. Bottom: Red 6462 (A) NYC and green 6462 (A) NYC. The gondola on the bottom left was earliest production, with three lines of weight data and "NEW 2-49"; it included steps at the four corners and brake wheels. E. Dougherty Collection.

	Gd	VG	Ex	LN

of Magnetraction. The train had an engine with Magnetraction (either a 2035 or a 2036), fourteen gondolas, and a caboose. These gondolas had Scout trucks but typical magnetic couplers; most were uniquely painted red, silver, or yellow. The display came with a special feature that allowed the entire train to disappear into a 2-foot tunnel. After the holiday season, many stores sold their gondolas separately. The following variations result from this display.

(C) Red-painted body with white heat-stamped lettering.

	110	230	350	500

(D) Silver-painted body with black heat-stamped lettering.

	100	210	325	450

(E) Yellow-painted body with black heat-stamped lettering.

	110	225	340	475

2452 PENNSYLVANIA: 1945–47. Short gondola; black-painted body with white heat-stamped lettering; "PENNSYLVANIA" overscored by line on top, also numbered "347000"; stylized PRR logo in circle; four lines of technical data at far right, with "G27" in last line. Metal underframe with steps at the four corners; body held to frame by four fillister-head screws; typically with brake wheels; staple-end trucks with coil couplers. Earliest production included small wooden barrels that opened, but most examples came without any load. All 1945–46 production had Type Ia body mold; 1947 examples had Type Ib body mold. Early production has "2452" rubber-stamped on frame.

(A) Type Ia body, small "G27".

	8	13	18	25

(B) Type Ib body, small "G27".

	8	13	18	25

(C) Type Ib body, large "G27".

	8	13	18	25

2452X PENNSYLVANIA: 1946–47. See 2452 listing. This short gondola was an O27 gauge set component that did *not* include brake wheels or come with barrels. "2452X" rubber-stamped on frame.

2452 (A) Pennsylvania gondola. Observe the brake wheel at upper right and the steps at lower corners.

SHORT GONDOLA BODY MOLDS

Type Ia. Rectangular opening approximately 2 inches by 1 inch in center of floor of body; does not go through metal frame; body fastened to frame by large flathead slotted screws. The opening was designed to fit a frame supporting the Electronic Control unit found in 4452.

Type Ib. Round opening approximately 1 inch in diameter in center of floor of body; does not go through metal frame; body fastened to frame by smaller round-head slotted screws.

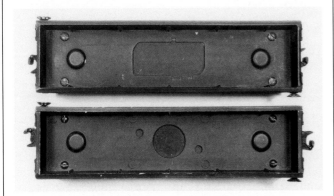

Shown are the Type Ia (top) and Type Ib (bottom) body molds. Note the two extra holes added to the Type Ib mold and the different sizes of screws fastening the body to the frame.

	Gd	VG	Ex	LN
(A) Type Ia body, small "G27".				
	5	10	20	25
(B) Type Ib body, small "G27".				
	5	8	10	15
(C) Type Ib body, large "G27".				
	5	8	10	15

3444 ERIE: 1957–59. Long animated gondola; unpainted red Type IIa body with white heat-stamped lettering; various shades of tan-colored crates conceal the operating mechanism; bar-end trucks.

Note: The cop and hobo figures were attached by U-shaped brackets to a continuous loop of 16mm film; the film encircled two spools with sprockets that were powered by a vibrator motor. A manual on-off lever projected through the molded plastic crates.

30	45	60	90

The 3562 Gondolas

Lionel introduced the 3562 operating barrel car in 1954. All models came with a metal unloading trough and an unloading bracket to which was attached an upright rubberized figure. Also included were a box of six brown-strained barrels, an unloading bin, and a controller.

In 1955 a small plastic tab was added to the mold to lock the unloading bracket when the car was not in the operating mode. Earlier models lacking the bracket tab tended to randomly dump the barrels trackside during normal operation of the train set.

3562-1 A. T. & S. F.: 1954. Long operating barrel car; black-painted body with white heat-stamped lettering; actually numbered "35621"; "NEW 5-54"; all examples without bracket tab; bar-end trucks.

(A) Body with yellow trough that matches color of the 3656 operating stockyard.   **75   100   175   225**

(B) Body with black trough.

75	100	175	225

3562-25 A. T. & S. F.: 1954. Long operating barrel car; gray-painted body with heat-stamped lettering; actually numbered "356225"; "NEW 5-54"; bar-end trucks. Although not cataloged, a frequent component of 1955 sets.

(A) Body with red lettering (very scarce); no bracket tab.   **125   225   325   525**

(B) Body with royal blue lettering; no bracket tab.

20	40	55	70

(C) Body with dark blue lettering; no bracket tab.

20	40	55	70

(D) Body with dark blue lettering; bracket tab.

20	40	55	70

Look carefully at the lettering to the right of the PRR Keystone logo on each of these 2452 gondolas. The last line of car data in the top example has a small "G27", while the lower car has a large "G27". See page 229.

Underside of the 2452X gondola, showing rubber-stamped "2452X".

3444 Erie animated gondola.

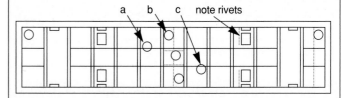

LONG GONDOLA BODY MOLDS

Chart redesigned by Harold J. Lovelock

Type I. Note ejector pin marks labeled a, b, and c.

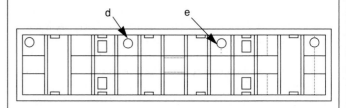

Type IIa. Note different placement of ejector pin marks labeled d and e.

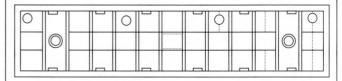

Type IIb. Trucks riveted directly to body; faint circular plug lines visible at the four points where former underframe retaining clips were located.

	Gd	VG	Ex	LN

3562-50 A. T. & S. F.: 1955–56. Long operating barrel car; yellow body with black heat-stamped lettering; actually numbered "356250"; "NEW 5-54"; bar-end trucks.

(A) Yellow-painted body; no bracket tab.	35	50	85	100
(B) Yellow-painted body; bracket tab.	35	50	85	100
(C) Unpainted yellow body; bracket tab.	20	40	55	65

3562-75 A. T. & S. F.: 1957–58. Long operating barrel car; unpainted orange body with black heat-stamped lettering; actually numbered "356275"; "NEW 5-54"; all examples with bracket tab; bar-end trucks.

	35	50	65	85

4452 PENNSYLVANIA: 1946–49. Short gondola. Special model that was included with the Electronic Control Set. Similar to 2452, but numbered "4452"; gray Electronic Control decal and Electronic Control receiver attached to underside of frame.

(A) Type Ia body.	40	75	100	125
(B) Type Ib body.	40	75	100	125

6002 NYC: 1950. Long gondola; unpainted black Type I body with white heat-stamped lettering; "N" in second panel; "6002" underlined; two-line weight data with "NEW 2-49"; came without barrel load; Scout trucks with magnetic couplers. See sidebar on New York Central gondola lettering.

	4	9	14	22

6012 LIONEL: 1951–56. Short gondola; unpainted black body with white heat-stamped lettering. Did not include brake wheels or load. All 1951 and early 1952 examples had staple-end trucks and magnetic couplers, replaced in 1952 by bar-end trucks and magnetic couplers.

	2	5	8	12

6032 LIONEL: 1952–54. Short gondola; unpainted black body with white heat-stamped lettering; did not include brake wheels or load. Scout trucks with magnetic couplers.

	2	4	6	8

6042 LIONEL: 1962–64. Introduced in 1959 advance catalog. Short gondola; unpainted body with white heat-stamped lettering. Arch-bar or AAR trucks, usually with two fixed couplers. Typical load (if any) was two unmarked canisters or cable reels.

Note: The 6042 model introduced a new short gondola body style (mold number 6112-86) with a detailed undercarriage and a molded brake wheel (also see 6142).

(A) Black body.	2	4	6	8

(B) Blue body. Cataloged in 1962–63 as 6042-75 with

Operating barrel cars. Top: 3562-1 (A) and 3562-1 (B). Middle: 3562-25 (A) with scarce red lettering and 3562 (B). Bottom: 3562-50 (C) and 3562-75.

4452 Pennsylvania gondola fitted with a receiver on the underside for use with the Electronic Control Set.

6012 Lionel gondola.

6032 Lionel gondola.

In 1959 Lionel introduced a new 8-inch gondola with a molded brake wheel and a detailed undercarriage identified with mold number 6112-86. Top: 6042 with two unmarked white canisters. Middle: Unstamped example designated 6042 (C). Bottom: 6142 with two unmarked red canisters.

	Gd	VG	Ex	LN

two cable reels, but the "-75" suffix does *not* appear on the car.

	2	4	6	8

(C) Cataloged in 1964 as an unstamped example in blue (shades vary); referred to as 6042-250.

	5	8	11	15

6042-75. See 6042 (B).
6042-250. See 6042 (C).

6062 N Y C: 1959–62, 1969. Long gondola; typically unpainted glossy black body with white heat-stamped lettering; "N" in third panel; "6062" underlined; typical three-line weight data; AAR trucks with operating couplers. Usual load was three orange cable reels.

(A) Type IIa unpainted body with "NEW 2-49". **Note:** The metal undercarriage was eliminated with the introduction of the 6062; however, this example is an exception that utilized "old" unfinished bodies and a metal undercarriage similar to 6462.

	15	20	35	50

(B) Type IIb black-painted body with "NEW 2-49".

	7	12	18	25

(C) Type IIb unpainted body without "NEW 2-49".

	7	12	18	25

(D) 1969 production. Same as (C), but one fixed and one operating coupler; truck types vary.

	7	12	18	25

6112 LIONEL: 1956–58. Short gondola; unpainted body with heat-stamped lettering; no brake wheels; 1956 production with bar-end trucks, replaced with AAR trucks for 1957 and future production; always with load of four red or white canisters with lettering. Component boxes with suffixes "-1", "-85", and "-135", but suffix does *not* appear on car.

(A) Black body with white lettering.

	3	5	7	9

(B) Blue body with white lettering.

	4	7	9	12

(C) White body with black lettering.

	10	18	25	35

6142 LIONEL: 1963–66, 1969. Short gondola; unpainted body with white heat-stamped lettering. Came in many shade variations, especially true of green models. The heat-stamped green examples came in two shades, and so did unstamped green bodies; one shade was the scarce bright translucent green. Various AAR and Arch-bar truck combinations, usually with one fixed and one operating coupler. Typical load was two white or red unmarked canisters. Cataloged with various suffixes as described below. **Note:** All examples came with a detailed undercarriage and molded brake wheel (mold number 6112-86). See 6042.

(A) Black body; cataloged as 6142 and listed in the Lionel Service Manual as 6142-25.

	3	5	7	9

(B) Unstamped common green body; listed in Lionel Service Manual as 6142-50 without load.

	7	10	14	20

NEW YORK CENTRAL GONDOLA LETTERING AND DATA STAMPING

by Paul V. Ambrose

All New York Central gondolas are long (9⁹⁄₁₆-inch) models. By and large, they have two lettering schemes. The first, used from 1949 to mid-1954, has small serif-lettered "N Y C", with the "N" in the second panel. This format (applicable only to 6002 and 6462) has three variations (listed chronologically):

Three lines of weight data and "NEW 2-49"
Two lines of weight data and "NEW 2-49"
Two lines of weight data *without* "NEW 2-49".

Sometime in mid-1954 a new heat-stamp tool was designed. This *later* format has large sans-serif–lettered "N Y C", with a line above each letter (overscored) and the "N" in the third panel. Except for the number, the lettering layout on *all* post-1954 long NYC gondolas is the same. Similar models are the mid-1954 and later versions of 6462, 6062, 6162, 6342, and 6562. The *late* format has two variations:

Three lines of weight data and "NEW 2-49"
Three lines of weight data *without* "NEW 2-49".

All NYC gondolas (regardless of lettering scheme or stock number) came with one of the following data formats:

Three lines of data	CAPY 140000
	LD LMT 158700
	LT WT 51500

Two lines of data	CAPY 140000
	LD LMT 158700

Note: The information printed in both formats was the same and remained so for the entire postwar era. The only variable was whether the three-line or the two-line heat-stamp tooling was used. Furthermore, the use of "NEW 2-49" was not consistent. See individual listings for usage.

Comparison of 6462 gondola heat stamps. Top: "N" in NYC is in second panel. Bottom: "N" in NYC is in third panel.

6112 (C) Lionel gondola.

Top: 6062 (C). Middle: 6162 (A) with "NEW 2-49" below the "C" in NYC. Bottom: 6162 (C) without "NEW 2-49".

6342 (A) N Y C culvert gondola.

The 6452 (B) gondola has the third version of the "G27" stamping with sans-serif "G". Compare with the lettering shown on page 225.

	Gd	VG	Ex	LN

(C) Unstamped bright translucent green body.

| | 3 | 5 | 7 | 9 |

(D) Blue body; cataloged as 6142-75.

| | 3 | 5 | 7 | 9 |

(E) Green body; cataloged as 6142-100.

| | 3 | 5 | 7 | 9 |

(F) Blue body; cataloged as 6142-125 without load.

| | 3 | 5 | 7 | 9 |

(G) Blue body; cataloged as 6142-150 with two orange cable reels.

| | 3 | 5 | 7 | 9 |

(H) Unstamped olive body; listed in Lionel Service Manual as 6142-175.

| | 4 | 6 | 8 | 10 |

6142-25: See 6142 (A).
6142-50: See 6142 (B).
6142-75: See 6142 (D).
6142-100: See 6142 (E).
6142-125: See 6142 (F).
6142-150: See 6142 (G).
6142-175: See 6142 (H).

6162 N Y C: 1959–68. Long gondola; typically unpainted blue Type IIb body with white heat-stamped lettering; "N" in third panel; "6162" underlined; typical three-line weight data; usually AAR trucks with varying coupler combinations. Typical load was three white unmarked canisters.

(A) Common blue body with "NEW 2-49".

| | 5 | 9 | 12 | 16 |

(B) Teal body with "NEW 2-49".

| | 5 | 9 | 12 | 16 |

(C) Blue body (shades vary from light to dark) without "NEW 2-49".

| | 5 | 9 | 12 | 16 |

(D) Red body (shades vary) without "NEW 2-49". Same mold as used for 6342 culvert gondola. Moderately scarce.

| | 40 | 75 | 105 | 125 |

6162-60 ALASKA: 1959. Long gondola; unpainted yellow Type IIb body with dark-blue heat-stamped lettering; "6162-60" underscored; three-line weight data; AAR trucks with operating couplers. Usual load was three red canisters with lettering.

| | 25 | 40 | 65 | 80 |

6342 N Y C: 1956–58, 1966–69; uncataloged 1964–65. Special long gondola for culvert loader and unloader accessories. Unpainted red body with white heat-stamped lettering; "N" in third panel; "6342" not underscored; typical three-line weight data; black metal culvert channel and seven culvert pipes.

(A) 1956–58 production. Type IIa dark red body with metal undercarriage; "NEW 2-49"; bar-end trucks.

| | 9 | 16 | 25 | 35 |

(B) Type IIb light red body; without "NEW 2-49"; AAR trucks.

| | 9 | 16 | 25 | 35 |

(C) Type IIb medium red body; without "NEW 2-49"; AAR trucks.

| | 9 | 16 | 25 | 35 |

6452 PENNSYLVANIA: 1948–49. Short gondola, identical to 2452, except for number. This model did not

	Gd	VG	Ex	LN

include brake wheels. As the 6000-series number implies, it came with magnetic couplers. All examples had Type Ib body.

(A) 1948. Numbered "6462" on side and rubber-stamped "6452" on frame. **9 15 20 30**

(B) 1949. Numbered "6452" on side and usually without "6452" on frame. **6 12 18 25**

The 6462 Gondolas

The 6462 model was introduced in 1949 and cataloged through 1957, when it was replaced by the similar 6062 and 6162. Most 1949 production came on frames with steps at the four corners, but the steps were soon eliminated to reduce costs. Separate-sale gondolas and those included with O gauge outfits usually included brake wheels, while most of those that came with O27 gauge sets did not. Brake wheels were completely eliminated by early 1954.

Pre-1954 cars came with six unstained large wood drums with two hoops and top and bottom rims; later models came with six smaller round barrels, usually stained a shade of brown, that were developed for the 3562 operating barrel car. Some of the lower-priced sets from the early 1950s included gondolas *without* any barrels.

All 6462 gondolas came with a metal underframe and trucks and had "6462" underscored, regardless of

whether the "N" in NYC was in the second or third panel; early issues had staple-end trucks, which were replaced by bar-end trucks late in 1951. The initial tooling for the $9^9/16$-inch–long body (designated as Type I) was used until mid-1954; the tooling was then modified into the Type II body, which was further modified in 1959 for use with plastic AAR trucks. See the boxed diagram of long gondola body molds.

6462 N Y C: 1949–56. Long gondola. Listings are organized according to color.

Black Gondolas: 1949–54. All examples with "N" in second panel. All are Type I bodies except as noted.

(A) Black-painted body; three lines of weight data with "NEW 2-49"; usually with steps and brake wheels. **6 10 15 18**

(B) Black-painted body; two lines of weight data with "NEW 2-49". **6 10 15 18**

(C) Same as (B), except unpainted black body. **5 7 10 12**

(D) Unpainted black body; two lines of weight data. **5 7 10 12**

(E) Type IIa black-painted body; two lines of weight data. **5 7 10 12**

Red Gondolas: 1950–57. "N" in second panel through early 1954; then "N" in third panel for remainder of production.

Top: 6462-500 NYC from the Girls' Set and green 6462 (B) NYC with "N" in the third panel. Bottom: Rare preproduction gray NYC gondola numbered "6462", not the typical 6562, and red 6462 (F) NYC with "N" in the third panel, which dates the car to late 1954. The red 6462 (F) came with brake wheels. E. Dougherty Collection.

Gray 6562 (A) and red 6562 (B). Observe the different color lettering on the red canisters. The canisters on the left have common white heat-stamped lettering, while those on the rights are decorated with scarce black rubber-stamped lettering. A single unbroken canister with black lettering is valued at approximately $25. Black-lettered canisters have also been verified with 6112 (A) and substantially add to values listed. E. Dougherty Collection.

	Gd	VG	Ex	LN

Second-panel "N"; all Type I bodies except as noted:

(A) Tile red–painted body; three lines of weight data with "NEW 2-49"; usually with steps and brake wheels.

	5	9	12	15

(B) Tile red–painted body; two lines of weight data with "NEW 2-49".

	5	9	12	15

(C) Distinctly different glossy tile red–painted body; two lines of weight data with "NEW 2-49".

	5	9	12	15

(D) Tile red–painted body; two lines of weight data.

	5	9	12	15

(E) Distinctly different true red–painted body; two lines of weight data; Type IIa body.

Third-panel "N"; all Type IIa body with three lines of weight data and "NEW 2-49".

	5	9	12	15

(F) True red–painted body.

	5	9	12	15

(G) Red-orange–painted body.

	5	9	12	15

(H) Unpainted red body (shades vary).

	5	9	12	15

Green Gondolas: 1954–57. All examples with Type IIa body. Lionel Service Manual designation is 6462-25 ("-25" does not appear on the car).

(A) Green-painted body with "N" in second panel; two lines of weight data.

	7	12	18	25

(B) Green-painted body with "N" in third panel; typical three-line weight data with "NEW 2-49".

	7	12	18	25

6462(-500) N Y C: 1957–58. Long gondola; pink-painted body with blue heat-stamped lettering and "N" in third panel; the -500 suffix does *not* appear on car; typical three-line weight data with "NEW 2-49"; bar-end trucks. Exclusive component of Girls' Set. Instead of the usual load of wood barrels, this model came with four white canisters that had typical black heat-stamped lettering.

	65	110	170	250

6562 N Y C: 1956–58. Long gondola; Type IIa body; "N" in third panel; "6562" *not* underscored; typical three-line weight data with "NEW 2-49"; bar-end trucks. Usual load was four red canisters with lettering.

(A) Unpainted gray body with maroon or red heat-stamped lettering. Lionel Service Manual and component box designation 6562-1.

	12	25	35	50

(B) Unpainted red body with white heat-stamped lettering. Lionel Service Manual and component box designation 6562-25.

	12	25	35	50

(C) Unpainted black body with white heat-stamped lettering. Lionel Service Manual and component box designation 6562-50.

	12	25	35	50

9

HOPPERS
AND DUMP CARS

Introduction by Roger Carp

Lionel's postwar hoppers have much in common with its gondolas. To begin, both are deceptively simple-looking models whose complexity becomes apparent only after some investigation. Also, one road name and a handful of color schemes prevailed for much of their production history. A dominant decorating scheme can mislead collectors into dismissing hoppers and gondolas as dull. However, further study uncovers a number of subtle variations of each kind of freight car. Frames and graphics changed on the basic hopper; even its body was altered to expand the line with a covered model referred to as a "cement car."

In addition, hoppers, like gondolas, were modified to create operating versions that work well independently or in conjunction with accessories. In fact, if dump cars are taken into consideration, Lionel's postwar line can be said to have boasted an operating hopper before it had a non-operating one. The existence of many variations and operating hoppers and dump cars prods collectors and operators to pay attention to these rugged and dependable models. Fortunately for enthusiasts, most variations of these cars can be acquired without spending too much time or money.

Hoppers share another trait with gondolas: Both were obvious additions to the Lionel line. After all, children wanted models of the cars they frequently saw, and they couldn't help seeing hoppers and gondolas on virtually any prototype railroad in the United States. Railroads depended on open hoppers to transport loose materials that wouldn't be harmed by exposure to the elements. Covered hoppers carried items that needed protection: primarily cement and sugar in the 1950s, grain and plastic pellets later. Kids knew that hoppers, like gondolas, made terrific toys. They filled the models with small rocks and pennies. The lucky boys who owned dump cars enjoyed filling them with stones, marbles, or Lionel's coal and then supervising their unloading.

When it was time to bring toy trains back to the market in 1945, Lionel's engineering and sales personnel checked over the hoppers and dump cars cataloged right before the war. As was true with gondolas, Lionel had listed several colorful models in its O and O27 gauge lines in the late 1930s and early 1940s. Taking hoppers, for example, there were two stamped sheet-metal cars painted red or black and loaded with brass or nickel details (the 816 and 2816). Larger and more impressive was the scale-detailed model Lionel had developed in 1940. Cast with zinc alloy, the 716 came painted black and rubber-stamped in white for the Baltimore and Ohio Railroad, a prominent line in the Northeast and Midwest. This handsome hopper, which featured manually operated double doors at the bottom of each of its four bays, fit beautifully with the 700-series boxcar, tank car, and caboose that Lionel released at the same time.

The development of the 716 and a counterpart equipped with tinplate trucks and couplers (the 2956) meant Lionel's engineers had at their disposal a realistic O gauge model ready to be updated for the postwar line. When they sought to put together a freight outfit for the holiday season of 1945, they might justifiably have included a hopper. Why they did not can't be determined, although it seems likely they wanted to feature one completely new item. The 2452 gondola served that purpose. Putting a hopper and a gondola in the same set probably seemed unnecessary to executives because both cars function as carriers of loose material. Better, they concluded, to mix in a boxcar, tank car, and caboose with the new gondola to make up a freight train that would have the greatest appeal. Interestingly, Lionel tended not to pack a hopper with a gondola in its postwar sets; low-end O27 outfits were the usual exception.

When the 1946 consumer catalog was distributed after Labor Day, kids could feel confident that a good-looking hopper was on its way. The top-of-the-line O gauge freight outfit was shown with a reincarnation of the 716. A black four-bay Baltimore and Ohio hopper, the 2856, was advertised as a set component as well as a separate-sale item. No such car was ever offered, not in 1946 or the following year, even though Lionel pictured it again in the 1947 catalog (this time, it was depicted as silver and described as an 11½-inch–long "scale, die-cast reproduction of the 70-ton quadruple hopper used by the B & O Railroad." Why Lionel abandoned its plans to manufacture this magnificent hopper remains a mystery. Perhaps the costs were greater than anticipated or the resources of the engineering department had to be diverted to projects deemed more important. Whatever the reason, Lionel didn't market a hopper in the years immediately after World War II.

Instead, the firm cataloged a pair of dump cars. By a stretch of the imagination, these models can be considered operating hoppers. As happened with its crane, Lionel started by reviving a prewar O27 car that left no doubt about its being a toy. The 3659 dump car had been cataloged from 1938 through 1942; fitted with new couplers and trucks, it returned to the line as the 3559 in 1946. Like its predecessor, the new model featured a metal frame painted black and bin painted red, along with a Bakelite housing for the dumping mechanism. Unloading was easy: position the car over a section of remote-control track and press a button on the track's controller. It activated a solenoid on the car that caused the bin to tilt forward and dump its load of 206 coal (really, pellets of Bakelite) into a tray or a bin at the base of a 97 coal elevator.

Although the 3559 looked out of place with the larger and more realistic models included in the 1946 line, its bright red paint and reliable operation made it worth reviving for the O27 line. Besides, doing so was relatively easy. Engineers brought it up to date by adding trucks and couplers and had it ready less than a year after toy train production resumed. Whether any new parts had to be manufactured for this car is unknown; most likely, Lionel used up leftover inventory when producing the 3559 dump car, which meant costs for cataloging it were low.

At the same time, engineers were finishing a longer dump car for the O gauge line. Their design held more coal and looked more realistic. They based it on a prototype owned by the Delaware, Lackawanna and Western Railroad and pictured in the November 1940 issue of *Model Builder* magazine, put out by Lionel. Two versions of the new operating car entered the line in 1946: the 3459 for the regular line and 5459 for the radio-controlled 4109WS Electronic Control Set. Both came painted black and heat-stamped white for Lionel Lines. The catalog depicted the 3459 in unpainted aluminum and lettered in black for the Baltimore and Ohio. A highly desirable unpainted variation did appear in 1946, but it was lettered for Lionel Lines. In addition, one painted dark green was included with set 2137WS in 1948. Regardless of color, the 3459 was a winner and worked beautifully with the 97 coal elevator as well as the 397 operating diesel-type coal loader brought out in 1948.

The most notable change in 1948 was the introduction

of a genuine hopper. Actually, two versions of a two-bay hopper (the 2456 and 6456) appeared and were listed in the catalog, but they differed only in the trucks installed on them. The car looked good, but paled in comparison to the planned 2856. It had half as many bays and lacked the opening doors. Moreover, at 8⁹⁄16 inches in length, it was almost 3 inches shorter. Still, the new injection-molded car had a lot going for it: a metal brake wheel, extensive heat-stamped graphics, and magnetic couplers. It was painted black and decorated for the Lehigh Valley, a coal-hauling railroad whose tracks ran by the Lionel factory in northern New Jersey.

The next version of Lionel's hopper did come with doors that opened—automatically! The engineering staff devised an operating car in 1950 to be used with an exciting new accessory. For the 3456 hopper, they modified the basic shell to accommodate an assembly with magnetically operating hatches. This attractive model, painted black and heat-stamped white for the Norfolk and Western Railway, was cataloged as a separate-sale item, which is somewhat misleading. For it to operate as intended, a 456 coal ramp was necessary. On large layouts, a 397 operating diesel-type coal loader stood nearby to facilitate complex loading and unloading of coal.

What is most striking about Lionel's hoppers and dump cars from the early 1950s are three things that *didn't* happen. First, engineers made no effort to develop a hopper for the inexpensive Scout line. Once more, having a gondola probably was enough. Second, after dropping the 3559 in 1949, no attempt was made to bring out an O27 dump car. Instead, Lionel tended to restrict its remaining dump car, renumbered as 3469, to O gauge outfits. Third, nothing was done to expand the line with a genuine O gauge hopper longer than the 6456. If the goal was to hold the line on expenses, then Lionel again adopted the obvious solution: It cataloged this short hopper in both O27 and O gauge sets.

Obvious is the right word to describe Lionel's next move regarding hoppers. Prototype railroads in the Middle Atlantic region were making increasing use of covered hoppers manufactured by American Car and Foundry and Pullman-Standard. Designers at Lionel watched as these hefty cars transported cement not far from their offices. Then in 1953, The A. C. Gilbert Company, Lionel's chief competitor during the postwar period, added a covered hopper to its S gauge American Flyer line. All of a sudden, developing an O gauge model became a top priority at Lionel. With no time to spare, engineers introduced the 6446 cement car in 1954. This model featured a new body shell that had four hoppers, which made it look longer. Lettered for the Norfolk and Western, it came painted gray with black heat-stamped markings or black with white markings.

Just as Lionel expanded its fleet of 6462 gondolas by giving them new colors rather than new road names, it brought out open hoppers painted in different hues between 1954 and 1957. First came a 6456 painted gray and heat-stamped dark red so it matched the 2321

Delaware, Lackawanna & Western Train Master that pulled it as part of set 2219W. Also in 1954, Lionel offered two prized versions of the 6456 painted glossy red with either white or yellow graphics. Black and maroon models remained in the catalog through 1955.

The short two-bay hopper was superseded sometime in 1955 by an O gauge open quad hopper that amounted to nothing more than a cement car without its roof. Early examples of the 6436 came painted black or maroon and heat-stamped white. Next came the most desirable of these open hoppers, one painted lilac and heat-stamped maroon for the pastel 1587S Lady Lionel (better known as the Girls' Set) in 1957. Of course, even before this celebrated outfit was released, designers had been experimenting with other colors for the short hopper and its covered companion. Samples of the 6446 and 6456 hoppers have been observed painted coral, mint green, pink, and medium yellow.

While playing around with colors, the engineering staff presented Lionel with a new and more modern design for an O gauge dump car. In 1955 it unveiled the 3359, which had an unpainted gray body holding two separate dumping compartments. A rotating cam enabled the car to unload one bin at a time into a plastic tray or a 397 operating diesel-type coal loader or 497 coaling station. Based on a prototype that was owned by the New York Central Railroad and illustrated in the November 1940 issue of *Model Builder*, the 3359 looked more sophisticated than the 3469, which was deleted in 1956. The new car ran through 1958. Then it and the last of Lionel's coal-related accessories were themselves dumped. Sales executives might have done this because they worried that loading coal was synonymous with the steam engines of the past and not the diesel locomotives of tomorrow or assumed that kids wanted more exciting animation on their layouts.

The straightforward history of Lionel's short hopper twisted and turned after 1956. That's when designers modified its body, omitted the brake wheel, and all but stopped painting the cars. The first of these stripped-down models, the 6476, made its debut in 1957. It typically featured an operating coupler at each end. The color combinations varied—black body with white lettering, gray body with black lettering, and red body with white lettering. From 1959 on, the 6476 had a new shell that enabled workers to rivet trucks directly to its body. The motive behind most of these changes was plain: Lionel wanted to cut manufacturing and decorating costs wherever possible on its most basic models.

Number 6076 appeared in 1961. Its color combinations varied, as did the graphics heat-stamped onto its bodies. What cars with this number generally have in common is a fixed coupler at each end. Exceptions, however, have been reported. Hoppers labeled 6076 were cataloged through 1963, but some were put in cataloged and uncataloged outfits for a couple more years.

To add to the confusion, Lionel gave yet another number (6176) to some of its short hoppers, beginning in 1964.

The aim was to identify models equipped with one fixed and one operating coupler. It sounded feasible, but exceptions eventually were assembled that had two fixed couplers. Meanwhile, more of the heat-stamped graphics were eliminated until some examples of the 6176 came without markings of any kind. Lionel intended to use these unlettered hoppers as components in uncataloged and promotional outfits, with the goal again being to reduce expenses.

Operators often turn up their noses at the many short hoppers produced during the 1960s. They prefer the detailed Lehigh Valley models of the 1950s and the open quad hoppers attractively decorated to match motive power painted and lettered for the Minneapolis & St. Louis Railway (the 6536) and the Alaska Railroad (the 6636). Collectors, however, enjoy acquiring and studying the later short hoppers. They examine them to learn more about Lionel's marketing and production strategies. For either group of enthusiasts, hoppers and dump cars offer more than first meets the eye.

SHORT HOPPERS

The 8⁹⁄16-inch–long hopper was a Lionel staple from its introduction in 1948; with various modifications, it had a 21-year production life, through 1969. Lionel used six different body molds: four represented significant changes; the other two featured slight differences in rivet detail. Nonoperating Types I and III are nearly identical, as are operating Types II and IV (see the accompanying chart).

All 2456 and 6456 hoppers came with either Type I or Type III body molds and were always painted. Painting generally ceased with the introduction of the 6476 Type V body mold in 1957. When decorating the 8⁹⁄16-inch hoppers, Lionel relied on heat-stamping exclusively. Considering the very large quantities produced, it seems surprising that Lionel cataloged only two road names, Lehigh Valley and the operating 3456 Norfolk and Western.

All Type V hoppers were numbered 6476 and most often came with AAR trucks. Each truck was attached to a special bracket that included steps; after the truck bracket was properly positioned, a tab that fit through a slot molded into the body was bent to secure the assembly. Manufacturing costs were further reduced in 1959 with the introduction of the Type VI body style. All Type VI hoppers had trucks riveted directly to the body. Consistency was the norm for hoppers manufactured prior to 1959; there were very few variations. With 1959 and later Type VI production variations abound.

Exceptions became the rule with 6076, 6176, and 6476 Type VI hoppers. However, even this group of cars had some constants. All designations shared the same body part numbers, lacked a brake wheel, and were unpainted with heat-stamped lettering. Color combinations were as follows: red body with white lettering, black body with white lettering, gray body with black lettering, and yellow

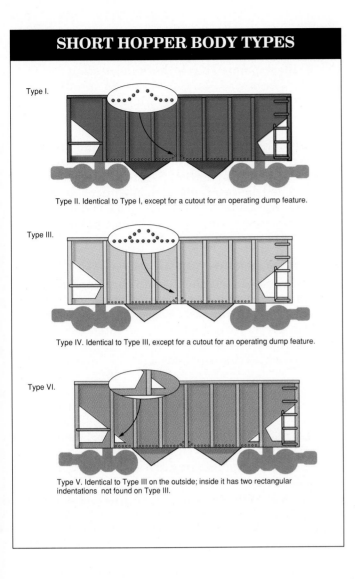

SHORT HOPPER BODY TYPES

Type I.

Type II. Identical to Type I, except for a cutout for an operating dump feature.

Type III.

Type IV. Identical to Type III, except for a cutout for an operating dump feature.

Type VI.

Type V. Identical to Type III on the outside; inside it has two rectangular indentations not found on Type III.

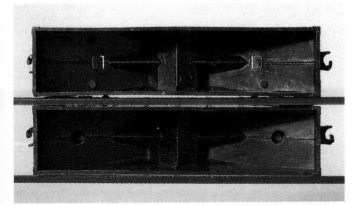

Inside views of the Type V body (top) and the Type VI body (bottom). On the Type V body each truck is secured with a unique bracket that was fitted through open slots in the body cavity. The Type VI style has the trucks riveted directly to the body.

body with black lettering. *No yellow hoppers were numbered either "6076" or "6476". No black or red hoppers were numbered "6176".*

Consistency stopped here as variables came into the picture. The 6076 designation typically meant fixed couplers, while 6176 implied one fixed and one operating coupler, although exceptions were commonplace. Examples numbered 6076 were routinely observed with an operating coupler, and 6176 models sometimes appeared with two fixed couplers.

Until about 1964 all Lehigh Valley hoppers included "NEW 1-48" and "BUILT 1-48 / LIONEL [applicable number]". Sometime in 1964 "NEW 1-48" disappeared from the hoppers. Shortly thereafter the applicable number was deleted, and then "BUILT 1-48 / LIONEL" was eliminated from the heat-stamping process. By 1965 the number stamped on the car (or its absence) was no longer pertinent; regardless of stamping, cars were designated by coupler type. Any hopper with one fixed and one operating coupler was considered 6176; any one with two operating couplers was called 6476. Even unmarked cars were identified by coupler type.

Note: When applicable, the word "complete" is used in the introduction to Lehigh Valley entries (for example, "complete white heat-stamped Lehigh Valley markings"). "Complete" means the item includes "NEW 1-48" and "BUILT 1-48 / LIONEL [applicable item number]". The photographs give the details of markings, logos, and technical data.

QUAD HOPPERS

The large quad hopper, with its new design of underside chutes, was introduced in 1954 and ran without major modifications, except for road names, until 1968. The Lionel Service Manual states that it was a scale reproduction of a 70-ton covered hopper used by the Norfolk and Western Railway. Lionel coined the term "cement car" to differentiate a covered hopper from an open model. The open hopper body was identical to the covered hopper body but simply had no roof. To prevent warping of unsupported car sides, Lionel added two small holes to the mold at the top center area of the sides and fit a special brace into them. Collectors use the terms "spreader brace" and "spreader bar" interchangeably.

Covered hoppers produced in the mid-1950s were not supposed to have spreader-brace holes, while open hoppers were. There were scarce and collectible variations of certain stock numbers, relating to either the presence or absence of spreader-brace holes. Beginning with 1957 production, all quad hoppers, whether covered or open, came *with* spreader-brace holes.

UNMARKED: 1963–69. Short hopper; Type VI unpainted body; varying truck and coupler combinations, but most often with one fixed and one operating coupler (which implies 6176 designation); usually an uncataloged set component.

	Gd	VG	Ex	LN
(A) Bright yellow body.	**20**	**30**	**45**	**60**

(B) Dark yellow body; cataloged with 1964 outfit 11430 as 6176, even though unmarked.

	Gd	VG	Ex	LN
	10	**15**	**25**	**30**
(C) Red body.	**15**	**25**	**40**	**50**
(D) Black body.	**15**	**25**	**40**	**50**

(E) Gray body; cataloged with 1963 outfit 11311 and listed in the Lionel Service Manual as 6076-100.

	Gd	VG	Ex	LN
	10	**15**	**25**	**30**

(F) Olive body; listed in the Lionel Service Manual as 6176-100.

	Gd	VG	Ex	LN
	20	**40**	**70**	**90**

2456 LEHIGH VALLEY: 1948. Short hopper; Type I black-painted body; complete white heat-stamped Lehigh Valley markings; brake wheel; staple-end trucks with coil couplers.

Note: This newly designed hopper was also offered as "6456" for the O27 gauge line, but had to be cataloged with coil couplers (hence the first digit "2") for O gauge. All O gauge outfits from 1948 came with the nonmagnetic principled RCS.

	Gd	VG	Ex	LN
(A) Dull black body.	**7**	**15**	**20**	**30**
(B) Semigloss black body.	**7**	**15**	**20**	**30**

3359 LIONEL LINES: 1955–58. Twin-bin coal dump car; unpainted gray body with black heat-stamped lettering; car actually numbered "335955"; unpainted red motor housing assembly attached by means of tabs and slots to frame; bar-end trucks.

Note: The 3359 unloading bins are dumped alternately in a stepped sequence by means of a special rotating cam. Unlike other dump cars, which are metal, the 3359 model is basically made of plastic. A complete car comes with a 90 controller, two OTC contactors, and a long 160 plastic receiving bin.

	Gd	VG	Ex	LN
	18	**35**	**52**	**65**

3456 N & W (Norfolk and Western): 1950–55. Short operating hopper; black-painted body with white heat-stamped lettering; brake wheel; pre-1952 examples with staple-end trucks and magnetic couplers; later issues with bar-end trucks and magnetic couplers.

Note: A modification was made to the hopper tooling to accept an assembly with magnetically operated bottom hatches. Included with the 456 coal ramp and available for separate sale.

	Gd	VG	Ex	LN
(A) Type II body.	**15**	**25**	**50**	**60**
(B) Type IV body.	**15**	**25**	**50**	**60**

3459 LIONEL LINES: 1946–48. Coal dump car; aluminum unloading bin with heat-stamped lettering described below; car also lettered "AUTOMATIC / DUMP CAR"; black-painted die-cast frame with integral motor housing assembly; brakestand at each end; staple-end trucks with coil couplers.

Note: Most examples came with a short 160 Bakelite receiving bin; however, some 1946 models came with a chemically blackened steel receiving bin.

	Gd	VG	Ex	LN
(A) Aluminum-finished bin with blue lettering.				
	100	**175**	**275**	**325**
(B) Black-painted bin with white lettering.				
	15	**35**	**50**	**75**
(C) Green-painted bin with white lettering.				
	20	**45**	**65**	**85**

3469 LIONEL LINES: 1949–55. Coal dump car; black-painted aluminum unloading bin with white heat-stamped lettering; car also lettered "AUTOMATIC / DUMP CAR"; black-painted die-cast frame with integral motor housing assembly; brakestand at each end; staple-end trucks with magnetic couplers into 1951, then bar-end trucks for remainder of production.

	Gd	VG	Ex	LN
	12	**30**	**45**	**60**

(3559) UNMARKED: 1946–48. Coal dump car (prewar design); red-painted sheet-metal bin with Bakelite mechanism housing; black-painted sheet-metal frame with steps at the four corners; usually rubber-stamped "3559" in silver or white on underside; staple-end trucks with coil couplers.

	Gd	VG	Ex	LN
(A) Black mechanism housing.				
	15	**28**	**40**	**50**
(B) Brown mechanism housing.				
	15	**28**	**40**	**50**

5459 LIONEL LINES: 1946–49. Electronic Control coal dump car; black-painted aluminum unloading bin with white heat-stamped lettering and green Electronic Control decal; car also lettered "AUTOMATIC / DUMP CAR"; black-painted die-cast frame with Electronic Control receiver concealed inside motor housing assembly; brakestand at each end; staple-end trucks with coil couplers.

	Gd	VG	Ex	LN
	55	**115**	**175**	**225**

6076 A T S F (Santa Fe): Uncataloged, 1963 and later. Short hopper; Type VI unpainted gray body with black heat-stamped lettering; varying truck and coupler combinations; originally issued with set 19263, a Libby's promotional outfit from 1963. (See *Greenberg's Guide to Lionel Trains 1945–1969, Volume IV: Uncatalogued Sets.*)

	Gd	VG	Ex	LN
	10	**15**	**22**	**35**

6076 LEHIGH VALLEY: 1961–63, but also appearing as a sometime 1964–65 set component. Short hopper; Type VI unpainted body; complete heat-stamped Lehigh Valley markings, except where noted (red and black bodies with white lettering, gray body with black lettering); usually with fixed coupler arch-bar trucks, but black and gray examples often appear with one fixed and one operating coupler.

	Gd	VG	Ex	LN
(A) Light red body.	**7**	**10**	**14**	**20**
(B) Dark red body.	**7**	**10**	**14**	**20**
(C) Black body.	**7**	**10**	**14**	**20**
(D) Black body without "NEW 1-48".				
	7	**10**	**14**	**20**
(E) Gray body without "NEW 1-48".				
	7	**10**	**14**	**20**

Top: 2456 (A) Lehigh Valley and 3456 (A) Norfolk and Western. Second: 6076 (A) uncataloged A T S F and red 6076 (A) Lehigh Valley. Third: Black 6076 (D) Lehigh Valley and gray 6076 (E)

Lehigh Valley. Neither of these examples included "NEW 1-48". Bottom: Unmarked 6076 (F) olive drab and unmarked (E) gray. E. Dougherty Collection.

6076(-75) Catalog listing for a Type VI black body with arch-bar trucks; see 6076 (D).

(6076-100) Catalog and Lionel Service Manual listing for UNMARKED (E).

6167-1967 T. T. O. S. (Toy Train Operating Society): Uncataloged, 1967. Short hopper; Type VI unpainted olive body with unique gold heat-stamped lettering; car

actually numbered "6167-1967"; AAR trucks typically with one fixed and one operating coupler. This hopper was specially commissioned by the Toy Train Operating Society. We assume it was erroneously numbered; the number should have been 6176 (the correct designation for a hopper), because 6167 is an appropriate number for an SP-type caboose! Apparently the "76" portion of the number was transposed to "67", thereby creating 6167.

3359 Lionel Lines twin-bin dump car. Note that the car is actually numbered "335955".

3559 (B) coal dump car.

5459 Lionel Lines from the Electronic Control Set.

	Gd	VG	Ex	LN

Note: The 6176 designation means one fixed and one operating coupler regardless of whether the number "6176" appears on the car. Even the unmarked olive hopper is designated 6176 in the Lionel Service Manual because it was equipped with one fixed and one operating coupler.

	25	50	75	100

6176 LEHIGH VALLEY: 1964-66, 1969. Short hopper; Type VI unpainted body; heat-stamped Lehigh Valley markings with varying data, as noted; AAR trucks generally with one fixed and one operating coupler.

(A) Bright yellow body; "BUILT 1-48 / LIONEL 6176".
	3	7	10	15

(B) Bright yellow body; "BUILT 1-48 / LIONEL".
	3	7	10	15

(C) Dark yellow body; "NEW 1-48" and "BUILT 1-48 / LIONEL 6176".
	3	7	10	15

(D) Dark yellow body; "BUILT 1-48 / LIONEL 6176".
	3	7	10	15

(E) Dark yellow body; "BUILT 1-48 / LIONEL".
	3	7	10	15

(F) Dark yellow body without new date, built date, or "LIONEL" and number. See 6476-185.
	3	7	10	15

(G) Gray body; "NEW 1-48" and "BUILT 1-48 / LIONEL 6176".
	3	7	10	15

(H) Gray body; "BUILT 1-48 / LIONEL 6176".
	3	7	10	15

(I) Black body without new date, built date, or "LIONEL" and number. See 6476-160.
	3	7	10	15

Note: Variations (F) and (I) are listed with the 6176 entry because they do appear with one fixed and one operating coupler and were components of 1969 outfits 11720 and 11730 as well as uncataloged sets from the late 1960s.

(6176-100) Catalog and Lionel Service Manual listing for UNMARKED (F).

(6346) 634656 ALCOA: 1956. Covered quad hopper; silver-painted body with heat-stamped lettering; car actually numbered "634656"; ALCOA adhesive emblem on each side; brake wheel; typically without spreader-brace holes; bar-end trucks.

	Gd	VG	Ex	LN

(A) Blue lettering; common version.
	20	30	45	65

(B) Red lettering; rare variation.
	300	500	750	1000

(C) Black lettering; exceptionally scarce.
	75	125	200	250

6436(-)1 LEHIGH VALLEY: 1955–56, 1966. Open quad hopper; black-painted body with white heat-stamped lettering; car actually numbered "64361"; brake wheel; bar-end trucks. The black quad hopper was not shown in consumer catalogs but is a known component of cataloged sets.

(A) Body without spreader-brace holes.
	35	50	75	100

(B) Body with spreader-brace holes and spreader brace.
	15	20	35	50

6436(-)25 LEHIGH VALLEY: 1955–57. Open quad hopper; maroon-painted body with white heat-stamped lettering; car actually numbered "643625"; brake wheel; bar-end trucks.

(A) Body without spreader-brace holes.
	35	50	75	100

(B) Body with spreader-brace holes and spreader brace.
	15	20	35	50

6436(-110) LEHIGH VALLEY: 1963–68. Open quad hopper; red-painted body with white heat-stamped lettering; car numbered only "6436"; brake wheel; spreader-brace holes and spreader brace; AAR trucks, usually with two operating couplers.

(A) Body with "NEW 3-55" centered on car sides.
	25	40	60	80

(B) Body without new date.
	17	20	30	50

(6436-500) 643657 LEHIGH VALLEY: 1957–58. Open quad hopper from the Girls' Set; lilac-painted body with maroon heat-stamped lettering; car actually numbered "643657"; brake wheel; bar-end trucks.

(A) Body without spreader-brace holes.
	200	325	500	650

(B) Body with spreader-brace holes and spreader brace.
	75	150	225	325

6436-1969 T C A (Train Collectors Association): Uncataloged, 1969. Open quad hopper; red-painted body with unique white heat-stamped lettering and convention data; car actually marked "TCA / 6436-1969"; brake wheel; spreader-brace holes and spreader brace; AAR trucks, usually with two operating couplers. This hopper was specially commissioned for the TCA national convention in 1969.
	50	75	110	150

(6446) 546446 N & W: 1954–55. Covered quad hopper; either gray-painted body with black heat-stamped lettering or black-painted body with white heat-stamped lettering; car actually numbered "546446"; brake wheel; bar-

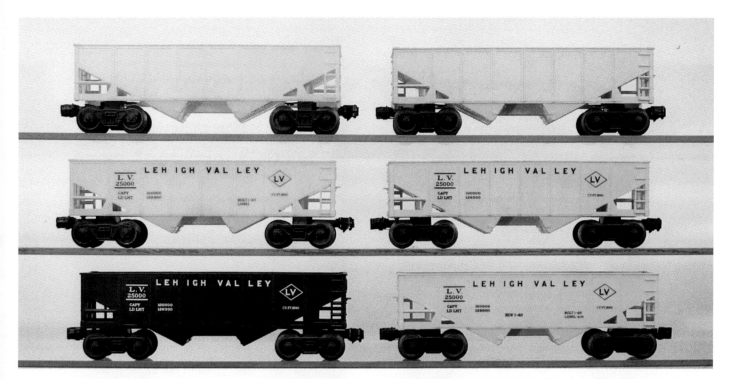

Lionel issued some cars without any markings and others with limited markings but no catalog number. Top: Unmarked (A) bright yellow, and unmarked (B) dark yellow. Middle: Yellow Lehigh Valley examples 6176 (E) and 6176 (F). Bottom: Black 6176 (I) Lehigh Valley and yellow 6176 C) Lehigh Valley. Examine the subtle differences between the three yellow examples with Lehigh Valley markings. The model on this shelf has the complete decorating scheme that includes "NEW 1-48" and "BUILT 1-48 / LIONEL 6176". E. Dougherty Collection.

	Gd	VG	Ex	LN

end trucks; sometime during 1955 the number on the heat-stamp plate was changed to read "644625". See 6446-25.

(A) Gray body without spreader-brace holes.

| | 18 | 25 | 45 | 60 |

(B) Black body without spreader-brace holes.

| | 18 | 25 | 45 | 60 |

(C) Black body with spreader-brace holes.

| | 25 | 50 | 75 | 100 |

6446(-)25 N & W: 1955–57, 1963. Covered quad hopper; typically either gray-painted body with black heat-stamped lettering or black-painted body with white heat-stamped lettering; car numbered "644625"; brake wheel; bar-end trucks. See 6446.

(A) Gray body without spreader-brace holes.

| | 18 | 25 | 45 | 60 |

(B) Gray body with spreader-brace holes.

| | 25 | 50 | 75 | 100 |

(C) Black body without spreader-brace holes.

| | 18 | 25 | 45 | 60 |

(D) 1963 reissue with *unpainted* gray body and spreader-brace holes; AAR trucks with two operating couplers; scarce variation.

| | 50 | 75 | 115 | 150 |

(E) Unpainted royal blue body with white heat-stamped lettering and spreader-brace holes; 1970 MPC production with a postwar stock number; listed and pictured for reference only.

	Gd	VG	Ex	LN

(6446-60) LEHIGH VALLEY: 1963. Covered quad hopper; identical to 6436-110 (A), except for the cover, hence the 6446 designation; while the body is painted red, the roof and hatches are *unpainted*; scarce variation.

| | 60 | 100 | 150 | 200 |

6456 LEHIGH VALLEY: 1948–55. Short hopper; painted body; complete white heat-stamped Lehigh Valley markings; brake wheel; pre-1952 examples with staple-end trucks and usually magnetic couplers; 1952 and later production with bar-end trucks and magnetic couplers.

(A) Type I black body.	6	9	12	15
(B) Type III black body.	6	9	12	15
(C) Type I dull maroon body.				
	5	7	11	15
(D) Type III dull maroon body.				
	5	7	11	15
(E) Type III semigloss maroon body.				
	10	15	22	30

6456(-25) LEHIGH VALLEY: 1954–55. Short hopper; Type III gray-painted body; complete dark red or maroon heat-stamped Lehigh Valley markings; brake wheel; bar-end trucks.

| | 15 | 25 | 40 | 50 |

6456(-50) LEHIGH VALLEY: 1954. Short hopper; Type III glossy red-painted body; complete *white* heat-stamped

Top: 6346 (A) Alcoa and 6436-500 (B) Lehigh Valley from Girls' Set. Second: 6436-25 (B) Lehigh Valley and maroon 6436 Lehigh Valley preproduction paint sample numbered "643657", the same as the Girls' Set hopper. Third: 6436-110 (B) Lehigh Valley without "NEW" date, and 6436-1 (A) Lehigh Valley without spreader bar holes. Bottom: 6436-110 (A) Lehigh Valley with "NEW" date (improper bar-end trucks are on this example), and 6436-1 (B) Lehigh Valley with spreader bar holes. E. Dougherty Collection.

Top: Gray 6446 (A) N & W (numbered 546446) and black 6446 (B) N & W (also numbered 546446). Second: Gray 6446-25 (D) N & W with spreader bar hole and black 6446-25 (C) N & W. Third: 6446-25 (E) N & W from MPC production with postwar number and 6536 (B) M St L. Bottom: 6636 Alaska and 6736 (A) Detroit & Mackinac. E. Dougherty Collection.

	Gd	VG	Ex	LN

Lehigh Valley markings; brake wheel; bar-end trucks. The white lettering makes this a very scarce item.

	200	**350**	**500**	**700**

6456(-75) LEHIGH VALLEY: 1954. Short hopper; Type III glossy red-painted body; complete yellow heat-stamped Lehigh Valley markings; brake wheel; bar-end trucks. Not to be confused with 6456-50, this moderately scarce item has yellow lettering. **50   75   115   150**

6476 LEHIGH VALLEY (Type V body): 1957–58. Short hopper; unpainted body; complete heat-stamped Lehigh Valley markings (red and black bodies with white lettering, gray body with black lettering); early 1957 issues with bar-end trucks, soon replaced by AAR trucks (each truck attached to truck bracket, which included steps).

Note: Type V bodies are easily identified, as a slot was molded into each side of the slanted portion of the underbody; after the truck bracket was properly positioned, a tab was bent to secure the assembly to the body.

(A) Red body; listed in the Lionel Service Manual as 6476-25. **4   10   15   20**

(B) Gray body; listed in the Lionel Service Manual as 6476-50. **4   10   15   20**

(C) Black body; listed in the Lionel Service Manual as 6476-75. **4   10   15   20**

Note: Although the number 6476 appeared in the consumer catalog from 1957 through 1969, 1963 was the last year in which it was used as part of the decorating process. Future versions of the 6476 designation were numbered "6176" or left unnumbered. To describe each item more thoroughly, the Type VI versions are listed below by the appropriate suffix.

6476-1 TOY TRAIN OPERATING SOCIETY: Uncataloged, 1969. Short hopper; Type VI unpainted gray body with unique blue heat-stamped lettering; car actually numbered "6476-1"; AAR trucks usually with two operating couplers. Specially commissioned by the Toy Train Operating Society. **25   50   75   100**

6476(-25) LEHIGH VALLEY: 1959–63. Short hopper; Type VI unpainted red body; complete white heat-stamped Lehigh Valley markings; AAR trucks with two operating couplers except 1963 production with one fixed and one operating coupler.

Note: The -25 suffix was not listed in the consumer catalog from 1959 to 1962, but 6476-25 appears as a component with the listing for outfit 11331 from 1963.

(A) Coral-pink opaque body. **10   15   25   30**

(B) Medium red opaque body. **4   7   10   15**

(C) Light red translucent body. **4   7   10   15**

(D) Dark red translucent body. **4   7   10   15**

Top: Two shades of maroon 6456 (C) with Type I bodies. Middle: Very scarce 6456-50 with white lettering and moderately scarce 6456-75 with yellow lettering. Both of these hoppers typically came with Type III bodies. Bottom: Two shade variations of 6476 (A) with Type V bodies. E. Dougherty Collection.

Two examples of a Type V body. Gray 6476 (B) Lehigh Valley and black 6476 (C) Lehigh Valley. E. Dougherty Collection.

	Gd	VG	Ex	LN

6476(-50): Lionel Service Manual listing for 6476 (Type V body) (B).

6476(-75) LEHIGH VALLEY: 1963. Short hopper; Type VI unpainted black body; complete white heat-stamped Lehigh Valley markings; AAR trucks with either two operating couplers or one fixed and one operating coupler. This hopper, the only Type VI black example numbered 6476, is somewhat scarce. **10 15 25 30**

(6476-125): Consumer catalog listing in 1964 for a Type VI yellow body. The -125 suffix also appears in the Lionel Service Manual; see next entry.

(6476-135) LEHIGH VALLEY: 1964–66, 1968. Catalog listing for a Type VI yellow body; however, there are no yellow hoppers numbered "6476"! (It was given the 6476 designation because of two operating couplers.) Typical black heat-stamped Lehigh Valley markings, but varying use of the new date, built date, and number heat-stamps; included with O gauge outfits and available for separate sale. See 6176 for yellow bodies and applicable values. **3 7 10 15**

(6476-160) LEHIGH VALLEY: Catalog listing in 1969 for 6176 (I), Type VI unpainted black body with operating couplers at both ends. **10 15 25 30**

(6476-185) LEHIGH VALLEY: Catalog listing in 1969 for 6176 (F) Type VI unpainted yellow body with operating couplers at both ends. **10 15 25 30**

6536 M St. L (Minneapolis & St. Louis): 1958–59, 1963. Open quad hopper; red-painted body with white

	Gd	VG	Ex	LN

heat-stamped lettering; brake wheel; spreader-brace holes and spreader brace.

(A) 1958 production with bar-end trucks.
20 30 50 65

(B) 1959 production with AAR trucks.
20 30 50 65

(C) 1963 production with AAR trucks and one fixed and one operating coupler. Apparently this minor variation was completed from existing inventory of body shells.
20 30 50 65

6636 ALASKA RAILROAD: 1959–60. Open quad hopper; black-painted body with varying shades of yellow heat-stamped lettering; brake wheel; spreader-brace holes and spreader brace; AAR trucks.
15 25 45 60

6736 DETROIT & MACKINAC: 1960–62. Open quad hopper; red-painted body with white heat-stamped lettering; brake wheel; spreader-brace holes and spreader brace; AAR trucks.

(A) Body with clearly defined face of figure in Mackinac Mac logo. **15 25 45 60**

(B) Body with partially obliterated face in Mackinac Mac logo, caused by a flawed heat-stamp plate; technically a factory error, but a common variation. Page 54 of the 1961 catalog even features the 6736 with a blotched face.
15 30 45 70

335955: See 3359.
546446: See (6446).
634656: See 6346.
643657: See (6436-500).

10

TANK AND VAT CARS

Introduction by Roger Carp

The O and O27 gauge tank cars produced by Lionel, like real tankers, have a beauty all their own. The blending of curved and straight lines, of soft and sharp angles, sets them apart from boxcars and flatcars. Their sleek, cylindrical tanks make them pleasing to the eye. And the solid color scheme, broken by the splashy hues of their owner's name and herald as well as the lines of car data, creates a distinct appeal. The various details added to top-of-the-line models make them desirable to collectors and operators.

Having great aesthetic appeal was necessary for the tank cars because Lionel didn't dare make them functional. Generally speaking, Lionel and its competitors found ways for their rolling stock to imitate its full-sized siblings. They created artificial coal for hoppers, tiny barrels for gondolas, and even miniature cows for stock cars. Liquids, however, were another story. Children could pretend there was milk in the metal cans unloaded from milk cars and wonder whether the clear plastic cubes used with the 352 icing depot would melt on a hot day. But other than putting colored fluid in the 38 pumping water tower in order for it to simulate filling a steam engine's boiler, Lionel had stayed away from using liquids with its trains. Water and electricity don't mix, and anything that spilled and stained might leave the parents of young engineers boiling mad.

To make tank cars desirable, therefore, Lionel depended on their unique shape and eye-catching graphics. Even with an engineering staff celebrated for its inventiveness and whimsy, the company never offered tank cars with moving parts or operating features. Instead, Lionel innovated by devising a vat car with four small yet colorful vertical tanks mounted on a glorified flatcar. Its tank and vat cars weren't earth-shattering, yet children apparently were captivated by them during the postwar era. Sales personnel trusted that packing a double-dome car into most sets added a touch of realism to any freight train, no matter how short. Over the years, Lionel expanded its fleet of tankers in key ways, although the variety of models offered at one time was never great.

The company picked up after World War II about where it had been prior to the conflict, with a single-dome tank car. Models built on metal frames and having fat sheet-metal tanks had been parts of the O27 and O gauge lines since the 1920s. Around 1932, Lionel negotiated a licensing agreement with the Sun Oil Company that allowed it to decorate its tankers with Sunoco graphics. Silver tanks with bright yellow and red heralds became the rule on the 654 and 804 and later the more detailed 815, 2654, and 2815. In 1939 and 1940, Lionel offered tank cars painted orange and lettered red for Shell, another petroleum producer. The two years following saw a return to Sunoco on Lionel's sheet-metal cars.

As nice as larger tank cars like the 2815 might look, engineers agreed that none was worth reviving in 1945. Fortunately for them, another alternative beckoned. The advances in metal blanking and die-casting that had enabled Lionel to produce its scale-detailed boxcar, hopper, and caboose also paved the way for an outstanding tank car in 1940. The 9-inch–long 715 and its twin, equipped with tinplate trucks and automatic box couplers (the 2955), featured a magnesium alloy frame and a body painted black and decaled first for Shell and then Sunoco. Similar features, along with handrails, ladders, steps, and placard holders, distinguished the 2755 oil car released in 1941. Less expensive to make, because its tank was stamped aluminum and its dome was compression-molded Bakelite, this Sunoco model looked like its scale companions yet sold for less.

The scale-proportioned 2755 seemed to sales and engineering personnel the best choice to update for the freight outfit Lionel planned to advertise for 1945. They assigned the number 2555 to the new oil car, but leftover decals with the old number were applied to the silver models and collectors usually refer to it as the 2755. The location of the Sunoco decal and a few subtle details, not to mention postwar couplers, differentiated this car from its predecessor.

With more time to devote to the 1946 line, Lionel's designers responded by tripling the number of tank cars in the catalog. Their wish to supplement both the O27 and O gauge lines was evident. In the former, they introduced the 2465, a double-dome car that, with the exception of 1957, appeared in the line continuously for the following 20 years. The new model departed from other Lionel tank cars by having a sheet-metal frame painted black and injection-molded tank, dome caps, and end pieces painted silver. Decaled car data and a Sunoco herald changed slightly over the next 2 years.

For the O gauge line in 1946, Lionel again offered an aluminum single-dome tank car, now correctly numbered as the 2555. As with the 2465, modifications of the herald could be detected on cars from 1947 and 1948. Meanwhile, the most desirable of all postwar tank cars was making its debut in 1946, the black-painted 2855. All the details removed from the 2555, including steps and extra placard holders, remained on this Sunoco tanker. Its decoration brought back memories of the scale-detailed Shell car cataloged before the war. The stark color of the 2855 contrasted with its vivid yellow herald to produce a car whose beauty continues to attract attention. A less valuable version, which came painted gray, appeared in 1947. Then Lionel deleted this superb model from its line.

When Lionel had brought out its first postwar set for the 1945 holiday season, it put a tank car in the four-car consist. Three years later, sales personnel selected the same types of rolling stock for the initial outfit in the new, inexpensive Scout line. Engineers developed an 8-inch–long single-dome tank car to accompany the Scout's boxcar, gondola, and caboose. The sheet-metal frame of the new 1005 was painted black, and the injection-molded body was left unpainted gray plastic. The handrails and dome cap were part of the tank molding, which had a rubber-stamped Sunoco herald and minimal Lionel Lines data. The 1005 was available for 2 more years and then was dropped as Lionel prepared to give up the Scout line.

Also in 1950, Lionel cataloged a metal single-dome oil car for the last time. This was significant for two reasons, one sentimental and the other practical. First, the 6555 (a version of the 2555 updated with magnetic couplers and renumbered in 1949) and the three incarnations of the 2625 *Irvington* heavyweight Pullman were the only cars left that boasted a direct link with the prewar period. All were gone after 1950, as Lionel was determined to enter its second half-century with new and more exciting trains.

The deletion of the 6555 was important for a second reason. Dropping it and the 1005 left Lionel with only one tank car for 1951: its plastic double-dome model, updated as the 6465. Company executives had broken their unwritten rule of striving to catalog different versions of the same kind of freight car in the O27 and O gauge lines. Even the 6456 hopper and 6462 gondola, which also appeared in sets cataloged for either line, weren't the only versions of those car types being produced. In addition, Lionel was cutting back on tank cars just when a potential rival, Thomas Industries, was developing some beautifully detailed kits for assembling O gauge tank cars with one, three, or even six domes. Lionel couldn't miss seeing the Thomas models, though its sales staff might have argued that kits would appeal to older, more experienced hobbyists and not detract from the sales of ready-to-run train sets to families.

All the same, recognizing that its tank car fleet was skimpy, Lionel took steps to remedy the situation. In 1952, the low-end of its O27 line gained the 6035, an updated Scout tank car. Two years later, designers changed the look of Lionel's 8-inch–long single-dome tanker from unpainted gray plastic to yellow and renumbered the Sunoco car as 6015. By then they had taken care of the top end by introducing an injection-molded triple-dome model based on a Union Tank Car Company prototype. Although the 6415 resembled Lionel's double-dome car, its production required such new parts as an injection-molded plastic frame and body. The result was a highly detailed car whose unique style and colorful rubber-stamped Sunoco herald and lettering left no doubt it was a premium item.

Having three different types of tank cars, at three different price levels, must have satisfied the officers at Lionel. But nothing ever seemed to stand still there. New versions of the small single-dome tanker (the 6025) and the triple-dome car (the 6425) made their debut in 1956, each decorated for the Gulf Oil Company. No precise reason for the switch to Gulf can be attributed; most likely, Lionel, Sunoco, or both chose not to renew their licensing agreement, and a newcomer stepped in. Another factor in Lionel's turning to Gulf might have been the extensive use of that firm's name and emblem on the S gauge single-dome tank cars marketed as part of the rival American Flyer line by The A. C. Gilbert Company.

From the perspective of kids in the 1950s and enthusiasts today, the change to Gulf was only positive for Lionel. Having the name of another petroleum refiner on its tank cars added needed variety to what was available. The 6025, molded with black, gray, and orange bodies between 1956 and 1958, looked especially good and found its way into several O27 outfits. In the meantime, designers introduced another type of tank car, also decorated for Gulf. Beginning in 1956, Lionel cataloged the 6315, an injection-molded single-dome model that replicated a tank car intended to transport chemicals. With its black tank partially painted orange and separate dome platform and ladder, this was a handsome model indeed. Here, however, Lionel was running behind Gilbert, which had brought out two eye-catching chemical tank cars since 1954.

The connection with Gulf lasted through 1958, and then Lionel dropped its 8-inch–long single-dome model and temporarily retired its triple-dome tanker and chemical car. Only the 6465 double-dome tank car survived, decorated for Gulf in 1958 and Lionel Lines in 1959. Executives appeared to conclude that the appeal of these cars was too limited. Few of the high-priced O27 outfits or the O and Super O freight sets featured a tank car anymore. At a time when children demanded action and animation, a tanker detracted from a train, regardless of how attractive or detailed the car might be.

The prevailing frame of mind probably explained why Lionel paid so little attention when other toy train manufacturers unveiled a slew of realistic models in S and O gauges. Between 1957 and 1959, Gilbert introduced stunning tank cars decorated for Baker's Chocolate, Mobilgas, and Pennsylvania Salt. Also in 1957, Kusan-Auburn, a toy producer in Tennessee, expanded its line of O gauge rolling stock with a near-scale single-dome car. The Kusan model, based on a General American Transportation Corporation prototype, came neatly decorated for a few chemical and petroleum firms. Lionel looked on and merely shrugged its shoulders.

Then its engineers got to work and built something entirely new for 1960. Nothing like the 11-inch–long 6475 vat car existed on the O gauge market, although there was at least one HO scale model of this odd car designed to transport pickles. Lionel cataloged its pickle car in both O27 and Super O outfits in 1960 and 1961. The cargo changed to pineapple in 1963. That's when Lionel modified the 6475 for uncataloged set 19263, which promoted Libby's canned foods.

Promotional outfits were one way to push Lionel trains in the 1960s. Space sets were another. The firm developed a huge array of rolling stock and accessories that capitalized on America's fascination with sending rockets and satellites into space. In 1962, it released a double-dome tank car labeled to carry rocket fuel. The 6463 car claimed attention because it reflected the mood of the early 1960s and may be the only Lionel item based on a model marketed first by Louis Marx and Company. Sometime in the late 1950s, Marx, the largest toy manufacturer in the world, produced an O gauge white tank car lettered in red, "Chemical Rocket Fuel". Although Lionel's model differed slightly (it had two domes, Marx's had one), the similarities between the two tankers were too obvious to be ignored.

Designing a vat car was about as innovative as Lionel wanted to be with tank cars in the 1960s. It did bring back the triple-dome Sunoco tanker and reissued the chemical car as an unpainted orange car lettered for Lionel Lines. It even put new names on the reliable double-dome tank car. An agreement with Cities Service, another petroleum refiner, led to the introduction of the 6045 and 6465 painted green and rubber-stamped white. Models with the same numbers appeared between 1959 and 1966 decorated for Lionel Lines. Versions of the 6045 were components in uncataloged sets.

The tank cars produced in the final decade of the postwar era certainly don't measure up to earlier ones in terms of detail and value. But like Lionel's gondolas and hoppers from the 1960s, they surpass them in color. They suggest that while financial and market considerations forced Lionel to retreat in the quest for authenticity, it continued to emphasize the need to produce trains that would appeal to children as toys. That's the main reason collectors enjoy the later tank cars and vat cars and operators insist on acquiring them to spice up freight trains. These models are just too neat to ignore.

DELUXE SINGLE-DOME TANK CARS

The deluxe single-dome style was developed in the prewar era. Four items, all basically similar, were produced when Lionel resumed production after World War II; the first release was 2755 in 1945, followed by 2555, 2855, and finally 6555 in 1949.

The tank car body was sheet metal and included separate sheet-metal end pieces and a separate plastic dome cap. Cars are held together by a single long screw positioned at the underside of the frame that goes through the tank and threads into the dome. All models utilized a die-cast frame, and some parts, such as a ladder, air brake, and step, retained their prewar numbers. Even though the Lionel Service Manual lists the frame as part no. 2755-17 for all examples, all frames are marked "PART NO. 955-6" and "NO. 2955 MADE IN U.S. OF AMERICA" and include "LIONEL CORPORATION NEW YORK". The frame also included holes for steps at the four corners and four slots for placard holders along the perimeter.

TWO-DOME TANK CARS

The two-dome style is by far the most common of all postwar tank cars. Production began in 1946 with the 2465 Sunoco and continued through 1966, with the exception of 1957. All two-dome models utilized a molded plastic body; dome caps and end pieces were molded separately and glued to the body. The Sunoco examples were detailed well for inexpensive items; they included a body secured by two screws to a sheet-metal frame, wire handrails, and a visually appealing decorating scheme. All 2465 and early-production 6465 frames included steps at the four corners; frames with steps were generally painted black, while those without steps were either painted (1948–50 production) or chemically blackened for later issues.

8-INCH SINGLE-DOME TANK CARS

The 8-inch single-dome model with a molded plastic body was introduced as 1005 in 1948. The dome cap and simulated railing were integral to the mold; the end caps were separate pieces that were glued to the basic body. All examples were rubber-stamped. The body was attached to a sheet-metal frame by means of two flexible tabs that were part of the frame. The earliest frames were painted glossy black and included steps at the four corners. Steps disappeared sometime during 1949, and most future production from the series came on chemically blackened frames without steps.

THREE-DOME TANK CARS

Lionel introduced the plastic-body three-dome tank car in 1953 with Sunoco markings; it was a highly detailed

TWO-DOME CAR FRAMES

by William Schilling

At least eight minor frame variations appear with the Sunoco model. All are similar because they include four rectangular holes and attach with two screws. However, the presence or absence of steps and varying amounts and positioning of circular holes account for the eight variations. Frame Types Ia, b, and c include steps, while Types IIa, b, c, d, and e do not. Keep in mind that frames are easily changed, which affords collectors and sellers the possibility of "creating."

In 1956 Lionel dropped the Sunoco name from its line of tank cars; we assume the licensing agreement between the two companies had expired. A two-dome 6465 was cataloged in 1956, but the car illustrated on page 32 of the consumer catalog did not feature the Sunoco logo. We further assume Lionel cataloged the 6465 to deplete existing inventory but deleted the Sunoco logo from the catalog illustration to avoid any legal consequences.

The two-dome tank car was not cataloged in 1957, but it reappeared in 1958 with major modifications to both the body and the frame. On the 1958 model, Lionel replaced the wire handrails by simulated railing and gave this version a body cavity specifically altered for use with the new Type III frame. The new frame was chemically blackened and included six rectangular slots, along with two tabs that fit into large round openings on the underside of the body and new aligning slots at each end. After the body was properly positioned on the frame, the tabs were bent to secure the body in place; this method of attaching body to frame was initially developed in 1948 for 8-inch single-dome models. The Type III frame and plastic AAR trucks became the norm for 1958 and all future production.

Type Ia frame

Type Ib frame

Type Ic frame. Note: This frame, without steps, is also Type IIa.

Type IIb frame

Type IIc frame

Type IId frame

Type IIe frame

Type III frame, introduced in 1958

model of an actual 70-ton gas and oil carrier. Amazingly, 6415 and 6425 were the only stock numbers from the series. Since this model was a new design, tooling had to be developed. The end caps and dome caps were separately molded pieces that were glued to the basic body.

CHEMICAL TANK CARS

The plastic-body, single-dome chemical tank car was introduced as part of the 1956 line. There are three distinctly different versions, yet all are numbered 6315. Lionel was able to save on design costs by utilizing the plastic frame and truck support that were developed for the 6415 three-dome tank car.

VAT CARS

The vat car, introduced in 1960, was an imaginative and new design. Because it was a new concept, Lionel had to make unique tooling. The company made two regular-production models—the pickles vat car (cataloged) and Libby's (uncataloged); both had the number 6475. There even exist examples with Heinz 57 labels; however, the postwar Heinz cars are *not* genuine Lionel production. Detailed information on this and other unique items is found in *Greenberg's Guide to Lionel Trains 1945–1969, Volume V: Rare and Unusual.*

Top: 1005 (A) Sunoco with small lettering. Bottom: 1005 (B) Sunoco with large lettering.

Top: Rare 2465 (A) Sunoco from early 1946. Second: 2465 (B) Sunoco with eight lines of technical data and 2465 (C) Sunoco with name extending beyond diamond. Third: 6015 (B) Sunoco and 6025 (E)

Gulf with orange tank. Bottom: 6025 (D) Gulf with gray tank and 6025 (A) Gulf with black tank. E. Dougherty Collection.

	Gd	VG	Ex	LN

1005 SUNOCO: 1948–50. 8" single-dome tank car; unpainted gray body; three-color rubber-stamped Sunoco herald and rubber-stamped lettering; frame information discussed below; Scout trucks and couplers.

Note: There are two distinctly different frames for 1005, and each came in two variations. Earliest frames included steps at the four corners and were usually painted glossy black; later frames came without steps and were most often chemically blackened.

(A) Medium blue lettering with small "LIONEL LINES / 1005". **3 5 10 12**

(B) Dark blue lettering with large "LIONEL LINES / 1005". **3 5 10 12**

2465 SUNOCO: 1946–48. Two-dome tank car; silver-painted body; various decorating schemes, typically with "SUNOCO" on left and technical data on right; handrails, black-painted Type I sheet-metal frame (see box with listing 6465) with steps at the four corners, "2465" rubber-stamped on frame; staple-end trucks with coil couplers.

(A) 1946; Sunoco decal with small (within the diamond) "SUNOCO" centered on car side; decal with "GAS" above and "OILS" below "SUNOCO". Very scarce.

Note: Fraudulent pieces exist, created by stripping and repainting a rubber-stamped 2465 (D) and applying an original replacement Sunoco decal, which can still be obtained. However, these replacement decals generally do *not* have "GAS" above and "OILS" below "SUNOCO". Reproduction decals are also available. Caution is advised.

	50	100	175	225

(B) Sunoco decal with small "SUNOCO" within the diamond; eight-line technical data decal.

	5	10	17	25

(C) Sunoco decal with large "SUNOCO" extending beyond the diamond; six-line technical data decal.

	5	10	17	25

(D) Three-color rubber-stamped Sunoco herald; six-line blue rubber-stamped technical data; "SUNOCO" extends beyond the diamond on all rubber-stamped examples. This identical rubber-stamped decorating scheme was carried forward to the 6465. **4 7 10 15**

2555 SUNOCO: 1946–48. Deluxe single-dome tank car; silver-painted sheet-metal body; Sunoco decal on left, "S.U.N.X. 2555" or generic decal with Lionel logo on right; handrails, die-cast frame, air brake, ladders, brakestand;

Top: Two versions of the 2555 Sunoco. Variation (A) on left and (B) on right without "GAS / OILS" decal. Second: 2555 (D) Sunoco with number on bottom and 2755 (A) Sunoco. Third: Gray 2855 (C)

Sunoco and black 2855 (A) Sunoco with "GAS / OILS" decal. Bottom: 6555 (C) Sunoco and 6555 (A) Sunoco with "GAS / OILS" decal. E. Dougherty Collection.

	Gd	VG	Ex	LN

typically without steps; usually placard holders on sides only; staple-end trucks with coil couplers.

(A) Sunoco decal with "GAS" above and "OILS" below "SUNOCO"; "S.U.N.X. 2555" decal.

	15	**25**	**40**	**60**

(B) Sunoco decal without "GAS / OILS"; "S.U.N.X. 2555" decal. **15 25 40 60**

(C) Sunoco decal with "GAS" above and "OILS" below "SUNOCO"; six-line generic decal with circled-L Lionel logo; "2555" rubber-stamped on frame.

15 25 40 60

(D) Sunoco decal without "GAS / OILS"; six-line generic decal with circled-L Lionel logo; "2555" rubber-stamped on frame. **15 25 40 60**

2755 SUNOCO: 1945. Deluxe single-dome tank car; silver-painted sheet-metal body; Sunoco decal on left with "GAS" above and "OILS" below "SUNOCO" on all variations, "S.U.N.X. 2755" decal on right; handrails, die-cast frame, air brake, ladders, brakestand, steps at the four corners; usually placard holders on sides only; staple-end trucks with coil couplers.

Note: This tank car came with set 463W. The 1945 catalog actually illustrated a prewar gray 2755 yet listed 2555 as the intended component! However, Lionel still had an adequate supply of 2755 decals and decided to deplete them with the tank car included with set 463W. There are two versions each of the "SUNOCO" and the "S.U.N.X." decals.

(A) Thin-letter Sunoco decal with straight bottom; large-letter S.U.N.X. decal usually with notched bottom.

35 75 125 200

(B) Thick-letter Sunoco decal with notched bottom; large-letter S.U.N.X. decal usually with notched bottom.

35 75 125 200

(C) Thin-letter Sunoco decal with straight bottom; small-letter S.U.N.X. decal usually with straight bottom.

35 75 125 200

2855 SUNOCO: 1946–47. Deluxe single-dome tank car; sheet-metal body; Sunoco decal on left, "S.U.N.X. 2855" or generic decal on right; handrails, die-cast frame, air brake, ladders, brakestand, steps at the four corners; typically with placard holders on all four sides; staple-end trucks with coil couplers.

(A) Black-painted body; Sunoco decal with "GAS" above and "OILS" below "SUNOCO" and white-lettered technical data; "S.U.N.X. 2855" decal.

65 125 200 325

(B) Black-painted body; Sunoco decal without "GAS / OILS" and white-lettered technical data; "S.U.N.X. 2855" decal.

65 125 200 325

(C) Gray-painted body; Sunoco decal without "GAS / OILS" and black-lettered technical data; six-line generic decal with circled-L Lionel logo; "2855" rubber-stamped on frame. The generic decal, because it did not include a number, was also used on some versions of 2555.

50 100 175 250

	Gd	VG	Ex	LN

6015 SUNOCO: 1954–55. 8" single-dome tank car; typically unpainted yellow body; two-color rubber-stamped Sunoco herald and black rubber-stamped lettering; chemically blackened frame without steps; bar-end trucks.

(A) Earliest production with gray body mold painted yellow. Very scarce variation; depletion of unused 6035 bodies. **35 60 90 125**

(B) Medium yellow body. **4 6 8 10**

(C) Dark yellow body. **4 6 8 10**

6025 GULF: 1956–58. 8" single-dome tank car; typically unpainted body; three-color rubber-stamped Gulf herald with rubber-stamped lettering; chemically blackened frame without steps; 1956–early 1957 production with bar-end trucks, followed by AAR trucks.

Note: The rubber-stamping of the Gulf herald was a three-step process. All examples came with either an orange or red-orange background; variations were created depending on whether white or navy ink was used during the second phase of the decorating process.

(A) Black body with white lettering; red-orange background with white "GULF" over navy; usually bar-end trucks. **5 10 15 20**

(B) Black body with white lettering; orange background with navy "GULF" over white; usually bar-end trucks. **5 10 15 20**

(C) Black-*painted* body with white lettering; red-orange background with navy "GULF" over white; usually AAR trucks. **5 10 15 20**

(D) Gray body with blue lettering; either red-orange or orange background with white "GULF" over navy; AAR trucks. Even though the body was not painted, the end caps were usually painted gray. **5 10 15 20**

(E) Orange body with blue lettering; either red-orange or orange background with white "GULF" over navy; AAR trucks. **5 10 15 20**

6035 SUNOCO: 1952–53. 8" single-dome tank car; unpainted gray body; three-color rubber-stamped Sunoco herald and dark blue rubber-stamped lettering; chemically blackened frame without steps; Scout trucks with magnetic couplers. **4 6 8 10**

6045 LIONEL LINES: Uncataloged, 1959–64. Two-dome tank car; unpainted body with rubber-stamped lettering; large circled-L Lionel logo; Type III frame (see box with listing 6465) with tabs; fixed coupler arch-bar trucks.

(A) Gray body with blue lettering; "BLT 1-58 / BY LIONEL". **15 20 25 35**

(B) Beige body with blue lettering; "BLT 1-58 / BY LIONEL". **15 20 25 35**

(C) Orange body with black end caps and black lettering; "BLT / BY LIONEL". Aside from trucks and number, this car is identical to orange 6465 Lionel Lines.

15 25 42 60

6045 CITIES SERVICE: Uncataloged, 1960–61. Two-dome tank car; green-painted body with white

Top: 6035 Sunoco and 6045 Lionel Lines (A) with gray tank. Second: 6045 green Cities Service and 6045 Lionel Lines (C) with black ends. Third: 6465 Cities Service and 6463 rocket fuel.

Bottom: 6465 Lionel Lines (B) with orange tank and 6465 Lionel Lines (A) with black tank. E. Dougherty Collection.

	Gd	VG	Ex	LN

rubber-stamped lettering; Type III frame (see box with listing 6465) with tabs; fixed coupler arch-bar trucks. Aside from trucks and number, this car is identical to 6465 Cities Service. **12 20 35 50**

6315 (early) GULF: 1956–58. Single-dome chemical tank car; unpainted black body and end caps with orange-painted detail; rubber-stamped lettering (black on orange and orange "BLT 1-56" on black); handrails; dome platform; ladders; unpainted black plastic frame; brakestand; bar-end trucks (each truck attached to a truck support, and truck supports fastened to frame with a single screw).

(A) Glossy burnt-orange body.
40 60 90 125
(B) Semigloss burnt-orange body.
20 35 50 70
(C) Flat burnt-orange body. Most common production.
20 30 45 60

(D) Distinctly different true orange body; finishes vary from glossy to semigloss. **40 60 90 125**

6315 (reissue) GULF: 1968–69. Single-dome chemical tank car; unpainted orange body with orange end caps; black rubber-stamped lettering; other particulars are the same as early 6315, except for late AAR trucks, usually with two operating couplers.

Note: The Gulf logo returned to the chemical tank car in 1968 after a 10-year absence; however, the 1968 consumer catalog mistakenly showed the item with discontinued Lionel Lines markings.

(A) Without built date. Most common version.
30 40 60 80
(B) With rubber-stamped "BLT 1-56" positioned near ladders. Scarce. **40 50 75 100**

6315 LIONEL LINES: 1963–66. Single-dome chemical tank car; typically unpainted orange body with orange

Top: 6415 (D) Sunoco with "8000 GALS" and "6415", and 6415 (E) Sunoco with "6600 GALS" and "6415". Second: 6415 (C) Sunoco with "8000 GALS" and "TANK", and 6415 (A) Sunoco with "6600 GALS" but without either "TANK" or "6415". Third: 6315 Gulf (C) with burnt-orange and black body and scarce 1969 issue of 6315 Gulf (A). Bottom: 6315 Lionel Lines (B) and 6425 Gulf. E. Dougherty Collection.

	Gd	VG	Ex	LN

end caps; black rubber-stamped lettering; no built date; handrails; dome platform; ladders; unpainted black plastic frame; brakestand; AAR trucks (each truck attached to a truck support, and truck supports fastened to frame with a single screw). While most examples came with two operating couplers, some 1963–64 production came with one fixed and one operating coupler.

(A) Very scarce variation with orange-painted body.

	100	**125**	**190**	**250**

(B) Most common version with unpainted orange body.

	12	**15**	**25**	**35**

6415 SUNOCO: 1953–55, 1964–66, 1969. Three-dome tank car; silver-painted body; three-color rubber-stamped Sunoco herald and rubber-stamped lettering that varies from black to blue-black to medium blue; circled-L Lionel logo; handrails; ladders; unpainted black plastic frame; brakestand; 1953–55 production with bar-end trucks and 1964–66 reissue with late AAR trucks and operating cou-

plers at both ends (each truck attached to a truck support, and truck supports fastened to frame with a single screw).

Note: There are three variations of data stamping: five lines only, five lines with "TANK", and five lines with "6415". There are two Sunoco heralds: with "CAPACITY 8000 GALS" and "CAPACITY 6600 GALS"; the latter was early production, which was followed by the 8000-gallon herald, which in turn was succeeded by the return of the 6600-gallon herald. There are two versions of the circled-L Lionel logo: white L on a blue circular background with an additional blue circle, and white L on a blue circular background. The silver brakestand predates the black version.

(A) 6600 gallons; five lines of data only; circled-L Lionel logo with additional blue circle; silver brakestand; bar-end trucks.

	10	**15**	**30**	**35**

(B) 8000 gallons; five lines of data with "TANK"; circled-L Lionel logo with additional blue circle; silver brakestand; bar-end trucks.

	10	**15**	**30**	**35**

6465 Gulf / Lionel Lines (A) with moderately scarce black body.

	Gd	VG	Ex	LN

(C) 8000 gallons; five lines of data with "6415"; circled-L Lionel logo with additional blue circle; silver brakestand; bar-end trucks.

	10	15	30	35

(D) 8000 gallons; five lines of data with "6415"; circled-L Lionel logo without additional blue circle; either silver or black brakestand; bar-end trucks.

	10	15	30	35

(E) 6600 gallons; five lines of data with "6415"; circled-L Lionel logo without additional blue circle; black brakestand; AAR trucks.

	10	15	30	35

6425 GULF: 1956–58. Three-dome tank car; silver-painted body; rubber-stamped Gulf herald on orange field with blue "GULF" and medium-blue rubber-stamped lettering; handrails; ladders; unpainted black plastic frame; black brakestand; bar-end trucks (each truck attached to a truck support, and truck supports fastened to frame with a single screw).

	15	25	40	50

6463 ROCKET FUEL: 1962–63. Two-dome tank car; white-painted body with red rubber-stamped lettering; Type III frame (see photographs) with tabs; AAR trucks (1962 production with two operating couplers and

	Gd	VG	Ex	LN

1963 versions with one fixed and one operating coupler).

	10	20	40	50

6465 CITIES SERVICE: 1960–62. Two-dome tank car; green-painted body with white rubber-stamped lettering; Type III frame with tabs; AAR trucks with operating couplers.

	12	15	30	35

6465 GULF / LIONEL LINES: 1958. Two-dome tank car; typically unpainted body with rubber-stamped lettering; three-color Gulf herald on left, "BLT 1-58 / BY LIONEL" at center, and "LIONEL LINES / 6465" on right; Type III frame with tabs; AAR trucks with operating couplers.

(A) Black body with white lettering.

	25	50	75	100

(B) Black-painted body with white lettering.

	25	50	75	100

(C) Gray body with blue lettering.

	10	15	25	30

6465 LIONEL LINES: 1959, 1963–66. Two-dome tank car; unpainted body with rubber-stamped lettering; large circled-L Lionel logo; Type III frame with tabs; AAR trucks.

(A) 1959; black body with white lettering; "BLT 1-58 / BY LIONEL"; two operating couplers.

	10	20	30	50

(B) Orange body with black end caps and black lettering; "BLT / BY LIONEL"; generally with one fixed and one operating coupler.

	5	10	15	20

6465 SUNOCO: 1948–56. Two-dome tank car; silver-painted body; handrails, three-color rubber-stamped Sunoco herald on left and six lines of blue rubber-stamped technical data on right; sheet-metal frame (1948–49 production with Type I frame and steps at the four corners, later versions with Type II frame); pre-1955 production usually with "6465" on frame; pre-1952 models with staple-end trucks and magnetic couplers, 1952 and after

Top: 6465 Sunoco (B) with staple-end trucks and 6465 Sunoco (B) with bar-end trucks. Bottom: 6465 Sunoco (D) with "6465" on last line of data and 6465 Gulf (C) with gray tank. E. Dougherty Collection.

	Gd	VG	Ex	LN

production with bar-end trucks and magnetic couplers.

(A) Technical data with "TANK"; Type I frame; staple-end trucks. 4 8 12 15

(B) Technical data with "TANK"; Type II frame; either staple- or bar-end trucks. 4 8 12 15

(C) Distinctly different glossy silver-gray–painted body; technical data with "TANK"; Type II frame; staple-end trucks. 10 15 25 35

(D) Technical data with "6465"; Type II frame; bar-end trucks. 7 10 18 25

(E) The last version of the Type II frame (newly defined as Type IIe) with "6455" rubber-stamped on bottom; tank data inconsequential. 7 10 18 25

6475 PICKLES: 1960–62. Vat car; unpainted tan body with steps at four corners and brown-painted roof; green heat-stamped lettering; brake wheel; four unpainted yellow vats with red heat-stamped "PICKLES" and black rubber-stamped hoops and staves (black often appears as brown when a vat has been stamped with an insufficient quantity of ink); AAR trucks usually with two operating couplers. Examples also surface around 1963–64 in uncataloged sets with varying truck and coupler combinations. The plastic steps were molded as part of the body; they were fragile and often are found broken.

(A) Light brown-painted roof. 15 25 45 60

(B) Dark brown-painted roof. 15 25 45 60

(C) Vats with "PICKLES" but no hoops or staves. 25 50 75 100

6475 LIBBY'S CRUSHED PINEAPPLE: Uncataloged, 1963–64. Vat car; unpainted blue body with steps at four corners; white heat-stamped lettering; no brake wheel; four vats with silver adhesive Libby's emblems; usually with fixed coupler arch-bar trucks. First issued with set 19263, Libby's promotional outfit from 1963. (See *Greenberg's Guide to Lionel Trains 1945–1969, Volume IV: Uncatalogued Sets.*)

Top: 6475 pickles (A) vat car. Middle: 6475 pickles (C) vat car with no hoops or staves. Bottom: 6475 Libby's (B).

	Gd	VG	Ex	LN
(A) Aqua body.	25	50	75	100
(B) Medium-blue body.	18	25	45	60

6555 SUNOCO: 1949–50. Deluxe single-dome tank car; silver-painted sheet-metal body; Sunoco decal on left, "S.U.N.X. 6555" decal on right; handrails, die-cast frame, air brake, ladders, brakestand, no steps; usually with placard holders on ends only; staple-end trucks with magnetic couplers.

(A) Sunoco decal with "GAS" above and "OILS" below "SUNOCO"; large-letter S.U.N.X. decal. 15 25 40 60

(B) Sunoco decal without "GAS / OILS"; large-letter S.U.N.X. decal. 15 25 40 60

(C) Sunoco decal without "GAS / OILS"; small-letter S.U.N.X. decal. 15 25 40 60

11

PASSENGER CARS

Introduction by Roger Carp

Passenger cars presented a special challenge to Lionel during the postwar era. Anecdotal evidence, not to mention hard data, had convinced the company's sales staff that they sold one passenger outfit for every ten freight ones. Consequently, developing new passenger cars wasn't a top priority in the years immediately after the close of World War II. Designing new locomotives and freight cars understandably took precedence. But overlooking the segment of the market that wanted toy passenger trains or trying to satisfy it with prewar carryovers weakened Lionel's dominance. Outside firms threatened to capture the passenger niche by offering stylish O gauge models of the latest passenger equipment.

As expected, Lionel eventually answered this threat and managed to overwhelm nascent rivals in the late 1940s and early 1950s. But new challengers appeared, introducing O gauge and S gauge passenger trains that some modelers liked more than Lionel's. In response, Lionel poured its resources into bringing out elegant models that captured the look of a few of the most-celebrated streamlined trains in America. Enhancing the appeal of Lionel's passenger cars were the diesel and electric locomotives that served as their motive power. Outfits that were cataloged in the 1950s and early 1960s, pulled by powerful F3s or GG1s, have become classics.

For many children 40 years ago and collectors today, Lionel's best efforts never quite matched the color and majesty of certain competing lines. It kept trying, however, and Lionel's passenger trains, especially when available as boxed outfits, stand out as among its most desirable postwar items. They command high prices and raise the quality of any collection.

Especially desirable are the scale-detailed passenger cars cataloged between 1946 and 1950. These magnificent models of heavyweight Pullman cars represented modified versions of the 2623 and 2624 from 1941 and 1942. The 14¼-inch–long models had Bakelite bodies that were painted Tuscan red and heat-stamped white. They featured detailed frames and six-wheel trucks. As such, they were the most realistic and technically

advanced of all prewar passenger cars and were intended as counterparts to the 700-series freight cars produced at the same time. As Lionel brought two of those models into its postwar line (automobile boxcar and single-dome tank car), it also revived the coach typically referred to as a "Madison" or an "Irvington" car. Initially, Lionel relied on a single number, 2625, to specify any of three illuminated Pullmans with different names. Then in 1948 it went to three numbers, with 2625 being the *Irvington*, 2627 the *Madison*, and 2628 the *Manhattan*.

Besides keeping the scale-detailed coaches in its O gauge line through 1950 (the longest of any prewar rolling stock), Lionel brought out another type of prewar passenger car after World War II. The painted sheet-metal coach and observation car offered between 1938 and 1942 were updated with new trucks and couplers for the O27 line. Before the war, Lionel had cataloged these cars with different couplers and paint schemes. In 1946 and 1947, Lionel offered new versions of the coach and observation car in blue with a silver roof, green and dark green, and all-Tuscan red (the 2430 and 2431, 2440 and 2441, and 2442 and 2443, respectively). The last two pairs, which had lights, remained in the line through 1949 with improved trucks and couplers.

In 1948, Lionel introduced two new Pullmans and a matching observation car, the 2400, 2401, and 2402. These were superb additions, with injection-molded bodies painted green and yellow and heat-stamped white, gray roofs, and interior lighting. Just as it had in the mid-1930s, Lionel was offering models of the latest streamlined passenger equipment. The 2400-series cars were lettered for Lionel Lines (by contrast, the sheet-metal cars had no road designation). As a further touch of realism, each car had its own name, being christened for towns in northern New Jersey located near the company's factory.

After working so hard to finish these three models, Lionel's designers must have been stunned to learn that a small firm in Indiana was offering larger, more realistic O gauge models of streamlined passenger cars. American Model Toys stirred the toy train market in 1948 with 14-inch–long sand-cast Pullmans and an observation car that came painted and lettered for both the New York

Central and the Pennsylvania Railroad. These models, complete with interior illumination and working drumheads, ran on three-rail track and had couplers compatible with Lionel's.

In the meantime, travelers were being dazzled by streamlined passenger trains comprised of stainless-steel cars. Gleaming coaches, diners, and observation cars, made principally by the Budd Company, distinguished the *Super Chief* on the Atchison, Topeka & Santa Fe and the *Zephyr* on the Chicago, Burlington & Quincy. Modelers clamored for models of these new streamliners, and entrepreneurs saw opportunities to grow rich. Two hobby shop owners in Rochester, New York, pooled their resources in 1947 to develop O gauge models under the Kasiner Hobbies trade name. Not long after, another pair of go-getters established U & R Manufacturing Company to build ready-to-run aluminum models aimed at the O27 market.

Lionel's chief response was to promote silver-painted versions of the new coach and observation car (the 2421, 2422, and 2423). These shiny cars made their debut in 1950, along with a special and highly desirable set of yellow and red-striped models produced to celebrate the company's golden anniversary. Other notable changes to the 2400-series cars were made later in the 1950s. For example, designers changed the heat-stamped lettering from black to red, developed a matching Vista-Dome, and selected new car names in 1954. Two years later, they painted wide red stripes through the windows on the silver bodies and created a consist of four cars (the 2442, 2444, 2445, and 2446). Curiously, Lionel cataloged these beauties in 1956 only. Even odder, it used one of the Pullmans as well as the Vista-Dome and observation car solely as components in a single outfit, 1562W, which is actively sought by collectors.

Competition kept getting hotter in the O gauge arena. One source of heat continued to be American Model Toys. It spoiled Lionel's 50th anniversary by introducing a set of near-scale models of stainless-steel streamliners. Before 1950 ended, AMT had eight different near-scale car types lettered for the Santa Fe or New York Central to tempt modelers. Judging from the response in hobby magazines in the early 1950s, many enthusiasts fell for the new cars and ran them with Lionel F3s.

At Lionel, engineers studied blueprints of Budd streamliners (and probably stripped apart some AMT models) so they could put into production in 1952 four gorgeous extruded aluminum cars: the 2531 observation, 2532 Astra-Dome, and 2533 and 2534 Pullmans. They worked under the direction of assistant chief engineer Morris Zion, who received patents for the dome and observation cars. As first depicted in the black-and-white advance catalog, the streamliners were lettered for the *California Zephyr*, which ran partly over the Western Pacific Railroad. Lionel most likely planned this scheme to make the cars fit with its latest F3, the 2345, which was decorated for the Western Pacific.

When regular-production models appeared, however, their markings indicated they belonged to Lionel Lines. A generic name would appeal to consumers everywhere. This ploy contrasted with AMT's practice of decorating its models for prototype railroads. In fact, its observation cars had drumheads promoting specific trains. But Lionel wanted to reach the largest audience and so stuck with Lionel Lines. However, it did choose car names taken from ones on the Chicago, Burlington & Quincy, which pulled the *California Zephyr* on part of its journey. The same heritage was evident in 1954, when Lionel added a baggage car to its roster. The 2530 looked much like streamlined cars in the Burlington's fleet.

A second rival to Lionel in the passenger train market, one that endured longer than American Model Toys, was The A. C. Gilbert Company. It outdistanced Lionel with the streamlined sets cataloged in its S gauge American Flyer line. For kids who begged for a passenger train, Gilbert's offerings could tip the scales in favor of the smaller gauge. One notable advance occurred in 1954, when Gilbert released sleek streamliners with blue, chestnut, green, or red bands painted through their window sections. These attractive cars were cataloged with matching Alco PA diesel units decorated for the Santa Fe and fictional trains with exciting names like the *Comet*, the *Rocket*, and the *Silver Flash*.

Lionel answered in 1955 with a truly unforgettable outfit, the 2254W *Congressional*. The company broke with its postwar habit of decorating passenger equipment for Lionel Lines. Perhaps someone at its New York headquarters remembered the legendary Standard gauge *Blue Comet* and the O gauge models of articulated Union Pacific and Milwaukee Road streamliners from the prewar years. Back then, Lionel had offered sets that modeled contemporary trains; market considerations said it was time to return to this practice. The *Congressional* captured in miniature the stately qualities of its prototype, a Pennsylvania Railroad streamliner that linked New York with Washington, D. C. For this set, Lionel reissued its GG1 (painted Tuscan red) and modified its extruded aluminum cars to accommodate metal decorative stripes with gold lettering above and below the windows.

Gilbert upped the ante in 1956, when it released the first of its painted streamliners. Five cars decorated in two tones of green and lettered for the Northern Pacific came in a set pulled by a matching Alco PA ABA combination. Lionel countered the following year with another outfit that has become a highly prized classic, replacing the *Congressional* with an unnamed streamlined train that matched its new 2373 Canadian Pacific F3s. The aluminum cars were given chestnut stripes with gold lettering that proclaimed them to be part of the Canadian Pacific system. An outstanding set (the 2296W) contained three identical Vista-Domes and an observation. Distributors and retailers sometimes balked at this consist and substituted one or both of the separate-sale Pullmans.

Gilbert released more painted streamlined sets in 1958 and 1959. Lionel never tried to match the classic

American Flyer Missouri Pacific and Union Pacific trains, but instead launched a three-pronged attack to hold onto the passenger train market. First, it again modified its O gauge streamliners, adding red stripes to match the cars with the 2383 Santa Fe F3s. This tactic enabled the firm to promote what it claimed was a model of the celebrated *Super Chief* without having to invest in new tooling or authorize complicated and expensive decoration. The same desire to avoid heavy expenditures explained Lionel's second action. It revamped the silver O27 cars simply by painting a blue stripe across their windows and heat-stamping them blue for the Santa Fe.

The third change for 1959 did represent a new direction. Lionel had been striving for years to model the latest locomotives and rolling stock. In doing so, it neglected a segment of the market interested in old-time railroading. Thomas Industries, a firm based in New Jersey and then Oklahoma, had identified this gap and sought to fill it in the late 1940s and 1950s with O gauge versions of late-19th-century engines and rolling stock. Thomas had never worried Lionel, but with westerns booming on television and the centennial of the Civil War on the horizon, executives concluded the time was ripe for an old-time set.

Lionel announced a series of models based on cars from the 1860s and 1870s. The 1865 and 1866 coach and mail-baggage car were supposed to look as though they were made of wood. Their bodies were painted yellow, their roofs brown. Decals and other details gave these O27 cars an antiquated look. Super O versions were also cataloged in 1959; an uncataloged blue-painted coach appeared in the desirable (and unnumbered) Halloween outfit a year later.

None of the three kinds of passenger cars offered in 1959 proved overwhelmingly popular. The old-time cars were dropped from the line after 1962. The O27 Santa Fe streamliners ran through 1963 and then were offered without blue window stripes. These low-end versions (the 2404, 2405, and 2406) had been stripped of lights and window silhouettes. In 1966, Lionel put back these features in upgraded cars numbered 2408, 2409, and 2410. When these additions didn't increase sales, they were dropped.

The O gauge Santa Fe extruded aluminum cars, so valued by collectors today, were all but ignored in 1960 and 1961. Lionel deleted them, only to bring out another series of streamliners the next year. Decorative stripes, made of gold-colored paper rather than metal, specified the type of car above the windows. Below they spelled out the name of an American president from the late 19th century. No railroad name was listed during the five years the 2521, 2522, and 2523 were cataloged.

Unlike The A. C. Gilbert Company, Lionel never produced an operating passenger car. The special effects that made the American Flyer mail pickup cars, operating baggage cars, and animated station coach so enjoyable to watch and play with failed to entice Lionel. The closest it came to cataloging an operating passenger car were

motorized injection-molded plastic models of the Budd Company's Rail Diesel Cars. First to duplicate one of these popular commuter cars was the 400, which was introduced in 1956. The next year, Lionel added the 404, a baggage-mail carrier. Nonpowered versions also were cataloged for the first time in 1957 (the 2550 and 2559). All four came painted silver and heat-stamped blue for the Baltimore and Ohio Railroad.

Time has not been a friend to real passenger trains, but it has certainly helped Lionel's. The values of virtually all its heavyweights and streamliners have risen steadily over the last two decades. Collectors search for boxed outfits, while operators are satisfied to run colorful trains behind steam engines and diesels. Though never a major part of the postwar product line, Lionel's passenger cars fascinate and entertain enthusiasts today.

2000 TINPLATE SERIES

Sheet-metal passenger cars originated in the prewar period. Postwar examples from this series were cataloged in three color schemes from 1946–1949: blue with silver, green with dark green, and solid brown. As a group, the cars are relatively common. However, it is not an easy task to acquire a complete set in Like New condition, especially the 1946 editions with rubber-stamped lettering.

The cars were well made and exceptionally detailed for inexpensive items. All examples included celluloid window strips and all, except 2430 and 2431, were lighted. However, the exterior carried only a modest amount of lettering. Neither a road name nor Lionel Lines was part of the decorating scheme; all models were named only "PULLMAN" or "OBSERVATION".

The green cars and brown cars underwent a number change in 1948 and 1949 respectively. As 6000-series cars they routinely feature staple-end trucks with magnetic couplers. Keep in mind that trucks are easily and often changed; also, out-of-production old stock was used until depleted. Some 6000-series cars even came with coil couplers as issued from the factory.

2400 STREAMLINED SERIES

Lionel introduced the 2400-series molded plastic streamlined passenger cars in 1948. Based on a Pullman-Standard design, the series ran basically unchanged—except for color scheme—through 1966. All pre-1959 production was designated "LIONEL LINES" and, except for the 2436 lettered "MOOSEHEART", all cars were named for New Jersey towns near the Lionel factory. Beginning with the blue-striped cars in 1959, later production exclusively carried the Santa Fe road name.

All 2400-series cars came with Type VII four-wheel die-cast passenger trucks. In 1954 the original issue sole-noid (coil)-type light passenger trucks were changed. The new-issue cars included magnetic coupler(s), and only one truck per car came with a contact roller assembly.

Some of the earlier passenger cars pose a special problem to collectors; they are usually Pullman numbers 2400, 2402, 2421, 2422, 2429, 2481, and 2482. The rainshields, present at one end of the roof, should be positioned over the doors; however, factory personnel sometimes attached the roof with the rainshields at the wrong end.

1800 GENERAL SERIES

The 1800-series cars made their debut in 1959, along with the 1862 and 1872 wood-burning General locomotives. Instead of creating something modern, Lionel engineers turned back the pages of history and copied a Civil War design. Six different stock numbers were made, and it was the 1800-series for which Type V arch-bar trucks were developed.

All cataloged cars except 1875 are quite common. The General series was only moderately successful, as sales expectations were not met. Mint examples of most items were available at the original Madison Hardware in New York through the 1980s.

MADISON CARS

The Madison cars were the cream of the early postwar passenger fleet. Strictly speaking, the postwar cars should have been called "Irvington" because the 2625 *Irvington* was the only item available in 1946. But collectors christened the postwar group "Madison" to avoid confusing them with prewar examples.

Bakelite, which is granular in nature, was the material used to mold bodies and end pieces. Each separately attached end piece was fitted with painted right-hand and left-hand functional doors. All Madison car frames were black-painted and included an interior frame and decorative air brake; frames were fitted with six-wheel articulated light coupler trucks at each end. All cars were lighted and came with celluloid window strips, plain from 1946 to 1949 and with silhouettes for 1950 production. Each car required four window strips (two per side) each held in place by a clamp bracket.

Because Madison car parts are readily interchangeable and production changes occurred every year between 1946 and 1950, the study of these cars can be confusing even to an experienced collector. Also remember, the Lionel factory continued to use obsolete parts, which included painted and heat-stamped bodies, until they were depleted.

To assist collectors in dating items, we offer a few general guidelines. Typically, in 1946–48 production, the first "L" in the Lionel Lines heat stamp along the roofline was distinctly positioned to the left of the first window in the center group of windows. Sometime in 1949, the lettering was realigned; the first "L" was

positioned over the first window of the center group for the remainder of production.

2500 EXTRUDED ALUMINUM SERIES

The major innovation of the 1952 product year was the introduction of the extruded aluminum 2500-series passenger cars. (Extrusion is a process whereby molten metal is forced through a die to create a long continuous shape or form.) Lionel used three basic aluminum passenger car bodies (observation, Vista-Dome, and Pullman) throughout the series. They introduced a companion baggage car in 1954. All models came with Type VIII die-cast O gauge passenger trucks and, except the baggage car, were lighted and came with appropriately numbered left-hand and right-hand silhouetted window strips. The observation car came with a unique rear end that included a plastic roof and skirt; these parts are often broken or scratched and in some instances have been post-factory repainted.

The original body design included ribbed or fluted channels above and below the car windows. To provide mounting space for the decorative metal stripes bearing the markings used by the Pennsylvania Railroad for its *Congressional* cars, Lionel modified the bodies in 1955 to eliminate some of the fluting above and below the windows. Nonfluted or flat-channel bodies became the norm for the rest of production. All *Congressional*, Canadian Pacific, Santa Fe, and Presidential cars included separate decorative stripes for both the road name and car name.

Be aware that the decorative stripes for *Congressional*, Canadian Pacific, and Santa Fe cars have been masterfully reproduced. Frauds permeate the marketplace, as 2530-series flat-channel cars have been altered into name-series cars and many other cars have had deteriorated original stripes replaced by reproductions.

2520 Presidential Series

The Presidential cars debuted in 1962; even though the lowest-numbered, they were the last issues in the name series. Unlike their predecessors, Presidential cars were not named for a real railroad but were simply called observation, Vista-Dome, and Pullman. Furthermore, the decorative Presidential stripes were no longer metal; instead they were made from a gold-colored paper base. Presidential cars were cataloged through 1966 and are readily available in the marketplace.

2530 Super Speedliner Series

This group of cars has numerous variations; it is exceedingly difficult to obtain a fully matched set of passenger cars even when purchasing factory-packaged outfits from 1952 to 1955.

The very earliest production had a lamp socket assembly wired directly to the collector roller. This soon gave way to a metal contact assembly that eliminated the wire leads. Lionel also experimented with hexhead screws, rivets, and glue as means of attaching nameplates.

Gd   VG   Ex   LN

Because of the complexity of the procedure, hexheads were probably used for initial production.

Most ribbed-channel cars have a satin finish, and most flat-channel cars have a glossy finish. Variations also exist with specific reference to examples with or without colons on the nameplates. However, the Lionel Service Manual does not make any differentiation between nameplates for anything other than name. Likewise, our listings do not take into account data pertaining to colons because glued nameplates are easily changeable.

2540 *Congressional* Series

The *Congressional* series was the second group of extruded aluminum cars issued and the first in the name series. They debuted with the Pennsylvania Railroad name in 1955 and were cataloged again in 1956; they were pulled by a Tuscan red GG1 in the top-of-the-line outfit each year. The decorative *Congressional* metal stripes (nameplates) were Tuscan red with gold lettering.

2550 Canadian Pacific Series

The Canadian Pacific cars were the second group issued in the name series; they were introduced in 1957 and ran for one year only. The decorative Canadian Pacific metal stripes (nameplates) were chestnut with gold lettering.

2560 Santa Fe Series

The Santa Fe road name was the third release in the name series. The cars debuted to a lukewarm welcome in 1959 and were cataloged through 1961. The decora-

tive Santa Fe metal stripes (nameplates) were red with silver lettering. Even though cataloged for three years, these cars are every bit as scarce and desirable as the more notable Canadian Pacific cars.

BUDD RAIL DIESEL CARS

The models of self-propelled Rail Diesel Cars are based on designs made by the Budd Company for commuter service on real railroads. Powered unit 400, first made in 1956, simulated Budd RDC-1, while powered unit 404 was a model of Budd RDC-4 baggage-express and mail car. With the exception of numbers, the body of 400 is identical to nonpowered 2559, and 404 is identical to nonpowered 2550. Amazingly, the nonpowered 2550 and 2559 are scarcer and valued more highly than their motorized counterparts, with the 2550 being extremely scarce.

400 BALTIMORE AND OHIO: 1956–58. Motorized passenger Rail Diesel Car; silver-painted body with blue heat-stamped lettering; "BUDD / RDC-1" adhesive nameplate; ornamental horn each end; silhouetted window strips; lens and window piece each end; two-axle Magnetraction; three-position E-unit; lighted with three lamps; horn; battery cover; operating couplers each end.

125   150   250   300

404 BALTIMORE AND OHIO: 1957–58. Motorized baggage-mail Rail Diesel Car; same description as 400,

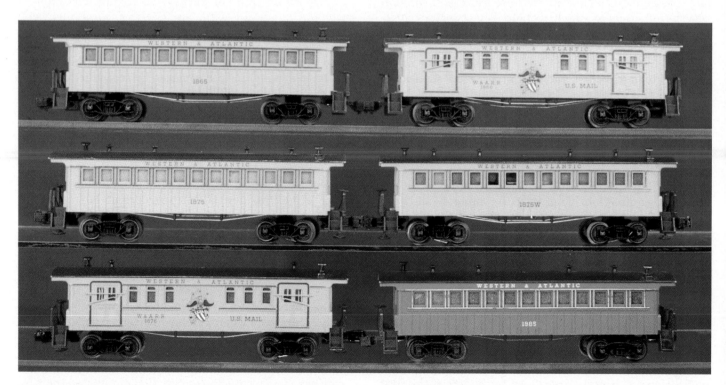

Top: 1865 Western & Atlantic and 1866 Western & Atlantic.
Middle: 1875 Western & Atlantic and 1875W Western & Atlantic.

Bottom: 1876 Western & Atlantic and 1885 Western & Atlantic.
E. Dougherty Collection.

	Gd	VG	Ex	LN

except with "BUDD / RDC-4" adhesive nameplate.

	165	200	300	400

1865 WESTERN & ATLANTIC: 1959–62. Simulated wood coach; yellow-painted body with brown-painted roof; brown heat-stamped lettering; opaque window shell; not lighted; two smokestacks and four roof ventilators; brake wheel each end; wire trusses; arch-bar trucks with fixed, nonself-centering die-cast couplers. Cataloged as O27 gauge.

	18	28	40	50

1866 WESTERN & ATLANTIC: 1959–62. Simulated wood mail-baggage car; yellow-painted body with brown-painted roof; brown heat-stamped lettering; eagle and flag decal; opaque window shell; not lighted; two smokestacks and two roof ventilators; brake wheel each end; wire trusses; arch-bar trucks with fixed, nonself-centering die-cast couplers. Cataloged as O27 gauge.

	18	28	40	50

1875 WESTERN & ATLANTIC: 1959–62. Simulated wood coach; yellow-painted body with brown-painted roof; brown heat-stamped lettering; opaque window shell;

	Gd	VG	Ex	LN

lighted; two smokestacks and four roof ventilators; brake wheel each end; wire trusses; arch-bar trucks with self-centering operating couplers. Cataloged as Super O. Available only for separate sale.

	125	150	250	300

1875W WESTERN & ATLANTIC: 1959–62. Simulated wood coach with whistle. Same as 1875, except special opaque window shell with cutouts that provide an escape for the whistle sound.

	85	125	175	200

1876 WESTERN & ATLANTIC: 1959–62. Simulated wood mail-baggage car; yellow-painted body with brown-painted roof; brown heat-stamped lettering; eagle and flag decal; opaque window shell; lighted; two smokestacks and two roof ventilators; brake wheel each end; wire trusses; arch-bar trucks with self-centering operating couplers. Cataloged as Super O.

	30	40	75	90

1885 WESTERN & ATLANTIC: Uncataloged, 1960. Simulated wood coach; blue-painted body with brown-painted roof; white heat-stamped lettering; opaque window shell; not lighted; two smokestacks and four roof

Top: 2400 Maplewood and 2404 Santa Fe. Second: 2408 Santa Fe and 2414 Santa Fe. Third: 2421 (B) Maplewood with silver roof and 2421 (A) Maplewood with gray roof and black stripes. Bottom: 2432 Clifton and 2436 Mooseheart. E. Dougherty Collection.

	Gd	VG	Ex	LN

ventilators; brake wheel each end; wide trusses; arch-bar trucks with fixed, nonself-centering die-cast couplers. Exclusive component of the uncataloged Halloween General outfit. (See *Greenberg's Guide to Lionel Trains 1945–1969, Volume IV: Uncatalogued Sets.*)

	95	150	275	350

2400 LIONEL LINES / MAPLEWOOD: 1948–49. Pullman; green-painted body with two narrow yellow stripes and window outlines; gray-painted roof; white heat-stamped lettering; nonsilhouetted window strips; lighted; cataloged as both O27 and O gauge.

	60	85	150	175

2401 LIONEL LINES / HILLSIDE: 1948–49. Observation; matches 2400.

	60	85	150	175

2402 LIONEL LINES / CHATHAM: 1948–49. Pullman; matches 2400.

	60	85	150	175

2404 SANTA FE: 1964–65. Vista-Dome; silver-painted body and roof; blue heat-stamped lettering.
Note: The 2404, 2405, and 2406 were *not* lighted and did *not* include silhouetted window strips as issued from the factory.

	30	50	70	90

2405 SANTA FE: 1964–65. Pullman; matches 2404.

	30	50	70	90

2406 SANTA FE: 1964–65. Observation; matches 2404.

	30	50	70	90

2408 SANTA FE: 1966. Vista-Dome; silver-painted body and roof; blue heat-stamped lettering; silhouetted window strips; lighted.
Note: The 2408, 2409, and 2410 were upgraded versions of the 2404, 2405, and 2406.

	35	60	75	100

2409 SANTA FE: 1966. Pullman; matches 2408.

	35	60	75	100

2410 SANTA FE: 1966. Observation; matches 2408.

	35	60	75	100

2412 SANTA FE: 1959–63. Vista-Dome; silver-painted body with wide blue-painted window stripe; silver-painted roof; blue heat-stamped lettering; silhouetted window strips; lighted.

	25	50	85	100

2414 SANTA FE: 1959–63. Pullman; matches 2412.

	25	50	85	100

2416 SANTA FE: 1959–63. Observation; matches 2412.

	25	50	75	90

2421 LIONEL LINES / MAPLEWOOD: 1950–53. Pullman; silver-painted body; black heat-stamped lettering;

silhouetted window strips; lighted. Cataloged as O gauge in 1950 and as O27 gauge in 1951–53.

(A) 1950–51, gray-painted roof; two narrow black stripes and window outlines on body.

	40	60	85	125

(B) 1952–53, silver-painted roof; no stripes or window outlines.

	40	50	75	115

2422 LIONEL LINES / CHATHAM: 1950–53. Pullman.
(A) 1950–51, matches 2421 (A).

	40	60	85	125

(B) 1952–53, matches 2421 (B).

	40	50	75	115

2423 LIONEL LINES / HILLSIDE: 1950–53. Observation.
(A) 1950–51, matches 2421 (A).

	40	60	85	125

(B) 1952–53; matches 2421 (B).

	40	50	75	115

2429 LIONEL LINES / LIVINGSTON: 1952–53. Pullman.
(A) Matches 2421 (A), but *not* typical production. The 2429 *Livingston* was not cataloged until 1952. Lionel may have experimented with the Livingston name in 1951 and decorated some shells with black stripes and window outlines. Verified examples appeared on the market as unassembled bodies and could be factory replacement items.

				NRS

(B) Matches 2421 (B). The *Livingston* is the least common car in this series.

	50	85	120	175

2430 PULLMAN: 1946–47. Sheet-metal Pullman; blue-painted body with silver-painted roof; silver-painted doors and window inserts; nonsilhouetted window strips; not lighted.
(A) 1946, silver rubber-stamped lettering.

	20	45	65	100

(B) 1947, white heat-stamped lettering.

	20	40	60	80

2431 OBSERVATION: 1946–47. Sheet-metal observation; matches 2430, but with silver-painted observation deck.
(A) 1946, silver rubber-stamped lettering.

	20	45	90	125

(B) 1947, white heat-stamped lettering.

	20	40	70	100

2432 LIONEL LINES / CLIFTON: 1954–58. Vista-Dome; silver-painted body and roof; red heat-stamped lettering; silhouetted window strips; lighted. Though not cataloged in 1959, the *Clifton* was available for separate sale.

	20	30	48	75

2434 LIONEL LINES / NEWARK: 1954–58. Pullman; matches 2432.

	20	30	48	75

Blue and silver were the first color combination offered in the 2000 tinplate series. All 1946 production was decorated with silver rubber-stamped lettering, while 1947 models typically came with white heat-stamped lettering. Top: 2431 (A) observation and 2430 (A)

Pullman. Bottom: Two pristine examples of 2430 (B) Pullmans. Observe the clarity and crispness of the heat-stamped lettering as opposed to the "grainy" features of the lettering on the examples on the top shelf. R. Swanson Collection.

	Gd	VG	Ex	LN

2435 LIONEL LINES / ELIZABETH: 1954–58. Pullman; matches 2432.

	30	40	75	125

2436 LIONEL LINES / SUMMIT: 1954–56. Observation; matches 2432.

	25	35	60	100

2436 LIONEL LINES / MOOSEHEART: 1957–58. Observation; matches 2432. Though not cataloged in 1959, the *Mooseheart* was available for separate sale.

	20	35	60	100

2440 PULLMAN: 1946–47. Sheet-metal Pullman; green-painted body with dark green-painted roof; cream-painted doors and window inserts; nonsilhouetted window strips; lighted.

(A) 1946, silver rubber-stamped lettering.

	20	30	55	70

	Gd	VG	Ex	LN

(B) 1947, white heat-stamped lettering.

	20	30	55	70

2441 OBSERVATION: 1946–47. Sheet-metal observation; matches 2440, but with silver-painted observation deck.

(A) 1946, silver rubber-stamped lettering.

	20	30	50	70

(B) 1947, white heat-stamped lettering.

	20	30	50	70

2442 PULLMAN: 1946–48. Sheet-metal Pullman; brown-painted body and roof; gray-painted doors and window inserts; nonsilhouetted window strips; lighted.

(A) 1946, silver rubber-stamped lettering.

	20	35	70	100

(B) 1947–48, white heat-stamped lettering.

	20	35	65	80

Green with dark green was the second color combination offered in the 2000 tinplate series. Rubber-stamping was the norm for 1946 production, while later models were decorated with white heat-stamped lettering. Top: 2440 (A) Pullman, and 2441

observation. Notice the "grainy" features of the rubber-stamped lettering. Bottom: 6440 Pullman, and 2441 (B) observation. R. Swanson Collection.

Top: Two examples of 2444 Newark. The model on the right has a distinctly glossy red-painted stripe. However, it is possible to "brighten" the appearance of a flat stripe with paste wax and a cotton ball. Bottom: 2436 Summit and 2483 Livingston, an exclusive component of outfit 1464W from 1950 (known as the Anniversary Set and headed by complementary yellow and gray 2023 Union Pacific Alco AA units). E. Dougherty Collection.

	Gd	VG	Ex	LN

2442 LIONEL LINES / CLIFTON: 1956. Vista-Dome; silver-painted body with wide red-painted window stripe; silver-painted roof; red heat-stamped lettering; silhouetted windows strips; lighted.   **45   75   100   175**

2443 OBSERVATION: 1946–48. Sheet-metal observation; matches 2442 Pullman, but with silver-painted observation deck.

   (A) 1946, silver rubber-stamped lettering.
         20   35   70   100
   (B) 1947–48, white heat-stamped lettering.
         20   35   60   80

2444 LIONEL LINES / NEWARK: 1956. Pullman; matches 2442 *Clifton.*   **45   75   100   175**

2445 LIONEL LINES / ELIZABETH: 1956. Pullman; matches 2442 *Clifton.* Available only for separate sale.   **55   100   190   225**

2446 LIONEL LINES / SUMMIT: 1956. Observation; matches 2442 *Clifton.*   **40   75   100   175**

2481 LIONEL LINES / PLAINFIELD: 1950. Pullman; yellow-painted body with two narrow red stripes and window outlines; gray-painted roof; red heat-stamped lettering; silhouetted window strips; lighted.

   Note: The 2481, 2482, and 2483 were released with outfit 1464W; they are commonly called the Anniversary Cars because 1950 was Lionel's golden anniversary. These were the first passenger cars to feature silhouetted

Brown was the third color scheme available in the 2000 tinplate series. Like the green examples, the brown cars underwent a number change when the last runs were fitted with magnetic couplers. Top: 2443 (A) observation and 2442 Pullman. Both of these models have silver rubber-stamped lettering. Bottom: 6443 observation and 2442 (B) Pullman. Both of these models have white heat-stamped lettering. R. Swanson Collection.

	Gd	VG	Ex	LN

window strips (referred to as litho or lithographed windows in the Lionel Service Manual).

	105	150	275	375

2482 LIONEL LINES / WESTFIELD: 1950. Pullman; matches 2481. **105 150 275 375**

2483 LIONEL LINES / LIVINGSTON: 1950. Observation; matches 2481. **85 125 230 325**

2521 OBSERVATION / PRESIDENT McKINLEY: 1962–66. Observation; flat-channel extruded aluminum body, with paper-based decorative gold stripes with black lettering; lighted; Type VIII O gauge passenger trucks. **80 125 180 250**

2522 VISTA DOME / PRESIDENT HARRISON: 1962–66. Vista-Dome; matches 2521. **80 125 180 250**

2523 PULLMAN / PRESIDENT GARFIELD: 1962–66. Pullman; matches 2521. **80 125 180 250**

2530 LIONEL LINES / RAILWAY EXPRESS AGENCY: 1954–60. Baggage car; extruded aluminum body with ribbed upper and lower channels and flat middle channel; two plain ends; not lighted; Type VIII O gauge passenger trucks.

Note: Large-door versions were early 1954 production; a construction change was soon made to strengthen the car sides by making the door openings smaller. Small doors were used for the balance of production. The glued REA nameplate has a dot at each of the four corners to simulate rivet detail and usually was positioned on the ribbed portion of the lower middle sides. Late production of car bodies distinctly glossier than early production.

(A) Large doors; "LIONEL LINES" nameplate attached with hexhead screws. **250 400 550 750**

(B) Large doors; glued "LIONEL LINES" nameplate without colons. **250 400 550 750**

(C) Small doors; glued "LIONEL LINES" nameplate either without (early) or with (later) colons. **100 150 175 250**

(D) Small doors; no "LIONEL LINES" nameplate; REA nameplate positioned on flat middle channel of car sides, most often with glossy finish. **125 175 225 275**

2531 LIONEL LINES / SILVER DAWN: 1952–60. Observation; extruded aluminum body; lighted; Type VIII O gauge passenger trucks.

(A) Ribbed channels; nameplates attached by hexhead screws. **75 100 140 165**

(B) Ribbed channels; nameplates attached by small roundhead silver rivets. **65 85 110 150**

(C) Ribbed channels; nameplates attached by large roundhead silver rivets. **65 85 110 150**

Top: Railway Express Agency baggage cars 2530 (B) with large doors and 2530 (C) with typical small doors. Second: Lionel Lines / Silver Range examples 2532 (B) and 2532 (F). Third: 2522 Vista-Dome / President Harrison and 2562 Santa Fe / Regal Pass. Bottom: 2552 Canadian Pacific / Skyline 500 and 2542 Pennsylvania / Betsy Ross. R. Shanfeld Collection.

	Gd	VG	Ex	LN

(D) Ribbed channels; nameplates attached by large roundhead black rivets. **65 85 110 150**

(E) Ribbed channels; glued nameplates. **65 85 110 150**

(F) Flat channels; glued nameplates. **90 125 160 200**

2532 LIONEL LINES / SILVER RANGE: 1952–60. Vista-Dome; matches 2531. The term Vista Dome first appeared on the downsized version (no cardboard liner) of the Middle Classic box in 1955; previously, this car was referred to as Astra-Dome.

(A) Ribbed channels; nameplates attached by hex-head screws. **75 100 140 165**

(B) Ribbed channels; nameplates attached by small roundhead silver rivets. **65 85 110 150**

(C) Ribbed channels; nameplates attached by large roundhead silver rivets. **65 85 110 150**

(D) Ribbed channels; nameplates attached by large roundhead black rivets. **65 85 110 150**

(E) Ribbed channels; glued nameplates. **65 85 110 150**

(F) Flat channels; glued nameplates. **90 125 175 250**

2533 LIONEL LINES / SILVER CLOUD: 1952–59. Pullman; matches 2531.

(A) Ribbed channels; nameplates attached by hex-head screws. **75 100 140 165**

(B) Ribbed channels; nameplates attached by small roundhead silver rivets. **65 85 110 150**

(C) Ribbed channels; nameplates attached by large roundhead silver rivets. **65 85 110 150**

(D) Ribbed channels; nameplates attached by large roundhead black rivets. **65 85 110 150**

(E) Ribbed channels; glued nameplates. **65 85 110 150**

(F) Flat channels; glued nameplates. **90 125 175 250**

2534 LIONEL LINES / SILVER BLUFF: 1952–59. Pullman; matches 2531. The 2534 is the least common item in the series.

(A) Ribbed channels; nameplates attached by hex-head screws. **75 100 140 165**

(B) Ribbed channels; nameplates attached by small roundhead silver rivets. **75 100 140 165**

(C) Ribbed channels; nameplates attached by large roundhead silver rivets. **75 100 140 165**

(D) Ribbed channels; nameplates attached by large roundhead black rivets. **75 100 140 165**

(E) Ribbed channels; glued nameplates. **75 100 140 165**

(F) Flat channels; glued nameplates. **125 175 275 350**

2541 PENNSYLVANIA / ALEXANDER HAMILTON: 1955–56. Observation; flat-channel extruded aluminum body with metal decorative Tuscan red stripes with gold lettering; lighted; Type VIII O gauge passenger trucks. **75 125 200 275**

2542 PENNSYLVANIA / BETSY ROSS: 1955–56. Vista-Dome; matches 2541. **75 125 200 275**

2543 PENNSYLVANIA / WILLIAM PENN: 1955–56. Pullman; matches 2541. **75 125 200 275**

2544 PENNSYLVANIA / MOLLY PITCHER: 1955–56. Pullman; matches 2541. **75 125 200 275**

2550 BALTIMORE AND OHIO: 1957–58. Nonpowered baggage-mail Rail Diesel Car; silver-painted body with blue heat-stamped lettering; "BUDD / RDC-4" adhesive nameplate; ornamental horn each end; silhouetted window strips; lens and window piece each end; lighted with three lamps; battery cover; operating couplers each end. **200 350 550 700**

2551 CANADIAN PACIFIC / BANFF PARK: 1957. Observation; flat-channel extruded aluminum body with metal decorative chestnut stripes with gold lettering; lighted; Type VIII O gauge passenger trucks. **100 150 250 325**

2552 CANADIAN PACIFIC / SKYLINE 500: 1957. Vista-Dome; matches 2551. **100 150 250 325**

2553 CANADIAN PACIFIC / BLAIR MANOR: 1957. Pullman; matches 2551. **175 225 375 500**

2554 CANADIAN PACIFIC / CRAIG MANOR: 1957. Pullman; matches 2551. **150 225 350 500**

2559 BALTIMORE AND OHIO: 1957–58. Nonpowered passenger Rail Diesel Car; same description as 2550, except with "BUDD / RDC-9" adhesive nameplate. **150 200 305 400**

2561 SANTA FE / VISTA VALLEY: 1959–61. Observation; flat-channel extruded aluminum body with metal decorative red stripes with silver lettering; lighted; Type VIII O gauge passenger trucks.

(A) "SANTA FE" 2¹³/₁₆" long on stripe. **100 150 245 325**

(B) "SANTA FE" 3⅛" long on stripe. **100 150 245 325**

2562 SANTA FE / REGAL PASS: 1959–61. Vista-Dome; matches 2561.

(A) "SANTA FE" 2¹³/₁₆" long on stripe. **125 200 310 425**

(B) "SANTA FE" 3⅛" long on stripe. **125 200 310 425**

	Gd	VG	Ex	LN

2563 SANTA FE / INDIAN FALLS: 1959–61. Pullman; matches 2561.

(A) "SANTA FE" 2¹³⁄₁₆" long on stripe.

	125	200	310	425

(B) "SANTA FE" 3⅛" long on stripe.

	125	200	310	425

Note: It is not uncommon to find these cars with one shorter version and one longer version of the Santa Fe nameplate.

2625 LIONEL LINES / IRVINGTON: 1946–50. Pullman; Tuscan-painted Bakelite body; white heat-stamped lettering; lighted; Type VI six-wheel trucks.

(A) 1946–48 production; first "L" in "LIONEL LINES" to the left of first window in center group; plain window strips; usually untaped couplers; visible wire leads on underside. **95 150 220 350**

(B) 1949 production; first "L" in "LIONEL LINES" usually to the left of the first window in center group; plain window strips; taped couplers; wire leads pass through frame. **95 150 220 350**

(C) 1950 production; first "L" in "LIONEL LINES" usually over first window in center group; silhouetted window strips; taped couplers; wire leads pass through frame. **105 180 275 400**

2625 LIONEL LINES / MADISON: 1947. Pullman; matches 2625 (A) *Irvington*. **95 175 235 425**

2625 LIONEL LINES / MANHATTAN: 1947. Pullman; matches 2625 (A) *Irvington*.

	100	175	240	425

2627 LIONEL LINES / MADISON: 1948-50. Pullman; same description as 2625 *Irvington*.

(A) Matches 2625 (A). **95 150 220 350**
(B) Matches 2625 (B). **95 150 220 350**

2551 Canadian Pacific / Banff Park observation.

	Gd	VG	Ex	LN

(C) Matches 2625 (C). **105 180 255 400**

2628 LIONEL LINES / MANHATTAN: 1948–50. Pullman; same description as 2625 *Irvington*.

(A) Matches 2625 (A). **95 150 220 350**
(B) Matches 2625 (B). **95 150 220 350**
(C) Matches 2625 (C). **105 180 260 400**

6440 PULLMAN: 1948–49. Sheet-metal Pullman; same description as 2440, but with magnetic couplers, white heat-stamped lettering. **20 30 45 70**

6441 OBSERVATION: 1948–49. Sheet-metal observation; same description as 2441, but with magnetic couplers, white heat-stamped lettering.

	20	30	45	70

6442 PULLMAN: 1949. Sheet-metal Pullman; same description as 2442 Pullman, but with magnetic couplers, white heat-stamped lettering.

	20	30	50	90

6443 OBSERVATION: 1949. Sheet-metal observation; same description as 2443, but with magnetic couplers, white heat-stamped lettering.

	20	30	50	90

GLOSSARY

Note: Definitions and illustrations of types of trucks and boxes are provided in Chapter 1.

A unit: lead unit for certain diesel locomotive designs, such as F3s; has cab for crew.

AA: combination of two A-unit diesel locomotives.

AB: combination of an A and a B unit.

ABA: combination of an A unit, a B unit, and a second A unit.

advance catalog: a catalog for wholesale and retail distributors that indicated what would most likely be available for sale.

Alco: an acronym for American Locomotive Company, manufacturer of locomotives for full-size railroads; made FA units popularized by Lionel.

Alnico: the raw (magnetic) material essential for use in Magnetraction (see below).

Anniversary Alcos: the Also diesel model was first introduced in 1950, to commemorate Lionel's 50th anniversary.

armature: rotating part of the electric motor, consisting of center shaft, the motor poles and their windings, and a commutator that completes the circuit.

AT&SF: abbreviation for Atchison, Topeka and Santa Fe.

B unit: trailing unit for certain diesel locomotive designs, such as F3 diesels; has no cab or windshield.

Bakelite: trade name for a compression-molded plastic powder which, because of its resistance to heat, was used in stoves; Lionel has used it for transformer casings and rolling stock.

Baldwin disk: drive wheel designed and manufactured for real railroads by Baldwin Locomotive Works. Used on some steam locomotives by Lionel in the late 1940s.

bay window caboose: caboose with no cupolas but with extended side bay windows.

Berkshire: type of steam locomotive with a 2-8-4 wheel arrangement.

boxcab: electric-outline locomotive with a rectangular body, such as the 520 introduced in 1956.

brushplate: location of the electrical conductors that make a sliding contact between the moving and stationary parts of an electric motor; they rub on the commutator portion of a rotating armature.

Bucyrus Erie: manufacturer of heavy equipment and crane cars used by real railroads. Modeled by Lionel as 2460, 6460, and others.

Budd RDC: self-propelled Rail Diesel Car: resembles a passenger car; modeled by Lionel as 400 and 404.

C unit: a term used by Lionel in catalogs and on boxes to identify their B units.

chassis: another term for frame; see below.

chemically blackened: treated with chemicals applied to metal in order to achieve a painted or blackened look.

clerestory: raised center section of passenger car roof with windows or openings on the sides.

coil coupler: type of coupler activated by a sliding shoe; more costly to manufacture than magnetic couplers.

Columbia: type of steam locomotive with a 2-4-2 wheel arrangement.

consist: the makeup of a train's rolling stock; the cars pulled by the motive power.

consumer catalog: a catalog offered to the general public to promote Lionel trains.

contact: term, most commonly used regarding postwar Lionel items for electrical pickup rollers.

cotter pins: common bendable hardware items used to attach trim such as handrails.

couplers: mechanical devices used to connect cars; see chart in Chapter 1.

crossheads: smaller portion of drive-wheel hardware near the steam chests; used in conjunction with drive rods; note in 1001-type Scout engines.

Delrin knuckle: nonmetal knuckle introduced by Lionel in the early 1960s for use with AAR trucks.

die-cast: a method of manufacturing in which molten metal is forced into a die and cooled, creating an object that takes the shape of the die.

drawbar: hooklike device that attaches a steam engine to its tender.

dummy: nonpowered locomotive; often the B units in AB combinations.

E-unit: Lionel's name for the mechanism that provides the reverse sequence; there are two-position models and three-position models with a neutral position.

Electronic Control Set: unique train set that used radio frequency waves to control direction and whistle of locomotive and to couple and uncouple rolling stock; cataloged by Lionel from 1946 through 1949.

EMD: abbreviation for Electro-Motive Division of General Motors, manufacturer of locomotives for real railroads.

EP-5: type of electric locomotive with a cab on each end and no walkways.

F3: type of diesel locomotive manufactured by EMD that has a rounded noses and no walkways.

FA: type of diesel locomotive manufactured by Alco that has a rounded nose and eight wheels.

FM: abbreviation for Fairbanks-Morse, manufacturer of locomotives for real railroads; produced by Train Master, which Lionel helped to popularize.

fixed coupler: a coupler that does not operate; has components that are fixed in place; either plastic or die-cast.

frame: bottom part of a car or locomotive; as generally used in this book, the part to which wheels or trucks are attached. Chapter 7 on flatcars uses the term to refer to that lower portion that constitutes the "body" of a flatcar.

gauge: distance between the rails; various model train manufacturers use different terms and gauges; postwar Lionel is generally O gauge.

GE: abbreviation for General Electric, manufacturer of real railroad locomotives; Lionel's model of the 44-ton center-cab diesel was based upon a GE design.

Geep: railroader's slang for GP-series locomotives.

GG1: popular electric locomotive used by the Pennsylvania Railroad; modeled by Lionel and others.

GP7 and GP9: types of general-purpose diesel locomotives manufactured by EMD that have a boxy shape and feature walkways around sides.

handwheel: common term often used instead of brake wheel; also used to describe the hand cranks on crane cars.

heat-stamping: process of lettering using heat and colored tape, making a slight impression on plastic or metal surfaces.

Hudson: steam locomotive that has a 4-6-4 wheel arrangement.

knurled pin: an approximately 3-inch steel pin with knurls or small knobs at one end; used to secure some motors to 200-series Scout engines.

lithography: process of applying paint or ink to sheet metal.

Magnetraction: patented term for special design element of Lionel locomotives using magnetized components to improve traction and pulling power and speeds on curves.

marker jewels: small rhinestones (red or green) used to simulate market lights on better-quality steam engines.

marker lens: synonymous with number board: The clear plastic part(s) used at the nose end of many diesels to simulate the number board detail used on real engines.

master carton: the exterior carton used to package separate-sale F3 and Alco units, as well as steam engine and tender pairs.

MKT: abbreviation for Missouri-Kansas-Texas.

NW2: type of diesel switcher modeled by Lionel.

O27 track: Lionel's lightweight track that is 7/16 inches high.

P unit: designation for powered diesel locomotives.

Pacific: type of steam locomotive with a 4-6-2 wheel arrangement.

pantograph: A diamond-shaped device with large sliding shoe at top for the collection of electrical power from an overhead wire on real railroads; modeled by Lionel and others.

porthole caboose: center-cupola caboose with round windows; based on N5c type on Pennsylvania Railroad.

promotional set: train set made up to promote a certain manufacturer or retailer.

quad hopper: larger hopper with four unloading bays, hence the term "quad."

RCS: remote controlled uncoupling/operating section without electromagnet.

rectifier: term often used to refer to some electric-outline locomotives; commonly used to identify Lionel's 2329.

rubber-stamping: process of lettering toy trains using rubber pads.

scale: proportion of model to prototype; O scale is, for example ¹⁄₄₈ actual size, or 1:48 scale; most Lionel models were slightly less than scale.

Scout: first used in 1948 catalog, refers to the 1001 engine and tender; it is commonly any inexpensive 0-4-0 or 2-4-2 steam engine.

semiscale: in Lionel terminology, almost scale detailed; does not use all the accent pieces utilized in full scale.

semi-Scout: any rolling stock and tenders that have the combination of Scout trucks and magnetic couplers.

solenoid: electrical device consisting of an electromagnet with a metal rod inside its core; when current is introduced, the rod moves and so does anything attached to its end.

SP: abbreviation for Southern Pacific. Lends itself to type of caboose that has square cupola, with cupola position toward rear.

speed nut: a rectangular fastener with flexible prongs that is pushed (not screwed) into the part it is to secure.

spreader brace/bar: a steel bar used on many quad hoppers to keep the side walls from collapsing inwards.

Super O: Lionel's specialized track system introduced in 1957; consists of plastic ties with a copper contact strip in place of the third rail; twelve sections form a circle with a diameter of 38 inches measured from outer rail to outer rail.

switcher: light-duty locomotive usually used in railroad yards.

T unit: designation used for trailing or nonpowered diesel engines.

tab frame: low-cost frame that eliminated the use of a screw to attach the cab to its chassis.

technical data: the load limit, capacity, etc.; information that Lionel used to decorate much of the rolling stock.

three-rail: track system popularized by Lionel, featuring two outside running rails (electrically grounded) and a single rail along the center that provides the positive current.

tinplate: tin-coated steel, used in many early toy trains, especially lower-priced items.

Train Master: see FM above.

truck: the wheel and axle assembly of a car.

turbine: type of steam locomotive based on Pennsylvania Railroad's class S2 with 6-8-6 wheel arrangement; modeled by Lionel.

UCS: uncoupling/operating section of track that allows automatic operation of couplers by means of an electromagnet; replacement for the RCS ; introduced in 1949.

Vista-Dome: passenger car with central raised windowed observation dome; also called Astra-Dome.

INDEX

This index lists all Lionel Postwar cars (excluding HO, which is covered in two separate Greenberg Guides). It includes both catalog numbers (usually the number which also appears on the side of a car) and any numbers appearing on the car, when these differ from the catalog numbers. Because of irregularities in the inclusion of hyphens in Lionel numbers, this index is sequenced according to the first four digits (disregarding hyphens as well as any letter which might precede the number). The actual listings make clear whether hyphens appear on the car or not. Since this index is a complete listing, it will not only aid you in finding a specific Postwar item, it will provide an inventory checklist as well. Postwar accessories are covered in Volume VI, and sets are covered in Volumes III and IV.

The item number is given in **bold** type. The page numbers following each item number indicate the beginning of the textual listing in this volume; there may be more than one page number given, indicating separate versions of an item. Page numbers in *italics* indicate the appearance of a photograph of the item. Tenders, which are not listed separately, can be linked to locomotives in photos and captions as well as listings in Chapter 2.

6434: 128; *114*
6436: 238
6436-1: 238; *240*
6436-25: 238; *240*
643657: 238
6436-110: 238; *240*
6436-500: 238; *240*
6436-1969: 238
6437: 160; *161*
6440: 203, 265; *205, 262*
6441: 265
6442: 265
6443: 265; *262*
6445: 128; *122*
6446/6446-1: 238; *240*
6446-25: 239; *240*
6446-60: 239
6447: 161; *161*
6448: 128; *127*
6452: 229; *229*
6454: 128; *123, 130*
6456: 239; *241*
6456-25: 239; *241*
6456-50: 239; *241*
6456-75: 241; *242*
6457: 161; *160*
6460: 168
6460-25: 168; *169*
6461: 183; *205*
6462: 230; *224, 230*
6462-25: 231
6462-500: 231; *230*
6463: 252; *250*
6464: 128, 129
6464-1: 128; *133*
6464-25: 129; *133*
6464-50: 129; *133*
6464-75: 129; *133*
6464-100: 129; *133*
6464-125: 129; *133*
6464-150: 129; *133*
6464-175: 131; *133*
6464-200: 131; *133*
6464-225: 131; *133*
6464-250: 131; *133*
6464-275: 132; *133*
6464-300: 132; *134*
6464-325: 132; *134*
6464-350: 134; *134*
6464-375: 134; *134*
6464-400: 135; *134*
6464-425: 135; *134*
6464-450: 135; *134*
6464-475: 135; *137*

6464-500: 136; *137*
6464-510: 136; *137*
6464-515: 136; *137*
6464-525: 136; *137*
6464-650: 136; *137*
6464-700: 136; *137*
6464-725: 136; *137, 138*
6464-735: 137
6464-825: 137; *138*
6464-900: 137; *138*
6464-1965: 137
6465: 252; *250, 252*
6466T/6466W: *47*
6466WX: *31*
6467: 203; *206*
6468: 138; *138*
6468-25: 138; *138*
6469: 203; *206*
6470: 138; *127*
6472: 139; *120*
6473: 139; *140*
6475: 253; *253*
6476: 241; *241, 242*
6476-1: 241
6476-25: 242
6476-50: 242
6476-75: 242
6476-125: 242
6476-135: 242
6476-160: 242
6476-185: 242
6477: 204; *206*
6480: 139; *127*
6482: 140; *120*
6500: 204; *206*
6501: 204; *206*
6502: 204; *206, 208*
6502-50: 205; *206*
6511: 205; *208*
6511-series: 183
6512: 206; *208*
6517: 162; *163*
6517-75: 162; *163*
6517/1966: 162; *163*
6518: 218; *208*
6519: 218; *208*
6520: 168; *169*
6530: 140; *122*
6536/-25: 242; *240*
65400: 112; *128*
6544: 219; *220*
6555: 253; *248*
6556: 140; *114*
6557: 162; *160*

6560: 168; *169. 170*
6560-25: 170
6561: 219; *220*
6562: 231; *230*
6572: 141; *114*
6630: 207; *209*
6636: 242; *240*
6640: 207; *209*
6646: 141; *140*
6650: 207; *209*
6651: 207; *210*
6654W: *41*
6656: 141; *140*
6657: 162; *160*
6660: 207; *210*
6670: 208; *210*
6672: 141; *140*
6736: 242; *240*
6800: 208; *210*
6801: 209; *210, 212*
6802: 210; *212*
6803: 211; *212*
6804: 211; *212*
6805: 211; *213*
6806: 211; *213*
6807: 211; *213*
6808: 211; *213*
6809: 211; *213*
6810: 211; *215*
6812: 212; *215*
6814: 163; *163*
6816: 213; *215*
6817: 214; *216*
6818: 214; *216*
6819: 214; *216*
6820: 215; *216*
6821: 215
6822: 170; *169*
6823: 216; *216*
6824: 163; *163*
6825: 216; *217*
6826: 217
6827: 217; *218*
6828: 217; *218*
6830: 217; *219*
6844: 218; *219*
81000: 128
96743: 128
Unmarked short hopper: 235; *239*
UnmarkedSP-type caboose: 155; *156*
Unmarked work caboose: 155
Unnumbered work caboose: 155; *163*
Unnumbered flatcars: 220